I0813407

Western Frontiersmen Series
XXXVIII

Andrew Dawson (1820–72),
the last "king of the high Missouri." Artist not identified.

Courtesy of the Montana Historical Society Research Center Photograph Archives, Helena.

This Far-Off Wild Land

The Upper Missouri Letters of Andrew Dawson

by
Lesley Wischmann
and
Andrew Erskine Dawson

THE ARTHUR H. CLARK COMPANY
An imprint of the University of Oklahoma Press
Norman, Oklahoma
2013

Also by Lesley Wischmann

Frontier Diplomats: The Life and Times of Alexander Culbertson and Natoyist-Siksina (Spokane, Wash., 2000)

Frontier Diplomats: Alexander Culbertson and Natoyist-Siksina among the Blackfeet (Norman, Okla., 2004)

Library of Congress Cataloging-in-Publication Data

Wischmann, Lesley.

This far-off wild land : the upper Missouri letters of Andrew Dawson / by Lesley Wischmann and Andrew Erskine Dawson.

pages cm. — (Western frontiersmen series) (Western frontiersmen series ; XXXVIII)

Includes bibliographical references and index.

ISBN 978-0-87062-419-3 (hardcover : alk. paper) 1. Dawson, Andrew, 1817–1871. 2. Dawson, Andrew, 1817–1871—Correspondence. 3. Fur traders—Missouri River Valley—Biography. 4. Fur traders—Missouri River Valley—Correspondence. 5. Frontier and pioneer life—Missouri River Valley. 6. Fur trade—Missouri River Valley—History—19th century. 7. Missouri River Valley—History—19th century. 8. Missouri River Valley—Biography. I. Dawson, Andrew Erskine. II. Title.

F598.D25W57 2013

977.8'03092—dc23

[B]

2012046843

This Far-Off Wild Land: The Upper Missouri Letters of Andrew Dawson is Volume 38 in the Western Frontiersmen Series.

Set in Caledonia, a typeface inspired by early nineteenth-century Scotch Roman type.

The paper in this book meets the guidelines for permanence and durability of the Committee on Production Guidelines for Book Longevity of the Council on Library Resources, Inc. ∞

1 2 3 4 5 6 7 8 9 10

To Larry, for making everything possible
—LW

❧

To the Dawson families
—AED

Contents

Illustrations

FIGURES

Map

Preface

ANDREW DAWSON, A TALL, REDHEADED SCOT, ARRIVED ON the upper Missouri in 1847. Destined to become the "Last King of the High Missouri," Dawson has been largely overlooked by historians, although it was he who figuratively turned out the lights on the upper Missouri fur trade when he retired in 1864. Through his letters, we can learn much about the denouement of the Upper Missouri Outfit of the American Fur Company.

Dawson spent his early years (1847–54) at two of the AFC's least documented forts: Fort Berthold and Fort Clark, which served that region's settled agricultural tribes. The villages of the Mandan, Hidatsa, and Arikara had once been the commercial hub of the upper Missouri Indian world. But their importance faded after the 1837 smallpox epidemic decimated their tribes. Afterwards, the nomadic tribes increasingly relied on the white traders for their manufactured goods and bypassed the traditional tribal middlemen. With the settled tribes no longer receiving large numbers of pelts in barter, the traders also became less interested in what those tribes had to offer.

By the 1840s, the two forts existed primarily to remind the nomadic warriors that the white traders had no plans to cede dominion. The mere presence of Forts Clark and Berthold helped to keep the river open by discouraging hostile warriors from attempting to hijack the vessels filled with trade goods. Andrew Dawson's letters bring life and occasional high drama back to these oft-forgotten posts.

Dawson moved to Fort Benton in 1854, where, in accordance with the 1855 Blackfeet Treaty, he embraced the region's development. No longer simply a fur trader, Dawson became, by default, an unpaid representative of the American government. The Indians, often bypassing their frequently absent agents, turned to Dawson for help with annuity distribution and treaty enforcement. While handling these functions paid well in prestige and goodwill, they added little to the American Fur Company ledgers or Dawson's own bank account.

Thus Dawson, a shrewd businessman, turned to freighting and outfitting to pad those accounts. When gold was discovered nearby, Dawson grubstaked untold numbers of prospectors. His assistance proved critical to the completion of the Mullan Road, linking east and west across the Continental Divide. When the steamboats finally reached Fort Benton, they ensured that Dawson's new commercial ventures would have a bright future.

Unfortunately, a catastrophic accident cut short Dawson's ability to capitalize on his own vision. Nevertheless, Dawson succeeded in transforming Fort Benton into the region's outfitting center, truly the "birthplace of Montana," and this led to his memorialization in the murals of the Montana state capitol.

Writing home, Andrew Dawson frequently alluded to his fear of being forgotten. Although members of his family were "daily cheered and comforted with almost hourly intercourse with each other," Dawson, a "poor hapless devil," was "scarce able to sleep at nights," so sure was he that he was "now nearly out of mind at home."

To avoid that fate, he spent hours crafting letters to keep his family both informed and entertained. This required "some little ingenuity," since he knew each letter would be read by his mother and each of his siblings "and the same song sung five times does sound rather tiresome."[1] His letters, he insisted, were to be shared, "a letter to one [was to be considered] a letter to all."[2] Still, he worried that these missives might never reach their destination, "so very suspicious [had he] become of the men" with whom he worked.[3] Fearing

[1]Letter 27.
[2]Letter 23.
[3]Letter 21.

that anything of value sent through the AFC would never reach its destination, Dawson found alternative delivery methods whenever possible.[4]

Contrary to his doubts, the Dawson family clearly prized his letters. After circulating them as instructed, Dawson's mother stowed them away in an old desk. But the letters became an afterthought, untouched for generations, after Dawson retired and returned to Scotland to live out his days at Glenesk, his brother Ebenezer's Dalkeith home.

Glenesk remained in the Dawson family until 1950, when the home was sold and its contents apportioned to Ebenezer's grandsons. His grandson Roy, then living in Vancouver, British Columbia, inherited the old family desk, which his brother dutifully shipped to Canada. Years later, when the widowed Roy returned to Scotland, the desk made another transatlantic voyage.

In 1975, Roy died and bequeathed the desk to Hamish, his brother James's son. A shoebox accompanied the desk, and inside Hamish discovered the unexpected letters of his great-great-uncle, Andrew Dawson. Hamish knew nothing of this relative or his letters. Perusing the letters, Hamish became fascinated by the story they told. For Christmas 1978, Hamish gave his siblings typescript copies of the thirty-seven well-traveled, century-old letters.[5]

The letters also intrigued Hamish's younger brother, Andrew.[6] Hoping to learn more about this familial namesake, Andrew, after his 1988 retirement, delved into researching the American fur trade. Two decades later, he had amassed enough information to imagine a book of Dawson's letters. At the Arthur H. Clark Company, he found a publisher, Bob Clark, who immediately saw the potential in this firsthand account of the fur trade's waning years, an assessment shared by several fur trade historians.

But the project was not without obstacles. Living in England, Andrew had no experience with the upper Missouri and only a limited understanding of the complexities of the fur trade. Clark also pointed out several more recent works on the fur trade that Andrew

---

[4]Hand delivery by someone visiting Scotland was preferred, but a large number of letters were sent through his brother's New York employer.

[5]By the time Hamish found them, the letters had crossed the Atlantic three times: the original posting, the shipping of the desk to Vancouver, and its return trip to Scotland.

[6]To distinguish between the two Andrew Dawsons, the front matter refers to the co-author as Andrew and the fur trader as Dawson.

had overlooked. Of these, Andrew was especially taken with *Frontier Diplomats*, the 2000 biography of Dawson's good friend Alexander Culbertson. Andrew was delighted to learn that Clark had also published that work.

In 2008, Andrew asked Clark to approach Lesley Wischmann, the author of *Frontier Diplomats*, to gauge her possible interest in collaborating on the Dawson project. After reviewing Dawson's letters, Lesley agreed, excited by this rare glimpse into a fur trader's private musings. Very few personal journals written by traders have survived.[7] Most of the writings by traders that remained were business-related. By contrast, Dawson's letters were wonderfully human, suffused with raw emotion and uncluttered by the requisite bravado of the 1800s fur trade.

The co-authors enjoyed an exceptionally rewarding collaboration. Andrew had completed the bulk of the research long before Lesley became involved. Her research illuminated and expanded on several known events but uncovered little that Andrew had not already discovered. Lesley's primary role was in crafting the narrative and providing historical context for Dawson's letters.

The letters themselves, first transcribed by Hamish Dawson, were transcribed anew by Andrew and then again by Lesley. This third transcription was crosschecked against Andrew's and then carefully reviewed again. That final version is the one contained herein. Every surviving letter has been included. Unfortunately, no letters exist from June 1850 to January 1852 or from January 1859 to April 1861.

The letters, as presented, have been rendered as faithfully as possible with Dawson's spelling, punctuation, and grammar preserved. Occasionally paragraphs have been inserted for clarity, especially to replace long spaces employed by Dawson to denote a change in focus.

Dawson's handwriting left very few words impossible to decipher. In those rare instances where this did occur, we have inserted our best guess in the body of the letter and acknowledged the ambiguity

[7]Alexander Culbertson entrusted his journal to his youngest son, Joe. After Joe's children scribbled on the pages, an embarrassed Joe destroyed it. Dawson's own journal was lost when the *Chippewa* exploded.

in a note. On several letters, sealing wax or its remnants obscured one or more words. These are noted with [obscured by sealing wax].

To indicate "etc., etc., etc.," Dawson frequently used multiple repetitions of a symbol similar to an ampersand. More rarely, Dawson used an actual ampersand. Therefore, &c has been used to denote Dawson's ampersand-looking "etc." The reader will recognize this from its multiple serial usage.

Letters 1, 2, 6–13, and 24, as well as parts of 3, 17, 20, and 22, were written in the space-saving crosshatched style common to that era. The writer would compose his letter as usual before turning the page ninety degrees and beginning again, writing across the previous section. While words are fairly easy to decipher in this style, punctuation is trickier. We have done our best to be faithful to Dawson's punctuation but acknowledge that some may have been unintentionally misinterpreted.

It had been our hope to publish Dawson's letters unedited. Unfortunately, space limitations made that impossible. The letters were shortened by editing out materials pertaining solely to Dawson's family and friends in Scotland. We removed no material regarding Dawson's American family nor did we omit family matters directly affecting Dawson's story. What is missing is the commentary expected of an absent relative: congratulations on births and marriages, condolences on deaths, questions about friends, concerns about siblings' employment, inquiries about loved ones' health, and similar material. In all, across the thirty-seven letters, some ten thousand words were cut. Deleted material is indicated by the typical ellipses.

Recognizing that any deletions will leave some researchers uneasy, the Dawson family has graciously agreed to place pdf scans of the original letters in three research facilities, each of which provided the authors with much appreciated assistance: Fort Union Trading Post National Historic Site, Williston, North Dakota; the Montana Historical Society Archives, Helena; and the Overholser Historical Research Center, Schwinden Library, Fort Benton, Montana. We encourage concerned researchers to consult the scanned originals.

Dawson's surviving letters were written to his immediate family, including his mother, Grace Scott Dawson; his older brother, Ebenezer (Eben); his older sister, Christian (Tit); his younger brother, Alexander (Aleck); and his youngest brother, Abraham (Abram).

The reader will quickly discover that Dawson's letters do not always present him in the most favorable light. When his feelings were hurt, he expressed his distress. When he felt neglected, he did not hesitate to complain. Moreover, his attitude toward his business partners—both white and Indian—were not always complimentary. The letters reveal a complex man whose feelings and attitudes shift and evolve depending on what is occurring around him. The reader is encouraged to remember that these letters span two decades, and therefore such an evolution is to be expected. Nevertheless, the tone of Dawson's letters sometimes makes him a less than sympathetic character. But that uncensored quality is precisely what makes these letters both unique and compelling.

Finally, we would like to explain our decision to refer to Dawson's employer as the "American Fur Company," despite its legally correct name being Pierre Chouteau, Jr. & Company.

John Jacob Astor founded the American Fur Company (AFC) in 1808. Multiple subdivisions handled the business across the continent. Soon after Ramsay Crooks opened their St. Louis office in 1822, the AFC entered into a contract with that city's fur barons, including Pierre Chouteau, Jr. In December 1826, Bernard Pratte & Company, with Chouteau as a partner, became the western agents for Astor's American Fur Company.

Meanwhile, Kenneth McKenzie and his Columbia Fur Company had become a powerhouse on the upper Missouri. Always eager to co-opt any viable competition, the AFC entered into negotiations with McKenzie. In 1827, McKenzie agreed to sell Astor the Columbia Fur Company, which was then rechristened the Upper Missouri Outfit (UMO) of the AFC's Western Department. With Pierre Chouteau, Jr., as chief executive of the Western Department and Kenneth McKenzie managing the UMO, the AFC quickly dominated the St. Louis fur trade.

Then, in 1834, Astor withdrew from the business and sold the American Fur Company name to Ramsay Crooks, who ran the Northern Department. The Western Department, with its powerhouse Upper Missouri Outfit, officially became Bernard Pratte &

Company. After Pratte died, the company became Pierre Chouteau, Jr. & Company.

But for most people, including the average upriver trader, all these shifts and permutations meant little. If they worked for Astor, Pratte, Chouteau, or McKenzie, they worked for "the Company." Everyone else was "the opposition."[8] Although Ramsay Crooks went bankrupt in 1844, the year Dawson arrived in America, and took the American Fur Company name with him, its lingering vitality is evident in Dawson's first letter home.[9] Since this book does not pretend to be a history of the business of the fur trade and, despite the legalities, the "American Fur Company" remained the common appellation for the outfit operated by Pierre Chouteau, Jr., and Kenneth McKenzie, we have chosen to use that designation, with our sincere apologies to those fur trade scholars who will be offended by its technically improper usage.

---

[8]Barbour, *Fort Union*, 14–18.

[9]Letter 1: the "American C^oy^ had no opening whatever for anyone . . ."

Acknowledgments

ANDREW ERSKINE DAWSON

I am deeply indebted to numerous archivists, genealogists, and librarians, including Eleanor Corbett, Manitoba Genealogical Society Inc., for histories of Robert Morgan and Andrew Dawson, Jr.; F. B. MacLowick, Cultural, Heritage, and Citizenship, Legislative Library, Winnipeg, for information on the Red River Settlement and the history of St. François-Xavier Municipality; Betty Somers, Manitoba Historical Society, for *Genealogy of the First Métis Nation*; Charles Armour, Dalhousie University Libraries, Halifax, Nova Scotia, Alice Thacker, Lloyd's Register of Shipping, London, and Robert Urquhart, Mitchell Library, Glasgow, for information about the barque, *Adam Carr,* its cargo, and sailing schedules; John English, general editor of the *Dictionary of Canadian Biography Online*, for the biographies of Scottish-born fur traders; Eppie Edwards, National Library of Jamaica, for the wording on the burial plaque for Squadron-Surgeon Ebenezer Scott, MD, RN, Naval Cemetery, Port Royal.

I also thank His Grace The Duke of Buccleuch, Selkirk, for information on North American buffalo on his Dalkeith estate; Rosamond Brown, Regional Library Headquarters, Selkirk, and Susan Donaldson, Scottish Borders Council, Hawick, for locating the family and farms of Laidlaw, Murray, and Potts; Marion Richardson, Ken Bogle, and Alex Fitzgerald, Midlothian Council Library Headquarters, Loanhead, for providing extracts from Dalkeith *Old Parish Records* and for Ken Bogle's help with illustrations of old Dalkeith, and David

Smith, editor, Dalkeith History Society, for access to Society publications; Jo Curry, Edinburgh University Library, Sheena McDougall, and Andrew Bethune, Edinburgh Room, Central Library, and Betty Iggo, genealogist, Edinburgh, for family histories of Combe, Dawson, Erskine, and Scott; Scott Collins, Historical Search Room, Scottish Record Office, Edinburgh, for copies of Dawson family wills and inventories; *ScotlandsPeople Online*, Edinburgh, for census extracts; Catherine Smith and Angela Schofield, Advocates Library, Edinburgh, for information on the careers of David Constable, Sr., and Thomas Potts; John Chalmers, Edinburgh, for research on John James Audubon; and Donald MacCormaig, antiquarian book dealer, Edinburgh, and Spike Hughes, rare books, Innerleithen, Peeblesshire.

I am grateful to Julie Gardham, University of Glasgow Library, for the definition of "tea paper" chapbooks; Betty Hendry, James Watt Library, Greenock, for family details of Daniel Lamont; Jeremy Duncan, A. K. Bell Library, Perth, for information on Sir William Drummond Stewart of Murthly Castle; Kathleen MacLeman, Avoch Heritage Association, The Black Isle, Ross and Cromarty, and Alistair Macleod, genealogist, Inverness Library, for family histories of Sir Alexander Mackenzie and his kinsman Kenneth McKenzie; Liza Verity, National Maritime Museum, Greenwich, for listing the battleships on which Ebenezer Scott, MD, RN, served; Mary Sampson, archivist, Royal Society, London, for confirmation of the election of Robert Erskine, FRS; Janice Hall, Cunard Line Limited, Southampton, for records of transatlantic liners *Persia*, *China*, and *Scotia*; Janet Smith, Liverpool Record Office, David Rogers, Warrington Library, and Francesca Anyon, Wirral Archive Services, Birkenhead, for census data on Alexander Dawson and Christian Drummond.

Thanks also to Helen Barnes, Central Library, Bristol, and the Receptionist Librarian Bodleian Library, Oxford University, for kindly allowing research access; P. Hatfield, Eton College, Windsor, Public Record Office, Kew, Surrey, Keith Haines, Head of History, Campbell College, Belfast, for kindly replying to letters; and to the receptionist librarian, School of Medical Sciences Library, Bristol University, for book reading facilities on cholera, scurvy, and smallpox.

My contacts in America have been rewarding, and my very special thanks are due to Carol Frasier, Dorothea Simonson, Kathryn Otto, Montana Historical Society, Helena; John Lepley, Museum of the Upper Missouri, Fort Benton, MT; George Lane, Photographer, Helena; Margaret Summers, Antiquarian Book Dealer, Helena; James Sperry and James Davis, State Historical Society of North Dakota, Bismarck; LaVera Rose, South Dakota State Historical Society, Pierre; Laura Robinson, Missouri State Archives, Jefferson City; Emily Miller and Dennis Northcott, Missouri Historical Society, St. Louis; Mark Cedeck, St. Louis Mercantile Library; The Archivist, Circuit Court of Clay County, Probate Division, Liberty, Missouri; Louise Hawkins, Clay County Archives & Historical Library Inc., Liberty; Phyllis Heath, Researcher, St. Joseph, Missouri; Graham Beal, former Director, Joslyn Art Museum, Omaha; Patricia LaPointe, Memphis/Shelby County Public Library and Information Center, Memphis; Genella Olker, Tennessee State Library and Archives, Nashville; Ira Glazier, Director, Temple University, Balch Institute, Center for Immigration Research, Philadelphia; Edward Skipworth, Special Collections and Archives, Rutgers University Libraries, New Brunswick; Ruth Schallert, Smithsonian Institution Libraries, Washington, DC; and Kathleen Baxter, National Anthropological Archives, Smithsonian Institution, Washington, DC.

It is with the greatest pleasure that I thank my sisters and brothers for their support over two decades. Elsie and her husband, David Foreman, from Vancouver, British Columbia, visited the Montana Historical Society Library, Helena, in 1988, to initiate my family research on our great-great-uncle, Andrew Dawson. Joy and her husband, Douglas Whybrow, in Dorset, drew my attention to sources of information in North America. Eben and his wife, Margaret, in Glasgow, were enthusiastic about my detailed research in Scotland. Above all, my special thanks are due to Hamish and his wife, Dorothy, in Ayrshire, for rediscovering and transcribing Andrew Dawson's letters. Hamish generously requested that facsimile copies of these historic letters should be deposited in archives in the United States. I only wish Hamish (1925–2007), my brother-in-law, Douglas Whybrow (1921–2009), and Eben (1927–2012) had lived to see this work come to fruition. My special thanks are also due to Ian Chapman, CBE, a long-standing friend of the Dawson family. Ian had a very distinguished career as a publisher in the United Kingdom and in the United States. My introduction to the University of Oklahoma Press was triggered by his professional support and encouragement.

Working with Lesley, my co-author and editor, has been inspirational and exciting. Together, we have opened new doors and made new discoveries. It has been a pleasure and a great privilege working on this transatlantic project. My siblings and I thank her for all her research and dedicated professional skill in achieving our joint goal.

We also thank Bob Clark for his foresight, wisdom, and friendly introductions, thus ensuring that Andrew Dawson's historic letters are more widely read in *This Far-Off Wild Land*.

Lesley Wischmann

I wish to express my gratitude to many librarians and archivists, including Dennis Northcott, Missouri Historical Society, St. Louis; Sarah Walker, North Dakota State Archives, Bismarck; and everyone who has contributed to the extensive historical holdings at the University of Wyoming's Coe Library and the staff that makes working there a pleasure.

The whole crew at the Montana Historical Society deserve special recognition: Barbara Pepper-Rotness, Emiley Jensen, Jodie Foley, Ellie Arguimbau, Brian Shovers, Rich Aarstad, and especially Zoe Ann Stoltz. They make working in their archives a sheer joy. Every request is met with a smile, and the staff members always make you believe that they find your topic eminently interesting. Moreover, this facility is one of those rare places where researchers are invited to browse the vertical files to see what turns up. This is such a delight as discoveries often happen serendipitously. Unfortunately, that kind of access has become increasingly rare. I hope Montanans never lose their welcoming attitude and open sensibility.

Very special thanks also to the Friends of Fort Union and the fellowship they bestowed upon me, enabling me to spend a wonderful week at the very special Fort Union Trading Post National Historic Site. The staff members were always willing to help, even as they scurried about, preparing for rendezvous. Special thanks to Lisa Sanden, for perpetual cheerfulness; Dominique Alhambra, for showing me Fort Union's wonderful collection of artifacts; Chuck Jones, for numerous cart trips that spared my legs the long hike from Montana (smile); Loren Yellow Bird, for allowing me access to his materials on the Fort Berthold tribes; Andy Banta, for letting me enjoy the porch; Tony Brown, Audrey Barnhart, and Dave Clark, for their general hospitality; and Randy Kane, for all of his many kindnesses and for sharing his extensive knowledge of Fort Union and the fur trade.

The Fort Union Muzzleloaders, with their living history encampment, made the week extra special. A special thanks also to Michael Cohan, reenactor, for sharing with me the fascinating broadside about Alfred Cumming. Erik Holland, supervisor at Fort Buford State Historic Site, came to my rescue by allowing me to use their microfilm reader while also adding immensely to my understanding of the roles played by Forts Clark and Berthold. Fellow writer and researcher Doreen Chaky of Williston is both my friend and a constant source of information and encouragement. I thank her especially for letting Larry borrow her car so that he had one day off from playing chauffeur.

Everyone at the Fort Whoop-Up fur trade symposium helped keep me focused on the research at hand. I especially want to thank Doran Degenstein and Gord Tolton of Fort Whoop-Up as well as Nancy Thornton, Friends of the Old Agency on the Teton; Gail DeBuse Potter and James Hansen, Museum of the Fur Trade; and Pat McCormack, University of Alberta, Edmonton. It was also a great pleasure finally to meet Rodger Touchie, who provided a lot of interesting information regarding Dawson's relationship with Jerry Potts as well as subsequent assistance in locating the Potts portrait.

I can never thank all my friends in Fort Benton enough. You always make me feel at home, and maybe one of these days I really will be a Fort Bentonite. In the meantime, my deep appreciation to Jack and Sue Lepley, Ken Robison, Bruce "Burnt Spoon" Druliner, Dave Parchen, and especially Bob Doerck, who would not even let me pay for all the copies made at the Overholser Research Center. I also want to thank Cheryl Gagnon for the elegant remodel of the Grand Union, which always makes my stays in Fort Benton special.

A number of people were also very helpful in assisting us in acquiring the included images. For their help, I would like to thank Amanda Streeter Trum and Rebecca Kohl at Montana Historical Society, Alexandra Lane of the White House Historical Society, Sara Przybylski of the State Historical Society of Missouri–Columbia,

Michelle Maxwell of the Thomas Gilcrease Museum at the University of Tulsa, Kay Johnson of the Joslyn Art Museum, and Doug Cass of the Glenbow Museum.

Jessica Walker of the University of Oklahoma Press always had a joyful attitude, even as she prodded me to get the work done. Bill Swagerty braved his "dungeon" to try to answer a last obscure question for us. Paul Hedren once again flattered me with his faith in my ability to flesh out the life of a lesser-known trader.

Gloreen Culbertson Strausser and her sister honored me by coming to Fort Union to hear me talk, yet again, about their ancestor and spend several hours visiting. I hope that one day I will have the pleasure of speaking about Dawson while one of his descendants sits in the audience.

I also want to thank my friends with the Alliance for Historic Wyoming, who never complained when I had to put AHW work on the back burner in order to tend to book commitments. You'll soon get my full attention, I promise!

Words cannot express my gratitude to my co-author, Andrew, and the extended Dawson family, who graciously trusted me to bring this project to fruition. I have so enjoyed getting to know your relative. I thank you for offering me this opportunity and for understanding when several wonderful discovered tidbits regrettably had to be cut in the end.

Without question, Bob Clark is the best editor a writer could have. He was always there to answer questions and provide encouragement. He understood when deadlines were missed and at every turn expressed endless faith in this work. At our only serious bump in the road, Bob came up with an elegant solution that satisfied everyone. I am proud to call him my editor, my publisher, and my friend. It is bittersweet to know that this book will be one of the first volumes to be published by Arthur H. Clark Co. without a Clark at its helm. I sincerely hope that this book will add luster to the reputation of that noble press, nurtured so carefully by three generations of the Clark family.

Nevertheless, Bob Clark left us in very capable hands. Moving toward copy editing can be a bit nerve-racking. But Emily Jerman and Elaine Durham Otto made the whole experience easy and pleasurable. Elaine's notes on our work were always kind and thoughtful, and her contributions undoubtedly helped to make this a better book. Emily was always available to answer our questions in clear language that helped us negotiate all the subtle nuances of the publishing process. From day one, both of them seemed like old friends, and we will always appreciate their painstaking attention to making this the best book possible. While we never had to turn to Chuck Rankin for assistance, it was nice to know that, at the end of this very long process, such a well-respected editor was available to us, if needed.

I accomplish nothing significant without the support of my dear sister, Margaret Mathews, and my loving husband, Larry Jansen. On this project, Larry drove me to North Dakota, Canada, Montana, and Oklahoma while Margaret offered me a West Virginia refuge to hide away as I thought through the structure of this work. Larry kept our Laramie home safe and warm so I would have the time, energy, and physical and mental health to pursue my writing. Both of them do an excellent job of pretending to listen while I rattle on and on and on as I work out a problem. Both are experts in helping me solve technical problems, and both are wonderful critics who make my words sharper. Both try not to laugh too hard when I prove how stupid an ostensibly bright person can be. And both know just how to talk me down when I become convinced I cannot write. Both bring me enormous joy. Both love me unconditionally. Both enrich my life in ways I sometimes doubt I deserve. Few people are lucky enough to have one such strong supporter, and I am blessed with two. I love you both and can't imagine my life without either of you. Thanks for always being there for me.

Abbreviations

AD	Andrew Dawson
AFC	American Fur Company
CSHSND	*Collections of the State Historical Society of North Dakota*
ExDoc	Executive Documents
FtB	Fort Benton, MT
LoC	Library of Congress
MiscDoc	Miscellaneous Documents
MOHS	Missouri Historical Society
MTHS	Montana Historical Society
NAM	National Archives Microfilm
ORL	Overholser Historical Research Center, Schwinden Library and Archives
UMO	Upper Missouri Outfit
VF	Vertical file

PART I

Biographical Sketch

1

Treachery on the Frontier

THE MYSTIQUE OF THE AMERICAN FRONTIER HAD LONG beckoned dreamers. One of those who caught the fever was a boy named Andrew Dawson, born in Scotland in 1820. The stories and art of adventuring relatives, a visiting ornithologist, and fellow countrymen who had joined America's entrepreneurial fur traders fed his curiosity about the American wilds. But as Dawson would discover, the fictions of our imagination rarely survive their confrontation with reality. Even as Dawson was dreaming of a swashbuckling future, those then living on the frontier were jeopardizing the entire enterprise.

In the summer of 1843, the American Fur Company reshuffled their upper Missouri operations.[1] Alexander Culbertson, the Company's newest wunderkind, protested the shake-up, believing it a dangerous mistake.[2] Having spent a decade among the Blackfeet, Culbertson knew their loyalties remained tenuous. Moreover, the extreme isolation of Fort McKenzie, the Upper Missouri Outfit's Blackfeet

[1]Actually its formal name was Pierre Chouteau, Jr. & Co. This fur company was commonly known as the American Fur Company (AFC). This was often shortened to simply "the Company." Their operations on the upper Missouri were known as the Upper Missouri Outfit (UMO). For more, see the preface.

[2]Born outside Chambersburg, Pennsylvania, in 1809, Culbertson joined the AFC in 1833 and was immediately assigned to the Blackfeet post. He became chief trader there in 1834, and in the ensuing decade, he survived a siege by the Crow and the 1837 smallpox epidemic. He built a thriving trade with the Blackfeet, the last upper Missouri tribe to engage with the AFC. Culbertson's own career blossomed, and he soon became a minor partner in the AFC. For more, see Wischmann, *Frontier Diplomats*.

post, often resulted in brittle relationships among the traders.[3] Fort McKenzie needed a constant and steady hand to remain on an even keel, and Culbertson did not trust those whom the Company proposed to place in charge.

But the Company, blinded by the possibility of solving three separate problems, refused to listen. They ordered the even-tempered, genial Culbertson to Fort Union to host the renowned ornithologist, John James Audubon, who would be spending the summer studying upper Missouri wildlife.[4] For years, the AFC had opened their upriver forts to American and European artists and scientists, thereby acquiring powerful strategic allies who rushed to their defense whenever political fights threatened the Company's hegemony. Audubon would be the first important visitor in years, and the AFC partners were determined to satisfy his every need. This required deploying Culbertson to Fort Union.

And when the summer ended, Culbertson could accompany Audubon downriver to Fort Pierre before heading overland to his new posting at Fort Laramie on the Platte. Fort Laramie, one of the earliest western fur posts, had been acquired by the AFC five years earlier. Fort Laramie operated primarily by supplying smaller outlying posts and then, each spring, gathering and bundling the furs from those posts before shipping them east. But Fort Laramie's returns had been consistently disappointing. Since Culbertson had been so successful in developing the Blackfeet trade, the Company was convinced he could do the same at Fort Laramie.

Meanwhile, back on the upper Missouri, the Company could dispose of another headache by transferring Francis Chardon to Fort McKenzie.[5] Although experienced, Chardon was a temperamental

---

[3]The Blackfeet posts were located in the interior of what is now Montana, some forty miles northeast of present-day Great Falls. Fort McKenzie was about ten miles northeast of Fort Benton.

[4]Fort Union is located on the present-day border of Montana and North Dakota, approximately twenty-five miles west of Williston, North Dakota, and some 750 river miles downstream from the Blackfeet posts.

[5]Born in Philadelphia, Chardon's early roots are obscure. He first turns up out west after the War of 1812, in which he participated. Between 1815 and 1827, he lived with the Osage, marrying a woman of that tribe. Around 1827–28, he joined the AFC. He spent 1832 at Fort Union and moved in 1833 to Blackfeet country, where he helped establish a trading post at the junction of Porcupine Creek and Milk River. In 1834, he became bourgeois at Fort Clark. He had a succession of Sioux wives and a black slave. For more, see Swagerty's introduction to *Chardon's Journal*.

trader known for freely dispensing liquor, "befriend[ing] the wrong people," and leaving "a trail of tension" in his wake.[6] At Fort Clark, he had recently been accused of murdering a rival. Although he denied the charge, the AFC thought it best to transfer him.[7]

So Culbertson would entertain Audubon at Fort Union and then transfer to Fort Laramie, while Chardon took charge of Fort McKenzie—an elegant solution to three thorny problems. Or so the partners thought.

Departing for Fort Union in the spring of 1843, Alexander Culbertson temporarily left Fort McKenzie in the hands of Alexander Harvey.[8] Harvey had first come upriver in 1833. He quickly gained a reputation as the resident hothead. During the 1835 Crow siege of Fort McKenzie, Harvey had urged Culbertson to fire on the recalcitrant warriors. When Culbertson refused, preferring negotiation, Harvey advocated open insurrection. The siege ended before Harvey implemented his mutinous plans, but his notoriously short fuse had left many fearing for their lives. In 1839, Culbertson had implored Pierre Chouteau, Jr., to fire Harvey. But Harvey's intrepid midwinter trek to St. Louis so impressed Chouteau that Harvey returned to the Blackfeet post, rehired and brasher than ever.

In the four years since, Culbertson and Harvey had reached a tenuous peace, each understanding that the other was untouchable. But Harvey chafed at his second fiddle status. Whenever business called Culbertson away, Harvey assumed command while impatiently awaiting a permanent promotion.

Harvey's command of Fort McKenzie in the spring of 1843 lasted only until Francis Chardon arrived a few weeks later. Harvey resented Chardon's appointment and, almost certainly, worked to undermine the older trader's authority. Chardon, unfamiliar with the Blackfeet,

---

[6]Sunder, *Fur Trade on the Upper Missouri*, 61.

[7]On his deathbed, Chardon declared: "As I am going before my God, it was an accident." He claimed the two men had gone hunting, and while making their way through a dense thicket of willows, his gun accidentally discharged, killing his companion. Abel, *Chardon's Journal*, 267n252.

[8]Sunder, *Fur Trade on the Upper Missouri*, 87, describes Harvey as "a tall, well-built storybook hero . . . strong, bold, and brave." His origins are somewhat sketchy, but as a youth, he apprenticed with a St. Louis saddle maker. After they quarreled, Harvey joined the AFC.

relied on Harvey's knowledge of the tribe. This misplaced reliance led to disaster in January 1844 when a band of twenty Blood warriors visited Fort McKenzie.[9] Chardon and Harvey, for reasons they never explained, refused to admit them to the fort. The insulted warriors killed some fort livestock before retreating. This infuriated Harvey and Chardon who, with six Fort McKenzie employees, set off in hot pursuit.[10]

The warriors soon realized they were being pursued and set a trap. When the traders lost sight of their prey, Chardon sent his slave, Reese, ahead to reconnoiter. From atop a small hill, Reese slowly raised his head. The warriors fired, killing him instantly. The Blood rushed up the hill, grabbed Reese, scalped him, and taunted the Company men with the bloody scalp.[11] The outraged traders were helpless. After the Blood departed, they collected Reese's remains and returned to Fort McKenzie.

Now Chardon, who "set great store by" Reese, began plotting his revenge.[12] Together with Harvey, he developed a devilish plot. Knowing that many fort employees remained loyal to Culbertson, who had always advocated conciliation with the tribes, Chardon and Harvey confided their plot to very few. Their chillingly simple scheme required little assistance.

They would load the cannon at the fort's gates with half-ounce lead balls and then wait for the next trading party to arrive. When they did, the traders would invite the chiefs inside, knowing the rest of the tribe would gather at the gates, waiting for trade to begin. Inside, the traders would kill the chiefs, and then Harvey planned to fire his pistol into the cannon's vent. The resulting blast would kill those gathered at the gates. The traders would not only have their revenge but also their victims' horses, robes, and personal possessions.

Since Culbertson had cultivated a vigorous trade at Fort McKenzie, the conspirators did not have to wait long for a trading party to arrive. On 19 February 1844, an unsuspecting band of Northern Blackfoot stepped into the trap. As planned, Harvey and Chardon

---

[9]The Blackfeet Confederacy consisted of three subgroups: the Piegan or Pikuni, the Blood or Kainah, and the Northern Blackfoot or Siksika. After ten years in their country, Harvey certainly understood these distinctions.

[10]Kane, *Wanderings of an Artist among the Indians of North America,* 296, says the Bloods killed thirteen cattle. Bradley, "Affairs at Fort Benton," 235, says they killed one pig.

[11]Kane, *Wanderings,* 296.

[12]Larpenteur, *Forty Years,* 188.

invited the chiefs inside, and the tribe gathered. But the chiefs, sensing something was amiss, bolted. As they scrambled over the pickets, a frantic Chardon fired, breaking one chief's thigh.[13]

The commotion alerted the rest of the tribe. They began to scatter, but Harvey fired the cannon anyway, killing several, including women and children.[14] Although the number of dead was disappointingly small, the wicked traders did collect guns, bows and arrows, horses, and hundreds of abandoned buffalo robes.[15]

Harvey finished off several wounded and helpless warriors with his dagger. According to folklore, he then licked their blood from the knife before using it to scalp them. In a final fit of frenzy, Harvey raised the scalps and forced the fort's women to dance over his victims, their relatives.[16]

One witness wrote: "February 19, 1844. Fight with the north Blackfeet, in which fight we killed six and wounded several others: took two children prisoners. The fruits of our victory were four scalps, twenty-two horses, three hundred and forty robes, and guns, bows, and arrows."[17] That night Chardon and Harvey celebrated, but their dastardly scheme cost the American Fur Company dearly, and the Blackfeet never forgot their treachery.

Misfits have always found refuge on the American frontier. The petty criminal wanting a fresh start or the not so petty criminal seeking new prey found fertile ground in new climes. Those who had burned their bridges in civilization built new ones in a new land. Personality attributes shunned by staid society were welcomed in

[13]Ibid.

[14]The number killed varies. Larpenteur, *Forty Years,* 188, says three died. Bradley, "Affairs at Fort Benton," 3:237, gives the number as twenty-one. Kane, *Wanderings,* 297, says ten, "principally women and children." Ewers, *Blackfeet,* 67, says "ten or more." Abel, *Chardon's Journal,* 246n186, reprints the letter of an eyewitness that gives the number of dead as six. This most authoritative account comes from a "private journal of a man, now dead (1856), who was at that time in the employ of the company." The author was not further identified. Senate ExDoc 2, 34th Cong., 3rd sess., 875, 626.

[15]Abel, *Chardon's Journal,* 246n187.

[16]Larpenteur, *Forty Years,* 189; Bradley, "Affairs at Fort Benton," 237; Chittenden, *American Fur Trade,* 2:685.

[17]Report of the Secretary of the Interior, 1856, Senate ExDoc 2, 34th Cong., 3rd sess., 875, 627.

the rough-and-tumble borderlands. With few questions to answer, frontier newcomers could shed any past indiscretions. Ancestry and education meant little. If a new arrival could do the work, he found acceptance. The frontier offered second chances.

Misfits come in many forms. Familiar social forces of early nineteenth-century America cast Alexander Culbertson away. The third son of a third-generation planter who settled Pennsylvania's Cumberland Valley in the early 1700s, Culbertson understood from earliest childhood that his ancestral lands could be subdivided no further. With no patrimonial land grant awaiting, he could find a landed wife, pursue the ministry, become a skilled laborer, or head to the frontier. His need for adventure made his choice clear.

Alexander Harvey was another outcast. Born and raised in St. Louis, he likely came from the rough-edged laborer class that managed to eke out a living there in the early 1800s.[18] While still a minor, Harvey's "headstrong disposition" got him discharged from a saddlery apprenticeship. Soon after, he headed upriver, one of the American Fur Company's newest misfits.[19]

Andrew Dawson would follow his path in 1847. A solid man standing well over six feet, Dawson's healthy shock of red hair added to his conspicuousness. When he spoke, his deep brogue identified him as Scottish. The Indians would remember him as "Long Knife," in acknowledgment of the prized sword he had inherited from his uncle, Ebenezer Scott. Scott, a Royal Navy surgeon, had stirred his nephew's imagination with his tales of worldwide travel.[20]

The sword may have been Dawson's showpiece, but Dawson prized his gun even more. Manufactured by Manton & Company, London's specialty gunsmiths, the fowling piece, which Dawson dubbed "My Joe," had helped him earn top shooting prizes in the 1839, 1840, and 1841 Dalkeith Gymnastic Games.[21] Both pieces connected Dawson to his beloved and much missed homeland.

Dawson did not grow up dreaming of a future on the American

---

[18]Little is known about Harvey's parentage.

[19]Chittenden, *American Fur Trade,* 2:692.

[20]Ebenezer Scott, M.D. (1792–1838), squadron physician on the HMS *Cornwallis,* served with the Baltic, Mediterranean, North American, and South American squadrons on several famous flagships. He died 30 December 1838 of yellow fever and was interred with full honors in the Royal Navy cemetery, Port Royal, Jamaica. Dawson Family Papers.

[21]The First Prize Silver Medal, suitably inscribed, remains in the Dawson family's possession. See photo section.

frontier. That idea developed only after his temper got the better of him, eventually shaming his own family. With the best solution a redemptive absence, Dawson joined that most lonesome category of misfits: the exile. The "love of home," truly known only "to those in exile,"[22] often rendered him a "big baby."[23] Homesickness frequently spiraled into melancholia that even his beloved wife could not penetrate.[24] Only letters from home—which Dawson felt arrived all too infrequently—kept him from feeling "alone, unfriended, solitary, and in tears."[25]

Throughout his nearly two decades on the upper Missouri, Dawson never got beyond the gnawing reality that his family had sent him away.

---

[22]Letter 24.
[23]Letter 19.
[24]Letter 23.
[25]Letter 2.

2

Grand Ambitions and Noble Temperament

By the time Andrew Dawson was born in Dalkeith, Scotland, on 5 March 1820, the Scottish Reformation was well under way, liberating its citizens from their role as the persecuted stepchildren of an imperious overseer. The country was finally reaping the benefits of their disputatious union with England more than a hundred years earlier. Something more complex and vibrant was replacing Scotland's traditional rural economy.

Dalkeith, seven miles southeast of Edinburgh and the administrative center of Midlothian, was a "celebrated and ancient little town," "a favorite spot of the early Scotch [*sic*] kings."[1] The broad tree-lined High Street hosted one of Scotland's largest markets. Lodging houses, grand and modest, thrived on market traffic. By 1831, a rail line transported coal, minerals, and produce to Edinburgh.

On the town's northeast edge stands Dalkeith Palace, with its Corinthian pilasters and bracketed pediments. Home to the Duke of Buccleuch, the palace reminds the townspeople of their place in the monarchical hierarchy. Dawson's elders remembered when Bonnie Prince Charlie stayed there in 1745.

Dalkeith's grandest church, dedicated to St. Nicholas, dated to the 1400s. Just as Scotland had struggled through long, torturous shifts in religious identity, the church's congregation had worshipped variously according to Roman Catholic, Episcopal, and Reformed dictates. By the time Andrew Dawson was born, the elegant church's original purpose had been largely abandoned. Lofts now cluttered its interior,

[1]James Dawson, "Major Andrew Dawson, 1817–1871."

accommodating Dalkeith's growing mercantile sector. Inside, bakers, fleshers, skinners, weavers, tailors, shoemakers, and colliers peddled their wares.

Andrew, ruddy-faced and redheaded, was the fourth child of Andrew Dawson, Sr., and his wife, the former Grace Scott. Two more sons quickly followed.[2] Then in 1825, Andrew, Sr., died. He was just thirty-two, and his namesake had just turned five. Grace was left alone with six children. In the best of times, her husband's small leather business, Andrew Dawson and Company, had struggled. Without him, these were desperate times. Grace needed both business advice and a capital infusion.

Her brother-in-law, Abraham Combe, a well-to-do Edinburgh tanner, took pity on the young widow, lending her money and business expertise. George Combe, Abraham's younger brother and an Edinburgh solicitor, also helped out. Together, the brothers underwrote the children's education. Without this kindness, the older Dawson children might have been forced to leave school, and Andrew might never have started. Instead, shortly after his fifth birthday, Andrew enrolled in Dalkeith Grammar School.[3]

Outside school, the young boy could be somewhat reckless, especially when riding his velocipede, an early bicycle. One of his many accidents resulted in a head injury that left him bedridden.[4] This unwanted confinement fed his burgeoning love of books. Naturally curious, Dawson was drawn to ornithology and adventure stories. In the fall of 1826, George Combe took him to see an exhibit of bird sketches by a North American artist named John James Audubon in Edinburgh.

Audubon had come to Edinburgh to find an engraver. American publishers had rejected his ornithological studies, but scientists, writers, and artists were enjoying an Enlightenment heyday in Scotland. Audubon reveled in Edinburgh: "the great breadth of the streets, their good pavement and footways, the beautiful uniformity of the buildings, their natural grey coloring and wonderful cleanliness." Word of his impressive works spread quickly through the city's educated classes.

William Home Lizars, a respected engraver, soon offered to under-

---

[2]The six children were James, Christian, Ebenezer, Andrew, Alexander, and Abraham.
[3]Dawson, "Major Andrew Dawson."
[4]Ibid.

take the publication, which Audubon insisted had to be done "in size of life." The prints, engraved on copper sheets, were then hand-colored. It was a time-consuming and expensive process. As Lizars slaved over the engravings, Audubon exhibited his work at the Royal Institution for the Encouragement of the Fine Arts. An awestruck young Andrew Dawson toured the show with his mentor, George Combe.[5]

Uncle George impressed Dawson even more when he acknowledged having met Audubon.[6] Combe was an ardent practitioner of phrenology, a pseudoscience that claimed to be capable of discerning personality traits from the bumps and variations of a person's skull. Intrigued, Audubon had allowed Combe to search his head for the "miraculous bumps."[7] After measuring the skull "as minutely and accurately" as Audubon "measure[d] the bill or legs of a new bird" and recording each protuberance, Combe declared Audubon "a strong and constant lover," an "affectionate father" with "great veneration for high, talented men."[8] Combe even persuaded Audubon to sit for a phrenological mask.[9] Young Dawson marveled at this connection, grateful for such an interesting and talented benefactor.

In 1833, George Combe used his legal skills to defend the Dawsons when the Duke of Buccleuch alleged that their tanning pits, constructed without permission, were emitting offensive odors that annoyed the Duke's tenants. Solicitor Combe arranged a settlement, but soon thereafter, the Duke bought the ancient thatched Dawson Close and demolished it. The family moved to White Hart Street, and the leather business relocated to Croft Street, where it continued operations until 1904.

At fourteen, Andrew Dawson moved to Edinburgh to study accounting.[10] Under a standard six-year indenture, he worked for his uncle, Ralph Erskine Scott, and boarded with his family.[11] Andrew readily took to the work; numbers in neat rows, adding up just right, satisfied

---

[5]John Chalmers, M.D., *Audubon in Edinburgh*. http://www.audubonroyaloctavos.com/SITE/pages/Chalmers.html. Accessed March 2010.

[6]While not technically Dawson's uncle, that is how he regarded George Combe.

[7]Audubon and Coues, *Audubon and His Journals*, 1:191.

[8]Ibid., 1:168.

[9]Audubon's mask is now in the National Portrait Gallery of Scotland. For more on George Combe's career as a phrenologist, see Stack, *Queen Victoria's Skull*.

[10]His son, James, in his biography in *Contributions to the Historical Society of Montana*, vol. 7, claims that Dawson trained as a lawyer and, "not liking the lawyers profession," became an accountant. This has been repeated in almost all subsequent biographical accounts. However, the authors found no evidence of Dawson having trained as a lawyer.

[11]Scott ran a successful accounting practice on Great King Street.

his desire for order. On Saturdays, Dawson walked seven miles home to Dalkeith to enjoy a family dinner, returning on Sundays.[12]

Dawson also enjoyed Edinburgh's intellectual challenges. A voracious reader, he reveled in the local bookshops where he apparently met Andrew and Thomas Potts. In addition to their mutual love of books, the three shared a family connection. Years earlier, Thomas Potts, uncle to the Edinburgh brothers, had courted Dawson's mother.[13] Even after marrying Dawson's father, she remained friendly with the Potts family and was delighted to learn her son was continuing the tradition. Thomas Potts would go on to clerk for the Supreme Court,[14] while his brother, Andrew, would soon leave for America to enter the upper Missouri fur trade.[15]

In 1840, Dawson completed his internship and qualified as a professional accountant. He stayed on with his uncle in Edinburgh until 1842, when something ruptured their relationship. Exactly what happened is unknown, but an embittered and unemployed Andrew soon returned to Dalkeith, to his mother's chagrin.

About this time, James Dawson, the eldest son, died. With James gone, the family business fell to Ebenezer. But there was apparently no place for Andrew at the leather factory. Instead, he was soon headed to Warrington, England, where his cousin, George Combe, helped him land a position with a Mr. Garven.[16] The situation seemed like a good fit, but Andrew hated the dirty, sooty, industrial Warrington,

---

[12]Letter 24.

[13]Mr.Thomas Potts, Hawick, Roxburghshire, to Miss Grace Scott, Dalkeith, Midlothian, 25 November 1811, Dawson Family Papers. This letter refers to their romantic meeting in Dalkeith.

[14]Will and Testament of Thomas Potts, ScotlandsPeople. Accessed November 2009.

[15]*Edinburgh Directory: Pigot 1837*, "Scottish Book Trade Index" lists Andrew P. Potts as "bookseller, stationer, and circulating library," at 47 Broughton Street, Edinburgh, from 1834 to 1838. Touchie, *Bear Child*, 28, 37, says Potts came to the United States in 1832 and was on the first boat upriver in 1836. In correspondence with Wischmann, Touchie expressed interest in this new evidence and suggested his dates came from Hugh Dempsey's research. Dempsey, letter to the Montana Historical Society, 11 January 1956, says that Potts had been in the States for approximately four years before his death in 1842 (author's collection). Dempsey, "Jerry Potts: Plainsman," says Potts began working for the AFC in 1836, after living for a short time in Pennsylvania. Entries in the AFC ledgers for "Andrew R. Potts" begin in 1837 and end in 1845. Entries after his death in 1842 probably relate to his estate. Scottish records show his correct name to be Andrew Petrie Potts, not Andrew R. Potts.

[16]Dawson Family Papers. George was the eldest son of Abraham and Agness Dawson Combe. An Edward Garven, or Gaven, was employed at Bank Quay glassworks in Warrington during the mid-1840s. Whether or not this is the man for whom Dawson worked is unknown. Correspondence from David Rogers, Warrington Library, 11 March 1992.

and less than two years later, he was back home, unemployed. Years later, he would blame his termination on having "read in black and white accusations against [him] of the grossest nature," which "were nearly all lies."[17] But the cause mattered little. His apparent inability to hold a job had become a familial embarrassment.

A twenty-four-year-old, working-class male could not afford to be cavalier about work. Now the man of the family, Ebenezer Dawson confronted his younger brother. Andrew simply had to be more responsible, Ebenezer insisted, if not for his own sake, then for their mother's. After some heartfelt discussions, Andrew hit upon a plan. In Edinburgh, Dawson had met Robert Laidlaw, whose brother, William, worked in the American fur trade. Although Dawson shuddered at the idea of becoming "a wanderer in a foreign land," the shame he had brought on his family could not be ignored.[18] In America, he could prove himself again. With good fortune, he could even send his poor widowed mother money. The more he pondered the idea, the more appealing it became. Abroad, he could be fearless and shrewd, merry and thoughtful, honest and compassionate. He would become one of those legendary Scots about whom Robert Burns and Sir Walter Scott wrote so poignantly.[19] He would show that his heart was right and his convictions clear, just as his ancestors had.

The Dawson family tree included several notable Scots. His mother, descended from the fourth Earl of Mar, was the great-great-granddaughter of Henry Erskine, a well-known Covenanter.[20] Arrested in 1682 for heresy, Henry Erskine was imprisoned at Melrose, Jedburgh, and Edinburgh before appearing before the Privy Council with instruments of torture attached to his hands. Commanded to stop his open air preaching, Erskine declared: "My Lord, I have my commission from Christ, and though I were within an hour of my death, I durst not lay it down at the feet of any mortal man."[21]

[17]Letter 12.

[18]Letter 12.

[19]Maclean, *Scotland*, 202.

[20]The Covenanters banded together to resist the attempts of the Catholic Church to reassert control over Scotland in the seventeenth century. They became a key part of Scotland's decades-long battle to maintain some semblance of autonomy.

[21]Smellie, *Men of the Covenant*, 2:301.

His stubborn refusal led to confinement at the Bass Rock, where he remained until, his health deteriorating, his brother paid his fine.[22] Although freed, Erskine was banished from Scotland.[23]

Erskine continued his preaching in England, where many of his adherents joined him. After his death in 1696, his sons, Ebenezer and Ralph, took up the calling. Ebenezer, Andrew Dawson's great-great-grandfather, helped form the liberty- and democracy-preaching Secession Church, which eventually reached across the Atlantic and into Europe.[24] Known for his courage and honesty, Ebenezer Erskine preached to increasingly large congregations until his death in 1754.[25]

As a teenager, Andrew Dawson had read his great-great-grandfather's biography. With his brother Ebenezer, he had visited Bass Rock, the site of Henry Erskine's imprisonment. They had planned to examine the old prison's remains and observe the sea birds, including tens of thousands of nesting gannets, but Ebenezer had seized the opportunity to lecture his irresponsible younger brother.

Ebenezer could not have picked a better location to inspire his brother. On the isolated island, Andrew had no choice but to listen to his brother's scolding. As he did so, Andrew thought about his ancestor's sacrifices. He could feel the loneliness Henry Erskine experienced. Andrew felt an obligation to his ancestor, whom he regarded as bravery incarnate. The Erskines had faced death and imprisonment for their principles. All Andrew had to do was take responsibility for his own future. On that barren island, he resolved to put his life in order, to make something of himself, and to bring pride to the family name.

The Erskine bravery could help him stand tall for principles, speak out against injustice, and face adversity with courage. Lately, those traits had gotten him into trouble, but surely they could also serve

---

[22]Bass Rock is an island in the outer part of the Firth of Forth. The steep-sided volcanic rock was settled by early Christian hermits and later became home to an important royal castle. It subsequently became a notorious prison and was featured in Robert Louis Stevenson's novel *Catriona*.

[23]Crighton, *Memoirs of Rev. John Blackader*, 380–81.

[24]Erskine and Fisher et al., *Representations*. A curious side note: In 1800s Pennsylvania, a relative of Andrew Dawson's preached in a Seceder Presbyterian Church attended by author Wischmann's ancestor.

[25]Ebenezer Erskine was commended for his bravery in commanding Seceders at Stirling during the 1745 uprising of Bonnie Prince Charlie by His Royal Highness, the Duke of Cumberland. Fraser, *Life and Diary of the Reverend Ebenezer Erskine*, 444.

him well, especially if he were to embrace a more challenging life. Perhaps his problem had been expecting noble ambitions to triumph in what he considered an increasingly gloomy, industrial wasteland. Perhaps Scotland was no longer a place where a man of grand ambitions and noble temperament could flourish. Perhaps that place was America.

After all, his relatives had also paved that path. Ralph Erskine's son Robert had been one of Scotland's best engineers, making significant contributions to the industrial economy with his work in hydraulics. He had been elected to the Royal Society in 1771,[26] shortly before moving to America, where he became manager of the Ringwood, New Jersey, ironworks. The company thrived until the Revolutionary War intervened. Then, to the dismay of some of his Scottish relatives, Erskine sided with the beleaguered colonists, even organizing an ironworkers' militia. Erskine was eventually appointed the first geographer and surveyor-general of the Continental Army by his friend George Washington.[27]

Erskine created detailed surveys of New Jersey and New York to aid the colonists.[28] He also devised the means of closing off the Hudson River with an impenetrable barrier of huge iron chains crafted by his ironworkers. By preventing British warships from entering the Hudson River, Erskine helped keep the colonies united. But while surveying the Hudson Highlands, Erskine caught a chill, which escalated into pneumonia. He died on 2 October 1780.[29]

Andrew Dawson's great-grandmother had told him about her famous cousin, although she considered his stand during the war with the colonies wrongheaded. Dawson took only one lesson from the stories: here was another relative who had chosen a bold, adventurous life.

Dawson hoped to arrive in America with a hand up in his new career. For years, Scots had been making their way to America to seek

---

[26]Robert Erskine's Certificate of Election, dated 31 January 1771, was signed by six Fellows including Sir John Pringle, president, and Benjamin Franklin (author's collection).

[27]Congress approved the appointment on 28 July 1777. Heusser, *George Washington's Map Maker*, 161n1.

[28]The New York Historical Society owns some 120 maps produced by Robert Erskine. The Morris Township Library, Morristown, New Jersey, owns others.

[29]Ringwood Manor, where Erskine lived and died, is now a state park. New Jersey's Erskine Lake and Erskine River are named for him. George Washington attended his funeral and may have been at his side when he died. Heusser, *George Washington's Map Maker*, 218.

riches on the frontier and in the fur trade. In addition to Sir Alexander Mackenzie, the famous explorer, notable frontier Scotsmen included Alexander Ross, Alexander MacKay, Robert Dickson, Ramsay Crooks, Sir William Drummond Stewart, and Daniel Lamont.

The fur trade had always had a special allure for Scotsmen. Highlanders even shared many cultural connections with the indigenous people who formed the other half of the American trading partnership. Both lived in tribal societies with a strong warrior tradition and intimate ties to clan; both dwelled in a rugged landscape not easily conquered; both prized the strong social bonds that fostered survival in spite of frequent deprivation and hardship; both perpetuated their heritage through an oral history tradition; and both existed on the edge of empire.

Both held similar world views. Just as the Great Law of Peace of the Six Nations Iroquois Confederacy mandated that elders consider the seventh generation in decision-making, Highlanders charted their path forward only after considering those who had come before and those who would follow.[30]

Disruptive change came first to the Highlands. Resources extracted from new American markets fueled Scotland's industrial development. As these new market forces ruptured communal bonds that had bound the clans together for centuries, large numbers of Highlanders were driven from their ancestral lands. Industrialization and commercial agriculture spread, requiring more and more land and further denigrating tribal societies with more and more people displaced. This pattern would be repeated in the American West as the frontier was pushed back.

By the mid-nineteenth century, Indians on the upper Missouri were trading robes and pelts for woolens made in Yorkshire mills from the wool of sheep that grazed on lands expropriated from traditional Highlanders. Meanwhile, many sons of those same Highlanders, stripped of their traditional sheep-tending roles, set sail for America to work in the fur trade, selling those blankets to the natives.[31]

Although not a Highlander, Dawson capitalized on the long Scottish

---

[30]The Great Law of Peace of the Six Nations Iroquois Confederacy was the oral constitution that bound the Confederacy together.

[31]For a fascinating look at the similarities between Scottish Highlanders and American Indians, see Calloway, *White People*, and Szasz, *Scottish Highlanders*. The subject is also discussed in Herman, *How the Scots Invented the Modern World*.

ties to the American fur trade to advance his own plans. He knew that Andrew Potts, the Edinburgh bookseller whose shop Dawson had frequented, had traded in his genteel profession for the American frontier in the late 1830s. But Andrew's brother, Thomas, was still in Edinburgh, and Dawson asked him for a letter of introduction to the St. Louis bigwigs.

Potts happily obliged, writing Kenneth McKenzie, founding member of the august Upper Missouri Outfit, to recommend Dawson with his accounting skills to the Company. But Potts also had sobering news for Dawson, news that emphasized the dangers inherent in the younger man's proposed adventure. Andrew Potts had been killed at Fort McKenzie, the difficult Blackfeet post commanded by Alexander Culbertson.

Well-read and educated, Andrew Potts had quickly become a "universal favourite" among the traders.[32] He had married a daughter of the Black Elks band of the Blood named Crooked Back soon after his arrival.[33] These mixed marriages were common on the frontier, helping to cement ties between the Company and the tribes while offering the men obvious benefits.[34]

Then in early 1842, Mercereau, a French-Canadian *engagé*, had banished a belligerent Piegan named Weasel from Fort McKenzie.[35] This infuriated Weasel. On the evening of February 25, 1842, the Piegan banged on the fort's closed wicket, expecting Mercereau to answer.[36] When the wicket opened, Weasel shoved his flintlock in and fired. Unfortunately, Andrew Potts, not Mercereau, had answered the banging. Potts died instantly. When the Piegan elders learned of Weasel's intemperate act, they had him executed. But Weasel's

---

[32]Letter 6.

[33]Touchie, *Bear Child*, 57, gives her Indian name as Namo-pisi.

[34]These Indian wives were often known as "country wives" because many traders also kept a white wife in the States.

[35]Dempsey, "Jerry Potts: Plainsman," identifies this warrior as "One White Eye" and gives his Indian name as Ah-pah. Other sources call him Weasel.

[36]The date of Potts's death is usually given as 1840 based on Bradley, "Affairs at Fort Benton," 231. But Bradley's dates, which apparently came from Culbertson's notes and memories, are not always reliable. Wischmann, in researching *Frontier Diplomats*, often found them to be off by a year or more. The date 25 February 1842 comes from an announcement placed in the *Edinburgh Evening Courant* by Thomas Potts, October 10, 1842, 3: "Died at Fort Mackenzie, Upper Missouri, North America, on 25th February last, MR ANDREW POTTS, of the American Fur Company, formerly bookseller in Edinburgh." A wicket was a small opening in the stockade through which goods were dispensed.

summary dispatch offered little comfort to Potts's widow, Crooked Back, his young son, Jeremiah, or his family back in Scotland.[37]

Although shaken by news of his friend's fate, Dawson pressed on, committed to his plan of action. He next visited Robert Laidlaw, whose brother William had founded the Columbia Fur Company with Kenneth McKenzie. Robert Laidlaw agreed to write letters of introduction to his brother and McKenzie, and he also told Dawson about another friend and former schoolmate from Tweedsmuir named James Murray, who was engaged in the upper Missouri trade. According to Laidlaw, when Audubon visited Scotland in the 1830s, he stayed at the Murrays' Hearthstane Farm.[38] Dawson filed Murray's name away for future reference.

Dawson left Edinburgh with these letters of introduction in his pocket. Despite the disturbing news about Andrew Potts, he remained eminently, even naively, confident of his own abilities.

---

[37]The Potts family in Scotland learned of Andrew's murder when letters of condolence were received from his colleagues on the upper Missouri, including McKenzie, Laidlaw, Culbertson, Desautel, and Murray.

[38]Audubon and Coues, *Audubon and His Journals*, 2:33.

3

Look Forward in Confidence

FIGHTING HOMESICKNESS, ANDREW DAWSON BOARDED THE *Adam Carr* in Glasgow, Scotland, on 1 May 1844, bound for New York City. The single-decker, square-rigged, three-masted barque of black birch and spruce timbers carried 130 passengers along with bales of cotton, damask, worsteds, woolens, silks, and "125 gallons of whisky and 61 barrels of beer." Pig iron and firebricks were used as ballast.[1]

Dawson, traveling in steerage, provided his own meals and utensils. During the long crossing, American mythology loomed large for the steerage passengers: America offered the "little man" his chance at greatness; America, the land of milk and honey; America, the land of limitless riches.

But as these emigrants would discover, the throngs crowding America's eastern cities already strained the available opportunities. Even as the *Adam Carr* docked in New York, many Americans, tired of foul air and crumbling economies, were packing up and heading west across the soon-to-be legendary Oregon Trail, the newest siren song. Dawson, of course, had his own plan, counting on his letters of recommendation to land him a job in Saint Louis with the American Fur Company.

The *Adam Carr* reached New York in mid-June, having been delayed by strong headwinds and gales.[2] Stepping ashore, Dawson spied his mother's old friends David Paterson and James Scrymgeour,

[1]The *Adam Carr* was built in New Glasgow, Nova Scotia, in 1842. *Glasgow Registry of Shipping of 6 January 1844* lists the syndicate owners, including Captain Robert Scott. *Exports of the Clyde from Glasgow, April 30, 1844* lists her exports. Also see *Clyde Bill of Entry and Shipping List, Custom-House, Glasgow, May 2, 1844*.

[2]*Manifest of Passengers as Lodged with the Collector of the Customs for the District of New York*, signed by Captain Robert Scott, 13 June 1844.

recent emigrés from Edinburgh. He was heartened to find them waiting but concerned by the absence of his uncle, William Adams of Memphis. Adams had promised to meet Dawson in New York and then accompany him to Saint Louis. Dismayed to find his plans already going awry, Dawson tried to adjust. With his cash depleted, he reluctantly accepted $20 from Paterson and then prevailed on the *Adam Carr*'s captain to let him remain on board the vessel until his uncle arrived. Dawson hunkered down on the ship, waiting as his foodstuffs dwindled. Finally, three days later, Adams arrived, blaming business for his tardiness.

A robust Irishman with a ruddy complexion, Adams had married Alison Scott, Dawson's mother's youngest sister. Years earlier, Alison had quarreled with her family over something long forgotten and run off to Canada, where she met Adams. Now living in Memphis, Alison ran a boarding house while her husband dabbled in various business schemes. His most recent venture involved metal pen nibs, just then coming into vogue.

Dawson, still short of cash, accepted another loan from his uncle for trip expenses, including the cost of shipping his many possessions to Saint Louis. To ease his transition to a new country, Dawson had brought along family mementos, a large leather valise, a hinged portmanteau, his father's folding oak writing desk, a complete set of Shakespeare's works, the poems of Robert Burns, his Bible, various writing supplies, bedding and cooking utensils, and, of course, his prized gun, and his uncle's naval sword.[3]

To Dawson's surprise, Adams then announced he could only go part of the way to Saint Louis. The younger man tried to suppress his mounting trepidations and to concentrate on his uncle's guidance while it was available. Dawson was learning that Americans' often abrupt, ever restless habits would require him to rely on his own wits more than he had expected. Dawson and Adams caught a steamboat for South Amboy, New Jersey, where they boarded a westbound train. In Baltimore, Adams bid his nephew farewell as Dawson caught another train bound for Cumberland, Maryland. There he began the long trek westward on the National Road.

One of the first government-built, long-distance roadways, the National Road, begun in 1811, connected Cumberland, on the

[3]Letter 3 and Dawson Family Papers, MTHS.

Potomac, to Wheeling, Virginia (now West Virginia), on the Ohio. From there, patrons could continue overland or take riverboats west or south. The road, although masterfully engineered, still left passengers "most disagreeably uncomfortable" as the stagecoaches bounced across the rugged Allegheny Mountains.[4] But to Dawson's delight, a Scotsman named Weddell boarded in Baltimore bound for Cincinnati. The two discussed Dawson's prospects in this strange, new country in between reminiscences about Edinburgh. Weddell's own success buoyed Andrew's spirits.[5]

Dawson was surprised by all the small settlements they passed, having imagined America would be mostly wild and uninhabited. The long journey also exposed him to scenery far different from anything he had known in Scotland. From the steamer, he observed the power of the Ohio and Mississippi Rivers and marveled at all the wildlife on shore. The Mississippi had flooded that summer, overflowing its banks and extending several miles out from its natural channel.

In general, Dawson found Americans pleasant and was surprised to see how easily the classes mingled. He quickly came to realize the high regard in which most of his fellow passengers held the dollar. If there was a buck to be made, an American was there to make it. He often balked at prices, including the $7.85 charge for transporting his baggage from Cumberland to Wheeling. But with no other choice, he paid, grateful for the money in his pocket.

His journey of more than 1,500 miles lasted ten days and cost him $25.25. On 19 June 1844, Dawson finally reached Saint Louis with 75 cents in his pocket and great ambitions to pursue.[6]

Andrew Dawson only expected to remain in Saint Louis a few weeks at most. In fact, he hoped his entire American adventure would be over in a few years. He would land a fur trade position, go upriver, live courageously, redeem his reputation, make a fortune, and return to Scotland, once again his mother's pride and joy. With his exile

[4]Letter 1.

[5]Nothing more is known about this man.

[6]James Dawson, "Major Andrew Dawson, 1817–1871." James Dawson says his father gave 50 cents to "the cabman" and spent the other 25 cents on a locksmith after losing the key to his trunk. He then charmed a landlady into letting him rent a room with no money upfront.

surely temporary, Dawson had given little thought to St. Louis, a city built by the fur trade.

In August 1763, a fifteen-year-old New Orleans native named Auguste Chouteau left his hometown with his stepfather, Pierre LaClède. Chouteau served as LaClède's clerk as his stepfather's party searched for a proper site to build an upriver settlement. By December, the group had reached Saint Genevieve, and LaClède dispatched Chouteau to explore the Mississippi's western bank north to the Missouri River. A few miles from the junction of the two great rivers, Chouteau located a promising town site on a limestone bluff some eighty feet above the Mississippi. Rich alluvial soil capable of sustaining the envisioned settlement covered the plateau to the north and west. For several miles around, beautiful prairie grasses waved in the wind.[7] Chouteau sent for his stepfather, who arrived and declared, "I have found a situation where I am going to form a settlement which might become, hereafter, one of the finest cities in America."[8]

Thirty workmen arrived in February 1764 to clear the land. Soon after the first trees fell on 15 February, the men had their first building, a structure that would become the Saint Louis Market House.[9] Within a year, five hundred people lived in LaClède's settlement as Saint Louis quickly became the region's commercial center.[10]

In 1778, LaClède died and Auguste Chouteau inherited his business interests. Following the 1804 Louisiana Purchase, Chouteau became Saint Louis's premier citizen, a necessary contact for anyone of stature passing through the region. Meriwether Lewis consulted with him as the Corps of Discovery prepared for their epic journey. By 1816, the government itself was relying on Chouteau for reports on tribal conditions on the upper Mississippi and Missouri Rivers.[11]

The St. Louis that greeted Andrew Dawson had long since outgrown its frontier trappings. Although still lacking many refinements, the city had grown from 6,500 to 30,000 between 1830 and 1841.[12]

---

[7]Joseph N. Nicollet, "Sketch of the Early History of St. Louis," published as Senate ExDoc 237, 27th Cong., 2nd sess., and as House ExDoc 52, 28th Cong., 2nd sess., and reprinted in McDermott, *Early Histories*, 136.

[8]St. Louis City Plan Commission, *Physical Growth of the City of St. Louis*. http://stlouis.missouri.org/heritage/History69/#intro. Accessed April 2010.

[9]McDermott, *Early Histories*, 5; Thwaites, ed., *Early Western Travels*, 26:145–48.

[10]McDermott, *Early Histories*, 22.

[11]Ibid., 9.

[12]Population figures vary. The 1845 *St. Louis City Directory* puts the 1830 number at 5,000. Likely, the discrepancies reflect the pace of growth. Nicollet as quoted by McDermott, *Early Histories*, 161.

Worshippers could choose between several Protestant churches or a Catholic cathedral. The city offered both a waterworks and a public school system. St. Louis University, the first institution of higher learning west of the Mississippi, had opened in 1829. During the 1830s, the state legislature chartered new banks, railroads, insurance companies, a gas company, the chamber of commerce, and a medical society. The St. Louis Theater opened in late 1837, and the foundation was laid for the Planters' House Hotel. Retail operations opened up on Third and Fourth Streets as the city reached up and down the riverfront and headed westward.[13] By 1841, the city's tax base exceeded $8.5 million.[14]

The *Zebulon M. Pike*, the first steamboat to reach St. Louis, arrived on 27 July 1817.[15] Three decades later, hundreds of steamers might be moored at the levee while slaves loaded and unloaded freight on Front Street. The badly rutted roads turned into a sea of mud as handcart and wagon traffic increased. Such was the price of progress.

Life in St. Louis could also be hazardous. The Mississippi routinely flooded. Just before Dawson arrived in June 1844, the river covered the American Bottom, its agricultural floodplain, leaving unknown numbers dead. Farm animals were swept away and families left homeless. St. Louis became "a city of refuge." Disease, "induced by anxiety, exposure, & privations," swept away many more.[16]

Nonetheless, the city continued to grow. In 1845, the population reached 35,000. Churches continued to multiply, with one Baptist, four Catholic, three Methodist, and two Presbyterian houses of worship built in 1845 alone. Meanwhile, laborers finished the courthouse, and two new tobacco warehouses opened. The local reservoir expanded. And while the absence of gas streetlights was "severely felt," boosters assured St. Louis residents they could "look forward to [this] with confidence in the course of a few years."

When LaClède arrived in 1763, he carried a precious charter from the director-general of Louisiana Province granting him exclusive trading

[13]St. Louis City Plan Commission, *Physical Growth of the City of St. Louis.*

[14]Nicollet, as quoted by McDermott, *Early Histories*, 161.

[15]St. Louis City Plan Commission, *Physical Growth of the City of St. Louis.* Nicollet, as quoted by McDermott, *Early Histories*, 161, incorrectly puts the date as 1819.

[16]*Green's St. Louis City Directory, 1845*, xi.

rights with the upriver tribes. Louisiana Creoles had long traded with the tribes downriver, and now they planned to expand their dominion. Joseph Nicollet remembered those early Creole traders:

> They are half civilized and half savages; rebellious and submissive; possessed of great courage and power of physical endurance, they fear neither the inclemency of seasons, the pains of hunger, the arrows of the Indian, nor the danger of exposure to wild beasts; never despairing, and always cheerful, they are intelligent, honest, devoted, and gifted with the warmest feelings; they speak, as it were unconsciously, the idioms of the several Indian tribes among whom they have been; they know all the rivers; all the paths and by-paths, and all the recesses of the wilderness; they are intimately acquainted with the character and wants of the Indians, and possess a good knowledge of the haunts and habits of the wild animals; in a word, they are a class of men with whom no military or scientific expedition, nor trading caravan, no traveller of any description, can dispense.[17]

That description could also have been applied to most of the upper Missouri fur traders, including those who reported to the dominant Chouteau enterprise, which Andrew Dawson hoped to join.

The day after he arrived, Dawson visited the headquarters of Pierre Chouteau, Jr. & Co. Clutching his letters of introduction from Thomas Potts and Robert Laidlaw, Dawson asked to meet with either Kenneth McKenzie or William Laidlaw. Laidlaw, he learned, was at his home, north of the city. But McKenzie appeared to greet the twenty-four-year-old Scotsman. Dawson, large and lanky at 6'4", was not easily intimidated even by a personality as strong as that of McKenzie. When the familiar brogue tumbled from McKenzie's tongue, the young man felt a rush of familiarity. Dawson waited expectantly as McKenzie read the presented letters.

Sizing up this potential new recruit, McKenzie reached a quick decision. As confident as Dawson appeared, McKenzie doubted he understood the living conditions awaiting him on the upper river. Moreover, McKenzie was well attuned to how difficult the situation on the upper Missouri had recently become.

Only six months had passed since Chardon and Harvey's horrific massacre at Fort McKenzie. The partners, shaken by their employees' treachery, were hoping to persuade Alexander Culbertson to return

---

[17]As quoted in McDermott, *Early Histories*, 155–56.

to the Blackfeet post. The young Scots-Irish trader had gained the tribe's trust with his straightforward and respectful handling of the 1837 smallpox epidemic, and the partners hoped he could do the same now. But McKenzie suspected that persuading him to return would not be easy.

After his warnings regarding Harvey and Chardon had gone unheeded, Culbertson had accepted his posting to Fort Laramie only grudgingly. Now his worst fears had been realized, and McKenzie doubted the young trader would risk his own life to assuage the perfidy of others. Indeed, even as McKenzie was pondering Dawson's credentials, Culbertson was upriver, shunning entreaties from company partner Honoré Picotte to return to Fort McKenzie.[18]

On the upper Missouri, conditions remained deeply troubled. Chardon and Harvey, their bloodlust sated, had quickly found their position untenable. Abandoning Fort McKenzie, the now infamous traders had headed downriver, stopping at the mouth of the Judith River to construct a new post that Francis A. Chardon named after himself. But Fort FAC was soon besieged. The only Indians who approached came to harass the traders or drive off livestock. After several members of the garrison were killed, the rest of the men refused to leave the post to hunt or gather wood. Soon they were barricaded inside all day every day for their own safety, with few supplies and plenty of recriminations.

Of even greater concern to the AFC, the hostilities extended beyond Blackfeet country. Marauding bands of Blackfeet raided several other posts, including the base of upriver operations, Fort Union, where warriors led by Big Snake drove off forty horses and mules. Two AFC men died in another raid.[19] Animosities threatened to spread to other tribes. Despite intertribal conflicts going back centuries, the upriver tribes shared suspicion of the American Fur Company's trustworthiness following the Fort McKenzie massacre.

In the prevailing environment, McKenzie was cautious about sending inexperienced men upriver. The young man before him

---

[18]A French Canadian, Picotte joined the Missouri River fur trade around 1820. Married to a Sioux woman, he served mostly at Fort Pierre. It had been to Picotte that Culbertson complained about his 1843 reassignment to Fort Laramie. During 1844, Picotte was in charge of the UMO. For more on persuading Culbertson to return to the upper Missouri, see Wischmann, *Frontier Diplomats*, 113–14.

[19]Bradley, "Affairs at Fort Benton," 238.

seemed to have good intentions, and his letters offered strong recommendations. Still, Dawson had only just arrived in the States and knew nothing of the fur trade, conditions upriver, or Indians. The Company could not afford any more mistakes. McKenzie told the eager applicant there was "no opening whatever for anyone."

The pronouncement devastated Dawson. Had he come all this way only to meet another failure? How would he explain that? McKenzie, seeing Dawson's crestfallen expression, assured him that "in present circumstances, anything was preferable to the Indian Country."[20]

Hoping to keep the potential recruit indebted to him, McKenzie scrambled to find another option. McKenzie knew a nearby dry goods store that might need an experienced bookkeeper, he informed Dawson. McKenzie scrawled a letter of introduction, and Dawson headed off to find Tevis, Scott, and Tevis.

At the store, Dawson introduced himself to John C. Tevis. Impressed by the young man's credentials, Tevis offered him a one-month trial position.[21] Dawson gratefully accepted, convincing himself that this was the best outcome because it would allow him "to get settled amongst civilization" without being "in a manner buried" from his family in Scotland.[22]

Dawson enjoyed St. Louis. He took long walks, wandering freely thanks to the city's easily mastered street grid. Chouteau's Pond, at the end of Seventeenth Street, became his favorite destination, offering a quiet contrast to the center city bustle. On Lucas Row, opposite the impressive Planters' House Hotel,[23] Dawson noted the phrenol-

---

[20]Letter 1.

[21]Tevis and Dawson shared a passion for books. Tevis was a founding member of St. Louis's Mercantile Library Association. Ravenswaay, *St. Louis*, 353.

[22]Letter 1.

[23]In 1842, Charles Dickens stayed in the new hotel with his wife, Catherine, and recorded: "The Planters'-house is as large as the Middlesex-hospital and built very much on our hospital plan, with long wards abundantly ventilated, and plain whitewashed walls. They had a famous notion of sending up at breakfast-time large glasses of new milk with blocks of ice in them as clear as crystal. Our table was abundantly supplied indeed at every meal. One day when Kate and I were dining alone together, in our own room, we counted sixteen dishes on the table at the same time. The society is pretty rough, and intolerably conceited. All the inhabitants are young. I didn't see one grey head in St. Louis." Forster, *Life of Charles Dickens*, 1:376–77.

ogy offices of Messrs. Fowler & Arthur, recalling the kindly George Combe. With temperatures routinely soaring above 90° that summer, being outdoors was preferable even with the constant "annoyance from the musquittoes."[24]

Work consumed most of Dawson's time. Arriving before 7 A.M., he spent his day completing bills of sale and recording transactions. Twice a year, when regional merchants descended with their orders, employees tended to purchases by day and packing and paperwork by night. During those periods, Dawson sometimes worked until 3 or 4 A.M., always returning at 7.

Within a year, Dawson began to see a downside to American's vaunted independence. At first, he had been enamored of America's "equality system," awed by the realization that, in his newly adopted country, master and clerk were as equals, even engaging together in friendly games of ten pins.[25] But eventually a darker side revealed itself in the "hard hearted and selfish strangers" whose only "motives to exertion" were "Self [and] Dollars."[26]

Before leaving Scotland, Dawson had visited his father's gravesite with his mother. There he had promised to continue his spiritual pursuits. He kept his word after arriving in St. Louis by joining the Second Presbyterian Church under the leadership of the Reverend Dr. William S. Potts.[27] Housed in a Greek Revival structure at Fifth and Walnut with six front columns and a tall white stone steeple, the church had welcomed its first congregants in 1840.

Another Second Presbyterian communicant was Robert Campbell, an Irish fur trader who had entered the business in 1823 as a clerk to John O'Fallon. As Jedediah Smith's clerk, Campbell attended the first Rocky Mountain rendezvous in 1825. He worked for various fur companies until 1832, when he and William Sublette, whom he had met at the 1826 rendezvous, entered into a partnership to form their own trading company.

Three years later, Sublette and Campbell were eyeing the establishment of a St. Louis mercantile. Frequent illnesses had softened

---

[24]Letter 1.

[25]Letter 1.

[26]Letter 2.

[27]Ravenswaay, *St. Louis*, 264–65. Potts was not related to Thomas and Andrew Potts of Scotland but was the son-in-law of Senator Thomas H. Benton, a great patron of Pierre Chouteau, Jr.

Campbell's lust for the frontier. In addition, while visiting his brother in Philadelphia, he had fallen in love with a young woman from North Carolina. Anxious to marry and begin a family, Campbell settled down in St. Louis, establishing a dry goods firm to outfit western travelers, sell Indian goods, and ship goods to start-ups across the West. By 1843, both a businessman and banker, he had become one of St. Louis's leading citizens.

But Campbell remained fascinated by the fur trade. His rivalry with the Chouteaus was legendary, and upstart outfits hoping to take on the American Fur Company often found Campbell a ready source of capital. Campbell was also quick to recognize the steamboat's potential to revolutionize the upper Missouri trade, and he purchased several light vessels to ascend the river.[28]

Upon meeting Dawson and learning his story, Campbell offered him a fur trade position with his opposition company.[29] Although tempted, Dawson still felt loyal to Kenneth McKenzie and William Laidlaw. They were fellow Scots, and his letters of introduction were written to them, not Campbell. So, despite the temptation, Dawson declined Campbell's offer. Dawson had remained in touch with McKenzie, who had introduced him to Laidlaw before McKenzie headed upriver in October 1844 to tend to business.

Dawson's decision to remain in St. Louis may also have been influenced by something besides loyalty. Like Campbell, Dawson had met an attractive young woman whose presence in the city made the frontier seem less appealing. She and Dawson took long walks, attended the theater, and talked about their pasts and futures. Soon they began to speak of marriage.

First, his lady friend insisted, Dawson needed her brother's approval. This made sense to Dawson. He had been raised to respect familial ties. And when the two met, they got along swimmingly. The brother was a doctor, and he confided to Dawson his plans for a new business venture. St. Louis, the brother explained, needed a new pharmaceutical store. As a doctor, he had the skill and knowledge to run it, and with Dawson's training, he would be a natural to handle the business details. Dawson, his intended, and her brother spent

---

[28]Nester, *From Mountain Man to Millionaire*, 11, 13–15, 19, 59, 118–22, 133, 167, 176–77.

[29]This book uses "opposition companies" to refer to any fur trade operation besides the American Fur Company.

many nights discussing the prospect. The plan seemed sound, likely to reap good benefits.

There was only one problem. The brother needed an additional $750 investment.[30] He hesitated to suggest it, but perhaps Dawson would like to invest. The investment, the brother promised, would bring a 10 percent return. Dawson, who worried constantly about finances, had been adding to his "store of money" with each paycheck. Still, he was by no means flush. He had not yet sent his mother anything to clear up his "very small debts at home," fearing that to do so would leave him "penniless." But he owed "not a cent" in St. Louis, and this not only sounded like a good investment but also would endear him to his beloved.[31] So, overcoming his reservations, Dawson secured a bank loan for $750 at 6 percent interest.[32] Soon thereafter, when he called on his betrothed, Dawson discovered that she and her brother, the upstanding doctor, had absconded with his money. It was yet another hard-learned lesson in the "self and dollars" culture that thrived on the American frontier.[33]

---

[30]The equivalent of $17,135 in 2008 currency.

[31]Letter 2.

[32]Letter 8.

[33]Letter 2.

4

A Solitary and Lonely Life

By early summer 1845, the American Fur Company knew they had a serious problem. In October 1844, after Alexander Culbertson refused to return to Blackfeet country, Kenneth McKenzie had gone upriver to winter at Fort Union, hoping to gauge overall conditions and reach out to the aggrieved tribes.[1] McKenzie's presence soothed some of the traders' anxieties but did little to stem tribal disaffection. With Francis Chardon and Alexander Harvey hunkered down in their beleaguered fort on the Judith, the AFC feared their Blackfeet trade might be lost forever.

On McKenzie's return trip to St. Louis, he almost certainly detoured to visit his protégé at Fort Laramie. McKenzie had experience appealing to Culbertson's pride. Ten years earlier, when Culbertson had doubted his ability to command Fort McKenzie, the veteran trader had suggested that Culbertson was "too diffident of [his] own powers."[2] This time, McKenzie's appeal would be easier, since Culbertson now regarded the Blackfeet as "his" Indians. And with ten years now invested in the Company, Culbertson's own financial interests were now at stake. Whatever McKenzie said apparently had some effect, as Culbertson was soon headed to New York City to discuss the situation with Pierre Chouteau, Jr.

By fall, Culbertson was headed back to Blackfeet country with a small contingent of dependable men. After sending Harvey and Chardon downriver, Culbertson and his handpicked men continued past Fort McKenzie, now burned to the ground, until they found a

[1]Letter 2.

[2]Kenneth McKenzie to Alexander Culbertson, 21 January 1834, Fort Union Letter Books, MOHS.

suitable location for a new post.[3] Choosing a site slightly upriver from present-day Fort Benton, Montana, Culbertson and his crew set to work, hoping to remain undetected until a protective enclosure could be constructed. In late October, Culbertson reported the new location to Honoré Picotte, whom he proposed as the fort's namesake. Picotte, convinced that the post would "be benificial to the Company," demurred, suggesting that Lewis would be "more suitable and appropriate."[4] Culbertson acceded to Picotte's suggestion, despite the irony that it had been Meriwether Lewis's 1806 killing of a Piegan warrior near the junction of Two Medicine River and Badger Creek that had engendered much of the original Blackfeet enmity.[5]

In early 1846, several Northern Blackfoot arrived at the fledgling Fort Lewis. Culbertson offered them gifts and invited their chiefs to a council. A few weeks later, some fifty warriors, led by Big Swan, appeared. Culbertson, extremely cognizant of the symbolism, invited them inside. There, he assured the chiefs that the perpetrators of the massacre had been banished from the region and that "the great chief of the traders" had sent him to make amends. Big Swan listened carefully and then told his people: "The ground has been made good again by Major Culbertson's return, and the Blackfeet must not be the first to stain it with blood."[6]

Fort Lewis's first four months resulted in a brisk trade. That spring, Culbertson headed downriver with 1,100 packs of buffalo robes along with a good quantity of beaver, fox, and wolf pelts.[7] With the Blackfeet trade successfully reestablished, the AFC breathed a sigh of relief.

[3]Accounts differ as to whether Fort McKenzie was burned by Chardon and Harvey when they fled or by the Indians. The site, downriver from present-day Fort Benton, is still relatively pristine, having been privately owned since the late 1800s. The owners, acutely aware of the fort's history, scrupulously avoided plowing or planting near the actual site of the old fort. The grounds remain littered with trade beads, old glass, and other artifacts.

[4]Honoré Picotte to Culbertson, 18 December 1845, Fort Laramie as well as the Chouteau Collection at MOHS; McDonnell, "Fort Benton Journal," 239.

[5]Moulton, *Journals of Lewis and Clark Expedition Online*, 26 July 1806, http://lewisandclarkjournals.unl.edu/index.html. The Piegan later identified the slain warrior as He-That-Looks-at-the-Calf. Ewers, *Blackfeet*, 47–48.

[6]Bradley, "Affairs at Fort Benton," 242–43. "Major" was an honorary title often applied to chief traders.

[7]Ibid., 244.

Andrew Dawson spent nearly three years in St. Louis, his employment unexpectedly gratifying. The young Scot liked America's decimal system, finding it eminently easier than the pounds, shillings, and pence used in Great Britain. His salary, too, had grown, and partnership rumors had been heard. Nevertheless, by the spring of 1847, his "spirits" were "frequently very much depressed and [his] strength very much reduced," perhaps influenced by his lost love and wounded pride.[8]

Then, one day, AFC partner William Laidlaw stopped by the shop to see Dawson. Born in 1795, Laidlaw was raised on a tenant farm at Kingledoors Farm near Tweedsmuir, Peeblesshire, Scottish Borders. His first North American job had been managing an experimental farm for Lord Selkirk of the Hudson's Bay Company. Charged with crossbreeding buffalo and English cattle, Laidlaw oversaw the birth of one healthy crossbred calf. But since Laidlaw preferred "marching around the country to superintending his agricultural operations," his successes were few. Dismissed for being "thoughtless . . . dissipated and extravagant," Laidlaw joined Kenneth McKenzie and Daniel Lamont in forming the Columbia Fur Company, which later became the AFC's Upper Missouri Outfit.[9]

Laidlaw had long since become a partner in the American Fur Company, and while Dawson considered him a "very good friend,"[10] not everyone held him in such esteem. The notoriously sour Charles Larpenteur called him "that old tyrant" and "a fiery, quick-tempered old Scotchman," placing him atop the trinity of drunkards who ran Fort Union in 1840–41. Larpenteur claimed that Indians could trade with a drunken Laidlaw, then steal their robes back and trade them again. Although Laidlaw upbraided his underlings for drinking, according to Larpenteur, "Laidlaw was the greater drunkard."[11]

The more congenial Culbertson also disliked Laidlaw. In 1839, wishing to discuss the wild-tempered Alexander Harvey with his superiors, Culbertson had taken the last commercial mackinaw fleet

---

[8]Letter 3.

[9]Hafen, *Mountain Men*, 3:167; Jo Leonard file, Clay County (MO) Archives and Historical Library; *Liberty Tribune*, 22 December 1899; Vera Haworth Eldridge, "County Can Boast of a 'Real Indian Princess,'" *Liberty (MO) Sun* 14, no. 17 (12 January 1983); Schooling, *Hudson's Bay*, 90–92.

[10]Letter 3.

[11]Larpenteur, *Forty Years*, 137, 138, 183. Larpenteur's trinity was "Mr. Laidlaw the father, Mr. Denig the Son, and Mr. Jacques Bruguière the Holy Ghost."

to St. Louis. Laidlaw complained that this had "put us to great inconvenience" and that Culbertson had acted "contrary to [Chouteau's] instructions" in order "to look after his own private affairs."[12] The next year, Culbertson hesitated when offered a promotion because of his brittle feelings toward Laidlaw, explaining: "It is simply the fear of having someone placed over me under whom I might be unwilling to act."[13]

But when Laidlaw asked if Dawson still wanted to join the fur company, Dawson, in "the real American fashion, that is to say in an instant," responded positively, despite Tevis's offer of a $200 bonus to stay.[14] In preparation, Laidlaw recommended that Dawson perfect his equestrian skills, and so the young Scotsman spent many spring evenings cantering around St. Louis. Dawson did not know that he would be going upriver with a man controversial enough to cause other traders to eye the new recruit warily.

In addition, Laidlaw had "had some falling out with the Co." According to Dawson, the older man had "resolved to withdraw . . . next Spring" and "start an independent trade." Laidlaw even offered Dawson "fair inducements" to join him after the split.[15] Although still "in the dark"[16] about Laidlaw's plans months later, Dawson continued to weigh his options based on a perceived indebtedness to the older trader.[17] Eventually, though, the "independent trade" talk evaporated, and Dawson admitted to feeling "dissatisfied with Mr. Laidlaw and inclined to doubt [his] motives" in having brought the younger Scotsman upriver.[18]

But for now, Laidlaw represented Dawson's entrée to the frontier.

By late June 1847, Laidlaw was ready to depart. Dawson joined several other recruits on the journey to Hackberry Hall, Laidlaw's farm in Liberty, Missouri. It took them about four weeks to cover four

---

[12]William Laidlaw to Pierre Chouteau, Jr., 1 August 1839, Chouteau-Papin Collection, MOHS.
[13]Holterman, *King of the High Missouri*, 52.
[14]Letter 3.
[15]Letter 3.
[16]Letter 5.
[17]Letter 6.
[18]Letter 6.

hundred miles.[19] Dawson traveled on horseback while packhorses carried their supplies. Laidlaw rode in a carriage with his Sioux wife, Red Bird (also known as Mary Ann), "two other Ladies," and one of Laidlaw's children.[20] In addition to the Laidlaws' own five daughters, then at school in the States, they were raising the children of Jacob Halsey, a trader who had died near Liberty several years earlier.[21]

The travelers shared the dusty route with emigrants heading west and outfitters destined for Independence, the "jumping off" point for the newly popular Oregon Trail. Dawson marveled at the huge bull trains hauling large wagons laden with all manner of freight.

Not used to such long rides, Dawson rejoiced when Hackberry Hall finally appeared on a hill above Clear Creek. An impressive timber structure, its central vestibule led to rooms with large, welcoming verandas. Inside, artifacts and game trophies adorned the walls. Indian headdresses, war bonnets, pipes, and richly decorated buffalo robes spoke to Laidlaw's ties with the indigenous peoples.

Hackberry Hall proclaimed to all its owner's riches, an impression Laidlaw purposely cultivated with extravagant parties, including an "orchestra" of fiddlers for entertainment. His immaculately set tables overflowed with the choicest dishes while the best whiskey, wines, and brandy flowed freely. Guests ate from the best china using the finest cutlery while relaxing on well-crafted furniture. This opulence, however, carried a price. When Laidlaw died in October 1851, many, including Dawson, were shocked to learn that he was heavily in debt.[22] But for now, his generosity prevailed. Laidlaw, who loved racing ponies, gave Dawson a "fine Indian Poney," which, when added to

---

[19]Dawson's letters of 4 August 1847 and 18 September 1847 do not state clearly whether Laidlaw and Dawson were accompanied by the other four men all the way from St. Louis or only on the second half of their journey.

[20]Letter 3.

[21]Hafen, *Mountain Men*, 3:171–72. Laidlaw to Pierre Chouteau, Jr., 9 September 1842, describes Halsey's death: "Mr. H. was returning from Liberty in company with Mr. Dawson & Arrott and had proceeded about a mile from town, when in the act of descending a hill Mr. H. struck his horse which caused the Animal to run violently down hill, and in making a curve at the foot Mr. Halsey lost his Seat and as he fell was violently dashed against a tree, the right side of his head receiving so severe a blow as to cause his death." Abel, *Chardon's Journal*, 211–12. Some have identified this "Mr. Dawson" as Andrew Dawson, but he was still in Scotland in 1842.

[22]Schuler, *Fort Pierre Chouteau*, 50, and Letter 24. What happened to Laidlaw's expensive household goods is unclear, as his will mentions only everyday items. His many debts included a $6,000 note to Francis Chardon, executed 7 August 1844. Chouteau Collection, MoHS.

Dawson's own "beautiful horse," guaranteed the young trader would "have no fear of having much to walk."[23] Or so he thought.

Realizing his life would be in flux for the foreseeable future, Dawson decided to leave his portable desk, some clothes, and most of his books at Hackberry Hall. Finally, on 5 August, the party of five men set off for the upper river with Laidlaw and his wife. Dawson, believing his final destination to be either Fort Union or Fort Alexander, "enjoyed [the journey] vastly" although the "flat swampy" landscape left much to be desired, being "mostly covered with a long rank grass" reaching over their heads.[24]

Near Council Bluffs, Dawson got his first taste of the unpredictability of life in Indian country. "Hundreds of thousands" of Indians had gathered for the distribution of Pottawatomie annuities. As the Laidlaw party passed, a group of Otoe, who had recently lost thirty warriors in a battle with the Sioux, recognized Mrs. Laidlaw as a member of the enemy tribe. Angry over their losses, some fifty Otoe circled the carriage, threatening her. With Laidlaw off on business, an "excited" Dawson found himself in charge. "After jabbering about 5 minutes [the Otoe] all at once set off at full gallop," apparently content with having caused alarm. Dawson, his adrenaline pumping, realized that "instead of books," he now had "men to command," making him feel his "importance too very great." When Laidlaw heard what had happened, he decided that, instead of spending a week as planned at Council Bluffs, they should proceed along a different route.[25]

The next day, the group set out for Fort Vermilion, one of many small AFC satellite posts. The trip continued to be "so different from anything [Dawson had] ever either experienced or imagined." One morning after breakfast, as they crossed a creek, "something or other" got into Dawson's pony's head "and budge he would not." As Dawson prodded him, the pony reared up and dumped his rider headfirst into the mud. Dawson was stuck so firmly that he "had to be hauled out by the heels, and indeed came near to suffocating." While his companions hooted, Dawson nursed his bruised ego.

As they continued northward, Dawson's hunting skills, aided by his prized fowling piece, earned him praise for keeping his companions

---

[23]Letters 3 and 4.
[24]Letters 3 and 4.
[25]Letter 4.

supplied with fresh meat. Although he did not hunt big game, local Indians frequently traded them buffalo and deer meat.[26]

One night, Dawson watched with awe as the prairie burned. The natives had long used fire to cleanse the landscape, but the sight of flames dancing across the vast open spaces left Dawson speechless. It was the "grandest spectacle" he had "ever beheld," even if it meant losing sleep as they guarded their campsite.

Approaching Fort Lookout near the Missouri–White River confluence, Dawson saw the Sioux gathering.[27] White men, even those known and trusted by the tribes, rarely traveled through Indian country without being closely observed. These warriors had planned a special feast, a customary welcome for chief traders such as Laidlaw. But Dawson soon discovered there was a catch. The Indians would present each white man with fifteen or twenty pounds of meat, and if he could not consume this portion at one sitting, he became obligated to apologize with his own gifts.

The custom may have begun innocently. Natives, accustomed to starvation followed by gluttony, frequently consumed huge quantities of meat. Warriors may have originally offered what they considered a generous but reasonable portion, while embarrassed traders willingly offered goods to make amends for their waste. But by the late 1840s, it had become an accepted game that both traders and warriors understood. Thus did Dawson confront his first dog meat feast. Although "both dog and [his] appetite were most excellent," Dawson could not finish and "had to fork out."[28]

In December, the caravan finally reached Fort Pierre, built in the 1830s by Laidlaw.[29] Dawson had expected to be at Fort Union by November, but now found himself many miles downriver with Laidlaw intending to go no further. Frustrated, Dawson, who was "so much in the dark" about Laidlaw's plans, accepted one of the fur trade's most challenging assignments: running the express.

The express consisted of delivering needed goods and the much-awaited mail while simultaneously collecting outgoing missives. The job also entailed carrying messages between forts and keeping every-

---

[26]Dawson first saw buffalo in Dalkeith after the Duke of Buccleuch imported a small North American herd.

[27]These were most likely Teton Sioux, a Dakota band.

[28]Letter 5.

[29]Hafen, *Mountain Men*, 3:168.

one informed of overall conditions. It was lonely and dangerous work, usually assigned to low-ranking men who would not be much missed if something went wrong. On the upside, with everyone longing for communications from the outside world, the express man was much awaited at these remote outposts.

Dawson surely had little concept of what he was getting into when he volunteered for the express. But he was not the type to sit around idly. So, despite "a mere trifle" for compensation, he jumped at the opportunity.[30] The river had to freeze over before he could depart, however. So, as he waited, he balanced Fort Pierre's books.[31]

On 29 December 1847, Dawson and five others set out for Fort Clark with two sleighs laden with trade goods. While he had known snow and cold in Scotland, nothing had prepared him for the arctic winds and daunting midwinter blizzards of the northern plains. Many days, severe storms kept them from moving at all.

The new year brought brutally frigid temperatures with snow averaging two and a half feet or more. Traveling a single mile could take a couple of hours. On 3 January, one of their horses froze to death, and Dawson suffered severe frostbite to his face. That night, they camped a quarter mile from an Indian village with both unaware of the other, thanks to the frigid conditions.

Five days later, the temperature dropped even more and all the men "froze [their] faces." That night when they reached Fort Berthold, some 450 miles above Fort Pierre, Dawson discovered his left ear swollen to the size of two fists. Unable to speak and in excruciating pain, he was incapacitated for days. Meanwhile, the men waited for the express to arrive from Fort Union. When it did not, Dawson agreed to travel the additional 250 miles to the iconic post. By 11 February, he was back at Berthold, and following a short respite, he headed back to Fort Pierre, where he arrived on the 24th.

[30]Letter 5.

[31]James Dawson, "Major Andrew Dawson," SC 294, MTHS, tells a fanciful tale of Dawson's first trip upriver, claiming that he heard so many good things in St. Louis about life upriver that he set out with a friend, Robert Morgan, to make their own way to the fur trade posts. Dawson's letters home clearly disprove this. The younger Dawson may have confused some of the details of his father's stories, or perhaps, in storyteller fashion, Andrew Dawson inflated his experiences for his son's enjoyment.

While Dawson completed his successful express run, Fort Pierre had done a brisk business, leaving the post low on trade goods. Knowing Fort Union had goods to spare, Dawson agreed to head back upriver. He left for Fort Union less than two weeks after arriving at Pierre, this time traveling with Robert Morgan, another new recruit from Dunfermline, Fife, Scotland. The two traveled "entirely on foot," carrying packs weighing between twenty-five and sixty-five pounds, depending on their food supplies.

One misstep could spell trouble, as Dawson learned when he slipped and fell, injuring his foot severely enough to necessitate a four-day layover. With little food, he and Morgan "had to starve" until they found a frozen skunk. This unlikely meal turned out to be "the sweetest morsel." Later Dawson was struck by snow blindness. They managed to reach an outpost that night, but the fire's heat caused "excruciating agony." Dawson struggled to regain his sight for five days.

At some point on this long and torturous journey, the two Scotsmen became separated. Dawson searched for Morgan without success.[32] Alone and miserable, he soldiered on, traveling the final two hundred miles in solitude. At night, he sought camping spots among the thick brushwood and then dug a hole to sleep in. Despite his unfamiliarity with the region, the upper Missouri offered a true course. Walking on the frozen river was often easier than crossing the snowy prairie. He depended on melted river ice for water.

By the end of March, Dawson was once again at Fort Berthold.[33] There he visited the chief trader he had met two months earlier: Francis Chardon, the despotic trader who had nearly sacrificed the Blackfeet trade with his vengeful Fort McKenzie plot. After being removed from Fort FAC, Chardon had been given command of Fort Berthold, a rather sleepy outpost serving the Mandan and Hidatsa. Chardon had traded with the Mandan before, commanding Fort Clark before and during the 1837 smallpox epidemic.[34] After that outbreak severely reduced their numbers, the Mandan had moved north to join the Hidatsa near Fort Berthold. The reassignment kept Chardon far away from the Blackfeet.

---

[32]This is, undoubtedly, the source of James Dawson's story about Morgan and Dawson's upriver trip. "Major Andrew Dawson."

[33]Letter 6.

[34]For more on Chardon's time at Fort Clark, see Abel, *Chardon's Journal.*

Chardon, impressed by Dawson's tenacity on his first express run, had offered the young trader Fort Berthold's command if he returned that summer. Dawson had responded favorably, "on condition that Mr. Laidlaw did not consider [him] bound to [Laidlaw]."[35] While it is not clear whether Chardon had the authority to make this offer or what may have prompted it, it almost certainly explains why Dawson, after one arduous express run, offered to go north again so quickly.

Dawson clearly hoped Chardon's offer remained on the table, but first he had business to handle at Fort Union. He headed upriver on 27 March, arriving at Fort Union on 6 April 1848. When the river ice broke up on the 13th, Dawson took a mackinaw and headed downriver with the trade goods for Fort Pierre. On the 22nd, he tied up below Fort Berthold. Surprised to not be greeted by Chardon, Dawson yelled out to the traders: "How is Mr. Chardon, and why has he not come down to welcome me?" The answer stunned him: Chardon had died four hours earlier.[36] Although Dawson had believed him to be "in perfect health" a few weeks earlier, Chardon had become "very ill, with a violent attack of rheumatism."[37] Yet the "description" Dawson received led him to believe Chardon had died of scurvy.[38]

Whatever had swept Chardon away, his death left an opening that Andrew Dawson seized. Following his "good winter's work, having travelled 2700 miles entirely on foot," Dawson took command of Fort Berthold, settling in to what he quickly realized would be "a solitary and lonely life."[39]

---

[35]Letter 6.

[36]Letter 6. For the first time, Dawson provides an actual date and time (4 A.M.) for Chardon's death. John Palliser put the date at the end of May. St. Louis newspapers reported it as having occurred on April 20, apparently based on information from Alexander Culbertson, who arrived soon after Dawson. See Abel, *Chardon's Journal*, 269n254.

[37]Abel, *Chardon's Journal*, 266n252.

[38]Letter 6. For symptoms of scurvy, see Packer and Fuchs, eds., *Vitamin C*. No one else has suggested Chardon died of scurvy.

[39]Letter 6.

5

A Great Lot of Rascals

FOUR YEARS AFTER DISEMBARKING THE *ADAM CARR*, Andrew Dawson was at last a fur trader with his own post. But, as often happens when dreams meet reality, much about his new lifestyle was disconcerting. Living so near the natives, Dawson now realized how little he understood them. Moreover, he received less companionship from the other fort employees than he had expected. Everyone at Fort Berthold, except Dawson, spoke French. When he tried to learn the native tongue, he angered the interpreters, whose jobs depended on the language barrier. Loneliness, a lifelong problem, frequently overwhelmed him.[1]

On Sundays, his thoughts inevitably "revert[ed] to the many, many pleasant Sabbaths" of his youth. On the frontier, "there [was] no sound of the 'Sabbath Bell,' no church going, no evening walk with the family group . . . and above all else no evening chat by the family hearth." Comfort came only from "that within that has not changed."[2]

Still, Dawson found things to celebrate. Fort Berthold, built in 1845 by veteran trader James Kipp, was one of the newest posts. Located on a bluff high above the Missouri, the fort was "more beautifully situated than any place on the River." A "fine level Prairie" stretched for several miles to "a lovely ridge of little hills." From the post, one could see five miles up and down the river.[3]

Fort Berthold served the Mandan and Hidatsa, who along with their latter-day allies, the Arikara, represented a unique upper

[1]Letter 7.
[2]Letter 6.
[3]Letter 6.

Missouri culture.[4] Unlike their nomadic neighbors with their transportable skin lodges, the Mandan, Hidatsa, and Arikara lived in earth lodges arrayed in a circle on terraces above the river. Rather than following the hunt, these tribes farmed the rich alluvial lands, growing corn, squash, beans, sunflowers, and tobacco. The river offered up catfish, sturgeon, turtles, and freshwater mussels while the prairie supplied turnips, Indian potatoes, wild plums, grapes, chokecherries, and buffalo berries. The tribes also hunted big game nearby. In the winter, they moved down into the floodplain to escape the howling winds.

Exactly when and how these tribes came together is unclear, but by the beginning of the eighteenth century, the Mandan and Hidatsa had joined forces near the mouth of Heart River. Their geographic position, combined with their lifestyle, gave them a unique role in the region's socioeconomic system serving as middlemen for the nomadic tribes in a tribal trading system.

The first whites to visit these fabled villages were Frenchmen led by Pierre Gaultier de Varennes de La Vérendrye and guided by Assiniboine warriors who arrived on 3 December 1738. The Assiniboine had long been trading guns, axes, kettles, knives, awls, and other metal goods acquired from these mysterious light-skinned men in the Mandan villages. Their appetite for manufactured goods having been whetted, the Mandan welcomed the French visitors. La Vérendrye's visit validated the fantastic stories that white explorers had been told about the village Indians. Now assured that these settled tribes really existed, white traders rushed upriver to establish a trading relationship.

Fifty years later, the Mandan and Hidatsa had migrated north to the mouth of Knife River, where they lived in five villages. By 1787, three Frenchmen—René Jessaume, Pierre Menard, and Toussaint Charbonneau—lived in the villages as "tenant traders."[5] But contact with American traders remained limited until the Corps of

---

[4]Letter 6 says the post serves "the Gros Ventres . . . and Mandans." The Hidatsa were also called "Gros Ventre of the Missouri." Meyer, *Village Indians*, 10. In 1943, the Hidatsa tribal council officially changed the name of the largest tribal group on the Fort Berthold Reservation from Gros Ventre to Hidatsa. To avoid ongoing confusion between the Gros Ventre of central Montana and the Hidatsa, this work will use Hidatsa rather than Gros Ventre of the Missouri or Minataree, another name for the Hidatsa. See Meyer, 205.

[5]Meyer, *Village Indians*, 1–2, 15–16, 18, 27, 30, 35. See also Wilson, *Agriculture of the Hidatsa Indians*.

Discovery, led by Meriwether Lewis and William Clark, arrived in the fall of 1804.

The Mandan and Hidatsa long remembered those visitors. Not only had this large contingent stayed for several months but they had also been annoyingly stubborn. Eager to protect their trading network from competition by the whites, the Mandan had warned early traders about the ferocity of the other tribes, discouraging them from going further upriver. But these men refused to listen. They built their own fort, spent the winter there, and then, undeterred, headed west when spring arrived.

The Lewis and Clark visitors also looked different from the other whites they had met. One of their chiefs, the one who could cure, had strange orange hair. And his man had black skin. Having never seen such a man, the tribes decided he possessed very powerful medicine.[6] Nevertheless, the Mandan and Hidatsa failed to appreciate the changes this visit would precipitate.

On 18 June 1837, the world of the village Indians was turned upside down when the *St. Peters* docked at Fort Clark. On the journey upriver, a mulatto employee had taken sick near Fort Leavenworth. Shorthanded, Captain Bernard Pratte had refused to put him ashore. The employee had smallpox, and the "fully developed" disease killed several other employees on the upriver journey.[7]

Exactly what happened when the steamer reached Fort Clark remains unclear. Some versions claim an elderly Indian stole a blanket and refused to surrender it to Francis Chardon, the chief trader.[8] But Chardon's contemporaneous journal mentions neither the alleged theft nor any subsequent retrieval efforts. Chardon's first mention of the smallpox appears nearly a month later, on 14 July, when a young Mandan died "of the Small Pox."[9]

Company employees may have subsequently concocted the stolen blanket story to shift responsibility away from the Company, which

[6]In Indian parlance, "medicine" means powers.

[7]Joshua Pilcher to General William Clark, 5 February 1838, NAM M234/884.

[8]Bradley, "Affairs at Fort Benton," 222; Chittenden, *American Fur Trade*, 2:621; Holterman, *King of the High Missouri*, 49.

[9]Abel, *Chardon's Journal*, 121.

had callously brought the disease upriver. Most likely, three Arikara spread the disease. They had come upriver on the *St. Peters* before dispersing to the villages. Although stricken with the pox on the journey upriver, they had recovered before reaching Fort Clark. But the highly contagious virus can be transmitted both before a victim shows symptoms and after he recovers. In any case, once the disease struck, it "continued as long as there was any one left to attack."[10]

As the disease swept their villages, some Mandan vowed revenge, but in their weakened state, they could do little. With victims succumbing daily, the healthy begged for help, but the traders had nothing to offer. As casualties mounted, bodies were stacked in heaps and thrown off the cliffs into the river. By mid-August, Chardon had stopped counting, "as they die so fast that it is impossible."[11]

The Mandan subagent, William Fulkerson, worried that unless the smallpox "be checked in its mad career I would not be surprised if it wiped the Mandan and Rickaree Tribes of Indians clean from the face of the earth."[12] Fulkerson was not far off. By the end of 1837, only about one hundred Mandan from a pre-epidemic population of fifteen hundred remained. One observer summed up the tragedy:

> The few that are left are as humble as dogs. No language can picture the scene of desolation which the country presents. In whatever direction we go, we see nothing but melancholy wrecks of human life. The tents are still standing on every hill, but no rising smoke announces the presence of human beings, and no sounds but the croaking of the raven and the howling of the wolf interrupt the fearful silence.[13]

The Hidatsa lost 70 percent of their warriors.[14] The Arikara, away hunting when the disease appeared, lost half.[15]

Even after the disease ebbed, the aftershocks continued. Many survivors chose suicide over life without family and friends. Ninety percent of the survivors were scarred permanently by "the disfiguring

---

[10] J. A. Hamilton to Pierre Chouteau, 25 February 1838, Chouteau Collection, MOHS.

[11] Abel, *Chardon's Journal*, 126.

[12] W. A. Fulkerson to William Clark, 10 September 1837, NAM, M234/884. Rickaree was another name for the Arikara who had joined the Mandan.

[13] Thwaites, *Early Western Travels*, 23:35. The author is unidentified, but it probably was Alexander Culbertson or Edwin Denig.

[14] Bradley, "Affairs at Fort Benton," 222.

[15] J. A. Hamilton to Pierre Chouteau, Jr., 25 February 1838, Chouteau Collection, MOHS.

marks of this awful malady."[16] One trader explained: "The destroying angel has visited the unfortunate sons of the wilderness with terrors never before known, and has converted extensive hunting grounds, as well as the peaceful settlements of those tribes, into desolate and boundless cemeteries."[17]

In late March 1838, the Arikara moved into the Mandan village near Fort Clark. But when the Arikara began taking Mandan wives, the tribes found themselves at odds.[18] The smallpox had weakened all the tribes. Yet, once the immediate threat subsided, old rivalries resurfaced. In early 1839, Sioux warriors burned the Mandan village. Chardon noted: "Upwards of one hundred years it has been standing, the Small Pox last year, very near annihilated the Whole tribe, and the Sioux has finished the Work of destruction by burning the Village—the rest of the Tribe are scattered, some with the Minetarees [Hidatsa], and others with the Aricarees."[19] With their village destroyed, the Mandan moved upriver with the Hidatsa, sharing a village near the future site of Fort Berthold. The Arikara, meanwhile, settled in the rebuilt Mandan lodges and resumed trade at Fort Clark.[20]

By the time Andrew Dawson took command of Fort Berthold in 1848, the horrors of the smallpox epidemic had passed. The Mandan and Hidatsa now built their mud lodges within 150 feet of the fort, and lived with "plenty to eat and to drink . . . free from care or the anxieties or troubles that possess the whites." "On the whole," Dawson concluded, they were "much more comfortable and happy than the whites on whom they look as a very inferior race."[21]

For Dawson, so new to Indian country, the natives remained both intriguing and puzzling. Their "beautiful stories," even in translation, were enthralling, being "much grander than any story [he had] ever read or heard." Still, he could not fathom why the women tolerated

---

[16]Letter 13.

[17]Unsigned letter published as an appendix to Maximilian's account in Thwaites, *Early Western Travels*, 23:33.

[18]Meyer, *Village Indians*, 95.

[19]Abel, *Chardon's Journal*, 181.

[20]Meyer, *Village Indians*, 98–100.

[21]Letter 6.

their station. They had "to dress all the Robes, attend to all the household and family affairs, carry firewood from a distance of 1 mile at least, hoe all the Corn, Sow and Gather it etc." Why a woman "would rather die from fatigue than suffer the disgrace of seeing her husband carrying anything on his back" was a mystery to the Scottish trader.[22]

Soon after Dawson's arrival, he witnessed a wonderful spectacle when some seven hundred Crow came to visit their near relatives, the Hidatsa. The warriors, all "beautifully dressed" and "fantastically painted," danced, sang, and exchanged presents before "[eating] themselves to sleep." The morning brought a "very busy day [of] trading."

Dawson did find companionship with John Palliser, an Irish explorer and geographer, who had come to the area on a "distant hunting expedition."[23] Palliser had been the only literate man in the fort when Chardon fell "very ill, with a violent attack of rheumatism."[24] At Chardon's request, Palliser had recorded his last will and testament. Palliser soon became a favorite of the traders, thanks to his hunting prowess and willingness to share his bounty. Although Dawson's duties kept him from hunting bear with Palliser, the two became good friends.[25] Palliser even gave Dawson a horse when the Irishman left the upper river at the end of 1849.[26]

Meanwhile, downriver, conditions were deteriorating. On 13 June 1849, the steamboat *Martha* stopped at the AFC post on Crow Creek, in the lands of the Yankton Sioux. Several hundred warriors lined the shore. Those aboard the *Martha* included company partners Honoré Picotte and John Sarpy, as well as Alexander Culbertson and Gideon Matlock, the new Indian agent. A year earlier, the Yankton, believing "the U.S. is yet indebted to them," had threatened Matlock. The agent had agreed to try to "give them something next Spring," but warned that he could make no promises.[27]

The warriors, convinced the government intended only to cheat them, decided to attack. Within minutes of the steamer docking,

[22]Letter 6.

[23]Palliser, *Solitary Rambles*, vi.

[24]Ibid., 198, 262–63.

[25]Letter 7.

[26]W. D. Hodgkiss to Pierre Chouteau, Jr. & Co., 14 February 1850, Chouteau-Papin Collection, MOHS. Due to the death of James Murray, a fellow Scotsman, the horse was never delivered.

[27]Gideon Matlock to Thomas H. Harvey, 29 June 1847, NAM M234/754.

thirty warriors rushed aboard and doused the *Martha*'s engine fires as warriors onshore began shooting. One bullet passed "a few inches to the right of [Culbertson's] face" before killing a crewmember.

Matlock, hoping to resolve the conflict, went ashore to meet with Smutty Bear, a Yankton chief. With Alexander Culbertson acting as interpreter, Smutty Bear explained: "Our trader has advised us to rob & Steal from the other trader. The traders have not only advised us to do these things but in many instances paid us." Smutty Bear went on to describe the traders as "a great lot of rascals," insisting that "our Father cannot expect us to do any better so long as he continues to allow bad white men among us."[28]

Matlock subsequently investigated Smutty Bear's charges and determined that the opposition traders had convinced the Yankton that the AFC intended to cheat them out of their annuities. Angered by this duplicity, Matlock suspended all the licenses to trade with the Yankton. The AFC got their license back only after Culbertson was made partner.

In the short term, Matlock appeased the warriors with a feast and presents. With the bad feelings eased, the *Martha* continued its upriver voyage, reaching Fort Berthold ten days later. There, Matlock learned that the Yankton were not the only angry tribe.[29]

Andrew Dawson was still adjusting to Fort Berthold on 18 June 1848 when he witnessed "the most horrifying proceedings . . . human beings could be guilty of." That morning, some one hundred Teton Sioux "made a rush from the hills."[30] Palliser posted himself "on the highest point of the Fort with an excellent telescope" to "view the combat in safety." At first, the Irishman thought "the sight was very picturesque" as "the braves rushed backwards and forwards on horseback, appearing and disappearing by turns through clouds of [gunfire] smoke."[31]

The Sioux killed a Hidatsa, but "were unable to carry off any part

[28]Sunder, *Fur Trade*, 107–108.

[29]Report of Gideon Matlock to Thomas H. Harvey, 16 June 1848, NAM M234/884.

[30]Letter 7. Palliser, *Solitary Rambles*, 285, identifies them as "Sioux from the Teton River" and gives the date as July 1848. Dawson's timeline is almost certainly more accurate as he wrote his brother that day.

[31]Palliser, *Solitary Rambles*, 285–86.

of his body or scalp, the much prized war trophy."[32] They did manage to "carr[y] off 22 horses belonging to the Indians and the opposition Co." while the Hidatsa killed one Sioux and "secured his body." After the Sioux retreated, the Hidatsa "dragged [the dead Sioux] behind a horse for a distance of 3 miles, at full gallop and then delivered [him] over to the squaws." What happened next appalled Dawson and Palliser. Palliser reported that "the boys shot arrows into the carcase of their fallen enemy, while their women with knives cut out pieces of the flesh, which they broiled and ate." The women "kept dancing and singing," all while "keeping up a horrible screeching" until the body was thoroughly consumed. Then "the squaws collected in a circle all standing with their faces to the east, and commenced such a howling and screeching as to horrify" in honor of their own slain warrior. When the new widow saw her beloved's body, she "tore her hair and her face till she was bloody all over," while a female companion "kept cutting her head with a knife." Dawson found the display "truly shocking," while Palliser, "chilled with horror," found himself "haunted for hours, and frequently afterwards."[33]

Although "unsettled" by this event, Dawson still felt the "utmost cheerfulness" regarding his "future career." He had regained the "energy[,] activity[,] and sprightliness of [his] schoolboy days," and while he still doubted he would remain upriver "any length of time," he considered the experience "far from being time lost."[34]

As Dawson settled in for his third winter upriver, Fort Berthold and the other forts remained on edge thanks to "the Sioux who keep prowling around . . . in search of horses and scalps." With "a white man's scalp . . . just as good to dance to as an Indian," the AFC men were rendered "close prisoners."[35] Most refused to hunt, forcing everyone to "liv[e] on dried Buffo. Meat,"[36] or what they called "parchment & water."[37] At Fort Pierre, "things go on—bad enough" with "every things look[ing] gloomy indeed," including "nothing to eat, and no prospect of getting any."[38]

---

[32]Letter 7. According to Palliser, *Solitary Rambles*, 286, the Sioux did carry off the body and "dragged him ignominiously along the ground by leathern thongs till they reached their own party, where they scalped him in safety."

[33]Letter 7; Palliser, *Solitary Rambles*, 286.

[34]Letter 7.

[35]Letter 8.

[36]Letter 9.

[37]Letter 10.

[38]W. D. Hodgkiss to Andrew Drips, 30 January 1849, Chouteau Collection, MOHS.

Dawson, meanwhile, frustrated by the "extortion of the Co."[39] in the prices charged its employees, decided to trap wolves for some extra income. Although a large wolf pelt could bring one dollar, the venture also had inherent risks. Not infrequently, the wolves escaped, dragging away the traps for which the Company charged $10. That annoyed but did not surprise Dawson, since he had concluded that his bosses were "a grasping[,] close[,] niggardly set,"[40] little better than "a pack of fools and knaves."[41]

Since Dawson found "pleasure in stirring about and doing[,] as the Yankee says, something desperate," after several months of hunkering down from fear of the Sioux, he decided to take a sleigh to the Hidatsa winter village to see if they had any robes to trade.[42] When he returned, he learned to his dismay of several desertions. Moreover, the two newcomers who had brought the winter express now refused to "budge a foot further." Remembering his own successful run, Dawson decided to take the express himself to Fort Clark, some forty-five miles downriver. To protect the Company papers, he hid them inside a copper kettle.[43] At Fort Clark, he discovered that post to be even more poorly staffed than Berthold. When Dawson offered to continue the express to Fort Pierre, Fort Clark's commander, Joseph Desautel, refused, declaring Dawson too vital to Fort Berthold. Later, when Dawson learned that the Sioux had killed the man Desautel sent instead, he reflected soberly that "such might have been [his] fate."

Although Dawson had "been living in the impression that my Indians—the Gros Ventres—would not harm the whites," he now realized he had "been mistaken." The Hidatsa, "like all other tribes, will take advantage when they can, being like all others most ignorant and superstitious." Still, Dawson did not blame them alone. Their situation, he concluded, "reflect[s] very much against the American government and people . . . that no effort has ever been made . . . to bring about a better state of things with the many savage tribes in this great river." He expected nothing more from the AFC, since their

---

[39]Letter 7.

[40]Letter 8.

[41]Letter 9.

[42]Letter 8.

[43]This story, probably originally taken from James Dawson's biography, is repeated in a number of Dawson biographical sketches. While it is impossible to know exactly when he used this deception, it was probably on this run, since there was so much tribal turmoil.

"sole object [was] the amassing of as much wealth as possible . . . and the more ignorance the Indians are kept in, the more profitable is the trade." But he believed the situation ultimately untenable as "this country is becoming poorer and poorer yearly, the only trade in it now of any importance being the Buffo. Robes."[44] And those could not last forever. Dawson estimated that in 1848, 270,000 buffalo had been "destroyed," "certainly a most awful destruction," even though the "Indians . . . do not think they diminish any, and have an idea that others come out of the earth to replace those they kill."[45]

Despite the contradictions and the troubling intertribal strife, Dawson still had a job to do, and so he focused on keeping Fort Berthold profitable. In mid-July, the *Amelia* finally arrived and Dawson learned of the Company's other difficulties. In mid-May, a massive fire had swept the St. Louis levee, consuming twenty-three steamboats, including the fully loaded *Martha*, along with fifteen blocks of the business district. The total loss was estimated at between $3 and $6 million. Meanwhile, cholera had swept the city, killing between five and eight thousand, including the venerable Pierre Chouteau, Sr.[46] William Potts, Dawson's former pastor, had declared the fire and pestilence to be God's punishment for the city having sanctioned a Sunday newspaper.[47] But Dawson was more alarmed to learn that the *Amelia*, which had lost nine passengers and crew, had brought the disease upriver. Adding to his troubles, thirty new recruits, fearful of contracting cholera, had deserted.[48]

Dawson listened to St. Louis's woes, convinced that its residents had it easy compared with those on the frontier. Only a month earlier, Berthold had again been tested when more than seven hundred Sioux had "made a rush from the hills" nearby. Dawson had secured the horses and then gone "out in the Prairie . . . to witness the fight." But the warring tribes had advanced "in such a scattered manner" that the trader soon found himself "right between the two enemies" and "the principal object aimed at by the Sioux." When the Hidatsa offered no assistance, Dawson fired his rifle before he "wheeled and retreated."

---

[44]Letter 10.

[45]Letter 7.

[46]Sunder, *Fur Trade*, 117; Ravenswaay, *St. Louis*, 383–88.

[47]Ravenswaay, *St. Louis*, 391.

[48]"From the Yellowstone River," *St. Louis New Era*, 9 August 1849; Letter 13.

Back inside the fort, Dawson found the "yard and houses . . . crowded with all the women, children and cowards of the village." The trader gave the Hidatsa "a barrel of Powder and some balls" and then headed for the bastion where he saw the Sioux within "100 yards . . . and firing on us as well as the Indian village." Deciding it was now "quite time enough . . . to be active," Dawson "got the little cannon" and dragged it up "to an embankment close by, and gave them some 15 shots from it." Although quite "unskilled . . . in gunnery" and with "no one to assist [him] save [his] old Negro cook," Dawson believed "the noise alone served a good end, as it terrified the most away."[49]

Around 3 P.M., "the Sioux gradually retired." The Hidatsa thanked Dawson for "a great service," telling him that "had it not been for the whites and this Fort, all the village would have been swept away." Dawson accepted their thanks, although he believed that the "Sioux displayed much courage and a good deal of skill," while the Hidatsa, "being so very few in proportion, had recourse to that better part of valour called discretion."

The one Hidatsa casualty was a little boy whom Dawson described as "the ugliest object I ever looked upon, having his nose crushed into his skull." The child had "gone to the woods in the morning to gather berries and was there surprised and killed by the Sioux. They rendered him even more ugly cutting off his hands and feet and taking his scalp." In addition, five Hidatsa had been wounded and twenty-seven horses stolen. What Dawson found "very vexatious" was the fact that "most all their corn and pumpkins is destroyed." Reports indicated that the Sioux had lost three men and five horses. And their parting words gave no one comfort: "They babbled out to us that they would be in the neighbourhood all summer and would pay us many a visit."[50]

With that hanging over his head, Dawson was relieved to learn that he was being transferred. On 20 July, with a band of horses, the twenty-nine-year-old Dawson set off for his new assignment at Fort Clark, the Arikara post some forty-five miles downriver.[51]

---

[49]The cook was probably Jim Hawkin. See Hewitt, *Journal of Rudolph Friederich Kurz*, 101–102.

[50]Letter 13. "From the Yellowstone River," 9 August 1849, placed the number of Sioux at 1,200.

[51]Letter 10.

6

Among the Evil-Doers

ALTHOUGH PROUD OF HIS ACCOMPLISHMENTS BOTH IN St. Louis and on the upper Missouri, Andrew Dawson still felt like "an outcast . . . without a comforting voice from friend or foe." His "love for home" often made him act "very childish." When the express did not bring him letters from home, Dawson despaired, "all alone in a far off country."

When letters did come, he wept "like a little bairn," enjoying "a fine blubber."[1] Five years after leaving home, he still "fervently" wished to return. He admitted that, if his family had only asked, he would never have left. "Stand[ing] alone in this wide world" seemed like such harsh "punishment." Still, he feared that, if he did return to Scotland, he would only find "some subordinate situation" to "dwindle out" his days in a "second oblivion." Even worse was the possibility that "after the first excitement . . . there would be nothing but regrets."[2] So he remained an exile, haunted by his own loneliness.

Thus when he saw an opportunity to tie his life to another's, especially one much in need of guidance, he grabbed it. In the spring of 1848, as Dawson grappled with Chardon's unexpected demise, Alexander Culbertson arrived at Fort Berthold. When Culbertson learned that this new trader had known Andrew Potts in Scotland, the senior trader mentioned that Potts had left behind a young son named Jeremiah who was now being raised by the querulous Alexander Harvey.[3] Harvey had claimed Potts's widow, Namo-pisi, as his own following Potts's death, and Jerry had come along as part of the

---

[1]"Bairn" is a common Scots word for child.

[2]Dawson's loneliness and continuing fears that he would be forgotten by his family are evident in many of his letters home. See particularly letters 8, 11, 12, 14, 22, and 26.

[3]Alexander Culbertson wrote Potts's family after his death. Touchie, *Bear Child*, 57.

package.[4] Although Culbertson reported that Jerry was "a fine healthy boy . . . about 8 years old," he worried about the way "the poor little fellow" was being raised.[5]

After being banished from Blackfeet country following the Fort McKenzie massacre, Harvey had quit the Company, filed liquor trafficking charges against the AFC, and started an opposition company with Robert Campbell's backing. Harvey had then returned to Blackfeet country in the fall of 1846 with one hundred recruits and established Fort Campbell near Fort Lewis. His new company, Harvey, Primeau and Company, with its $50,000 worth of trade goods, had quickly become a serious competitor.[6] They had also established posts near Forts Berthold and Clark, and it had been Harvey's men who had incited the Sioux attack on Berthold earlier that year.[7] Now, to Dawson's chagrin, he learned that this hardhearted rival was raising his friend's orphaned son.

Thinking Jerry might be better off in Scotland, Dawson wrote his mother to suggest that, if she "saw fit," she should inform Andrew Potts's brother, Thomas, of his nephew's existence. Dawson, "consider[ing] it a means of repaying a small portion of his very great obligation" to Potts, would make all the arrangements if Potts wanted the child sent to Scotland.[8]

The situation, however, was tricky. Although mixed marriages were common on the frontier, proper Scots might not understand. Dawson begged his mother not to judge Potts too harshly for a marriage he assumed his friend had never divulged to his family. These marriages, Dawson assured his mother, were "almost an universal practice with the Clerks and Traders" who "all seem fondly attached to their Wives or Squaws and children." Although "not solemnised by a Minister or Priest," the marriages occurred "according to the only law of the Country." Dawson insisted it would be "an extra display of bigotry to cavil at the sinfulness." Besides, he explained, "All who can afford it, send their children below, to be educated, and they are recognised in society as much as we are, indeed, even more so."[9]

---

[4]Fardy, *Jerry Potts*, 8, as quoted by Touchie, *Bear Child*, 58. Namo-pisi was also known as Crooked Back. She was from the Black Elks band of the Blood.

[5]Letter 6.

[6]Wischmann, *Frontier Diplomats*, 138–42.

[7]Report of Gideon Matlock to Thomas H. Harvey, 16 June 1848, NAM M884/234.

[8]Letter 6.

[9]This interesting statement suggests that the fur traders were regarded as less than civilized by their city counterparts.

But Dawson's appeal for guidance went unanswered as he became more and more convinced that Harvey was an unfit guardian. Although Jerry was a "quick-witted, independent boy," he suffered from "bow-legs and stunted growth."[10] Concerned about the boy's development and anxious for his own family, Dawson had Jerry brought to Fort Clark where the trader "took a fatherly interest in the orphan and cared for him as if he were his own," imparting to him "all the values [Jerry] had not learned from Harvey," including English and survival techniques "that separated him from most of the mixed-bloods on the frontier." Under Dawson's tutelage, Potts prepared for his own exceptional career.[11]

Fort Clark brought Dawson another companion: Joseph Desautel, the Canadian nephew of James Kipp, one of the Company's oldest active traders. Although most men his age had long since retired, Kipp, who had built Fort Clark and helped to open the Blackfeet trade, remained upriver, often "morose" but addicted to adventure and "strong drink."[12]

Desautel had come upriver with his uncle around 1838 and had served at Fort McKenzie with Culbertson and Andrew Potts.[13] Witness to the 1844 massacre, he had fled with Harvey and Chardon and then traveled to Fort Union to report the incident.[14] In 1845, he took command at Fort Clark, trading with the Mandan, Arikara, Hidatsa, nomadic Crow, Yankton, and Yanktonai.[15] There he met and married Josette Garreau.[16] She was apparently the granddaughter of Joseph

[10]Cruise and Griffiths, *Great Adventure*, 73, as quoted by Touchie, *Bear Child*, 63.

[11]Touchie, *Bear Child*, 65. It is not clear exactly when Potts came to live with Dawson or what had happened to Namo-pisi, although she was clearly alive at this time. For a discussion of this, see Touchie, *Bear Child*, 64–65.

[12]Hewitt, *Journal of Rudolph Friederich Kurz*, 123. Kipp, who had an Indian family upriver, also kept a white wife and children in Parkville, Missouri.

[13]Desautel was one of the AFC traders who wrote letters of condolence to the Potts family in Scotland after Andrew's death.

[14]Larpenteur, *Forty Years*, 187, says he learned of the massacre from "Mr. Des Hôtel, one of the clerks, in whom full confidence could be placed."

[15]Williams, *Ethnohistory*, 267.

[16]Her name is also given as Kate, Kuta, and Yellow. Her mother, a mixed-blood Arikara, was also named Josette. Determining her lineage is difficult. Several accounts say her father was Antoine, but they also identify Antoine as the trader who met Lewis and Clark in 1805. Genealogical Information Online http://www.genrecords.net/emailregistry/vols/00001.html#0000031. Accessed June 2010. But Lewis and Clark scholars agree that (*continued*)

Garreau, who was credited as the first white man to settle in the Dakotas. Probably French Canadian, Joseph Garreau came upriver in the late 1780s or early 1790s, settling among the Mandan and Arikara, who did not always trust him.[17] Still there in 1805, he showed Lewis and Clark "the process used by those Indians to make beads."[18]

Josette's uncle was Pierre Garreau, an interpreter whom Dawson had known at Berthold.[19] Since Garreau spoke primarily French, his communications with Dawson had been limited. In addition, Garreau had inherited some of his father's less admirable qualities.[20] Described as "an unreasonable, self-conceited half-breed" who insulted and fought with "everybody who refused to drink with him," Pierre Garreau would not have been the kind of friend Dawson normally sought.[21] But Dawson did enjoy the garrulous Desautel and his many tales. And Jerry Potts, no longer the "fort urchin eating scraps," also found friends at Fort Clark, including Garreau's sons and Desautel's daughters.[22]

Although it was not as comfortable as Fort Berthold, Dawson found Fort Clark pleasant. Built around 1828, it stood on a terrace about thirty-five feet above the river and some nine hundred feet from Mit-tutta-hang-Kush, the Mandan village. The flood plain offered excellent farming opportunities while the river bottom provided abundant timber for cooking, building, and powering steamboats. The greatest hazard came from the weather. In 1833, Prince Maximilian, who spent six months at the post, noted that "the mercury in the thermometer was frozen for several days."[23] When the ice broke up, the

---

that was Joseph Garreau, not Antoine. See Tubbs and Jenkinson, *Lewis and Clark Companion*, 124; Moulton, *Journals of the Lewis and Clark Expedition Online;* Ronda, *Lewis & Clark*, 16, 248, 250. In the diaries, Garreau's name appears as "Garrow" (16 March 1805) and "Gurrow" (16 March 1804). Luttig, *Journal of a Fur-Trading Expedition,* notes, 64: According to Luttig, Antoine was Joseph's son and Pierre's brother. If Josette/Kuta was nineteen in 1851, it seems likely she was Joseph's granddaughter. Genealogical notes for the Dawson children (ORL, FtB) say she was Pierre's daughter. Fred Gerard, who knew the Dawsons, says (*CSHSND,* 1:363) Antoine Garreau's wife was Josette, and their daughter, Josette, married Dawson.

[17]Milton, *South Dakota*, 40; "Trudeau's Journal," 403n4.

[18]Moulton, *Journals of the Lewis and Clark Expedition Online,* 16 March 1804.

[19]Pierre is said to have been Joseph's son from his marriage to a Mandan. Exactly what became of Antoine is not known, as he is not mentioned in literature about this period.

[20]Maximilian in Thwaites, *Early Western Travels*, 3:35, called him "the perfidious old Garreau," and Trudeau, 410, "very strongly condemn[ed]" his morals.

[21]Hewitt, *Journal of Rudolph Friederich Kurz*, 84, 303.

[22]Touchie, *Bear Child*, 65.

[23]Williams, *Ethnohistory*, 25.

river could rise dramatically. On 26 March 1835, it had risen four feet overnight.[24]

Great herds of buffalo also roamed the area. James Kipp's son, Joe, described "the immense prairie back of [Fort Clark] look[ing] black [with buffalo] to the tops of the hills though the ground was covered with snow."[25] In 1838, Chardon mentioned the fort was "completely surrounded" by the animals.[26]

In late 1849, as winter approached, the greatest threat came from the restless upper Missouri tribes. With an increasing flood of emigrants heading west across the Oregon Trail, the Sioux felt particularly aggrieved. Earlier in the year, the Arikara had killed a Company man while the Sioux had badly wounded another.[27] Fear of Indian depredations kept most post hunters out of the field. There was even talk of a military company coming upriver to maintain order. Add to that Harvey, Primeau and Company's successful competition, and the AFC realized they would be lucky to accept "an equal division of robes."[28]

Nevertheless, Desautel, hoping to entice more trade, sent Dawson to winter in the Arikara village some ten miles away. Dawson did so well that when Desautel decided to visit his family in Montreal after fifteen years away, he left Dawson in charge of Fort Clark. Dawson was grateful for the opportunity, but "anxiously" awaited the return of "the most agreeable companion and best friend" he had "on this side of the Atlantic."[29]

Unfortunately, Desautel never would return. By mid-October 1850, he was at Fort Pierre "in a very low state of health" with "but little chance of . . . ever recovering." James Kipp planned to stay with him "until his fate is decided." Recognizing that Dawson had been "associated with Mr. Desautel for some time in the trade of Ft. Clark," the Company left the Scotsman in charge, with "every confidence" that Dawson would "make a good and profitable trade."[30]

The Company's trust was rewarded. By the end of 1850, the partners could report that "Dawson has done well with the Rees, he has

---

[24]Abel, *Chardon's Journal*, 26.

[25]Audubon and Coues, *Audubon and His Journals*, 2:146.

[26]Abel, *Chardon's Journal*, 146.

[27]Denig to Culbertson, 1 December 1849, Chouteau Collection, MOHS: "The Rees killed Jeffris & the Sioux wounded Carafel."

[28]Ibid.

[29]Letter 14.

[30]Letter to Andrew Dawson, 23 October 1850, Ft. Pierre Letterbook, Chouteau Collection, MOHS.

sent us down 300 Bushel of Corn and will be able to give us our principal supply for [indecipherable] 1851 to come down on Steamer—he has also on hand 105 Packs Robes."[31] But for Dawson, sadness tempered this success. Desautel had died in mid-November, leaving Dawson once again friendless but with added obligations.

Desautel had made Dawson promise he would marry Josette and raise their children as his own if anything were to befall him on his long and dangerous journey. Hoping that the need would never arise, Dawson had agreed. And now he kept his promise. In the summer of 1851, with the blessings of James Kipp and the Arikara chief, White Shield, Dawson married Josette Garreau Desautel.[32]

Dawson had little time to adapt to married life. The summer of 1851 would prove to be one of the most significant and chaotic since 1837 and the smallpox epidemic. For years, the superintendent of Indian affairs and the fur traders had implored the federal government to negotiate "treaties of peace and friendship" with the tribes whose lands were being negatively impacted by the westward emigration. Superintendent Thomas Harvey argued that "a trifling compensation" could "secure [the Indians'] friendship."[33]

But their appeals fell on deaf ears until 1849, when the California gold rush gave them new urgency. Thus in the spring of 1851, the government recruited traders to bring representatives from the "Prairie Tribes . . . residing South of the Missouri River and North of Texas" to a conference at Fort Laramie where a "just and humane" treaty "entirely for the benefit and future welfare of the Indians" would be negotiated. By dividing and subdividing the country into various geographical districts, the government hoped to stop the tribal wars.[34] The revered Jesuit missionary Pierre De Smet and Alexander

---

[31]Report to Pierre Chouteau, Jr., 4 December 1850, Ft. Pierre Letterbook, Chouteau Collection, MOHS.

[32]Sunder, *Fur Trade*, 139. Apparently Dawson "hinted" to his family about this marriage soon after it occurred, but no letters from 1851 have survived. On 6 July 1852, he confirms his marriage, saying, "I thank God your opinions coincide with my own" and that "without a priest marriage in my own circumstances can be as sacredly and as honourably performed as amongst you all in God's most holy Sanctuary." This suggests that Dawson's mother had accepted her son's marriage to a mixed-blood woman.

[33]Killoren, *"Come Blackrobe,"* 116.

[34]Ibid., reproduction of flyer facing 106.

Culbertson were enlisted to escort representatives of the upper Missouri tribes to the conference. Unfortunately, trouble erupted before they could even chart a route.

Culbertson, as was his custom, had left Fort Benton in early spring to meet the steamboat. He and Honoré Picotte were waiting near St. Joseph when they saw the *St. Ange* coming upriver. Although they flagged the approaching steamer, she passed them by. Confused, the traders continued upriver, still hoping to board. Thirty miles later, the *St. Ange* docked and the traders learned they had been ignored because the steamer carried cholera and the disease had already claimed thirteen lives.[35]

Rudolph Kurz, a young Swiss artist on board, wrote that the *St. Ange* had been converted into a "hospital for victims of cholera—the sick and the dying." The helpless crew had nothing to offer the stricken except for a potion of meal and whiskey.[36] Two Jesuit missionaries, Pierre De Smet and Christian Hoecken, were also on board, and they prayed for the victims until De Smet himself was stricken with a "bilious attack." De Smet, fearing he might die, asked Hoecken to hear his confession. Hoecken, simultaneously called to minister to a cholera victim, demurred: "I see no immediate danger for you; to-morrow we will see." But there would be no tomorrow for Hoecken. That night, he contracted cholera and died.[37]

Despite the pestilence, the steamboat continued upriver. At Fort Clark, Dawson was happy to see De Smet disembark. As the two chatted, White Shield, an Arikara chief, interrupted them with an urgent appeal: "It is very late in the season and no rain. Corn ought to be up now. We want the Black Robe to send us rain."[38] The kindly De Smet, knowing his limits, "laughed heartily" before instructing White Shield to gather his chiefs. Then, the missionary promised, he would "ask [the Almighty] to be merciful and grant your requests."

Once the Arikara chiefs had gathered, De Smet offered his prayers before everyone boarded the *St. Ange* for the customary feast. Later that afternoon, "there came up a heavy thunder shower which fairly deluged the place." De Smet knew "[t]hey will think I did it," and indeed, Pierre Garreau was soon offering "ten good horses" for the

[35]Bradley, "Affairs at Fort Benton," 265.

[36]Hewitt, *Journal of Rudolph Friederich Kurz*, 69.

[37]Chittenden and Richardson, *Father de Smet*, 2:640–41.

[38]Indians called the Jesuits "Black Robes" because of their frocks.

secret to "how Father DeSmet . . . made it rain." De Smet's answer almost certainly disappointed: "Be a good Christian."[39]

The good feelings evoked by the rain did not last. Immediately after the steamer departed, news of the cholera began to spread. At Fort Berthold, "a great number of . . . Gros Ventres were seized with a violent cold. The affection terminated fatally in a few instances. On the disappearance of this ailment, however, the Cholera introduced itself among them. Sixteen deaths occurred in forty-eight hours. . . . More than one hundred Indians were attacked."[40]

For Dawson, the disease-ridden *St. Ange* brought "a dreadful life of anxiety and trouble." Illness erupted at Fort Clark on 25 August. The "poor, ignorant" Indians, "thoroughly convinced it was our desire to kill them," blamed the Company as "the people [near Fort Clark], both whites and Indians, were attacked with an influenza, unusually severe in character, which proved fatal in three cases."[41] Twenty days later, "another malady" broke out. "Infinitely more fearful in its character and effects—its symptoms are identical with those of cholera. Yesterday, twenty-five Indians (Arickarees) died, and to-day . . . thirty-seven more fatal cases."[42]

Alone "in the Fort with only a single man, the remainder of the hands having gone to the *Shantee*,"[43] Dawson tried to vaccinate the panicked Indians and doctor them with his few crude supplies.[44] But as conditions deteriorated, Dawson moved inside "with closed doors, and . . . a careful watch for some treacherous assault." The Indians "refuse[d] to disperse," because "they ha[d] no lodges, and many of them no horses."[45] By early October, the Arikara, "dying . . . like flies under frost," were "in a fury." They "razed the block houses of the opposition [Fort Primeau] and [stole] their goods" before Dawson "[brought] into action his great guns (4-pound cannons) in order to protect himself."[46]

---

[39]Chittenden, *Early Steamboat Navigation*, 196–98.

[40]"Cholera among the Indians," *Missouri Republican*, 14 October 1851. "Affection" is the term used in the article. Whether this was meant to be "affliction" or whether there is a more colloquial understanding of that term is not known.

[41]Letter 16.

[42]"Cholera among the Indians."

[43]"The express has since returned," and "as he passed the *shantee*, he saw Dawson's people." This is almost certainly a corruption of "chantier," meaning a log hut or workshop. Ibid.

[44]Sunder, *Fur Trade*, 135–36.

[45]"Cholera among the Indians."

[46]Hewitt, *Journal of Rudolph Friederich Kurz*, 167. Kurz calls Dawson "Dorson," reflecting Dawson's heavy Scottish brogue.

Dawson finally learned that the "most cowardly" Harvey, Primeau and Company traders had "told the Indians" that he "had killed them and that [he] would kill many more . . . unless they killed [him]." The opposition traders pointed out that "not one of the whites" died, convincing them of the traders' "desire to kill them." "Innumerable attempts" were made to "kill any one" of the AFC men and Dawson in particular.[47] Blamed as "one among the crowd of evil-doers," Dawson survived two attempts on his life, thanks in part to "some friends" among the warriors.[48]

In the end, Dawson estimated that "at least a fourth" of the Arikara were "carried off" by the epidemic.[49] But, demonstrating just how thoroughly he had adjusted to the frontier, Dawson dismissed his daily life as "monotinous."[50]

In late September 1851, the Fort Laramie treaty was signed. For most tribes, its impact would be fleeting as new and more complex treaties replaced this one. But for the upper Missouri village Indians, the 1851 Horse Creek Treaty would permanently define their relationship to the American government, and its reverberations began almost immediately.

Under the treaty, the government promised the Arikara $1,500 in annual annuities "so long as they keep peace" with the traders and other tribes.[51] In the fall of 1852, Dawson made the first distribution, believing they would "have most beneficial effects," despite his "fear that sometime Uncle Sam will fail to fulfil his part of the contract and then will things be worse than ever."[52]

In fact, Dawson's premonition was already unfolding. The 1852 Arikara annuities had arrived only because a distressed Alexander

---

[47]Letter 16.

[48]"Cholera among the Indians." Unfortunately, no further details could be found about these threats or the Indian friends who protected Dawson.

[49]Letter 17.

[50]Letter 16.

[51]The figure $1,500 comes from Dawson's letters. Tribes were supposed to receive $50,000 in annuities annually for fifty years. Congress later arbitrarily reduced that to fifteen years. Why the Arikara would only have received $1,500 worth of annuities is unclear. Perhaps Dawson misunderstood, or perhaps as a small tribe, the Arikara had to share a $50,000 allotment with other village Indians.

[52]Letter 22.

Culbertson had traveled to St. Louis to complain to Superintendent of Indian Affairs David D. Mitchell. The upper Missouri tribes had been without an agent for almost four years, and Culbertson feared the annuities would not be distributed properly. The Assiniboin had already begun to ridicule Fool Bear, their representative to the conference, for having "come back from the White's country with a lie in his mouth" and having "sold their lands for a handful of goods."[53] Fearing a more severe backlash, Mitchell and Culbertson personally delivered that year's annuities.[54]

The treaty terms that benefited whites were implemented more promptly. These included "the right of the United States to form roads and establish military posts in [Indian] territory."[55] In March 1853, Congress, eager to connect the expanding nation, authorized surveys of possible transcontinental railroad routes. Isaac Ingalls Stevens, recently appointed governor of Washington Territory, was tapped to lead the northern survey.[56] Facing a congressional deadline of January 1854, Stevens wasted no time heading to Minnesota to begin his survey "over the Mountains to the Pacific."[57]

His "troop of Soldiers," which included Lieutenant John Mullan, represented the beginning of a flood of visitors to a region that was "getting to be a little more bustling." The 1854 arrivals also included John Tevis, Dawson's former employer in St. Louis, who would "pass the winter" at Fort Clark, "hunting deer[,] buffalo[,] and health."[58]

With Tevis in residence, Dawson must have breathed a sigh of relief as the "somewhat tranquil" Indians "attend[ed] better to their business—Robe making." The year before, as the tribes had recovered from the cholera, "they [had] made very few robes," resulting in "a very poor trade" and a "most inadequate" profit. "Happily," though, "the Company appreciated all the circumstances" and "instead of blame," Dawson had been "highly commended." Moreover, since the opposition company had "become such a poor affair," Dawson managed to "get at least 9/10ths" of the Arikara's new robes.[59] Impressed,

---

[53]Denig, *Five Indian Tribes*, 85.

[54]Wischmann, *Frontier Diplomats*, 213–15.

[55]Chittenden and Richardson, *Father de Smet*, 2:676.

[56]Report of the Commissioner of Indian Affairs, House ExDoc 1, 38th Cong., 1st sess., 129 (1863), 736.

[57]Letter 25.

[58]Letter 25.

[59]Letter 24.

the Company offered him a new two-year contract at "an increased Salary of $100 annually."[60]

Meanwhile, Dawson welcomed a new clerk, straight from "the Land of Cakes."[61] David Constable, "a fine straight forward 'up and down' Scotchman," was the grandson of a famous Edinburgh publisher. Another misfit, Constable had left Scotland "to fight his own battles." He and Dawson reminisced about their homeland, lamenting the need to leave home to find oneself. But before long, business required that Dawson send Constable to the winter villages to trade.[62]

Dawson's exceptional returns that winter brought even more favorable attention. In early June, Culbertson instructed Dawson to "prepare . . . to start for the Blackft. Country":

> Fully satisfied of the judicious and careful management of Fort Clark since it has been under your charge, we find your service will be now more necessary and beneficial to the Outfit by giving you a larger field to work upon. It has consequently been agreed upon by the gentleman of the house as well as myself to place Mr. [Charles] Galpin in charge of Fort Clark and you to accompany me to the Blackfeet preparatory to taking the permanent charge of Fort Benton.[63]

The new assignment shocked Dawson. He had become such a "fixture at old Fort Clark" that the idea of moving had "never entered" his head.[64] When Culbertson arrived, Dawson learned the promotion also came with a partnership share in the Company.

While Dawson was undoubtedly flattered by Culbertson's praise, he also suffered self-doubt. Fort Benton conducted "four fifths of all our trade," and Dawson would be commanding some 170 men, including many who were older than he. He quickly realized that "the next years trading . . . [would] be either [his] making or marring." The very thought of it left his head "in a whirl."[65]

---

[60]Letter 25.

[61]"Land o' Cakes" was used by Robert Burns to describe Scotland in the opening line of his poem, "On the Late Captain Grose's Peregrinations." The expression had also been used to describe Scotland by Robert Fergusson in his poem "The King's Birthday in Edinburgh." The phrase is believed to describe the Scots' fondness for oatcakes, once a staple of the Scottish diet.

[62]Letter 27.

[63]This excerpt of Culbertson's letter is included in letter 30. The original was not found.

[64]Letter 30.

[65]Letter 30.

But Culbertson never asked whether Dawson wanted the position. The assignment had come as orders and, with the steamboat's departure imminent, Dawson rushed to put his affairs in order. Although Dawson's wife dreaded leaving her mother, her life was now with Dawson and their two young children, James and Grace.[66]

Dawson, however, would be leaving behind another child. During the winter of 1851–52, while trading in the Brulé winter camps, he had fathered Andrew, who arrived with his father's distinctive carrot-top and a birth date embarrassingly close to that of his half-brother, James. Dawson was so ashamed of this indiscretion that he only mentioned Andrew, Jr., once in his letters home and only then, apparently, by mistake.[67] Instead, Dawson prevailed on his old friend Robert Morgan to raise the child in Canada's Red River Settlements.[68]

---

[66]James Scott Dawson was born 6 September 1852, Grace Dawson on 13 December 1853. It is not clear what became of Kuta's daughters with Desautel, although Dawson once alludes to possibly sending them to their grandmother in Montreal. They may also have gone downriver for schooling.

[67]Letter 22.

[68]Baptismal Records and the Manitoba Cemetery Index, Holy Trinity Anglican Church, Headingley, confirm that Andrew Dawson, Jr., was baptized on 9 September 1858 and died on 8 May 1932. He was not mentioned in his father's will.

7

Something of an Undertaking

DAWSON'S NEW POSITION BROUGHT WITH IT NEW PERQUISITES, including steamboat travel. "In a dream," he and his family boarded the *Sonora* in late June 1854, bound for Fort Union. Dawson had never before traveled by steamer—a luxury reserved for AFC higher-ups. As he lazed on deck, driven slightly "stupid" by the steamboat's "noise and racket," his only regret was that this promotion would mean a delay in his highly anticipated visit home.[1]

On 3 July, the *Sonora* reached Fort Union, and the very next day Dawson set off for Fort Benton with two mackinaws, each carrying some twenty-seven tons of freight. The long journey turned tedious almost immediately as the mackinaws had to be unloaded to portage at every rapid. As Dawson later admitted in a letter to his mother, "It was something of an undertaking." They finally reached Fort Benton on 19 September.[2]

Dawson had heard much about the Blackfeet posts, but had never seen them. Alexander Culbertson had established a new Blackfeet post after abandoning Fort McKenzie following the 1844 massacre. Culbertson had intentionally located that first replacement post, Fort Lewis, on the river's south bank, to protect it from the potentially still-hostile Blackfeet. But after the tribe accepted Culbertson's contrite overtures, he moved to a better location some fifteen miles downstream on the north bank of the Missouri in 1847. The post was soon rechristened as Fort Benton.

To Dawson's surprise, he adjudged Fort Benton, located "'furthest from nowhere' in the known Globe," to be "miserably situated" at

[1]Letter 30.
[2]Letter 31.

"the poorest spot . . . on the face of creation." Nonetheless, the fort was "by far the best, and the most commodious on the river." Nearby was "a fine view of the Rocky Mountains," although the basin-like topography restricted their sight line from the fort to less than one mile. Still, as he told his mother, Dawson looked forward to exploring the area, especially the "Great Falls of the Missouri."

In recognition of his new position, Dawson's recently signed contract had been replaced with one that awarded Dawson $500 a year, his goods at cost, and an exemption from all losses. In addition, he received a 1/24th share in the Company, which, while "not the greatest thing in the world," was clearly a "step to advancement" and evidence of "very flattering" prospects.[3]

A week later, on 28 September, Alexander Culbertson arrived with his much admired wife, Natawista, and her Piegan cousin, Little Dog.[4] Culbertson and Washington Territorial governor Isaac Stevens were making plans for a Blackfeet Treaty Council. Stevens, as a result of his governing position as well as his encounters with the tribes during his survey work, had become interested in ensuring peaceful relations among the Northern Plains tribes. The council had originally been scheduled for that fall but had to be postponed. Culbertson worried about the tribes' reaction to the delay. Adding to his concerns, the new superintendent of Indian affairs, Alfred Cumming, had awarded the 1854 annuities contract to the AFC's competitors.[5] Now it was all the more important "to make something out of the Blackfeet [trade]."[6]

On 29 September, the Culbertsons held the customary employees' ball at which, Dawson noted, "two only of the number made a sorry display of their reasons." Nonetheless, the next day's work had to be canceled since "the effects of intemperance [were] a little noticeable."[7]

Finally, on the 31st, Culbertson opened trade by introducing Dawson to the assembled Blackfeet chiefs. But the ever-restless Culbertson did not remain at Benton for long. The day after Christmas, following a "little jolification," Culbertson departed for St. Louis

[3]Letter 31.

[4]McDonnell, "Fort Benton Journal," 1.

[5]Correspondence between Cumming and George Manypenny and between Manypenny and David Mitchell, spring and summer 1853, NAM, M234/885.

[6]Alexander Culbertson to Charles Galpin, 6 September 1854, Chouteau Collection, MOHS.

[7]McDonnell, "Fort Benton Journal," 1. Dawson immediately began keeping the Fort Benton journal.

with John Tevis, Dawson's former employer, leaving the Scotsman in sole command of the Blackfeet post.[8]

As Dawson settled in and worked on improving his sign language, an incident six hundred miles away precipitated events that would roil the frontier. During July 1854, the Oglala, Miniconjou, and Brulé Sioux along with the Northern Cheyenne, gathered near Fort Laramie, awaiting their annuities. When their agent was delayed, the tribes grew increasingly impatient as their goods remained in storage.

In mid-August, as an emigrant party passed nearby, a lame cow from the wagon train wandered into the Indian camp and the hungry natives slaughtered it. Both the Indians and the emigrants reported this breach of the 1851 treaty to the authorities at Fort Laramie. When attempts to mediate the dispute failed, Lieutenant John Grattan pressed to arrest High Forehead, the Miniconjou cow-killer.

Authorized to pursue the complaint, Grattan rode out to the Indian encampment with an interpreter, two noncommissioned officers, and twenty-seven members of the Sixth Infantry.[9] There High Forehead refused to be taken into custody. The tribal chiefs tried to explain that one tribe could not compel a warrior of another tribe to surrender, but the encounter grew heated. A shot rang out and Conquering Bear, appointed chief of the Brulé, fell, mortally wounded. The Indians responded with fury, slaughtering Grattan and his men.[10]

For two days, the Sioux rampaged through the valley. Knowing now that their annuities would never be distributed, they seized "the whole of them" along with "a large stock of goods left from last year's trade, and an entire new stock just arrived from the Missouri, amounting to about twelve or fifteen hundred dollars" before retreating.[11] The violence left the soldiers at Fort Laramie badly shaken.[12]

The incident's repercussions extended far beyond Fort Laramie. Writing from Fort Pierre two months later, the usually sympathetic Indian agent Alfred Vaughan called the situation "perilous in the

[8]Ibid., 14; Letter 31.

[9]McChristian, *Fort Laramie*, 74.

[10]Paul, *Blue Water Creek*, 21–24.

[11]Report of the Commissioner of Indian Affairs, Senate ExDoc 1, 33rd Cong., 2nd sess., 746, 296.

[12]Paul, *Blue Water Creek*, 24–25.

extreme." Unless the government sent "a sufficient number of troops of the *proper kind*," Vaughan feared "there is no knowing to what extent [the Indians] will commit murder and depredations." In recent days, the Yankton, Hunkpapa, and Blackfeet Sioux had all refused Vaughan's overtures, "preferr[ing] the liberty to take scalps, and commit whatever depredations they pleased."[13]

By November, the "conduct and talk [of the Sioux] had produced the Greatest Excitement." They were "urging all the others to prepare to Join with them in defence against any U.S. Troops that may be sent," Vaughan reported, "stating that the ease with which they killed the unfortunate party at the Platte" proved they could "easily overcome" any troops sent against them. More alarmingly, the tribes were "untiring in procuring ammunition and guns, arrow points, and all implements of war." Vaughan continued: "The Brulées from the Platte, the Onkpapas[,] Blackfeet Sioux[,] a part of the Yantonais[,] Sans Arc[,] and Miniconjous Bands of the Missouri openly bid defiance to the threats of the Government and go so far as to say they do not fear the result should soldiers come to fight them."[14]

Commissioner of Indian Affairs George Manypenny forwarded Vaughan's report to the Senate along with his own cautions. Acknowledging the "melancholy and heart-rending" deaths of Grattan and his men, Manypenny nonetheless insisted that the emigrants should have been compensated with Indian annuities. "[N]o officer of the military departments was, in my opinion, authorized to arrest or try any Indian for the offence charged against him." While situations do "frequently arise in our intercourse with the Indians requiring the employment of force," Manypenny suggested that "the whites may be, and often are, the aggressors." A "force better adapted to the Indian service" would benefit everyone while "careful attention and kind and humane treatment will, generally, have more influence . . . than bayonets and gunpowder."[15]

[13]Alfred J. Vaughan to Col. Alfred Cumming, 19 October 1854, Senate ExDoc 1, 33rd Cong., 2nd sess., 746, 296–97. Italics in original.

[14]Alfred Vaughan to Alfred Cumming, 21 November 1854, NAM, M234/885. The Blackfeet Sioux are a subdivision of the Sioux not to be confused with the Blackfeet bands.

[15]Senate ExDoc 1, 33rd Cong., 2nd sess., 746, 224–25.

Unaware of the storms gathering along the Platte and spilling up the Missouri, Dawson set about to master Fort Benton's rhythms. While the pattern of life seemed familiar, the pace of events was brisk and the number of personnel dizzying. Traders assigned to multiple satellite posts came and went with supplies and trade goods. Wagons broke down, horses were stolen, accidents occurred, Indians visited and traded, illnesses struck, children were born, men got lost, half-dead men appeared while others perished. When opposition wagons returned empty from the Indian camps, Dawson cheered their apparent failure with a simple "Hurra for us."[16]

Meanwhile, the fort's men continued to rebuild Benton with adobe bricks whenever weather allowed. Dawson singled out one employee, "Nigger George," for his ability to do "three days work in one."[17] At the same time, Dawson oversaw construction of a new kitchen, a chicken coop, and a "fine little pig pen" for "one of our Sows having litered." With winter approaching, the men also stockpiled food and wood.[18]

Unfamiliar with nomadic tribes, Dawson was surprised by the constant comings and goings of war parties. Although he complained about life among the shiftless Indians and indolent employees, both of whom he labeled "a miserable set of beings," he knew that gaining the Blackfeet's trust would be critical to his own success.[19] To his delight, Dawson discovered that providing simple medical treatments earned him the desired respect. When a "noted Indian chief" gorged on a "heap big dish of roast dog," Dawson prescribed an emetic. The chief "vomited bone after bone," but recovered and became "one of Dawson's best friends." When the chief's favorite son became sick, the chief immediately brought him to Dawson, who again worked his magic.[20]

These skills convinced the superstitious warriors that Dawson had special powers. One warrior decided to test the trader by proclaiming his interest in becoming a white horse. Dawson thought about this before ordering the warrior to strip. He was then taken outside

[16]McDonnell, "Fort Benton Journal," 22.

[17]James Dawson, "Major Andrew Dawson, 1817–1871," 4. This name and the notation of his exceptional ability to shoulder such heavy workloads seem fraught with racial stereotypes.

[18]McDonnell, "Fort Benton Journal," 8. For a fascinating glimpse into the fort's day-to-day rhythms, this book cannot be surpassed.

[19]Ibid., 20.

[20]Dawson, "Major," 5.

and picketed in the open air and snow. When Dawson next saw the nearly frozen, snow-covered warrior, he had reassessed his desires.[21]

Unfortunately, Dawson's medical skills had their limits. In February, Kuta, Dawson's "good loving obedient wife and companion," lay "on her death bed," growing "feebler and feebler daily." To Dawson's dismay, she had "not enjoyed one days health" since leaving Fort Clark and was now "in the last stay of consumption and the dropsy." Dawson had planned to send her downriver as soon as the river opened, but he feared she could not "bear the fatigue." By 8 March she was "very low indeed," and three days later she was dead at the age of twenty-three. After burying her "back of the Fort," Dawson, "unnerved" and "unfitted . . . for any manner of business," took to his own bed to mourn the "most affectionate Wife as ever breathed the breath of lip." He sank into such a depression that he could not even care for his own children.[22]

Shortly thereafter, Dawson took James and Grace to live with their grandmother at Fort Clark. His friend David Constable also promised to look after the children. Dawson hated to leave them behind, but consoled himself with the hope that "in a year or two . . . should [they] be all spared," he would take the children with him to Scotland.[23]

At Fort Clark, Dawson anxiously awaited the overdue steamer, which finally arrived on 5 July 1855. Alfred Cumming, superintendent of Indian affairs, had come upriver on the *St. Mary* to preside over the upcoming Blackfeet Treaty Council with Isaac Stevens. Two such different men could scarcely be imagined. The West Point–educated Stevens was good-looking with dark hazel eyes, curly black hair, a straight nose, and a firm goatee-covered chin. Suffering from a mild form of dwarfism, he was also quite diminutive.[24]

By contrast, Cumming weighed over three hundred pounds, and his imperiousness matched his girth.[25] He had attained his lofty

---

[21]Ibid., 6.

[22]McDonnell, "Fort Benton Journal," 23–26; Letters 31 and 32.

[23]Letter 32. Dawson mentions taking the children "with me to the settlements," suggesting for the first time that Dawson may have considered settling in the States.

[24]Richards, *Stevens*, 6.

[25]Bradley, "Affairs at Fort Benton," 3:277.

position through socially prominent roots and political connections, despite having been charged with "*libel, Perjury* and *damages*" twenty years earlier. According to John Randolph of Louisiana, who also offered a $500 bounty, Cumming was nothing but a "*bloated, pusillanimous* Scoundrel" and "infamous Villain."[26]

Isaac Stevens would likely have endorsed Randolph's assessment. Stung at being denied sole conference authority, Stevens had also seen the government reject his railroad route as well as his proposal to purchase a government steamboat to ferry annuities upriver. The treaty council's delay, combined with the indignity of co-chairing it with Cumming, infuriated Stevens.[27] Coming east from Washington Territory, the governor reached Fort Benton on 26 July, where he found nothing in readiness.[28] Annoyed, Stevens headed downriver, searching for his co-commissioner and the council goods. On 15 August, he found Cumming camping with Alexander Culbertson at the mouth of Milk River.[29] At that first meeting, Cumming proposed jettisoning most of Stevens's preparations, developed over several years.[30]

As Stevens and Cumming argued, Andrew Dawson, James Kipp, and sixty other men "wend[ed] [their] way at a Snails pace up Stream" with the "immense pile" of treaty goods bound for Fort Benton, the proposed conference site. When mackinaws proved inadequate, the men built "four large Keel Boats, the largest that ever entered on these waters," to handle the supplies.[31]

But the headaches continued. With the water lower "than it was ever known to be," the commissioners accepted Alexander Culbertson's suggestion that the conference be moved downriver to the mouth of the Judith. This rare agreement mercifully shortened Dawson's

[26]"$500 Reward," 29 August 1835, John Randolph, Louisiana re: Alfred Cumming, *An American Time Capsule: Three Centuries of Broadsides and Other Printed Ephemera*, http://memory.loc.gov/cgi-bin/ampage?collId=rbpe&fileName=rbpe02/rbpe024/02401300/rbpe02401300.db&recNum=0&itemLink=r?ammem/rbpebib:@field%28NUMBER+@band%28rbpe+02401300%29%29&linkText=0. Emphasis in original.

[27]Sunder, *Fur Trade*, 167.

[28]McDonnell, "Fort Benton Journal," 38.

[29]Richards, *Stevens*, 230.

[30]Correspondence regarding the negotiations between Stevens and Cumming in preparation for the treaty council can be found on NAM, M234/30. No item was too small for them to argue over.

[31]Lepley, *Blackfoot Fur Trade*, 196; McDonnell, "Fort Benton Journal," 255n19. The boatmen included two of the river's best pilots, Michael Champagne and Paul Polach.

"labours[,] anxieties and troubles." As soon as the commissioners acknowledged receiving the goods, Dawson returned to Fort Benton, confident that the Company stood to "nett . . . a little over $35,000, a pretty little business," for transporting the council supplies.[32]

The Company had also recently made a tidy profit by selling Fort Pierre to the government. Despite inventorying the decrepit post at only $5,000, the AFC had gotten the government to pay $45,000 for it. All this left Dawson feeling smug about his first year as a partner. While he recognized that "our business . . . will be considerably injured by this war with the Sioux . . . this year we can afford it, and perhaps another year something else will cast up."[33]

Meanwhile, at the council grounds, the commissioners quickly concluded the negotiations. The tribes agreed to "a common hunting-ground" where, for ninety-nine years, all tribes could "enjoy equal and uninterrupted privileges of hunting, fishing and gathering fruit, grazing animals, curing meat and dressing robes" with "permanent settlements" barred.[34]

Other articles required the tribes "to remain within their own respective countries" unless traveling to the common hunting ground or visiting other tribes "for the purpose of trade or social intercourse." The treaty guaranteed emigrants safe passage while promising the tribes government protection from "depredations and other unlawful acts." In exchange, the Indians agreed to permit "travelling thoroughfares," including telegraph lines, military posts, agency buildings, missions, schools, farms, shops, and mills. Whites would also be permitted to "permanently occupy as much land as may be necessary" to support those facilities. The "navigation of all lakes and streams" would be "forever free to citizens of the United States."[35] The treaty promised ten years of annuities along with an additional $15,000 allocated annually to educate the children, "promoting their civilization and Christianization" and instructing them "in agricultural and mechanical pursuits." Finally, the treaty authorized compensation

[32]Letter 32. While McDonnell, "Fort Benton Journal," 38–49, is filled with entries detailing council preparations, there are no entries for 5–17 October. The decision to move the conference was reached on the 5th, and the conference got under way on the 17th, leading Anne McDonnell to conclude that the journalist attended the conference (273n90).

[33]Letter 32.

[34]Kappler, *Treaties,* 2:736.

[35]Ibid., 2:737.

for whites victimized by Indian depredations and the withholding of annuities for treaty violations.[36]

Piegan, Blood, Northern Blackfoot, Gros Ventre, Nez Perce, and Flathead representatives affixed their signatures on 17 October 1855. Apparently none paid much attention to Article XI, which proclaimed "their dependence on the Government of the United States."[37]

Following the conference, Culbertson accompanied Cumming downriver as he headed to Washington to try to persuade the Senate to ratify the treaty.[38] Meanwhile, Governor Stevens paused at Fort Benton, where he briefed Dawson on the new treaty.[39] In early November, Edwin A. C. Hatch, the Blackfeet's newly appointed agent, arrived. Although Dawson and Hatch had previously met, they had spent little time together. Hoping to solicit Dawson's advice regarding a location for his new agency, Hatch proposed a pleasure trip to the Missouri Falls (later known as the Great Falls). With that official veneer, Dawson accepted. Although "the distance is only 25 miles," the trip, begun on 6 December, lasted five days.[40] They "set out not to hurry but to enjoy [them]selves," a task easily accomplished thanks to some fishing, hunting, and the "very grand" falls.[41]

On New Year's Eve, Major Hatch, still ensconced at Fort Benton, threw a party that stretched into a second day, thanks to plentiful provisions. Dancing competed with a lottery and numerous prizes, leaving everyone "pleased and happy."[42] Despite the distractions, Dawson made 1855's trade "the biggest and most profitable . . . ever . . . in this country." To his delight, there was "plenty money[,] plenty robes[,] plenty everything."[43]

Dawson was already basking in his achievements when "the Old Sunn[,] Big Sun[,] Big Sitting Down[,] and The tail that goes up the Hill" appeared on 15 February 1856. These Northern Blackfoot chiefs

[36]Ibid., 2:738–39.

[37]Ibid., 2:738.

[38]The treaty was ratified on 15 April 1856. 11 Stat. 657.

[39]McDonnell, "Fort Benton Journal," 50.

[40]Ibid., 50, 55.

[41]Letter 33.

[42]McDonnell, "Fort Benton Journal," 58.

[43]Letter 33.

were making their "first formal visit" to the post "since the Canon was fired on them" in February 1844. For Dawson, this visit represented a coup that even the well-respected Culbertson had not achieved. After Dawson received them with all the graciousness he could muster, Hatch also "made them a very handsome present."[44] When Hatch explained the recently signed treaty, the chiefs were "greatly pleased when informed that they were to receive a portion of the benefits," their tribe being "much poorer" than the others.[45] The traders then got down to business, with the Northern Blackfoot trading in excess of 500 robes before departing with everyone "well satisfied."[46]

Meanwhile, trade had "fairly commenced," with some 350 lodges of Gros Ventre, encamped between the Milk and Missouri Rivers, trading more than 300 robes. The rest of the month saw equally large numbers. On 18 February, the traders collected over 600 robes and nearly 800 the next day. By the 20th, the "Stock of goods [began] to look down," but they still managed to purchase 550 robes. Over 250 came in on the 21st and more than 270 on the 22nd. The 23rd brought more than 400 robes with another 1,000 coming in over the next two days. The only thing that dampened the traders' spirits was fear that the opposition also "might have doubled" their take.[47]

Although Alexander Harvey had died in 1854, leaving his company in disarray, it had reorganized as Picotte and Company and was conducting a brisk trade with supplies freighted overland.[48] That April, when Joseph Picotte left Fort Campbell with three fully loaded mackinaws, Dawson, recognizing the companies' "most amicable terms," ordered the Fort Benton cannon fired, the "first time an opposition Bourgeois had such an honor paid him."[49] With his own bounty, Dawson could afford a little generosity.

Dawson inherited more from Culbertson than responsibility for Fort Benton. His ascension to "king of the high Missouri" included oversight

[44]McDonnell, "Fort Benton Journal," 63.
[45]Senate ExDoc 2, 34th Cong., 3rd sess., 875, 627.
[46]McDonnell, "Fort Benton Journal," 63.
[47]Senate ExDoc 2, 34th Cong., 3rd sess., 875, 625; McDonnell, "Fort Benton Journal," 63.
[48]Sunder, *Fur Trade*, 166; obituary, *Daily Missouri Republican*, 19 September 1854. The anti-Chouteau paper called Harvey "a brave, an honest, and a kindhearted man."
[49]McDonnell, "Fort Benton Journal," 70.

of all the upriver posts, mandating a grueling travel schedule. In early spring, with snows still deep, Dawson would travel overland to Fort Union to await the river's opening. From there, he would check on the downriver posts before meeting the northbound steamboat. Instructions from St. Louis dictated the rest of his summer schedule. Autumn often entailed a trip to St. Louis before quickly pushing back upriver. With luck, Dawson reached Fort Benton by Christmas.

In June 1856, Dawson was visiting his children at Fort Clark while he waited for the *St. Mary*, which finally arrived, carrying Alexander Culbertson, Alfred Vaughan, and Charles Chouteau. Dawson was delighted to learn that Chouteau had nominated him, along with several other AFC traders, to be corresponding members of the newly organized Academy of Science in St. Louis and that Culbertson had handled the necessary business in St. Louis, leaving Dawson free to return to Fort Benton with another distinguished visitor coming upriver in response to the new Blackfeet Treaty.[50]

Article X of Lame Bull's Treaty called for the "civilization and Christianization" of the Indians.[51] Although the traders had long worked with Jesuit missionaries, Culbertson apparently thought a Protestant presentation might benefit the Blackfeet.[52] Therefore, he had enlisted Elkanah Mackey, a Presbyterian minister, to come upriver. Mackey, a Pennsylvania native and graduate of Princeton Seminary, had brought along his new wife, Sarah Armstrong Mackey.[53]

Culbertson, Dawson, and the Mackeys traveled overland from Fort Union to Fort Benton, arriving on 15 August with Agent Hatch, whom they had met at Milk River. Word spread quickly about Sarah Mackey, the first white woman to visit the region. Although unendingly curious, the natives treated her with courtesy and respect.[54]

The AFC employees hoped to learn more about the newcomers at the ball customarily held to celebrate the return of the bourgeois. But to their disappointment, Culbertson canceled the festivities, perhaps because both he and Mrs. Mackey were feeling ill or perhaps because he feared the customary debauchery would offend the newcomers.

---

[50]Sunder, *Fur Trade*, 176.

[51]Kappler, *Treaties*, 2:738. The Blackfeet often refer to the 1855 Treaty as "Lame Bull's Treaty" after the first signatory.

[52]Culbertson's own stepbrother ran a Presbyterian mission in China and had graduated from Princeton Seminary.

[53]McDonnell, "Fort Benton Journal," 279.

[54]Ewers, *Blackfeet*, 195.

The Mackeys appeared to settle in well. On 17 August, Mackey preached two services, one for the fort employees and another for the tribes. On the 31st, he preached again before riding out to explore the countryside. But Sarah Mackey, having recently discovered she was pregnant, was in a "most distressing state of nervous derangement." Reluctantly, Mackey acquiesced to her wishes and agreed to leave the Blackfeet country. On 15 September, their brief residence came to an end.[55]

Unfortunately, something with more lasting impact also arrived that summer. Soon after the opposition steamboat *Clara* left St. Louis on 14 July, smallpox broke out.[56] Once again, the captain refused to put the victims ashore, and the disease soon struck the Arikara, Mandan, Hidatsa, and Assiniboine. Before winter could contain it, the disease spread to the Crow, the Blackfeet, and the Red River métis.[57]

While the 1856–57 death toll paled in comparison to the 1837 devastation, Alfred Vaughan witnessed ten deaths in twenty days at Fort William, Picotte's post near Fort Union. In the Arikara villages, the disease raged "at an alarming rate," killing sixty-three. Only "with difficulty" were the "much enraged" Indians restrained from "committing violence upon the traders." The "poor Mandans," numbering only 250, lost 17. In all, Vaughan estimated 2,000 casualties. Once again, he implored the government to vaccinate the upriver tribes.[58]

Nevertheless, as 1856 came to an end, Dawson could celebrate "the biggest and most profitable" trade ever. Moreover, his employees had finished Benton's adobe reconstruction and the post now boasted exterior walls fourteen feet high and three feet thick, a two-story kitchen, and one twenty-one-foot corner bastion.[59]

For the traders, spring arrived when the ice broke. "The explosion, as the water burst the rotten mass upwards, was like distant thunder."

---

[55]McDonnell, "Fort Benton Journal," 88, 90, 279; Harrod, *Mission among the Blackfeet*, 25.

[56]Alfred Vaughan identified the disease as "varioloid, or a modified form of the small-pox." Senate ExDoc 2, 34th Cong., 4th sess., 875, 636.

[57]Sunder, *Fur Trade*, 178–79.

[58]Senate ExDoc 2, 34th Cong., 3rd sess., 875, 637; House ExDoc 1, 35th Cong., 1st sess., 942, 408.

[59]Lepley, *Blackfoot Fur Trade*, 178–80.

The traders watched "the various sized packs of frozen blocks float by, roaring with a splendid sound as mass after mass passed onward[,] forcing aside all resistance and sweeping everything before it." The rushing ice could last for hours, "keeping up a continuous roar."[60]

Despite a decade of witnessing this awe-inspiring display, Dawson still found it liberating and never more so than in 1858. For years, he had plotted and planned a visit to his beloved Scotland. But something had always gotten in the way. Now, finally, the trip was happening. Leaving his senior clerks, Matthew Carroll and George Steele, in charge of Benton, Dawson headed downriver. At Fort Clark, he visited his children. Then, in St. Louis, he learned that Culbertson was retiring for good. But even this news could not divert him. Soon he was en route to New York where he caught the RMS *Persia* to Liverpool. There he was met by his brother Aleck and Aleck's wife, Margaret. Together they traveled to Birkenhead, on the west bank of the River Mersey, to visit their sister, Christian, affectionately known as Tit. She and Andrew shared the pain of having been widowed, and while neither had met the other's spouse, it comforted them to discuss their mutual sorrow.

Dawson enjoyed visiting with his siblings but was anxious to see his mother. Fifteen years had passed since his exile. Many times he had wondered if he would ever return to see her face shine on him again. Now a successful American fur trader, he looked forward to presenting himself on her doorstep again.

A train carried him to Dalkeith, where he stayed with his brother Ebenezer. Together they traveled to their mother's home in Bridgend on the North Esk. Andrew could not help but notice how much she had aged. Still, being with her brought such joy. His youthful impetuousness had been forgotten and his irresponsibility forgiven. To be together again meant everything.

While in Scotland, Dawson renewed old friendships and connected with the families of his American associates. In Edinburgh, he brought Thomas Potts news of his nephew, Jerry. Dawson traveled to Portobello, a beach resort east of Edinburgh, to visit David Constable's invalid father. Finally, he visited Belfast to see his cousin James Combe.[61]

---

[60]Palliser, *Solitary Rambles*, 202. Written in 1847 while Palliser was living among the village Indians.

[61]Informed speculation based on Dawson Family Papers.

The trip convinced Dawson that he had not been forgotten. When he returned to Fort Benton after eight months away, he wrote his mother a bittersweet letter, lamenting the "world of water and of land" that again separated them. The trip had been "just as [he] would have wished," although it left Dawson feeling "lonely[,] very[,] very lonely" and hoping soon to be reunited.[62]

Unfortunately, Grace Dawson would never read her son's letter because she died on 20 January 1859.[63]

---

[62]Letter 34.
[63]Dawson Family Papers.

8

The Undisputed Seat of Commerce

DAWSON'S TRIP HOME HAD BEEN AN UNQUALIFIED SUCCESS. He had returned from exile as the most important man at the most important frontier fur post on the upper Missouri.[1] Family and friends had welcomed him enthusiastically. His exciting tales thrilled newly met nieces and nephews. Families of men with whom he served had welcomed him, eager for any tidbit about their loved ones in America. Dawson's transgressions had been forgiven, perhaps even forgotten. Now no one could deny his success. This reception had washed away his long-smoldering fears of permanent exile. Only money now stood between him and a happy retirement in Scotland.

Still, back on the upper Missouri, he realized that this "far off wild land" had also become home. Stopping at Fort Clark to visit his children, he was welcomed by his many friends. Heading to Fort Union, he recalled that first winter's express run and felt overwhelming pride at his accomplishments. En route to Fort Benton, the weather turned wicked, leaving his "nose, cheeks and ears . . . pretty badly" frozen. But Dawson, now a hardened frontiersman, dismissed these as "incidents so common . . . as scarcely to call forth a remark." When he arrived at Fort Benton on 16 December 1858, a boisterous celebration greeted him. In addition to his underlings, his "red friends . . . crowd[ed] in to welcome [him] back." Although Dawson suspected they had also come to collect gifts, it still made his heart "soft."

But he soon discovered that, in his absence, "misrule and extravagance . . . had [had] its sway." Although distressing from a business

[1]While Fort Union had long claimed this title, by the late 1850s it properly belonged to Fort Benton.

standpoint, Dawson secretly relished the knowledge that, without him, the trade had "proved very much a failure." No matter. He felt confident that, under his firm hand, 1859 would bring "a very handsome return." With his interest in the Company now doubled, he looked forward to a healthy personal profit. With luck, he could retire in three years.[2]

More than Dawson's own fortunes were changing. He had brought a pistol from Scotland, a gift from Thomas Potts for his nephew. But during Dawson's absence, Jerry had been "enticed away to the Red River settlements." While Dawson fully expected him to return, he knew that his years of mentoring Jerry were coming to an end. With James and Grace at Fort Clark and Kuta in her grave, Dawson again faced a lonely existence. To stave off his morose tendencies, Dawson took a new wife: Pipe Woman, daughter of Running Fisher, an Atsina.[3] To his delight, Pipe Woman, who was also known as Mary Fisher, presented Dawson with his third son, Thomas Erskine Dawson, on 6 October 1859.[4]

Soon after returning from Scotland, Dawson set off again, this time headed for "the rough bosom of the far off Rocky Mountains," where he spent Christmas "snugly domiciled in the comfortable & commodious Agricultural Fort" at the Sun River Blackfeet Agency. His "intelligent companions" for this retreat to "civilized life" included the respected Blackfeet agent Alfred Vaughan, "Major" John Owen, "the enterprizing agent for the Flathead Indians," Angus MacDonald, "the quiet, intelligent & courteous Agent of the Hudson's Bay Co.'s Fort at Colville," and several "spirited & lively young men, companions of the latter gentlemen." Sitting "round the burning logs in the hospitable drawing room," they discussed the rapidly changing

---

[2]Letter 34.

[3]Thomas Dawson notes and "Life History," interview with Tom Dawson, received by Joel Overholser "with the Dawson piano," 1972, ORL, FtB. Also known as Gros Ventre of the Prairies, the Atsina numbered about 350 lodges in 1856 and occupied the country between the Milk and Missouri Rivers, extending up to the mouth of the Marias. Although loosely affiliated with the Blackfeet, they spoke a different language "said to be similar to the Arrapahoe." Senate ExDoc 2, 34th Cong., 3rd sess., 875, 625.

[4]Multiple obituaries for Thomas Dawson.

business environment while entertaining each other with old-fashioned storytelling.[5]

That such a gathering could take place illustrated the upper Missouri's continuing evolution. Just seven years earlier, Alexander Culbertson, attempting to deliver supplies to the Jesuit mission among the Flathead, had become hopelessly lost between the headwaters of the Missouri and Columbia Rivers.[6] Now Owen, MacDonald, and their companions made the journey without complications, thanks to the surveying done by the military engineers for the northern railroad survey. Routine intercourse between the two sides of the Rockies was beginning to seem eminently possible.

John Owen had been an Army sutler when he arrived in the West in 1849. After wintering at Fort Hall in what is now Idaho, Owen gave up that position to spend the summer trading with the Oregon Trail emigrants. That fall, he headed north and met the Jesuits at St. Mary's Mission in the Bitterroot Valley. His timing turned out to be propitious. The Flathead had recently become irate with the Jesuits for taking their "medicine" to the Blackfeet, the Flathead's mortal enemies. No longer welcome in the valley, the Jesuits were ready to sell out, and Owen was able to buy the mission, soon renamed Fort Owen, for $300.

With a favorable climate, rich soil, and fenced fields, the location proved perfect for Owen's new venture. His adobe and log fort supported an extensive farming operation, a flour mill and sawmill, and a few head of cattle trailed from Utah. By 1853, he was well situated to welcome Governor Isaac Stevens's northern transcontinental railroad survey. Impressed by Owen's operation and hospitality, Stevens granted him an Indian trading license.[7]

But supplying the post remained a challenge. Goods arrived either by pack train over the Clark Fork Trail from Oregon or were brought up from the Salt Lake valley on the trail past Fort Hall.[8] Both routes

---

[5]Notes attached to "Lodge Talk, No. 2," SC 294, MTHS. The agency had recently been established by Alfred Vaughan after numerous conflicts between whites and Indians visiting the old agency in Fort Benton. The agency was located on Sun River near present-day Great Falls, Montana.

[6]Pierre De Smet to Edwin T. Denig, May 1852; unattributed typescript notes in the Alexander Culbertson VF, MTHS.

[7]Hamilton, *From Wilderness to Statehood*, 105–106, 110.

[8]Ibid., 106.

were demanding. So Owen turned his sights east. Traveling to Fort Benton in March 1856, he asked Dawson about "obtaining supplies for his trade from this side [of the Continental Divide]." By October, he was back to borrow two wagons, four yoke of oxen, and two men for a trip to Sun River.[9]

Owen's interest in receiving supplies through Fort Benton had confirmed an idea Dawson had been entertaining since his arrival. He imagined Fort Benton transformed from an Indian post into the undisputed seat of regional commerce.

The upper Missouri fur trade had been built by steamboats. Without their efficiency in supplying the upriver posts and transporting the bulky robes to market, the trade could never have reached the heights it experienced in the 1840s and 1850s. The steamers had also helped intimidate the tribes, impressing them with the white man's technological achievements.

The steamboat had been especially critical in the Blackfeet trade. That tribe, leery of Americans following Meriwether Lewis's fatal encounter with the Piegan, had kept their trade north of the border, with the Hudson's Bay Company,[10] until the HBC became reluctant to handle the buffalo robes that increasingly dominated the market because of the long, difficult haul to the eastern markets. With steamers available for transport, the Americans eagerly embraced the robe trade.

But Fort Benton remained a step too far for steamboats. Boatmen dubbed the shallow and turbulent Missouri between Fort Benton and Cow Island, some 170 miles to the east, "the rocky river."[11] For years no one dared take a steamer beyond Cow Island. Goods had to be transported over that last critical stretch by keelboat or mackinaw.[12]

In 1851, Alexander Culbertson took the first wheeled cart to Fort Benton, traveling along the upper Missouri to the mouth of Milk River and then heading northwest before crossing the Milk near today's

---

[9]McDonnell, "Fort Benton Journal," 68, 93.

[10]Ewers, *Blackfeet*, 45.

[11]Overholser, *Fort Benton*, 33.

[12]A keelboat is a long, narrow, cigar-shaped riverboat capable of carrying about ten tons.

Havre, Montana. From there, he skirted the Bear's Paw Mountains before turning southwest to Fort Benton.[13] These options kept the Fort Benton trade humming, but visionaries, including Andrew Dawson, hoped that someday a steamer would tie up at Fort Benton itself.

Steamboats had been inching closer. In 1850, the *El Paso* set a new head of navigation some eight miles above the mouth of Milk River. But eight years later, the steamboat captains had only gained another fifty miles. Then, in 1859, with the elusive Fort Benton in mind, the Company sent the first "mountain steamboat," the *Chippewa*, upriver. Measuring 160 by 30 feet, with three boilers and two engines, the *Chippewa* could carry some 350 tons.[14] That year, the AFC, under contract both to deliver Indian annuities and to carry a military reconnaissance unit under Major William F. Raynolds, sent two steamers upriver, the *Chippewa* and the *Spread Eagle*.

Running in tandem, the two boats arrived at Fort Union on 1 July, just over a month after leaving St. Louis. The *Spread Eagle* carried several near celebrities: the venerable mountain man Jim Bridger; St. Louis physician Elias Marsh; geologist Ferdinand Hayden; Smithsonian-sponsored taxidermist John Pearsall; painter Carl Wimar; Blackfeet agent Alfred Vaughan; and Alexander Culbertson and his Kainah wife, Natawista. Andrew Dawson had joined them at Fort Pierre.

At Fort Union, Charles Chouteau, now in command of the AFC empire, purchased the *Chippewa* for $13,700, thereby assuming all financial risks for the next step. On 3 July, amid much fanfare, the *Chippewa* set off for Fort Benton. Under the able command of Captain John La Barge and a crew of ninety-five, she carried sixty tons of freight and had two mackinaws strapped to her sides for extra buoyancy. Chouteau, Dawson, Vaughan, and the Culbertsons boarded with great anticipation.

Three days later, the *Chippewa* reached the previous high point of navigation. Slowly she continued on, searching out the ever-shifting channel. Two full days were spent cordelling through the treacherous currents at Dauphin's Rapids. At Judith River, Chouteau cut loose the mackinaws after determining they created more drag than lift. On 17 July, the *Chippewa* reached old Fort McKenzie, a dozen miles

[13]Bradley, "Affairs at Fort Benton," 267. This route roughly parallels today's U.S. Highways 2 and 87.

[14]Lass, *History of Steamboating*, 16; Overholser, *Fort Benton*, 36–37.

below Fort Benton. But they could go no further, and after unloading the freight, the *Chippewa* turned back.[15] Short of—but tantalizingly close to—his goal, Chouteau set his sights on the next year.

And, indeed, 1860 would prove to be the magical year. That spring, three steamboats, the most ever, had set off from St. Louis, "amid the roar of cannon" and cheers that "rent the air." And finally, on 2 July, "in great commotion," the *Chippewa* and the *Key West* reached Fort Benton, where they landed "amidst the booming of the Cannon and the acclamation of the People."[16] Alfred Vaughan, commending "the untiring skill and energy displayed" by Captain La Barge, also praised Andrew Dawson "for his forethought and sagacity in having wood hauled some 10 miles below the Fort, which enabled the 2 gallant Drafts to land where no Steamer ever was landed before."[17]

In 1859, following the disappointing docking at old Fort McKenzie, Andrew Dawson gave his duly impressed boss, Charles Chouteau, a tour of the improved Fort Benton. About a week later, Dawson welcomed a weakened Pierre De Smet. For months, De Smet confessed, he had been suffering from a strange soreness in his throat. Now, contemplating the two thousand mile journey to St. Louis, he was overcome by exhaustion.[18] Relying on Dawson's "continued kindness and charity," De Smet asked if "a little skiff" might be built to take him downriver. With "very great kindness," Dawson arranged a boat, three oarsmen, and a pilot. Leaving behind his traveling companions—Father Nicholas Congiato, Father Adrian Hoecken, and Brother Vincent Magri—to establish the new Blackfeet mission, a grateful De Smet bid farewell to the "worthy" Dawson less than a week after arriving.[19]

That December, Dawson welcomed another regional luminary, First Lieutenant John Mullan. He had come upriver in 1853 with Isaac Stevens's northern transcontinental railway survey. Recognizing the need for a good wagon road to connect the Missouri and

---

[15]Sunder, *Fur Trade*, 205–206; Overholser, *Fort Benton*, 37–38.
[16]Sunder, *Fur Trade*, 211–13.
[17]Alfred Vaughan to Commissioner of Indian Affairs, 31 August 1860, M234/30.
[18]Terrell, *Furs by Astor*, 308.
[19]Chittenden and Richardson, *Father de Smet*, 772–74.

Columbia River watersheds, Stevens assigned Mullan to explore between the 45th and 48th parallels, a "perfect network of hills and mountains of vast extent."[20]

Mullan established Cantonment Stevens in the Bitterroot Valley in October 1853. By the next spring, one of his engineers had discovered "a trail . . . through a pass which even now will permit of the passage of an emigrant wagon." Stevens hopefully reported that this could compete "with the route through the South Pass" over which the Oregon Trail crossed the Continental Divide, postulating that "by steamers emigrants can probably ascend the Missouri river as far as Fort Benton . . . carrying with them their effects, and driving their cattle." From there, "good wagon routes lead to the passes of the mountains and to the St. Mary's valley."[21] In March 1854, Mullan took this route to Fort Benton where, with Dawson's assistance, he outfitted a wagon train, returning to Cantonment Stevens in a remarkable fifteen days.

But there the project languished until 1857, when the so-called Mormon War and Indian unrest in Oregon Territory convinced Congress of the importance of reliable supply routes to the more remote military outposts. Congress authorized work to resume in March 1858, but the project stalled once again when Mullan was called to active duty.

The project began again when Congress, responding to lobbying from Governor Stevens, authorized an additional $100,000 for the project in March 1859. By May, Mullan had assembled another road-building crew. Heading east from Fort Walla Walla, they built bridges, graded terrain, constructed ferryboats, laid four hundred feet of corduroy, and cut through three miles of dense timber before reaching the Coeur d'Alene Mission some two hundred miles to the east.[22] Separating them from the St. Regis de Borgia River, the Bitterroot Valley, and the wagon road to Fort Benton lay a dense forest, tangled with "the undecayed fallen timber of ages."[23]

These seemingly insurmountable obstacles were "attacked with determination—the axes were applied with unremitting industry,

[20]Bradley, "Mullen's Military Road," 162.

[21]Isaac I. Stevens to Geo. W. Manypenny, 5 April 1854, H MiscDoc 59, 33rd Cong., 1st sess., 741, 3.

[22]A corduroy road is made by placing sand-covered logs horizontally in the roadbed.

[23]Bradley, "Mullen's Military Road," 165.

the narrow passage through the forest daily lengthened, numerous bridges were laid across the streams that murmured through its dark recesses, the picks and spades polished anew, in thousands of grades and at last on the fourth day of December the valley of the St. Regis Borgia was gained." Mullan praised his men's "cheerfulness and zeal," emphasizing that his report could not do justice to "the industry and fortitude of the men while mastering this wilderness section."[24]

With spring 1860 approaching, Mullan traveled to Fort Owen to gather supplies for a trip to Fort Benton where Dawson happily sold him the rations for another season of work. After building and improving the road up the Clark Fork River, "the constant labor of 150 men for six weeks" allowed Mullan and his crew to conquer the last sixty miles over the Continental Divide through what would become known as Mullan Pass.[25] By the end of June, the only work that remained was some simple grading to connect with the existing route to Fort Benton. Finally, the Mullan Road was complete.[26]

In 1860, some three hundred soldiers under Major George Blake, along with a "due allowance of laundresses" requested by Mullan, landed in Fort Benton aboard the *Chippewa* and *Key West*.[27] That August, Mullan arrived to lead the troops west over his new road. They reached Fort Walla Walla in a remarkable fifty-seven days, having saved the government an estimated $30,000 in transportation costs.[28]

The opening of the Mullan Road kept Dawson busy. During that hectic summer of 1860, in addition to tending "numerous different Companys of troops," Dawson himself "happily" transported "some 4,000 lbs. across the Mountains, a distance of 340 miles" "at profitable rates." Another trip, to transport Flathead annuities to Fort Owen,

---

[24]Ibid.

[25]Ibid., 166–67. This Mullan Pass is near Helena. There is another one, the highest point on the road, about seven miles east of Mullan on the Idaho-Montana border.

[26]In Montana, the Mullan Road passed west from Fort Benton, north of Great Falls, then dropped south to cross the Continental Divide west of Helena, just north of the current U.S. Highway 12, along the Clark Fork River, passing near the ghost town of Bearmouth, until it was west of Garrison, where it joined the route of current-day Interstate 90 through the Missoula valley and into Idaho near Mullan.

[27]Sunder, *Fur Trade*, 211–13.

[28]Bradley, "Mullen's Military Road," 168. In all, the Mullan Road runs 624 miles, peaking at 6,000 feet on Mullan Pass. The four-span Blackfoot Bridge stretches 235 feet over Hell Gate Canyon. All together, it cost $230,000 to build. See Mullan, "Report of the Construction."

was delayed when "Vaughan and Owen [could not] agree." Dawson's last wagon train did not return to Fort Benton until 22 September.

As a result, 1860 was incredibly profitable, with Dawson "tak[ing] in a pile." He sent over $11,000 "to the House in Checks and Dfts" and still had "$3,000 on hand," plus $6,000 on loan, in "part Cash but mostly goods and Horses."[29] Fort Benton was no longer a lonely fur trade post. Thanks to the arrival of steamboats and the completion of the Mullan Road, it now laid claim to being the interior West's outfitting hub.

Despite these successes, Dawson's life had been forever changed by a catastrophic accident.[30] Most accounts agree that alcohol played a role, but how much is disputed. Some claim Dawson was extremely intoxicated, while others recall only modest consumption over a friendly game of cards.

In any case, earlier in the day, Dawson had been in the cellar, checking transactions in the Company's ledgers. After climbing the ladder back up to his bedroom, he apparently neglected to close the hatch. That night, with whiskey in his belly and sleep on his mind, he forgot the open trap, stumbled, and catapulted into the basement. There he lay on the cold earthen floor, stunned and badly injured, floating in and out of consciousness, through a long night of sub-freezing temperatures.

In the morning, when Dawson failed to appear, Matthew Carroll and George Steele, his trusted subalterns, began searching for him. Receiving no answer to his knocks, Carroll opened Dawson's door, saw the undisturbed bed and the open hatch. Scrambling down the ladder, he found Dawson prostate, barely conscious, and nearly frozen.

---

[29]AD to W. D. Hodgkiss, 25 September 1860, Chouteau Collection, MOHS.

[30]No contemporaneous accounts exist to explain the circumstances and, unfortunately, the letter Dawson must have written home about it did not survive. James Dawson, "Major Andrew Dawson, 1817–1871," 70–71, claims the accident occurred in the "winter of 1858," a date picked up by nearly all subsequent reports. Being able to date and document both Dawson's trip to Scotland and the Sun River agency, if the accident did indeed occur during the "winter of 1858," it was probably in early 1859. However, since James was a small boy at the time, his subsequent dating of the event should probably not be considered dispositive.

With help, the two clerks carefully extricated Dawson from the gloomy basement, tucked him into bed, and fed him hot drinks to raise his body temperature. With no doctor available, Dawson's employees employed frontier remedies to soothe his agonies. From the fort's native women, he received herbal potions.

But nothing could address the fearsome reality. The fall had badly damaged several lumbar vertebrae. The resulting nerve damage was permanent and progressive. In the immediate aftermath, Dawson retained full use of his legs, although he used a cane to walk. Eventually his men devised a special carriage for his long-distance travels. And to dull the chronic, often excruciating pain, Dawson turned to one of the frontier's most readily available painkillers: whiskey.[31]

His life would never be the same.

---

[31]Opiates, commonly stocked at frontier posts, were probably also available. However, it appears that Dawson's alcohol use increased after his fall. See Letter 36.

9

The Most Exciting, Bombastic, Furious Times

ON 25 MARCH 1861, DAWSON HEADED DOWNRIVER WITH A large mackinaw. He arrived in Saint Louis just in time to attend the funeral of the recently deceased Kenneth McKenzie, the AFC's first "king of the high Missouri."[1] With so many of the fur trade elite attending McKenzie's funeral, the *Spread Eagle* delayed its upriver voyage until after the burial. She departed for the upper Missouri on 1 May, six days behind the lighter *Chippewa*. On board was the customary assortment of luminaries, including Dawson, who was supervising Jack Culbertson, his friend's eldest son.

The teenaged Jack immediately struck up a friendship with William de la Montagne Cary, a young New York artist. The boys, while respecting "the awesome Major Dawson," were not easily tamed.[2] When the steamer tied up in Sioux country to take on wood, they decided to go hunting. They encountered several Sioux warriors who invited them back to their village where Jack persuaded Cary, "something of an athlete," to "turn some handsprings and somersaults." The chief, in appreciation of the performance, gave Cary "some beautiful moccasins." Later, Jack told the artist that the warriors belonged to a hostile band, and they had been receptive only because they knew Jack's father. Years later, Cary learned that Sitting Bull had been in the audience that day.[3]

---

[1]Obituary Notice and Death Announcement of Kenneth McKenzie, *Daily Missouri Republican*, 27 April 1861.

[2]Ladner, *Cary*, 31.

[3]Ibid., 36–37, 162–64.

Meanwhile, aboard the *Spread Eagle*, "nothing [was] talked of but soldiering." Passengers, organized into small militias, conducted "daily drill," and the men cut their hair military-style.[4] With rifles borrowed from the Yankton annuities, the militarists paraded on the deck, preparing to confront either Southern guerillas or errant Indians.

Dawson was not sure what to make of the war. While he expected that "once all the funds are expended and everyone has become bankrupt, [the Americans] will again come together and again spout of their glories of this great growing inseparable union," he nonetheless recognized that it was "the most exciting[,] bombastic[,] furious times here that any Country ever experienced what with these saffron visage lank Southerners and those gaunt[,] bony[,] tobacco-chewing Yankees of the North."[5] But the coming war also threatened business. The "commercial panic" had already reduced Dawson's expected "large fat dividends" to "nothing,"[6] and he feared that ultimately the war would result in "utter bankruptcy . . . to one and all."[7]

Aboard the *Spread Eagle*, Dawson discussed these concerns with John Mason Brown, one of the steamboat's more interesting passengers. A Yale graduate and member of the Saint Louis bar, Brown could also boast a distinguished family. His grandfather had been Kentucky's first U.S. senator. His half-brother was Benjamin Gratz Brown, a journalist who had sent awestruck dispatches from the 1851 Horse Creek Treaty conference.[8] Brown went on to become a U.S. senator, governor of Missouri, and the 1872 Liberal Republican vice presidential candidate. Their time aboard the steamer helped cement Dawson and Brown's growing friendship.[9]

As Dawson informed his sister, Christian, on 31 July (letter 37), the Fort Benton–bound passengers boarded the *Chippewa* at Fort Union for the remainder of their journey. Near dinnertime, on 22 June,[10] as

---

[4]Letter 36; Sunder, *Fur Trade*, 224.

[5]Letter 35.

[6]Letter 35.

[7]Letter 36.

[8]See "Letters from the Editor," *Republican* (St. Louis), fall 1851.

[9]Sunder, *Fur Trade*, 225; John Mason Brown biographical notes and letters, SC 294, MTHS.

[10]The date is variously given. Sunder, *Fur Trade*, 226, and Overholser, *Fort Benton*, 40, say 23 June. Perry W. McAdow says 21 June. Cary inexplicably says 19 May. Ladner, *Cary*, 39. The 22 June date is from Dawson's letter to his sister written 31 July 1861, the closest to a contemporaneous account.

the *Chippewa* rounded a bend below Poplar River, a fire broke out in the hold near some two hundred kegs of "ordinary black and giant" gunpowder.[11] Someone yelled, "Fire!" right before the hold erupted "in one blaze from stem to stern." The columns of smoke, leaping flames, and increasingly frantic screams "were enough to shake the nerves of the bravest men." As "panic ensued," Charles Chouteau and Andrew Dawson scrambled to contain the catastrophe. When the *Chippewa* neared shore, its captain, William Humphreys, his "instinct of self-preservation strongly developed," "leaped like a wild man," propelling her back into the river. Luckily, "the engineer managed to drive her up to the shore and held her there until all the passengers were safely off."[12]

The passengers took refuge behind some cottonwoods as the *Chippewa* "floated down stream[,] one entire sheet of flame." Ten minutes later, "she blew up and all was over." Everything was lost, except a few personal firearms grabbed by passengers.[13] One man was badly burned. "Had the boat been tied up or not drifted into the Stream," Dawson wrote, many likely would have died since "curiosity or a desire to save something would have induced many to approach her."

The shaken passengers passed an uncomfortable night "devising ways and means by which to get away from that part of the country."[14] Meanwhile, Dawson ordered his men to the Poplar River post to commandeer a seventy-foot mackinaw. The morning light "shed its rays on a most forlorn set of pilgrims."[15] Passengers and Indians alike worked to salvage cans of oysters and tomatoes, chunks of roast pork and corned beef, singed annuity blankets, and scraps of red flannel and cotton thrown ashore by the blast.[16] Around noon, Dawson's men returned with the mackinaw and everyone, except those who opted to travel overland, "crowded on board" to return to Fort Union. "The party was far from being sad" because, while "all were losers," they were happy to be alive.[17]

---

[11]Other sources suggest the amount of gunpowder could have been as much as three hundred kegs or nearly six thousand pounds. Sunder, *Fur Trade*, 226. Several sources ascribe the fast spread of the fire to the presence of alcohol, but Dawson never mentions this.

[12]Ladner, *Cary*, 40, quoting W. H. Schieffelin.

[13]Sunder, *Fur Trade*, 226.

[14]McAdow, "Perry W. McAdow," 43.

[15]Ibid.

[16]Ladner, *Cary*, 41.

[17]Letter 37.

Dawson had lost nearly everything: his trunk, clothing, and private stores as well as his personal letters and his hefty journals, which he had faithfully kept since arriving upriver. Over the years, several Scottish acquaintances had expressed interest in publishing his frontier adventures. But now those carefully recorded stories were gone. Most distressing to Dawson, his "old Joe Manton gun" lay at the bottom of the river along with his uncle's prized naval sword. Dawson told Christian that he feared the catastrophe augured "a sad year of trouble and anxiety" ahead.

Safely back at Fort Union, most of the pleasure-seekers decided they had had enough adventuring and happily accepted Chouteau's offer of transport back to Saint Louis. After bidding the travelers farewell, Dawson headed overland to Fort Benton, hoping to assemble wagons to transport whatever supplies he could gather for the winter trade. Within weeks, he was back.[18] But his troubles were not over.

Dawson was dismayed to find four thousand buffalo robes still in Fort Union's warehouse. "Anxious to send [them] below," he arranged a boat and crew to take them to St. Louis. Then, "at the eleventh hour," the crew balked, "allow[ing] no man to dictate what they will or will not do." Dawson fired the mutineers. Already short of men, he feared "appoint[ing] another crew as the result might prove the same." He resigned himself to leaving the robes at Fort Union while dourly admitting he was growing "most heartily tired of" "this miserable country." In that frame of mind, Dawson set off with twenty-one loaded wagons on his most ambitious freighting trip yet.[19]

Traveling with Dawson were "three young 'bloods' from New York"—William Cary, the artist acrobat, William Schieffelin, and Emlen

---

[18]How long this took is unclear. Dawson, in letter 37 from Fort Union dated 31 July, says that he has been to Fort Benton and retrieved the wagons and will head back as soon as his animals are rested. This is only nine days after the explosion, an impossible feat. The discrepancy is probably due to an acknowledged pause of unspecified length in Dawson's letter writing. Sunder, *Fur Trade*, 227, and Ladner, *Cary*, 42, say that Dawson's journey to Fort Benton and back was accomplished "within six weeks." This matches Schieffelin's account, "Crossing the Rockies," 17, which says they left "about August 10th."

[19]To fill twenty-one wagons, Dawson must have seriously depleted the Fort Union stores, perhaps demonstrating how much of the trade had shifted to Fort Benton. That Dawson had that many wagons at Fort Benton is also somewhat surprising, although some may have come from the Mullan road building crew.

Lawrence.[20] They carried their possessions in an old Red River cart. Their first attempts to erect a skin tipi purchased from the Indians near Fort Union greatly amused the natives until finally they had to admit their "inferiority" and "employ a couple of red women" to complete the job.[21]

Between Poplar River and Wolf Creek, the impressive wagon train passed a large Crow encampment. Dawson and the New Yorkers called on the chief, who invited them to join him in a meal. The young men enjoyed the "tender" meat with the "really delicious flavor" of what they assumed was "fawn or a kid antelope." Dawson stunned them by revealing that they were eating dog.[22]

As custom dictated, Dawson offered the chief gifts after eating and then departed. Back at the wagons, he discovered a tense situation unfolding. A Crow warrior had been run over as he attempted to steal a spare oxbow. His comrades were threatening to appropriate the entire wagon train, unless proper reparations were paid. Dawson sought a reasonable solution, but the warriors "paid little attention." His nerves already frayed, the trader finally "lost his temper and drew his revolver." Seeing this as "an excuse for open hostility," the Crow "immediately seized" Dawson and his companions. "About 200 of the Indians" aimed guns and arrows at the prisoners, "anxious for an excuse to fire." One captive remembered his "heart [go] down into [his] boots, or somewhere away from its right place." The Crow "danced round and round and threatened every moment to tomahawk or kill as they saw fit."[23] Things looked bleak until the chief with whom they had dined suddenly appeared and negotiated their release for "sundry blankets, provisions, etc."[24]

Dawson and his companions quickly departed. They had gone about a mile and were congratulating themselves on their escape when eleven naked warriors "in full war paint and feathers, their

[20] McAdow, "Perry W. McAdow," 42–43. McAdow lists the third man as "Seamon," not Lawrence. Seamon may have been with the group earlier. Lawrence accompanied Dawson, according to Schieffelin, "Crossing the Rockies," 15.

[21] Schieffelin, "Crossing the Rockies," 17.

[22] Ibid., 19.

[23] James Dawson, "Major Andrew Dawson, 1817–1871," 66–67. James Dawson's version differs from the eyewitness account of Dawson's companion. James Dawson claims that, during their capture by the River Crow, a Mountain Crow slipped away, returning with six hundred Mountain Crow to rescue the men. He probably conflated and confused the captivity, release, and subsequent appearance of the Gros Ventre.

[24] Schieffelin, "Crossing the Rockies," 19; Overholser, "Dangerous Freighting Trip."

horses covered with foam," appeared in the distance, approaching rapidly. The New Yorkers, their hearts still pounding, feared the worst, but Dawson knew better.

When the warriors reached them, the "noble-looking white-haired chief" dismounted and "threw his arms around Mr. Dawson." Even for Dawson, "an old Scotchman tough nut, accustomed to thrilling scenes of frontier Indian life . . . this was too much." Teary-eyed, the trader introduced the chief, his father-in-law, to his companions: "He heard we had been seized, and were about to be killed by the Crows: that he, with his ten warriors, could not do much against 3,000 Crows, but that they had come down to die with us." A mixed-blood boy had slipped away during the confrontation to alert the Gros Ventre. Knowing that entering Crow lands constituted an invitation to war, the warriors had come prepared to die. To everyone's relief, that had not been necessary.[25]

Early on, Pierre De Smet, the venerable missionary, had discovered that the beautiful lands inhabited by the fur traders contained something far more precious than furs: gold. Although De Smet could have used this knowledge to enrich his beloved Jesuits, he kept the secret, worried about the impact from an onslaught of gold-crazed miners. De Smet also cautioned the Indians against mentioning the "golden sands" that they, too, knew existed.[26] But John Owen, in the Bitterroot Valley, learned of the possibility. On 15 February 1852, he recorded in the *Fort Owen Journal*: "Gold hunting[,] found some."[27]

The dam finally broke in 1856 when John Silverthorne, an "old mountaineer," brought to Fort Benton some yellow dust he claimed was gold.[28] Short of money but needing supplies, Silverthorne offered the dust for $1,000 in goods. Alexander Culbertson agreed, but

[25]Schieffelin, "Crossing the Rockies," 19, 21.

[26]Laveille, *Father de Smet*, 319–20; Chittenden and Richardson, *Father de Smet*, 1:118.

[27]Stuart, *Forty Years on the Frontier*, 139n31; Overholser, *Fort Benton*, 146.

[28]The date is uncertain. Culbertson fixed the date as October 1856, but his dates were often off by a year or two. Bradley, "Affairs at Fort Benton," 277–78. Overholser, *Fort Benton*, 146, agrees on this date but probably bases that on Bradley. McDonnell, "Fort Benton Journal," 247, notes that Silverthorne came to Montana in 1856. Lepley, *Blackfoot Fur Trade*, 209, says October 1857. However, an October 1854 entry in McDonnell could also refer to this event.

queasy about his decision, he charged the goods to his own account. The next summer, Culbertson took the "remarkably pure" gold to the St. Louis assay office where he received $1,525.[29] The transaction generated little notice.

But with the gold centers of California, Nevada, and Colorado beginning to play out, prospectors were searching for the next big strike. Discoveries in modern-day Idaho caused an influx of miners who could travel upriver on the steamboats and then cross the mountains west of Fort Benton on the Mullan Road. First, however, the get-rich-quickers would see what the immediate vicinity could offer.

On 2 May 1858, James and Granville Stuart found placer gold near present-day Drummond, Montana.[30] A small settlement sprouted nearby on the aptly named Gold Creek. Then, in the summer of 1862, John White discovered a sizable deposit on Grasshopper Creek, setting off an authentic gold rush. By fall, some five hundred had settled at the "Grasshopper Diggings" on Beaverhead River. Soon to be renamed Bannack, the settlement became the region's first genuine boomtown.[31]

The next spring, an accidental discovery at Alder Gulch, 70 miles east of Bannack, led to an even larger strike when frustrated miners who had missed their appointed rendezvous decided to pan for tobacco money. Their first attempt yielded a small fortune, and eighteen months later, at least ten thousand people were working an area known as Fourteen-Mile City that included Virginia City and Nevada City.[32] By the mid-1860s, prospectors seemed to be finding gold everywhere, including in Last Chance Gulch, 150 miles west of Fort Benton. Located so close to existing transportation hubs and easily supplied with foodstuffs from the Prickly Pear Valley, these diggings gave birth to Helena.[33]

---

[29]Bradley, "Affairs at Fort Benton." 277–78; McDonnell, "Fort Benton Journal," 246–47. Silverthorne may have received the gold from Owen, who procured it from Oregon Trail emigrants. Overholser, *Fort Benton*, 375. Others suggest it came from Canada's Kootenai country. Stuart, *Forty Years on the Frontier*, 139n31.

[30]Stuart, *Forty Years on the Frontier*, 136–37.

[31]Malone, Roeder, and Lang, *Montana*, 65.

[32]Ibid., 65–66.

[33]Helena became the capital of Montana Territory in 1875 and the state in 1889.

The ever-shrewd Andrew Dawson quickly grasped the significance of the gold rush. The steady influx of greenhorns transformed Fort Benton into a rowdy, semi-lawless frontier town with attendant advantages and disadvantages. Dawson, still looking to build his retirement account, saw mostly upsides. Plenty of new arrivals needed, and received, a grubstake and horse from the old trader.[34] Dawson earned a hefty profit off most of those loans.

On the downside, the mass influx of often harshly prejudiced whites drove many Indians away. In the decade between the 1851 Horse Creek Treaty and the discovery of gold at Grasshopper Creek, Indian-white relations on the upper Missouri deteriorated dramatically. The tribes no longer saw the traders as equal partners; they had become accessories of the invading gold miners. The young warriors felt especially aggrieved, forbidden by the treaty from employing time-honored traditions to advance their tribal status.

Since the traders came upriver on the steamboats with the annuities and often participated in their distribution, the Indians also equated the traders with the government. The Indians felt totally justified in retaliating against the traders when their increasingly important government annuities were delayed or inferior. For their part, the traders happily embraced their profits from transporting annuities but fumed when held accountable for associated problems.

Attacks on AFC posts, especially in the Dakotas, began to accelerate. In May 1858, Yankton warriors fired on the *Spread Eagle*. While feasts temporarily calmed their rage, the nearly destitute Indians encountered between Forts Berthold and Union suggested additional problems to come.[35] That fall, Culbertson reported the Arikara to be "rather lukewarm in their friendship with the whites" while the Sioux near Fort Pierre were "in deplorable condition—bordering quite on starvation."[36] The next summer, military surveyors in the Yellowstone River valley engendered additional hostility from the Sioux.[37]

In 1860, the Sioux complained bitterly about being cheated by the government. At dawn on 22 August, they turned their frustrations against the fur company. Some 250 warriors, "well mounted and all caparisoned in their war costumes," rushed Fort Union. Failing to

[34]Dawson, "Major," 70.
[35]Wischmann, *Frontier Diplomats*, 288.
[36]Culbertson, "A Winter Trip across the Rocky Mountains."
[37]Sunder, *Fur Trade*, 205.

gain entry, they slaughtered cattle, ignited haystacks and woodpiles, and destroyed wagons, mackinaws, and outbuildings. Within hours, everything beyond the palisades had been demolished. Finally, with a dozen warriors marching toward the gates with firebrands and hatchets, the employees opened fire, killing one and wounding several. The Sioux withdrew, but their message left fur traders up and down the river shaken.[38]

In 1862, the Sioux began refusing their annuities. Only Bear's Rib, appointed at Horse Creek to lead the Hunkpapa, bucked this trend, simultaneously telling Agent Samuel Latta that it might cost him his life.[39] It did. The murderers of Bear's Rib warned Latta: "We notified the Bear's Rib yearly not to receive your goods, he had no ears, and we gave him ears by killing him. We now say to you, bring us no more goods. . . . If you have no ears we will give you ears. . . . If you do not stop [whites from travelling in our country], we will."[40]

That summer, some five to six hundred prospectors arrived in Fort Benton. Alexander Culbertson, summering at the Blackfeet Agency on Sun River, caught wind of a Blackfeet plan to harass the region's settlers. The retired trader enlisted Caroline Connoyer, a mixed-blood Piegan who had worked for him at Fort Benton, to warn the whites. The attack never materialized, but everyone regarded the rumor as cause for concern.[41] The new Blackfeet agent, Henry Reed, told the commissioner of Indian affairs that "not a few" of the recently arrived whites would scarcely "be tolerated in any civilized society."[42]

That same tumultuous summer, Sioux warriors had ruthlessly slaughtered three Arikara brothers near Fort Berthold. The brothers had been returning from a successful hunt when they stopped to adjust their take and found themselves surrounded. The Arikara fought bravely but were overcome, then scalped and mutilated. This news hit Dawson especially hard as the three brothers were cousins to his late wife, Kuta.[43]

---

[38]Bernard Schoonover to A. M. Robinson, 23 August 1860; Pierre Chouteau, Jr., and Company to A. M. Robinson, 2 January 1861, NAM M234/885; Pierre Chouteau, Jr., and Company to Charles Primeau, 6 February 1861, Chouteau Collection, MOHS.

[39]John Pattee to Brigadier General Blunt, 21 July 1862, NAM M234/885.

[40]Utley, *The Lance and the Shield*, 49.

[41]Wischmann, *Frontier Diplomats*, 296–97.

[42]Ewers, *Blackfeet*, 237.

[43]Boller, *Among the Indians*, 249–51.

The hope that whites and Indians could peacefully coexist finally came crashing down in August 1862 when four Santee Sioux killed five white settlers in Acton Township, Minnesota. It was now just a matter of time before the entire region succumbed to war.

Although the white newcomers often made no distinction, not all Indians were hostile. Little Dog, the Piegan cousin of Culbertson's wife, had watched with interest when Agent Alfred Vaughan had established a government farm at the Sun River Agency. Little Dog wanted to try farming. Vaughan, hoping the warrior could become a role model, gave him a small nearby parcel of land.[44] But Little Dog soon became frustrated with white man's work and abandoned his farm.[45]

Andrew Dawson cared less about Little Dog's attempts at farming than his earlier exploits. In the 1840s, the Piegan warrior had led a raid on an emigrant wagon train near Fort Hall. After killing the emigrants, including babies, Little Dog discovered a box of brass buttons "without eye holes" in the wagons. Seeing little value in them and not wanting to transport the heavy item, the warrior cached them in rocks overlooking the Snake River. Two decades later, Little Dog realized those buttons had been gold. Dawson, upon hearing the story, promised the warrior a hefty reward if he would retrieve the box. Little Dog agreed before changing his mind. Attacking the wagon train had been wrong, he told Dawson, and he could not now profit from that evil deed.[46]

Dawson, however, continued to look for gold profit. In the summer of 1862, a man named L'Heureux who claimed to be a Jesuit priest brought Dawson a package of gold-bearing sand. He asked Dawson to advance him $500 worth of supplies to pursue his claim. Promised quick repayment in gold, Dawson agreed. L'Heureux also promised to guide other fortune hunters, including Dawson's friend John Mason Brown, to the strike. But when the time came, L'Heureux

---

[44]Report of the Commissioner of Indian Affairs, 1860, 83; Ewers, *Blackfeet*, 232.

[45]Annual Report to the Commissioner of Indian Affairs, 1863, 179; Ewers, *Blackfeet,* 237.

[46]"Brass Buttons without Eyes," *Glacier County Chief*, 30 December 1935; Bradley, "The Oregon Trail"; Greenfield, "Little Dog," 24, 33. His own people would eventually kill Little Dog and his son, Fringe, outside Fort Benton, for being "too friendly with the whites."

was nowhere to be found. Brown and the other gold-seekers headed north alone, working every creek from the Marias to Willow Rounds, before returning, empty-handed, frustrated, and angry.

They did not blame Dawson, since he, too, had been duped. Pierre De Smet, after hearing that Dawson had given the phony priest $500, predicted the scam, but Dawson refused to believe him. A few days later, when an Indian arrived with a bundle from L'Heureux, Dawson presumed it contained the promised repayment and summoned De Smet to witness his vindication. After unwinding the considerable bundle of cloth, Dawson watched in dismay as a single English half-sovereign, worth about $2.50, fell out.[47]

Dawson did find other ways to make money for the Company and himself. With the fur trade declining, he focused increasingly on freighting and warehousing. In March 1862, Dawson received a letter from his friend Henri Chase, suggesting yet another venture: "do you remember what I wrote to you about two years ago, about laying out a town site at Benton & securing for me two lots[?] it is not too late yet, and if you do not take the first steps somebody else will." Chase, writing from Walla Walla, assured Dawson that "most of the necessaries of life can be shipped from St. Louis to the mines at lower figures than they can be from this side. Parties here are already talking of going over and locating on the Missouri so as to be in readiness for the great change which must take place during the coming season." Chase warned: "There are now at least 40,000 men preparing & en route for these mines from California, Oregon & New Mexico!! So govern yourself accordingly."[48]

Dawson knew change was coming. His only potentially viable competition, La Barge, Harkness & Co., had folded in 1863 after only a year of operations. Dawson jumped into the breach left behind, taking possession of their leftover goods while also agreeing to transport their freight, stranded upriver by low water, to Fort Benton. For an additional $1,000, he promised to store their goods until they could be liquidated to pay the firm's liabilities. Dawson also nabbed a new sawmill from the liquidation of his last opposition company.[49]

---

[47]Dawson, "Major," 71; Overholser, *Fort Benton*, 356.

[48]Henri M. Chase to AD, 15 March 1862. SC 294, MTHS. From Massachusetts, Henri M. Chase came west in 1851 and settled in Washington Territory, where he married a mixed-blood woman and had two children. He apparently knew and may have worked with John Owen.

[49]Sunder, *Fur Trade*, 251–52.

Still, the AFC's future remained bleak. In autumn 1862, after the Blackfeet and Gros Ventre feuded, the latter refused to come to Fort Benton to trade. To serve them, Dawson established an outpost fifteen miles above the confluence of the Musselshell, which Charles Chouteau dubbed Fort Andrew in honor of Dawson. George Steele was put in charge, and John Largent, a favorite of Dawson, became one of the post's most reliable hands.

That first winter, provisions at Fort Andrew ran perilously low, forcing the men to trap wolves and salvage corn kernels from the mice. On one hunt, hostile warriors surrounded Largent. His only escape route called for maneuvering his horse through a buffalo stampede. During another outing, Largent and a companion were captured by Blood warriors who demanded a bounty for the traders' release. Steele acquiesced, offering up blankets, coffee, tea, and tobacco. Largent quit the AFC soon afterward, but not before the penny-pinching company deducted the cost of his ransom from his own account. Fort Andrew, perpetually plagued by Indian raids and supply shortages, was abandoned after only a year of operations.[50]

---

[50]Ibid., 240; "John Largent Once Escaped from Indian Band by Riding Pony into Herd of Stampeding Buffalo," *Judith Basin County Press*, 16 May 1938.

10

The Old Country

IN AUGUST 1862, RECOGNIZING THE HANDWRITING ON THE wall, Andrew Dawson, Charles Chouteau, and Malcolm Clarke formed a partnership to "jointly carry on business as Indian traders and otherwise as they may deem profitable."[1] In other words, their primary interest from then on would be servicing the influx of miners and other potential settlers. The Fort Benton warehouses, built to store pelts, would now house tools, equipment, domestic wares, food, and clothing. Dawson's primary responsibility would be freighting. He routinely transported heavily laden wagons to the mining camps, advised newcomers on the best routes, and offered packing suggestions. With steamboat captains vying to be the first to reach Fort Benton each season, profits seemed assured.

The new venture also brought unexpected responsibilities. Lawlessness flourished in the boomtowns like Bannack, where stagecoach robbers, murderers, military deserters, gamblers, river pirates, con men, and prostitutes thrived under Henry Plummer's rule. When a particularly egregious crime demanded a trial, jurors understood evidence could be ignored to reach the desired verdict of not guilty. Charles Reeves, a Plummer ally, faced such a jury in January 1863.

Although the evidence of Reeves's guilt appeared overwhelming, the majority of jurors voted to acquit. But with N. P. Langford, the jury foreman, voting for the death penalty, the jury settled on a verdict of banishment. Rather than accept this outcome, Plummer's

---

[1]Partnership agreement between Pierre Chouteau, Jr., Andrew Dawson & Malcolm Clarke, 21 August 1862, SC 294, MOHS. Clarke came upriver in 1839 as Alexander Culbertson's protégé, trading primarily with the Blackfeet and often assuming command in Culbertson's absence. Dismayed when Dawson was promoted over him at Fort Benton, Clarke quit the AFC in 1854 to form an opposition company.

gang decided to kill everyone involved, including the acting sheriff, Hank Crawford, whom Plummer pledged to dispatch personally.

Shortly thereafter, Crawford noticed Plummer skulking across the street and, without hesitation, fired at Plummer, striking him in the arm. Plummer retreated temporarily. But rather than wait around for the inevitable next confrontation, Crawford fled to Fort Benton where he sought protection from Andrew Dawson. Dawson sheltered the refugee until he arranged safe transport downriver. Dawson's intervention helped save Crawford's life; within five months, twenty of the twenty-seven men involved in the trial had been killed or driven from Bannack.[2]

The dry spring of 1863 turned the upper Missouri into a slow running stream, stranding steamers at Fort Union and casting a pall over that year's prospects. With his summer outfitting and winter trade supplies four hundred miles downriver at Fort Union, Dawson organized a long and perilous bull train. With his best employees for labor and his adopted son, Jerry Potts, as scout, Dawson headed east that fall. By October 23, they were ready to head west again, their loaded wagons an inviting target for the hostile Sioux.

Three days later, at Ash Point, Potts spotted a band of Indians headed their way. Identifying them as Sioux, he advised circling the wagons. The Sioux stopped just beyond rifle range and a powerful-looking warrior approached, using sign language to indicate they came in peace. A wary Matthew Carroll walked out to meet him. The warrior extended his hand in peace while reaching for a hidden scalping knife. Pulling out his own hidden weapon, Carroll thrust his cocked six-shooter in the Indian's face. The warrior, shamed by Carroll's quick reaction, skulked away. Dawson reassembled the wagon train and continued the trek to Fort Benton, with the still-vigilant Potts bringing up the rear.[3]

Meanwhile, the war dominated news from the States. Clement Seaman wrote, bitterly:

> You who live in the "upper country" can have no conception—this fratricidal war has and will entail the most dreadful consequences

[2]Hamilton, *From Wilderness to Statehood*, 221–23.
[3]Touchie, *Bear Child*, 74–76.

> to us all—the Administration appear either crazy—monomaniacal—or—else—drunk with power which they use for the most illegitimate purposes—subverting our liberties—burdening us with taxes & rousing that spirit of public indignation which will result either in a redress of wrongs or a divided and perhaps bloody north—I cannot write on the subject without my evenness of temper but will leave the subject for your own bitter fancies.

Seaman urged Dawson to leave the region "unless you are determined to lay your bones back of Benton."[4]

John Shaw, a former steamboat captain, informed Dawson of "a big battle . . . going on at Fredericksburg, Va. between the 'Grand Army' and Lee's Confederate Army[.] [I]t bids fair to be a bloody affair."[5] John Mason Brown wrote from "the field, Camp of 10th Kentucky Cavalry" to tell his friend that "5 days after my return to Kentucky I found myself Major of the 10th Regiment of Kentucky Cavalry, busily engaged in drilling my men." He would soon be put in command of his own regiment." Being a cavalry officer meant "one day in Kentucky, the next probably in Tennessee—uncertain as to times and places."[6]

Dawson's opinion of the war remained unchanged: "utter bankruptcy will be the result to one and all."[7] But his concerns focused more on the personal. The previous summer, his younger brother, Alexander, had visited Fort Benton. Aleck, as he was known, claimed to want a wilderness adventure, and the two brothers did visit the Great Falls. But Aleck's real purpose was to check on Dawson's health, which was clearly failing. Dawson now relied on two walking sticks, and special arrangements had been made to accommodate him on the wagons. Aleck also noticed that Dawson increasingly relied on liquor as a painkiller. Although Aleck tried to persuade his brother to retire and return to Scotland, Dawson insisted he could not afford to do so. Rebuffed, Aleck headed home with Dawson's oldest son, James, crossing the Rockies and visiting Fort Walla Walla.[8]

---

[4]Clement M. Seaman to AD, 12 November 1862, SC 294, MTHS. Little is known about Seaman, who wrote from Glen Cove, Long Island. The *Montana Post*, 9 November 1867, says he was a clerk on the steamboat *The Only Chance*. The *Helena Herald*, 5 June 1867, calls him "master" of that boat.

[5]John S. Shaw to AD, 13 December 1862.

[6]John Mason Brown to AD, 15 March 1863.

[7]Letter 36.

[8]In England, James lived with his aunt in Liverpool and attended the Birkenhead school. Dawson Family Papers.

Dawson's friends shared Aleck's concerns. David Constable, now retired and living in St. Joseph, wrote of his sadness "to think that your legs are failing" and despaired of Dawson's complete recovery. Believing that "if anything in the world can help you it will be a trip home," Constable urged Dawson to spend "a year at home in the old country."[9] John Mason Brown also hoped that his health would be "greatly improved" and that Dawson's legs would be "again fully up to their duty."[10] Only the indefatigable Pierre De Smet seemed to hear good reports: "I learn with pleasure that your health is improving."[11] But any such improvements were temporary.

Entering his seventeenth year upriver, Andrew Dawson faced several harsh realities. By 1864, the rapid influx of whites, combined with an increasing military presence, had created enormous turmoil among the tribes. The Blackfeet were at war with the Crow, "making bloody work of it." But when they got "whipped," the Blackfeet "begged Mr. Dawson to send white men to help them rescue some of their friends." Malcolm Clarke "talk[ed] of going," but it was apparently "only talk."[12]

Meanwhile, the Piegans had "gone to war en masse" against the Gros Ventre, leading the Gros Ventre to abandon their trade at Fort Benton.[13] They would not even come for their annuities except as a war party. "Having considerable confidence in [his] influence" with them, Dawson rode "out alone to meet them but [had been] rather Severely used by some of the Younger of the Party who struck [him] with their lances and offered other indignities." Finally Dawson arranged to present his peace proposal to the elders.[14] Hoping "to quiet matters in the country," Dawson asked Acting Agent Jasper Viall to allow him to transport the supplies directly to the tribe.[15] The

[9]D. A. Constable to AD, February–March 1864, SC 294, MTHS.

[10]John Mason Brown to AD, 15 March 1864, SC 294, MTHS.

[11]Pierre De Smet to AD, 11 July 1863, SC 294, MTHS.

[12]Jasper Viall to Rev. H. W. Reed, 23 December 1862, M234/30.

[13]Ibid.

[14]AD to Gad Upson, 23 January 1864, M234/30.

[15]Jasper Viall to AD, 14 January 1864, M234/30. Viall was in charge of the Sun River farm, but he was also the de facto agent during this critical period between the tenures of Henry Reed and Gad Upson.

Gros Ventre received these, but a bureaucratic tussle broke out, and accusations flew about misappropriated goods.[16]

Adding to the turmoil was the rapidly escalating whiskey trade that created untold misery in the Indian encampments:

> The appetite of the Indians seems to have been formed for the sole purpose of prostituting him to the [illegible] influences of the "Spiritous Liquors." His horses, his cattle, the clothes on his back, his jewells, his wife and daughters, and even the dearest objects of his wifes affections are rung from him and all! all! are thrown down at the feet of this "fell destroyer" to satisfy the cravings of his morbid appetite. The heart rending scenes of every day life in the low vile sinks of prostitution in our populous cities, and the consequent evils to society resulting therefrom are but drops in the ocean compared with the scenes witnessed in the Indian camp and the evils entailed upon the poor untutored ignorant Savage from the effects of this infamous traffic.[17]

Confronted with all this turbulence and his own declining health, Dawson finally decided the time had come to return to Scotland. Although still lacking the retirement funds he had hoped to accumulate, he now doubted that additional time upriver would add much. So, in January 1864, Dawson loaded his final wagon train and headed to Fort Union.

Between the mouth of the Musselshell and the mouth of Milk River, "a large party of Sioux" attacked, "completed overpower[ing]" Dawson and his men. They killed Louis Dauphin, an independent French Creole trader, and appropriated "1,000 packs of buffalo robes and $4,088 worth of goods."[18] "This whole section of the country is in terrible foment," Dawson informed Charles Chouteau, with the Sioux gathering "in large crowds in the angle formed by the Yellowstone and Missouri."[19] Frederick Gerard, in charge of Fort Berthold II, confirmed vast numbers of hostile Sioux around the Yellowstone. Blackfeet agent Gad Upson had even heard rumors that the Sioux planned to destroy Forts Union and Berthold II.[20]

This obvious instability helped Dawson accept his decision to

---

[16]See correspondence between AD and Upson, 23 January 1864, and Upson and W. T. Dole, commissioner of Indian affairs, 25 January 1864, M234/30.

[17]Upson to Dole, 23 January 1864, M234/30.

[18]Sunder, *Fur Trade*, 188; McDonnell, *Fort Benton Journal*, 292n212. Dauphin had a small post near Milk River.

[19]AD to Charles Chouteau, 5 February 1864.

[20]*CSHSND*, 1:345.

leave despite the many friendships formed over nearly two decades on the frontier and the whispers of guilt he felt for abandoning his associates at such a perilous time. Those whispers roared as he bid farewell to his daughter, Grace. Although he had tried to arrange for her education in the States, her Arikara grandmother remained "very much averse to part[ing] with her." So the eleven-year-old remained "in the Country" as Dawson departed for Scotland with his four-year-old son, Thomas.[21]

After one final meeting with Charles Chouteau, Dawson and Tom boarded the *Yellowstone* for the journey downriver. In St. Joseph, they visited Dawson's old friend David Constable, who ran a St. Joseph mercantile. Dawson had invested in the business, in part as appreciation for Constable's kindness in looking after Dawson's son James when he went downriver to be educated.

Constable had had a "very prosperous" 1863 in "North Missouri," grossing $14,000 in profits. Business was increasing "rapidly," thanks to the Montana gold rush, but the Civil War made goods "so difficult to obtain." In addition, the cost of items sometimes increased a full 20 percent during transit, leaving Constable in constant need of cash. With hundreds of pairs of animals and oxbows on hand for the "very large emigration this season to Bannock" and "six or eight steamboats . . . going up to Benton," Constable hoped to clear at least $20,000 in 1864.[22]

Doing "famously" six weeks later, Constable raised his expected profit by $5,000. With financial help from Dawson, Constable had already sold $15,000 worth of goods, and "the profits hold out very well." Even when orders came in after the steamboats departed, he had secured "good facilities for shipping by wagon via Bannack & Virginia City." With the emigration "increasing every day," "mules, horses & work cattle [were] in great demand and [were] bringing large prices."[23]

By April, Constable was seeking "any money" Dawson "want[ed] to lend out" to build his own store. Constable promised him 10 percent

[21]Letter 37. There is no evidence that Dawson ever considered taking his second wife, Pipe Woman, to Scotland. She apparently stayed at Fort Benton or returned to her people, the Gros Ventre.

[22]Constable to AD, 7 February 1864, SC 294, MTHS.

[23]Constable to AD, 24 March 1864, SC 294, MTHS.

interest and "real estate security."[24] With everything convincing him that Constable was on the road to riches, Dawson jumped at this chance to increase his wealth. Alas, Dawson's faith was once again misplaced. Despite Constable's rosy predictions, eight years later the merchant still owed Dawson $13,000. Constable would die penniless, and the debt would never be repaid.[25]

In St. Louis, Dawson visited AFC headquarters to close his accounts. After seventeen years, he was owed $2,225.00. In New York, he collected an additional $1,418.21 from the McCombie & Child assay office for gold and silver he had carried east.[26] With his business complete, Dawson and Tom boarded the Cunard liner, RMS *Scotia*, bound for Liverpool.

Unlike his 1844 voyage, Dawson now traveled first class, receiving all the attention that status bestowed. An upholstered, wood-framed wicker wheelchair gave him needed mobility. Dining at the captain's table, he entertained the passengers with riveting frontier tales. Tom, meanwhile, had the run of the ship, delighting passengers with his youthful exuberance.

Aleck Dawson and his wife met the ship when it landed in Liverpool. Although only two years had passed since Aleck's visit to Fort Benton, he was shocked by his brother's decline. He insisted that Dawson spend a few days recuperating at their Liverpool home before traveling by train to Edinburgh. Meanwhile, Tom got acquainted with his Aunt Christian, with whom he would live while attending school.

In Edinburgh, Andrew was met by his older brother, Ebenezer. Years earlier, Ebenezer had been instrumental in pushing Andrew into the fur trade. But now he cheerfully welcomed him home. Together, they traveled to Bridgend, Dalkeith, where Ebenezer was now sole owner of Andrew Dawson and Company, Leather Merchants. Two years later, the increasingly frail Andrew moved into Ebenezer's new

---

[24]Constable to AD, 28 April 1864, SC 294, MTHS.

[25]James Dawson to his aunt, Marion Dawson, 26 March 1901. Constable's loan accounted for nearly 50 percent of Dawson's estate when he died. Dawson's brothers, as trustees, tried repeatedly to get the loan repaid, without success. In 2010 dollars, the loan amounted to nearly $300,000. Dawson Family Papers.

[26]ORL, FtB; SC 294, MTHS.

home, the impressive Glenesk, in Eskbank, Dalkeith. Beyond Glenesk's main gates, a graveled carriageway led to the main house with its ornate sandstone threshold and four bedrooms. Two gardeners tended the three-acre grounds, while house servants helped Andrew with his daily tasks.[27]

Dawson received many visitors at Glenesk, including old Dalkeith schoolmates and David Constable's Edinburgh relatives. Some fur trade colleagues even found their way to his door.[28] Occasionally he found the energy to visit Edinburgh, but increasingly he remained homebound.

Eventually Andrew required care beyond what Ebenezer, his family, and the servants could provide. In 1872, the old trader moved into Palmerston Villa, where Jane Heath, the resident nurse, oversaw his care. James Dawson, then employed by a Dalkeith draper, moved in to assist his father.

On 18 September 1872, at 11:45 P.M., Andrew Dawson, age fifty-two, passed away. James, Ebenezer, and Ebenezer's wife were at his bedside. His body was laid to rest in the family plot at Dalkeith.[29] In reporting his death, the *Rocky Mountain Gazette* praised his "cultivated taste," "generous heart," "fine conversational powers," and "singular charm."[30]

The region did not forget Dawson. Montana Territory had been created shortly before Dawson retired. Five years later, the territorial legislature established Dawson County, named in honor of the old trader. The county, stretching from Canada to the Dakotas, originally included some 18,000 square miles.[31] The first white man to see this area had most likely been William Clark, during the expedition's return trek.

---

[27]The gardeners lived in two-room cottages, traditionally known as a "but and ben." Co-author Andrew Dawson is Ebenezer's great-grandson. As a child, he visited Glenesk frequently. The home was sold in 1949.

[28]The American guests enjoyed Eben and Marion's lavish hospitality and especially the vintage claret. Notable features of the house were the light and airy rooms with large windows and high ornate plaster ceilings, the dazzling hall with an Italian polished marble floor in a black and white chequered pattern, and the magnificent panoramic views of the garden with its surrounding specimen trees giving a backdrop of kaleidoscopic greens, browns, and greys.

[29]Death certificate signed by Dr. Robert Lucas and witnessed by his niece, Katharine Dawson. Scottish Record Office, Edinburgh. His grave is marked only by the family plot headstone, which has been rendered illegible by the elements.

[30]Obituary of Andrew Dawson, *Rocky Mountain Gazette*, Helena, 28 October 1872, 2.

[31]Today, the county includes 2,383 square miles with Glendive as county seat.

But not everyone agreed with the legislature's choice of nomenclature. An 1882 Glendive editorial savaged the decision: "[I]t is a liberal estimate when we say that one half of the white population do not know why [the county] was named Dawson." After detailing Dawson's career, the anonymous editorialist continued: "Dawson was a hard drinker and was a helpless invalid for years previous to his death, which in a manner accounts for his extreme filth. He returned to Scotland where he died, detested by himself and everyone surrounding him."[32]

With no one claiming credit for the editorial, it is hard to say what Dawson did to deserve such a harsh judgment. But the opinion was not widely shared. A week later, the *Benton Weekly Record* defended the once exiled Scotsman:

> Dawson may have been a hard drinker, as most of the men of his day and circumstances were, but he was one of the most able men connected with the American Fur Company and enjoyed the respect and esteem of all who knew him personally. . . . He accumulated a large fortune and some of the most prominent business men of our territory to-day received their first start in a business career through the generosity of the man whom the above paragraph says was detested by himself and every one surrounding him. . . . Previous to [his becoming paralyzed] he was one of the finest looking and most energetic men that ever struggled for wealth in the early days of our territory, and even after his physical misfortune his mental capacities were unimpaired, and he directed the affairs of the company with as much vigor and skill as when enjoying full health and strength. Mr. John J. Healy, of this place, and Captain LaBarge, who is now in Benton, were personal friends of Dawson, and they say that a more whole-souled, conscientious or honorable man never breathed.[33]

And Montana had yet one more honor to bestow. In 1902, Governor Joseph K. Toole commissioned F. Pedretti's Sons of Cincinnati to design six murals for the new Capitol in Helena. The paintings, by a trio of Montana artists including Charles M. Russell, depicted the Louisiana Purchase, Lewis and Clark at Three Forks, Fathers Ravalli and De Smet at St. Mary's Mission, prospectors at Nelson's Gulch, Custer's Last Stand, and Andrew Dawson with Pierre Chouteau, Jr., at old Fort Benton.[34]

---

[32]"Dawson," *Times Supplement*, Glendive, Montana Territory, 15 June 1882.

[33]"Dawson," *Benton Weekly Record*, 29 June 1882.

[34]Lambert, Burnham, and Near, *Montana's State Capitol*, 23.

Epilogue

In addition to his rich fur trade legacy, Andrew Dawson left behind four children: Andrew, James, Thomas, and Grace, and his adopted son, Jerry Potts. Jerry Potts would leave the largest mark on the region.[1] Born of mixed Indian-Scots blood into a world of brutality, drunkenness, and exploitation, Jerry learned life's worst lessons early on. Only after his adoption did he discover childhood's joys. Dawson neatly balanced Jerry's two worlds, teaching him to read and write while also encouraging his native friendships. Under Dawson's tutelage, Potts visited Crow and Assiniboine camps, learning to view them as potential friends rather than perpetual enemies.

Jerry developed exceptional tracking and hunting skills, becoming a much sought after guide who knew every trail from Canada's Fort Edmonton down into the land of the Cheyenne and Apache. When others returned from a hunt empty-handed, Potts brought back enough to feed a small group. While often mistaken for white, thanks to his buckskins and Stetson, the stocky, bowlegged Potts was every bit an Indian. The Indians called him Ky-yo-kosi or Bear Child.

Beginning in his teens, Jerry spent increasing amounts of time with his Blood relatives. Potts's lethal accuracy with a weapon combined with his sometimes reckless courage quickly established his place in the tribe. While in his twenties, he endured a three-day Sun Dance, lashed to the pole before tearing loose. Afterwards, he became a minor Blood chief and member of several secret warrior societies.

---

[1]Touchie, *Bear Child*, 71.

In 1870, Potts led the Blood and Piegan in the last great North American all-Indian battle, the historic Battle of Belly River.[2] Under his leadership at Fort Whoop-up, the Blood forced the Cree to retreat to the rim of a coulee and down a steep cliff to the Belly River. Only a few escaped. In all, the Cree and Assiniboine lost between two and four hundred warriors while only about one hundred Blackfeet perished. During the battle, Potts counted coup sixteen times, later claiming: "You could fire with your eyes shut and be sure to kill a Cree."[3]

Following this battle, whiskey traders gained control of northern Montana and southern Alberta. In 1872, a drunken Blood killed Potts's mother. Distraught, Jerry hunted him down and returned the favor. Various accounts from this period paint Potts as both an avenger of those victimized by whiskey and an accomplice in the accursed enterprise. Such was the region's confused state in the early 1870s.

In September 1874, Jerry signed on as a guide, interpreter, and scout for the North West Mounted Police. That fall, he arranged the first meeting between Assistant Commissioner James Macleod and the two Blood chiefs, Crowfoot and Red Crow. Handsomely paid, he helped the Mounties site Fort Macleod and became an emissary between the new law enforcers and the region's tribes.

At age fifty-eight, Jerry developed throat cancer, dying at Fort Macleod on 14 July 1896. He was buried there with full honors. The next day, the *Macleod Gazette and Alberta Livestock Record* remembered him for enabling "a small and utterly insufficient force to occupy and gradually dominate what might so easily, under other circumstances, have been a hostile and difficult country. . . . Had he been other than he was . . . the history of the North West would have been vastly different."[4]

During his life, Potts married four times, fathering several children. Two of his sons, Henry and Tyrone, also served in the North West Mounted Police. Today, his descendants live among the Blackfeet both in Montana and Alberta.

---

[2]Alexander Culbertson's youngest son, Joe, was visiting Potts during this battle. Whether or not he participated is unknown.

[3]Dempsey, "Jerry Potts: Plainsman," 10.

[4]*Dictionary of Canadian Biography Online*, accessed fall 2009.

The least known of Dawson's children is Andrew, Jr. Born in the fall of 1852 to a Sioux woman, young Andrew represented one of his father's greatest embarrassments. Dawson had just married Kuta when he was dispatched to trade in the Sioux winter camps where he impregnated a native woman.[5] Nine months later, when she gave birth to a healthy baby boy with a bushy head of orange-red hair, it was impossible to deny Dawson's parentage. His own moral code caused much self-condemnation, probably more than he received from Kuta, who had grown up with polygamy.

Dawson only mentioned Andrew to his family once,[6] and even that may have been a mistake. He subsequently claimed that, when he mentioned a son named Andrew, he actually meant his son James.[7] In any case, Dawson enlisted his Scottish friend Robert Morgan to cover up his transgression. As soon as the child could leave his mother's lodge, Morgan assumed responsibility for him. Before long, the two moved to Canada's Red River settlements where Dawson sent money for his son's education and upbringing.

In February 1862, Morgan wrote to congratulate Dawson on having taken "your old friend Culbertson's place" as "king of Missouri." Apparently, Dawson had been slow to impart the news, which had not "astonished" Morgan as he "knew perfectly well if [Dawson] managed to unseat [Culbertson] that there was no one on the Missouri as fit for the position." Morgan offered to help out with Dawson's other children "on the Missouri," if Dawson had no "means of educating them there." Morgan could "come over in the Summer & bring them across," since he had "a good opportunity here of having them well educated." Andrew had had to be removed from boarding school the previous spring due to illness, but after "run[ning] wild all summer," he had "recovered . . . perfectly" and now attended a "day school . . . where he is getting on very well & is . . . quit[e] hearty & well."

Morgan had a "good large house," a "good sized farm under cultivation[,] a Good stock of Horses[,] Cattle[,] & Hogs[,] a moying & reaping machine & also a thrashing Mill for two Horses." But it had all "rather come hard," putting Morgan in debt for $500. A year's hard work "thrashing & reaping for others in my vicinity" had reduced

[5]James Scott Dawson claimed Andrew's mother was named Mary Scott. He didn't reveal his source.

[6]Letter 22.

[7]Letter 25.

that to $200, "but there it must stick until another crop comes of the ground." His only other recourse would be to "sell animals at ½ of what they cost . . . as it is hardly possible to get hold of an[y] money here just at this time." Morgan made sure his point was clear in a postscript: "If you co[d] manage to lend me $200 for a year or so you wo[d] greatly oblige your old friend."[8]

Dawson sent the money, which Morgan acknowledged: "I received your kind letter enclosing a remittance for 200 Dollars for which I again return you my hearty thanks." Assuming that Dawson "must have made [his] fortune by this time" and would "be thinking of returning and taking [his] ease," Morgan suggested he consider "coming to Red River to Settle." Although "it is not a place for a man to coin money," it was "a very good place for one with an Indian family to settle, & where one with a small capital can get along very well." Morgan downplayed the "good deal of expense & trouble" they had recently had with the natives.

As for Andrew, after a few months at home, he was "quite stout & healthy," although "get[ting] on very slowly with his education." Morgan hoped that, as he grew, he would "see the necessity of it, & stick closer to it." In any case, Dawson's old friend promised "to raise Andrew & provide for him as [he] wo[d] for a child of [his] own." "Very comfortably settled," Morgan "expect[ed] to spend the balance of [his] life" at Red River and hoped to "see some good men," such as Dawson, join him.[9]

But Dawson would return to Scotland while Morgan and Andrew obtained separate parcels of land near Fort Garry in the Red River Settlements.[10] Eventually Andrew married Morgan's half-sister, Annie, who was twenty years his senior.[11] Although he spent some time with his half-brothers, his father remained the stranger who sent his son into exile much as his own family had done to him.

Andrew Dawson, Jr., died on 8 May 1932 and was buried in the Holy Trinity Anglican Cemetery in Headingley.

---

[8]Robert Morgan, Selkirk Settlement, to AD, 24 February 1862, SC 294, MTHS.

[9]Morgan to AD, 15 March 1864, SC 294, MTHS.

[10]Sprague and Frye, *Genealogy*, table 5, lists Andrew Dawson, Jr., on 136 acres in 1877. Robert Morgan occupied the adjoining 363 acres.

[11]Annie Morgan Dawson was born in Dunfermline, Fifeshire, Scotland. She died 6 January 1924 at age ninety-five and was buried beside her husband.

Dawson and Kuta's second child, Grace, was born at Fort Clark on 13 January 1853 and named after the trader's mother.[12] Grace was the only one of Dawson's children to remain exclusively with her people, and her fate has proven elusive. The clues we have suggest that, at some point, Grace became known as Maggie and later as Aunt Snow. The boys, taken to Scotland at a young age, seem to have had little contact with her. James's obituary mentions a sister, Maggie,[13] while Tom Dawson, in an undated interview, says, "My sister is gone now."[14]

But James's obituary also includes some tantalizing clues about her fate: "His sister, Aunt Snow, still lives at Armstrong, N.D., and his nephew, Prof. C. W. Hoffman, at Shell Village, where he is an instructor in the government schools."[15] If this is indeed Grace, some additional details about her remarkable life are found in a 1952 *North Dakota History* article by Erling Nicolai Rolfsrud, "Rising Bear, Pioneer North Dakota Schoolteacher."

As a girl, Grace/Maggie married Charles Wheeler Hoffman, a white trader. Together they had a son, Charles Ward Hoffman, born at Like-A-Fishhook Village in 1868. The Arikara called him Ni-ku-ta-wi-kau-ta-ka or White Hawk. As a baby, White Hawk and his mother were "kidnapped by Indian relatives" while Hoffman was away. When Hoffman returned, he was told that his wife had deserted him and his son was dead. Moreover, he was not welcome on Indian lands, and if he set foot there, he would be killed. Devastated, Hoffman moved to Montana where he began a new life that included eighteen years in the Montana legislature, serving under a portrait of his father-in-law.

Back in the Arikara villages, Grace/Maggie grieved for the husband she believed had abandoned her.[16] Years later, after White Hawk was grown, Hoffman learned that his son was alive and living on the Fort Berthold Reservation. The elder Hoffman immediately returned to North Dakota, where father and son were reunited.

---

[12] Letters 26 and 29.

[13] The obituary says Dawson had three children: Maggie, Mary, and James. The reference to Mary is completely baffling unless this is Kuta's daughter by Joseph Desautel. Most likely the obituary was written by someone who had no actual knowledge of Dawson's family, since James knew both of his brothers, Tom and Andrew.

[14] "Life History," interview with Tom Dawson, interviewer and date unknown, received by Joel Overholser "with Dawson piano." ORL, FtB.

[15] "James Dawson, Dakota Montana Pioneer, Dies," *Van Hook Reporter*, 19 October 1925.

[16] Rolfsrud states that Hoffman's wife "died at an early age," which contradicts James's obituary.

Charles Ward Hoffman, a/k/a White Hawk and later Rising Bear, went on to become a pioneering North Dakota educator.[17]

Support for the supposition that Maggie is Grace comes from Fred Gerard, who knew Dawson. In biographical notes on Dawson, Gerard states that Dawson "returned to Scotland with his son, leaving his daughter, Maggie, at Fort Berthold."[18] Gerard's biography of Antoine Garreau also mentions Maggie: "His first wife was a half breed Arikara, named Josette; his children by this marriage were Josette, mother of Maggie Dawson and wife of Andrew Dawson."[19]

Fred Gerard's descendant, Howard, gives us a little more. Although never connecting Maggie/Grace with C. W. Hoffman, he believed that Maggie/Grace, later known as the "Matron of Fort Berthold," married Richard Irving, and together they had a daughter, Annie, in 1871. These dates would be consistent with Maggie/Grace marrying Hoffman, enduring the apparent abandonment, and then remarrying.

The Three Tribes Agency in Newtown, North Dakota, has enrollment papers for an Anna Dawson, born 7 May 1871. But these simply add to the confusion as they list Anna's father as Richard Irving and her mother as Enemy Woman. Her maternal grandparents are given as Add to It and Thunder Woman, names that do not seem to match Josette Garreau (Kuta) and Andrew Dawson. Anna says her mother died in January 1880, another contradiction. It is also unclear how Anna, daughter of Richard Irving, became Anna Dawson. Gerard speculates government schools changed her surname, but that seems tenuous.[20]

---

[17]Rolfsrud, "Rising Bear," 241. In 1908, Charles Ward Hoffman was named superintendent of Fort Berthold Indian Reservation and oversaw the establishment of Sanish, Van Hook, and Parshall. After moving to Poplar, Montana, to teach for one year, he returned and, with his wife, founded the Shell Creek Day School. There he received the name Rising Bear, which had belonged to one of the tribe's most revered chiefs. After retiring in 1933, the Hoffmans moved to Elmwood Ranch, seven miles south of Sanish on the Missouri's south side. This is very close to James Dawson's ranch, further suggesting a connection. Hoffman had to abandon his home in 1950 when the Garrison Dam was built. Hoffman's collection of Hidatsa relics, "one of the best in existence," is housed at the Museum of the North Dakota Historical Society in Bismarck. Rolfsrud, 247–48.

[18]*CSHSND*, 1:362.

[19]*CSHSND*, 1:363.

[20]Gerard further asserts that Kuta and his own Arikara wife were daughters of Son of the Star, an Arikara chief, and that "Dawsons son wintered with Gerard at Ft. Berthold in 1862 and Gerard took the boy to St. Louis in 1863." But by then, James, Dawson's Arikara son, had gone to Scotland with his Uncle Alexander. Tom, still a toddler, does not appear to have left Fort Benton during that time. Are Gerard's dates wrong, or might there be an unknown Dawson child? Howard Gerard to Joel Overholser, 1 October 1991, ORL, FtB.

After years of attempting to track Maggie Dawson, Howard Gerard declared simply, "I surrender."[21]

James Scott Dawson, born at Fort Clark on 6 September 1852, moved to Fort Benton with his father and mother when he was barely two years old. Later he acknowledged knowing very little about his ancestry. Although his mother, Kuta, was Arikara, James believed his parents had married at Fort Benton and that his mother was Blood.[22]

Following his mother's death in 1855, James returned to live with his Arikara relatives near Fort Clark. In his obituary, he says he spent 1858–61 at St. Ignatius Mission under the instruction of Father De Smet and Father Imoda. Then, in 1861, he went to St. Joseph, Missouri, to live with the La Barges and Constables while attending school. In 1862, his uncle Alexander took him to Scotland, where James attended Birkenhead School. He may also have studied with "private masters at Edinburgh."

Between 1870 and 1878, he "engaged in merchandising" in Glasgow and Edinburgh before returning to North America. After a brief stay in the States, James traveled to Winnipeg to visit his half-brother, Andrew. There he met Elizabeth Park, a native of Aberdeen, Scotland, and the two married. In 1881, they moved to North Dakota, farming an allotment James received as an enrolled member of the Arikara tribe.[23]

In 1885, James moved to Montana and went into business with Joe Kipp, the son of legendary AFC trader James Kipp.[24] In Montana, James "energetically conduct[ed] merchandizing, mining, etc., at Fort Conrad, Missoula and Blackfoot" while also serving as postmaster and justice of the peace. In 1910, he returned to North Dakota

---

[21]Gerard to Overholser, 2 April 1984, ORL, FtB. Despite our best efforts, the authors were not able to establish conclusively the facts of Grace's later life. We cannot even say with absolute certainty that Maggie is Grace. Since Dawson had one son whose existence was little known, it is possible that Maggie was another daughter never acknowledged in his correspondence home. Nonetheless, based on our research, we believe that Grace and Maggie are one and the same and that this is an accurate reconstruction of her adulthood.

[22]Blackfeet lineage books, ORL, FtB.

[23]"James Dawson, Dakota Montana Pioneer, Dies."

[24]James Scott Dawson to his aunt, Marion Dawson, at Glenesk, Dalkeith, 26 March 1901. Writing from Kipp, Montana, James states that he is in charge of Kipp's business affairs. Dawson Family Papers.

to farm with his sons James, William, and Harold. Once again an enrolled member of the Arikara tribe, he received an allotment "on a beautiful place about three miles southwest of Sanish, across the Missouri river in McKenzie County." He spent the rest of his life there, dying at his son Harold's home on 17 October 1925 at the age of seventy-three. He was buried in the Sanish cemetery.[25]

Andrew's youngest child, Thomas Erskine Dawson, was born in Fort Benton on 6 October 1859. When his father retired in 1864, Tom accompanied him to Scotland. Not quite five years old, Tom had "no memories" of the trip "except that they traveled on a sailing vessel." When Dawson returned to his hometown of Dalkeith, Tom stayed in Birkenhead with his aunt. His father's "great hope for Tom was an Oxford education," and so the young boy was enrolled in "a good preparatory school," Ruggs School in Birkenhead, and later Peebles School on the River Tweed.[26] Unfortunately, after his father's death, it became clear that bad debts combined with Dawson's terminal care costs had depleted the family finances.[27] With no chance to pursue his father's goal, Tom signed on as an apprentice with a Clydebank shipbuilder. Serving as ship's mechanic, he sailed to New York aboard the *Bolivia* in 1878 and stayed.[28]

Tom first worked in Troy, New York, before moving to Brainerd, Minnesota. Soon thereafter, his brothers sent him money to join them in Winnipeg. There he worked for the Bridges Construction Company and the Canadian Pacific Railroad.[29] Meanwhile, for the first time in their lives, the three brothers got acquainted.

But Tom, who remembered the Dawsons as "restless, adventurous souls," only stayed in Winnipeg for a year. Heading west, he worked

---

[25]"James Dawson, Dakota Montana Pioneer, Dies"; "The Passing of Pioneers," *Van Hook Reporter*, probably October 1925.

[26]"Tom Dawson, 92, 'Last of Mountain Men,'" *Great Falls Tribune*, 23 March 1952; "Life History," ORL, FtB. Tom also claims he attended Eton for one year, but Eton has no record of this.

[27]What remained of their father's bequest was finally lost in 1878 when the City of Glasgow Bank went bankrupt. "Life History," ORL, FtB. Tom also says that he was "surpassing the other uncles in school. The others got jealous and cut me off."

[28]"Tom Dawson, 92, 'Last of Mountain Men.'"

[29]"Life History," ORL, FtB.

in Cruxton, Minnesota, Fargo, North Dakota, and Billings, Montana, before spending time at Waterton Lakes with Kootenai Brown, Fred Kanouse, and several other notorious whiskey traders.[30]

Eventually he was recruited by the North West Mounted Police, then engaged in suppressing the Canadian métis uprising known as the Riel Rebellion. Tom, who as a child probably knew Jerry Potts, found himself working with his adopted brother. He engaged in several brushes with Riel's men, later wondering how he got away with "a whole hide."[31]

After his stint with the NWMP, Tom returned to Fort Benton, where "nothing looked familiar." Like his brother James, Tom teamed up with Joe Kipp, operating a store at the Old Agency on Big Badger Creek. He and Kipp frequently journeyed into the surrounding wilderness.[32] Tom built the first sawmill on upper Dupuyer Creek and occasionally worked for the Indian service as a mechanic.[33]

Then in February 1891, "right after Lent," at St. Peter's Mission near Birdtail Rock, he married Isabel Clarke, daughter of Malcolm Clarke, his father's former partner. Together they settled on land that would become the eastern edge of Glacier National Park. Tom helped conduct the park's first survey, worked with Major W. R. Logan, the park's first superintendent, and guided many notables through the park, including Henry Stimson, the Baring Brothers, Dr. Lyman Beecher Sperry, and Britain's Earl of Dudley.[34] Early maps of Glacier call the pass at the head of Nyack Creek "Dawson Pass" for Tom, who discovered it in 1896.[35]

In 1950, Tom posed for Winold Reiss. Reiss, a renowned portraitist, had painted lifelike images of Blackfeet to adorn the Great Northern Railway's calendars since 1932. The 1950 calendar, departing from tradition, featured Reiss's portrait of Tom, who by then had lived around Glacier for more than fifty years.[36]

Tom laughed remembering how Reiss pulled out a coonskin cap

---

[30]Ibid. Tom does not admit to being involved in the whiskey trade, but it is hard to believe he would have been welcomed into this company had he not been.

[31]"Highlights of Life of Distinguished Pioneer," *Cut Bank Pioneer Press*, 26 November 1953.

[32]Ibid.

[33]"Tom Dawson, 92, 'Last of Mountain Men.'"

[34]Ibid.; "Highlights of Life of Distinguished Pioneer."

[35]"Tom Dawson, 92, 'Last of Mountain Men.'" Lake Isabel was named for his wife and Lake Helen for his adopted daughter.

[36]"Tom Dawson—Mountain Man," Tom Dawson VF, MTHS.

and asked him to wear it. "There were, and are, no raccoons in this part of the country. Some of the mountain men from Kentucky or Missouri may have worn such caps in this part of the country, but I never saw them." Nevertheless, Tom donned the cap for the portrait and enjoyed hearing from people around the world who had seen it.[37]

Tom and Isabel adopted four children: Lorena (Mrs. William Meade), Helen (Mrs. G. W. Edkins), Malcolm, and Ned. Tom outlived both of the boys, finally dying at Lorena's home in Cut Bank on 20 November 1953. The last surviving child of Andrew Dawson, he was laid to rest in the Clarke-Dawson Cemetery in East Glacier Park, Montana.

Tom was remembered as "a natural story-teller who gives a listener mental images of the places and the incidents."[38] He told one interviewer that the key to a long life was to "have Scottish and Indian blood in your veins. Then spend your formative years, or at least a part of them, in a rugged frontier country."[39]

---

[37]"Tom Dawson, 92, 'Last of Mountain Men.'"
[38]"Highlights of Life of Distinguished Pioneer."
[39]"Tom Dawson, 92, 'Last of Mountain Men.'"

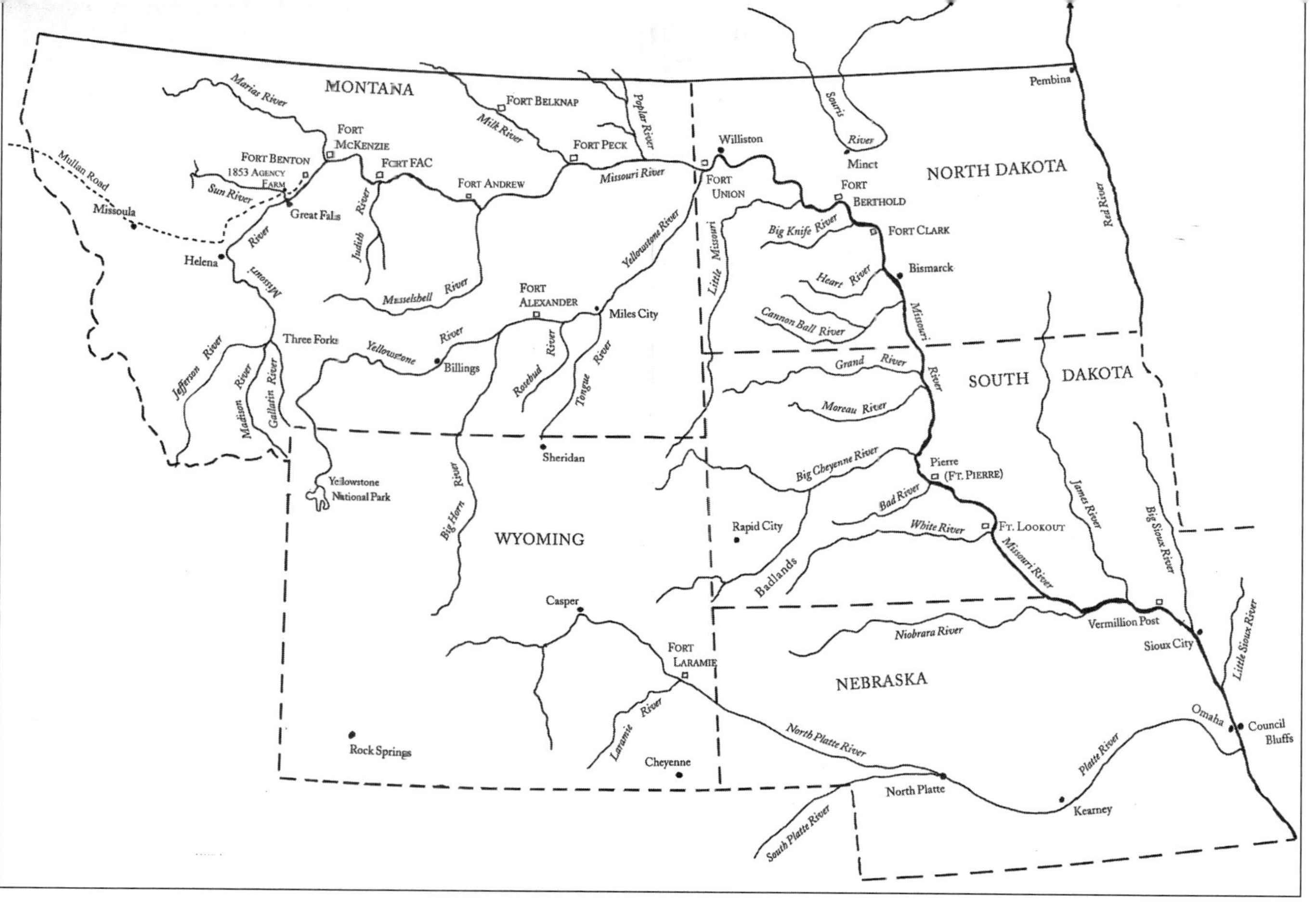

Mid-nineteenth-century upper Missouri fur trade sites.

(*above*) An overview of Dalkeith.

From Sir Walter Scott, *Provincial Antiquities and Picturesque Scenery of Scotland*, London, 1826.

(*below*) Dalkeith Church.

From Sir Walter Scott, *Provincial Antiquities and Picturesque Scenery of Scotland*, London, 1826.

(*left*) Grace Scott Dawson, 1794–1859, oil on canvas by William Bell Scott, 1855.

Courtesy of James "Hamish" Cooper Dawson, Dawson Family Papers.

(*below*) Ebenezer Dawson (1816–93).

Courtesy of James "Hamish" Cooper Dawson, Dawson Family Papers.

(*above*) The First Prize Silver Medal won by Andrew Dawson, age twenty, at the Dalkeith Gymnastic Games on 13 July 1840.

Courtesy of James "Hamish" Cooper Dawson, Dawson Family Papers.

(*below*) Glenesk, Avenue Road, Eskbank, Dalkeith, bought in 1866 by Eben Dawson, Sr. Andrew Dawson lived there until shortly before his death in 1872. Photo taken in 1949.

Copyright Douglas A. Whybrow.

F. Pedretti's Sons, "Old Fort Benton."
Andrew Dawson was honored for his role in Montana history with this portrayal in the Montana State Capitol. He is pictured at Fort Benton with Pierre Chouteau, Jr. Such a scene never happened, since Pierre Chouteau, Jr., died before Dawson arrived at Fort Benton.
Courtesy of the Montana Historical Society Research Center, Helena.

(*left*) John James Audubon, Edinburgh, November 1826, by John Syme. Dawson saw an exhibition of Audubon's prints at the Royal Institution for the Encouragement of the Fine Arts.

Courtesy of the White House Historical Association (White House Collection), 485.

(*right*) When Andrew Dawson arrived in St. Louis in 1844, he carried with him a letter of introduction to present to Kenneth McKenzie, a native Scotsman, who was in charge of the Upper Missouri Outfit of the American Fur Company.

Courtesy of the State Historical Society of Missouri, Columbia (013298).

Alexander Culbertson with his Kainah wife, Natawista, and youngest son, Joe, circa 1860. When Culbertson retired from the fur trade, Andrew Dawson was promoted to become the last "king of the high Missouri."

Courtesy of the Montana Historical Society, Helena.

"Fort Berthold on the Upper Missouri" by Phillipe Régis De Trobriand.
Courtesy of the State Historical Society of North Dakota, 12468.

(*above*) Mih-tutta-Hangkusch (A Mandan Village).
Sketch by Karl Bodmer. This village was located across the Missouri from Fort Clark, where Andrew Dawson was stationed from 1849 to 1854.

Library of Congress, LC-USZ62-28804.

(*below*) *Evening Bivouac on the Missouri*,
watercolor on paper, by Karl Bodmer, illustrates a typical encampment of fur traders on the upper Missouri.

From the Atlas accompanying Maximilian, Prince von Wied, Reise in das innere Nord-America in den Jahren 1832 bis 1834, *courtesy Biodiversity Heritage Library.*

Camp of the Gros Ventres of the Prairies on the Upper Missouri, by Karl Bodmer. This image illustrates a typical Indian encampment as seen from the opposite riverbank. Andrew Dawson's second wife belonged to the Gros Ventres of the Prairies (Atsina). Her father came to assist Dawson when he had a run-in with the Crow following the explosion of the *Chippewa*.

Library of Congress, LC-DIG-ds-00324.

(*left*) Thomas Erskine Dawson (1859–1953) was Andrew Dawson's youngest child by his second wife. This portrait, by renowned artist Winold Reiss, appeared on the 1950 Great Northern Railroad calendar, which, before then, had always featured indigenous peoples. Tom had never seen a coonskin cap before Reiss presented him with this one and asked him to wear it.

Photography courtesy of L. A. Jansen from a print in the Tom Dawson vertical file at the Montana Historical Society, Helena.

(*right*) Jerry Potts, circa 1870s, with his rifle. Andrew Dawson knew Jerry's father, Andrew Potts, in Scotland. Andrew Potts was killed at Fort McKenzie in 1842 when Jerry was a toddler. Dawson adopted Jerry in the late 1840s.

Photo courtesy of the Glenbow Archives, NA-1237-1.

(*above*) *"Fort Benton."* Taken from *Harper's Monthly*, October 1867, *'Rides through Montana,'* by Thomas F. Meagher, 570. Dawson spent his final years in the fur trade at Fort Benton, which he helped transform into the commercial hub of the evolving territory.

Photo courtesy of the Montana Historical Society, Helena.

(*left*) Andrew Dawson, circa 1866–70. Photograph by Robert Craigie, 1 West Glebe, Dalkeith.

Dawson Family Papers.

PART II

Letters

1

St. Louis, MO.
25th July 1844

My very dear Mother

It is with no common feeling that I am now able to inform you of my being once again able to earn my bite and sup by my own labour but strange to say this happy result has been succeeded by the lowest depression of spirits I ever experienced. Now that the anxiety to obtain employ is removed from my mind my thoughts of Home and of you all, of you my beloved kind parent, you whom it may be God's will I may never see again come upon me with tenfold more force than I ever thought they could. I know this feeling will ware off a little as time associates me with the things and people of this strange place but God forbid that the ardent love of home or the fond fond desire to be beside you all again or have you all here should ever leave me. Most manifest to me have been God's kind dealings towards me and my present position is another proof that I am not forsaken by him, and that should he spare me much social happiness is still in store for us all. Nor can I doubt that all the resolutions I made by your side, and over the grave of my dear, tho long lost father,[1] will yet be realised. May He bless you in the meantime.

I wrote you Christian and Eben[2] from N York, the latter I sent by the "Adam Carr"[3] which sailed on the 7th and all which letters I trust you have received. Here let me request you to be very particular when you write to state what letters you do receive, and what may appear to you to have gone missing if any. As stated in Eben's letter I left N York on the Tuesday[4] for this place and arrived on Friday last the 19th Inst. Having had the singular good fortune to get

[1] Andrew Dawson, Sr., born 1792, died in 1825 and was buried in the churchyard, St. Nicholas, High Street, Dalkeith.

[2] Dawson's older brother, Eben, confirmed steerage fare and provisions at £8 10s 9d (ca. $43). Dawson Family Papers.

[3] The *Adam Carr* was built in New Glasgow, Nova Scotia, in 1842; it had 130 passengers and approximately $43,000 (£8,590) in cargo; *Manifest of Passengers as Lodged with the Collector of the Customs for the District of New York*, signed by Captain Robert Scott on 13 June 1844, includes Dawson as a passenger; *Glasgow Registry of Shipping of 6 Jan 1844* and *Exports of the Clyde from Glasgow, 30 Apr 1844*, ship owners and trade goods for New York.

[4] He left New York on 16 July 1844.

uncle Adams as companion part of the way, he having only arrived on the evening before. My route and particulars of my journey I will give you in an after part of this Letter but in the meantime I must hasten to what I know will far more interest you, my situation. The American C^{oy} had no opening whatever for anyone but there is another C^{oy} started in opposition[5] and into which I might have got. Mr. McKenzie[6] of this place however knew of a situation and strongly recommended me to try for it and stated he thought that in present circumstances anything was preferable to the Indian Country,[7] and indeed I was far more desirous myself to get settled amongst civilisation, for otherwise my previous life would have been nearly lost and I would have been in a manner burried from you all. I did apply therefore, and this Mr. M's interest and my own exertions I have been successful, far more so than I expected to be and you will think so too, for I only arrived here on Friday last and I now have been 3 days in my situation whilst 10's that I have met—for poverty brings me into strange company—have been here for months, some for years without employment. My situation is as Bookkeeper, Clerk in a wholesale Dry Goods House or Clothiers—and tho I am only on trial for a month I have little fear of being found suitable only my entire ignorance of goods is grately against me. My Salary will be very moderate, I have no doubt for sometime as it is a very young business and my predecessor had only $300—about £60—but they stated to me they had no objections to give a little more than this, and as they improved so would they advance my Salary but notwithstanding all

---

[5]Any company that opposed the AFC was referred to as the "opposition." Several opposition companies were operating in 1844. Dawson was most likely referring to the Union Fur Company, organized by John Ebbetts, Fulton Cutting, and Charles Kelsey with financial backing from Bolton, Fox, and Livingston. While the threat was short-lived, the AFC did fear the competition from Ebbetts, Cutting, and Kelsey. Thus AFC employees tried to discourage talented young men, such as Dawson, from joining them. See Sunder, *Fur Trade,* 52ff.

[6]Kenneth McKenzie, born 1 August 1796 at Breachloch Farm, Parish of Urquhart and Logie Wester, the Black Isle, Ross and Cromarty, Scotland, was the son of Murdow and Mary McDonald McKenzie. Highland Regional Archives, Inverness Library, ScotlandsPeople, and Avoch Heritage Association. McKenzie joined the North West Company in 1816 and helped form the Columbia Fur Company in the early 1820s. In 1827, the AFC acquired the Columbia Fur Company, and McKenzie became chief trader on the upper Missouri. McKenzie married Mary Marshall on 26 June 1842 in Saint Louis. They had five children. McKenzie died in Saint Louis in 1861.

[7]McKenzie probably was wary because of the recent massacre at Fort McKenzie (see chapter 1), but he also wanted to discourage Dawson from signing on with an opposition company.

this, however trifling a sum they may give me I shall be contented. In the meantime, I am very poor as you may suppose, not having even as much as pay the postage of this Letter,[8] and I am desirous to keep my poverty to myself here which I think I will be able to manage, and in about a month I will be able to draw from the concern. Now I shall give you the particulars of my Journey in a concise Bookkeeper kind of a fashion, viz.:

Rout from N York to St. Louis	*Conveyance*	*Expenses*	*Distance (Remarks)*
South Amboy[9]	Steam Boat	$ 2.25	27 miles
Philadelphia	Railway		64 "
New Castle[10]			
Baltimore[11]	Steam Boat		35 "
Frenchtown[12]	Railway		16 "
Baltimore	Steam Boat	13.00	69 "
Cumberland[13]	Railroad		153 "
Wheeling[14]	Stage Coach		126 "
Cincinatti	Steamboat	4.00	358 "
St. Louis	d^o^	6.00	676 "
		$25.25	1,524 miles

The ten dollars from Wheeling to St. Louis included victualing but I had to pay for this the whole of the previous part of the journey, furthermore my luggage cost me ½ a dollar from N York to Phil. & $7.85 from Cumberland to Wheeling by Stage Coach, and which latter I thought a very great imposition. You will see from this statement that the money I had was considerably short of defraying these exp[n] with those I had to incur in New York—I had therefore to borrow $20 from D. Paterson[15] and my Uncle further assisted me with the loan of $10 on the way and without which I would have had to leave my

[8]Throughout his career, Dawson was deeply concerned about personal finances. His letters suggest that he had some creditors in Scotland who were apparently paid by his family, which weighed heavily on him.

[9]New Jersey.

[10]Delaware.

[11]This first mention appears to be a mistake. The route only makes sense if the first Baltimore is ignored.

[12]Maryland.

[13]Maryland.

[14]Then Virginia, now West Virginia.

[15]David Paterson, formerly of Edinburgh and a friend of Dawson's mother.

luggage behind. . . . [Mr. Adams and I] . . . travelled together so far as Baltimore where he had to remain a day on business and as economy was desirable with me and moreover I felt very dull in his C^{oy} so I e'en left him and toddled my weary way mself. I was introduced to an old Countryman by my Uncle and with whom I continued to travell as far as Cincinnati. If you wish to know the genuineness of a true Scot, seek for one far from home. This neighbour arrived in North Carolina about 17 years since with £7 in his pocket and he is now worth £1000s. There is encouragement for me, for if our money is to increase the more, the less we had on arrival, certainly I shall be a wealthy man ere long. This Countryman is a Mr. Weddell from Edin[burgh] and I am in future to keep up a correspondence with him.

In my route I have merely given you the principal Towns thro which I passed, for the Country is much thicker settled than you at home have any idea off. On the Ohio likewise the Scenery is very pretty indeed every where it is so very different to anything I have seen before that be it pretty or not, to me it appears to be so. The expense of travelling is very cheap and it is likewise very expeditious. The Railways are however, vastly different from ours and in no place are they fenced in, so that I am much surprised even more accidents do not occur. Every mile or two we have to slacken speed and sound the whistle to frighten the cattle of[f] the line. Of all the modes of travelling however, that by the River Steamboats is the most pleasant a thousandfold—You can sit walk read or sleep with as great comfort as on shore, and at the sametime the beatiful sceenery is constantly changing in appearance. The Sceenery on the Mississippi is however much the tamest and as it has very grately overflown its banks this year some of the poor emigrants present a most wretched appearance and the destruction to their stock & crops has been very great. In many places the river has been 10 and 15 miles wide where its proper width is only 1½ or so. It is now however grately subsided, and will very soon be to its proper level. Travelling by Stage which you will observe I did from Cumberland to Wheeling and which comprises the Aleghaney Mountains is most disagreeably uncomfortable. I am led to believe however I was in the best Stage Coach and on the best road in the States[16] and if so I pity those that have to travel by the worst of these. As for the Country, I like it in every respect very

[16]Dawson traveled on the National Road.

much and tho the manners of the people are vastly different from those at Home I have no doubt I will get reconciled to this likewise. There is, in the meantime, much about them that I like, and as a good sample of their equality system let me tell you that the Clerk by the master and by the public is every bit as much thought of as his employers, and here it is quite common for Clerks and Masters to play ten pins[17] and all manner of games together. What would Mr. Garven[18] say to this? . . . this is the only Letter I will be able to send home for a month or so, for as before stated I am without funds to pay the postage of this Letter. . . . In this Country I conceive there is a good deal of money to be made only one must proceed cautiously. . . . Manufactures here are treading fast on the English the people too arc calling loudly for a high protective tariff and beyond a doubt in the ensuing election of President in November next, Mr. Clay will be the man[19] and he is for protection. This House sells nothing but American Manufacture and assuredly things look well for it. After receiving this you must address me at Messrs Tevis Scott & Tevis 95 Main S^t^ here, and I will expect you to send me what Newspapers you can command. . . . I have had my hollidays sufficient in all conscience and as for mirth possibly I may still have my share of that

> "A last request permit me here
> When yearly ye assemble a'
> One round! I ask with a tear
> To him your Son that's far awa."[20]

The Weather is most unconsciously hot the glass being over 90 in the shade but the heat is nothing compared to the annoyance from the Musquittoes, which have bitten me all over. Time however will reconcile me to all these things—I shall anxiously long to have an answer to this letter so do not delay. . . . with every prayer for your comfort and happiness,

I reamain, My dear dear Mother, your most attached and most affec Son Andrew Dawson

---

[17]British for bowling.

[18]Mr. Garven was manager of the company for which Dawson worked in Warrington, England. Dawson worked for Garven before a dispute led to his dismissal.

[19]Despite Dawson's confidence, James Polk was elected president in 1844.

[20]This little poem, while in quotes, appears to have been composed by Dawson himself. Although torn, this is believed to be an accurate transcription.

[Enclosed with this letter was a newspaper clipping of the advertisement which Dawson placed in a local newspaper upon arrival in St. Louis:]

> SITUATION WANTED—By a highly respectable young man recently from Britain. He has been 8 years in an Accountant's office in the metropolis of Scotland, and subsequently two years as responsible Clerk in an extensive manufactory in the neighborhood of Liverpool. Is thoroughly conversant with book keeping and business in general. Address "Werdna,"[21] office of this paper. Je20 3t*[22]

2

Saint Louis, Mo.
2nd May 45.

My Dear dear Mother,

Yours of the 1st April is this morning to hand and I have not reaped more pleasure in the perusal of any letter from home than in it. Ah how inexpresably gratifying it is to think that tho so far away, and situated amidst hard hearted and selfish strangers as I am, there is yet those in this World to whom you are dear, and who take an interest in all your well doings. From your letter I find that there are some out of our own family circle to whom I am still of interest, and may God bless them all for "the kind word." . . . Self Dollars are the only motives to exertion here with one & all.

When I look at the letters I have received since I last wrote I know well that you are all scolding me for not having written sooner but you must not do so, for when I tell you that there is no pleasure left to me like that of writing to some one at home you will know that I am not too much to blame, no doubt I might have found an opportunity sooner but I have let it pass to do something I thought more pressing at the time. Our business this Spring has been very good and all things seem to be flourishing. We are still in the midst of the Spring business and it will be yet 6 weeks ere we can pause to take a breath. The general Breakfast hour in the City is 7 O clock and previous to that we are all at work, and this too has several times been the case

---

[21] Andrew spelled backwards.

[22] Apparently a newspaper code.

tho were kept up so late at 3 and even 4 in the morning. I enjoy the fun of working at night first rate and am generally the last to give in. You will wonder what keeps us up so late so I will tell you. Our Business is mostly entirely carried on with the Merchants in this State, Illinois, Wisconsin & Iowa, who visit us as it were in a body twice a year. During the day nothing can be attended to but the Selling, and in the Evening we have these goods to enter, and pack, all of which is done by Scott, his brother, another Salesman and myself. My business is chiefly to enter them in the Books and make the bills out, but I am ready to assist at anything should I get thro' with my share before the others. The Bills made by the different Merchants run from $100 to $2000 & sometimes $3000 tho' we consider $400 or $500 a pretty fair bill. They are paid for in Cash unless the party is particularly well known, for tho the credit business was very extensively carried on here about 5 years since, brother Jonathan[1] has found that it is not foreigners that alone suffer from repudiation. When not paid in Cash we take the partys note at 1 d/d or 1 to 6 Mos[2] as may be agreed upon, leaving 10 pr. Ct.[3] after maturity and these remain in with us till the party chooses to redeem them, which is generally pretty promptly, and indeed to secure the whole amount of those presently outstanding amounting to about $31,000—the concern would not pay $50 so securely is business conducted. We are in the most easy circumstances as regards money matters, having an inexhaustable fountain in old Mr. Tevis of Phila[4] (one of the partns)[5] to draw from, so that we never require to discount.

. . . We have many Churches here and many religions. There are three Presbyterian Churches and to one of these filled by a Mr. Potts, I go. He is a very able preacher and does much good. I am not personally acquainted with him tho in a short time I expect I shall become so, as I have a strong desire to become one of his Members, a desire which I believe will yield you some comfort.[6]

---

[1]Jonathan is presumably a brother of the partner, Scott.

[2]Months.

[3]Percent.

[4]Philadelphia.

[5]Partners.

[6]Dr. William S. Potts (1802–52) was the son-in-law of Senator Thomas Hart Benton, a great friend of the AFC. He was also John Charles Frémont's brother-in-law. Ravenswaay, 264, 344. He preached at the Second Presbyterian Church, on the corner of Fifth and Walnut Streets. *Green's Saint Louis Directory*, no. 1, 1845, xxxii.

. . . I have likewise had a long and a kind letter from Aunt Alison,[7] and if I can I will pay a visit to Memphis about August but as Mr. Tevis goes East this Sum^r^ and Mr. Scott electioneering (knocking about for customers) I think there is a very small chance of my being able. Doubtless it would be much for my interest. . . . Mr. Kenneth McKenzie went to the Mountains in October last, on some of the old Coy's[8] business and has not since returned, tho he is expected any day. A week or two previous to his starting he brought Mr. Laidlaw[9] in and introduced him to me, we were pretty busy at the time so he left promising to see me soon and here the old country cracks but I have never seen him since, and conclude he must have gone with McKenzie. He resides near Liberty about 500 miles above this, and very seldom comes here. I shall be glad when McKenzie returns as I think he is too good a friend to loose sight of. As regards myself—now—I feel very contented & happy each day I add a little to my store of money, and tho' to send you what I desire to do, would leave me pennyless, I am strongly promted to do so. A little time at least will put you in possession of some funds from me to clear of[f] some of my very small debts at home and if not sufficient to pay all why my passive creditors and you my dear Mother, the greatest of them all[10] must just appease themselves with the bone, till more provender can be supplied. I owe not a cent here but for the Boots ($7.50 by the way) which I have at present on, and which were sent yesterday and will be paid tomorrow. On the other hand there is a trifle owing to me (Credit money) which I suppose will neither be paid tomorrow or ever—but this does not ruin me—But I think you have a long enough budget[11] here for one time so you must now take your pen and scratch out Mother at the beginning substituting Sister Tit,[12] and hand it to you know whom to peruse. . . . With unbounded love to all who love me, and even a little of that same to those who do not,

[7]Alison Scott Adams of Memphis. Dawson appreciated the friendship of his aunt and her family after his falling out with other members of the Scott family. After having her own falling out with family members, Alison left Scotland for Canada, where she met and married William Adams.

[8]Company's. The American Fur Company. McKenzie was trying to restore relations with the Blackfeet following the Fort McKenzie massacre.

[9]AFC employee William Laidlaw (1795–1851) was born at Kingledoors Farm, Drummelzier Parish, Peeblesshire, the second son of Robert Laidlaw and Dorothea Turnbull Laidlaw.

[10]Apparently Dawson had borrowed money from his mother.

[11]Archaic term for letter.

[12]Nickname for his sister, Christian.

I remain, My own dear Parent
Your Most loving Son
And^{w} Dawson

I have perused this epistle and found as in the writing of it, as if I were with you all again, but now alas is my delusion over and I find myself alone, unfriended, solitary and in tears.

3

Hackberry Hall, Nr. Liberty, Mo.
4th August 1847

My Dear Mother

The date and contents of this I doubt not will surprise you, but I fear it will not be an agreeable one,—I left Bookkeeping and S^{t}. Louis, some six weeks since to carry out my original views in coming to this country, to wit, to go into the Fur trade,—This resolve I came to after the real American fashion, that is to say in an instant, having been strongly prompted by my very good friend M^{r}. Laidlaw to whom you will recollect I had letters of introduction both from his brother in Edin. and from Thomas Pots,[1] and whom I have reaped much kindness from ever since my arrival in the country.

Mr. Laidlaw has been in the Fur Co. for the past 31 years,[2] and has amassed considerable wealth—he has had some falling out with the Co.[3] of which he is at present a partner, and has now resolved to withdraw therefrom next Spring, and to start an independent trade himself in connection with which he offers me very fair inducements.

In the meantime, to make arrangements he starts for the mountains tomorrow, Sunday and I am one of five to accompany him. The trip in the meantime will be more like a pleasure one than anything else, M^{rs}. Laidlaw,[4] one of her children and two other Ladies accompanying us.

In all this I fear not, the change will ultimately prove to my benefit in a pecuniary point, as it already has to my health and spirits.

[1]Thomas Potts, Edinburgh, brother of Andrew Potts, formerly of the AFC.

[2]See Hafen, *Mountain Men*, 3:167–72, for Laidlaw's career.

[3]Written across this section, perpendicularly, is "Private—Private."

[4]The daughter of a Sioux chief, Laidlaw's wife's Indian name was Red Bird. He called her Mary Ann.

My prospects in S^t^. Louis were doubtless very good, and with some more years of hard toil might have resulted in something better than a Clerkship,—As a proof I was offered an advance of $200—to remain. Yet, tho I have had little or no sickness during my stay there, I have been far from enjoying perfect health, my spirits being frequently very much depressed and my strength very much reduced. In short there is but one thing that grieves me in the change, and that is the removal some two thousand miles further from you my dear Mother, and the hindrance to a frequent correspondence with you. Yet I strive to think that this should not so much affect me for to add any number of miles of land to the broad Atlantic people here think increases the distance from our much loved homes none. You know the character of the Americans. they think as little of a 500 miles jaunt as we at home do of one of 5 or say 50 and we foreigners soon get into their ways. Certainly if you had been located any where on this far extending Continent three years would not have elapsed without a visit from me.

Our destination is Fort Union on the Yellow Stone, to which place we travel on Horseback visiting most of the Forts, & trading posts South of that. It may be that M^r^. Laidlaw will proceed so far as the Crow nation[5] and if so I shall accompany him, but this is quite uncertain. To reach Fort Union will take us 80 or 85 days—say the 25th of Nov. and by that time you may reckon we will have experienced pretty severe cold and hardships on the Prairies. A Mountain man must learn to flinch nothing however. I have bot me a beautiful horse and can already brag a little of my riding having practised every day since being here. In all other respects my equipment is complete. We will be at Council Bluffs—say 200 miles from this in about 8 or 10 days and as that is the last place where I will be able to write you from for at least 6 Months, I shall strive to do so, and shall give you an account of our Journey that far. And as soon as I can write again after that rest assured the pleasure will not be omitted. It may be that I shall not return to the Settlements in Spring, tho I think it more than probable that I shall. Mr. Laidlaw however is certain to do so if he lives. I would have written to you of this determination of mine earlier, but I wished to be certain of our rout and also of the day of starting, and this last was only fixed yesterday. . . . When you write again, which need not be till the latter end of March, address to me here,

---

[5]The Crow lived south of Fort Union on the Yellowstone near the AFC's Fort Alexander.

and should I not be down they will be forwarded to me, you must not omit to send me a Newspaper or two also. My writing desk clothing Books & I leave here with the exception of my copy of Shakespear & one or two other [obscured by sealing wax]. . . . I shall certainly write from Council Bluffs tho it be but a line, tho you must not expect it in regular course as communications from there is far from frequent.

And now my dear Mother good bye till then— . . . I would much like to have a letter from one and all of you in the Spring if you can so manage it. It would be such a feast should I not return.

God bless one and all of our little band at home, and ever teach you to know the true affection of your fond fond Son.

And[w] Dawson

4

6 Miles North of Council Bluffs Mo.
18th September 1847

My Dear Mother

As I wrote to you we started from Mr. Laidlaw's on Sunday the 5th and arrived safe here without much of incident late last evening. We have remained here over today to recruit[1] Men and Horses, and tomorrow again start on our long travel.

Hitherto I have enjoyed myself vastly, tho I have only had the change of occupation and thoughts to thank for this as the Country we have passed thro is flat swampy and mostly covered with a long rank grass reaching over our heads when on horseback. We have met with no game hitherto either nor in fact was there anything to interest until yesterday.

This Government pays an annuity to the "Potiwattimy" (excuse spelling) tribe of indians in lieu of their lands. The payment takes place this year tomorrow at Council Bluffs and there is consequently hundreds and thousands of Indians collected in our neighbourhood, not only from the above tribe but from many others looking for what they may catch of the Spoils. Now some of the "Soux"[2] and the "Ottos" had a fight last Saturday in which some 30 of the latter were

---

[1]Rest.

[2]Presumably Sioux.

killed. M[rs]. Laidlaw you are perhaps aware is a "Soux" and in passing thro' the Bluffs yesterday the "Ottos" somehow became aware of this and the yelling and screaming that immediately immediately[3] took place surpassed description they collected about fifty of their number and surrounded the carriage, and from some of the interpreters we could make out that their intention was to kill her. Mr. Laidlaw was at that time absent and as I am next in authority I felt excited indeed. After jabbering about 5 minutes they all at once set off at full gallop and shortly after we were joined by Mr. L. and the Agent at the Bluffs. They instantly changed our rout and instead of remaining 6 or 7 days comfortably fixed at the Agent's House, we struck across the country and are in concealment. The Ottos are much weaker than the "Soux" and never venture further North than 10 miles from this at farthest so that by tomorrow evening we shall feel more comfortable—and in a day or two more we shall be amongst the Soux and therefore entirely free from further danger. You cannot conceive how my strength and Spirits are improved and I have an appetite equal to 10 Bullocks[4] I feel my importance too very great of course for instead of Books I have now men to command. Mr. Laidlaw has made me a present of a very fine Indian Poney and I have bot me a fine horse so that with the two I have no fear of having much to walk, as was poor And[w] Potts case.[5] By the way Fort Union our present destination is the place where Andrew was killed.[6] I have seen the two friends Murray[7] and Speirres[8] that came here with him the former of whom is still in the Fur trade and has a most excellent berth. I have commenced and shall continue to keep a Journal of our daily adventures, and shall give you a budget from it in the Spring[9]—you and all others on the other hand must not forget the March pakage. You know not, now that I have as I may say leisure to think, how frequently and how fondly my thoughts are turned upon you all. I feel

[3]The word is repeated at the bottom of one page and the top of the next.

[4]Castrated or young bulls.

[5]This reference is unclear. Perhaps Andrew Potts walked upriver on his first trip and his brother, Thomas, told Dawson that story.

[6]This is inaccurate. Andrew Potts was killed at Fort McKenzie.

[7]James Murray (1814–48) was born at Hearthstane Farm, Parish of Tweedsmuir, Peeblesshire, Scotland. He hunted game with John Palliser. Palliser, *Solitary Rambles*, 83, 84, 97, 98, 101, 108, 180, and 282.

[8]Unable to trace Speirres.

[9]Dawson means he will use his journal to refresh his recollection when writing letters to his family.

somehow as if I was again leaving home, but I must bear up. Mr. L. has concluded to send me back to the Bluffs on business so I must conclude this abruptly. May Heaven bless you all and assure you ever of the unceasing attachment of your very dutiful Son.

And^w Dawson

5

F^t. Pierre
1st Decr 1847.

My Dear Mother

I arrived thus far on my long journey about 6 weeks since, and have been waiting this long for the closing of the Mo River[1] so that we might proceed on the Ice. It is now all frozen to about the thickness of a foot, so that in a few days we shall start for F^t. Clark—about 400 miles north of this. We proceed in Sleighs.

I had made up my mind not to write to you at this time, as it will reach you but a very short time before my next,—if I am spared,—in June next, as it shall have to wait the opening of the Ice, about the latter end of March, when an express leaves this for St. Louis. Many things might happen to me also before that time—therefore my present resolve besides also the very great pleasure it is to me to write home. In St. Louis I had too much to do even to think of my own very immediate wants, but now that I have so much time—far too much—how very very often do these thoughts wing their flight across Prairie and Ocean, to you all, and oh how I do long now for a letter. June however is the first chance I have of receiving one. Do write all of you, and mind[2] some Newspapers.

Our trip thus far has been attended with such variety and so different from any thing I have ever either experienced or imagined that I know not what of all the many things to tell you of. Fancy your humble Servant dining on dogs and having to pay over to the noble Indian host (?)[3] any quantity of Tobacco &c &c as presents, because he could not cram down the 15 or 20lbs. set before him but had to cry halt at about the 10th lb. fact. but this is going ahead too fast.

---

[1]Missouri River.

[2]Scottish for "remember to send."

[3]Question mark in original.

I wrote you from M^{r}. Laidlaws about the 4th of Sepr. and again from Council Bluffs about the 18th of that Month, giving an account that far. We started from thence for Fort Vermillion on the 19th and reached there on the 28th.[4] This is another of the C^{os} Posts on the Mo. We experienced beautiful weather but tho the rain did not wet us we got soaked many a time in the Creeks we had to cross, over all which we had to construct either Bridges, make Rafts, or wade across sometimes to the neck half in mud and half in Water. One morning we had just started after a comfortable breakfast and having taken our last tost at the fire—for the mornings were always very cold, when we had a creek to across, all had got safe over but myself and another man, when something or other had got into my good little Poneys head that it was miry and budge he would not, but budge I determined to make him.—He gained the better part of the battle however for away he sent me plump into the mud head foremost, and so firmly did my Gun[5] and I stick there that I had to be hauled out by the heels, and indeed came near suffocating.

I assure you never did I feel more miserable in all my life and the comforts of your happy fireside came into my muddy head—I gradually cooled off however to the tune of *"Oh why left I my hame."* Such mishaps and with one or other they were of daily occurrence served however to laugh at over our camp fire in the evening. I enjoyed myself on the whole very much, and on this part of our Journey I kept the good folks in fresh meat what with Geese Ducks and Prairie Hens. From Vermillion to this we got into more variety, meeting daily with Indians Hunting—with Buffaloe—Deer—Antelope &c &c but none of us shot any of this larger game as it was too trying for the Horses, some of which had already begun to show symptoms of fatigue. We however procured plenty of the meat from the Indians, for a little Tobacco or a knife or some trifle. Much is talked of Buffalo meat and doubtless it is very good, but recomend me to a "biled gigget"[6] or a Sheeps head yet. I had the pleasure of witnessing on this part of our trip the grandest spectacle I think I ever beheld. A Prairie on fire at

---

[4]Fort Vermilion, below the mouth of the Vermilion River in present-day South Dakota, was an important trading post for the lower Sioux. Chittenden, *American Fur Trade,* 2:927.

[5]Dawson's prized Manton & Company fowling piece could be loaded with drop shot for prairie hens, ducks, and geese, or buckshot for deer, or a single large ball for buffalo or grizzly bear.

[6]Boiled leg of mutton.

night too, as it must be seen to be appreciated I shall forbear attempting a picture of it.[7] It burned right around our Camp and it required all our exertions and long to prevent it going right thro.[8] We called at "Fort Look Out" another of the Posts, on our rout and it was here I had or rather choose to eat the dogs.[9] A feast is generally given by the Indians when many are met together to anyone they may think highly of, by way of welcome, but of all their feasts a dog feast is the greatest compliment. This one was in honour of Mr. L. and we being in his Co. were also invited. At such a feast it is considered—over the left for they are a begging set[10]—a mark of disrespect to leav~~ing~~ anything on your plate—bason I should say[11]—and to make amends you must of necessity make them some presents.

To get these presents therefore, and which I conceive is the main object of the feast[12]—they set before you what is more than possible for any white man to stuff into himself.[13] I eat however right well for both the dog and my appetite were most excellent. It was no go however and I had to fork out. As to Mr. Laidlaw intentions I am as much in the dark as when I last wrote but all will come out in the Spring. In the meantime I have hired to the old Co.[14] to take some goods to Ft. Clark where I shall remain till the S.B.[15] arrives, and by it shall proceed to the Yellow Stone.[16] What I hire for is a mere trifle when compared with the rate they sell things here—but it is

---

[7]At that time of year, this fire may have been natural, as fall brings tinder dry conditions to the prairies. But Indians also commonly set the prairie on fire to foster new growth.

[8]Experienced frontiersmen would set a controlled fire to serve as a fire break around their camp.

[9]Fort Lookout was situated below the Great Bend of the Missouri River. Sunder, *Fur Trade,* 38. On October 2, 1804, Lewis and Clark named this area "Lookout Bend." Coues, *History of the Lewis and Clark Expedition,* 151.

[10]Newcomers commonly misunderstood Indians to be a "begging set." In fact, they routinely shared whatever they had with visitors, even when they had precious little and needed that for their own survival. But they expected guests to respond in kind. This was not "begging" but a mutual exchange of gifts.

[11]Written above "plate" in the original.

[12]This represents another misunderstanding. See footnote 10.

[13]The Indians routinely suffered through periods of near starvation broken by huge feasts when the game reappeared. So while Dawson correctly noted the inability of "white men" to eat these amounts, to an Indian warrior they might have seemed fairly normal.

[14]American Fur Company.

[15]Steamboat. The *Martha,* captained by Joseph La Barge, would come upriver in the spring.

[16]Dawson was apparently planning to take the steamboat further upriver, most likely to Fort Union, situated near the confluence of the Yellowstone and Missouri.

better than nothing.[17] In the meantime my health is quite restored and I feel strong as when I was in Ed^{r}.[18] When you write after receipt address to me at F^{t}. Clark care Pierre Chouteau Jr. & Co., St. Louis and wherever I may be it will be forwarded. Paper is out now so again adieu my dear Mother.

Believe me ever very affect^{ly} your Son
And^{w} Dawson

6

Fort Berthold I.T.
28th May 1848.

My Dear Mother

How strongly do my thoughts at this time revert to the many, many pleasant Sabbaths I have spent at home. This is Sunday, but alas what a change from the Sundays of early youth. Here there is no sound of Sabbath Bell, no church going, no evening walk with the family group by the sweet running Esk[1] or among the "Yellow Corn"[2] and above all else, no evening chat by the family hearth. Here the few white men around me even dream little of its being Sunday, and the many red men that are either out hunting or engaged in some of their Savage amusements or smoking, know of no such day. But tho' the outward scene and incidents around me be so sadly changed, there is that within which has not changed, or if at all it has changed to the better, and therein layeth my comfort.

I last wrote you from Fort Pierre on the 1st of December 1847 and since that time I have gone thro a great deal, but that you may judge I will relate all in order. We were to have started for F^{t}. Clark (60 miles below this) on or about the 3rd of Dec. with 5 Sleighs containing goods for that, this and lower posts, but on arrival on the 2nd from above reported the Ice not strong enough for Sleighs so the

---

[17]The high prices the AFC charged its employees were a common complaint. Working so far from civilization, the employees had no choice. With pay and expenses registered as accounting marks, it was not unusual for a low paid employee to find himself in debt to the AFC at the end of the year.

[18]Edinburgh. Dawson lived at 57 Great King Street from 1833 to 1842 while studying accounting and working for his uncle, Ralph Erskine Scott. This was the Scott home. Dawson Family Papers.

[1]The North and South Esk unite in Dalkeith and flow north to the Firth of Forth.

[2]Ripening cereal crops.

expedition was delayed. On the 19th of the same month, I started in charge of 2 Sleighs, the other goods having been sent to the nearer posts by land. The distance to this is 450 or 460 miles, and it took us 21 days in all, arriving here on the 8th of January 1848 many days however it was quite impossible to travel from wind snow and cold. I think of all the sufferings I ever experienced those of the 3rd and the 8th of Jany were the severest from cold. On the first of those days, I froze my face very badly and one of the poor horses was frozen to death. We camped in the evening too within ¼ of a mile of an Indian Village without either the Indians knowing of us or our knowing of them, a circumstance I suppose unprecedented for not only do the Indians keep constantly on the outlook for miles and miles around their camp, but the whites are also exceedingly cautious and from signs can generally tell when Indians are near. This neglect of course arose from the exceeding cold. On the 8th it was even colder and not only I but the 5 men with me froze our faces that day. One of the men had been 17 years in the country and had never before (before) been frozen. In the evening my left ear swelled up the size of my two fists and the pain was very great, but both subsided in 3 or 4 days. When I arrived at the Fort I could not speak. Nothing that day would have tempted me to make any further engagement to travel in the winter, but see how changeable we poor mortals are, in 10 days afterwards I had taken on hand and had started on another trip equally as severe. It is usual for the posts above this to send down about the 1st of the year with their requisitions for goods for the ensuing Summer &c and to take back with them what letters may have been brought up thus far from below. We waited some days after our arrival still no express came from above when the late Mr. Chardon (the Boss here) became impatient to have the Letters I had brought forwarded and offered me such inducements as I consented to take them the length of Fort Union 3 miles above the mouth of the Yellow Stone River, on the Missouri, and 250 miles from this by the Ice.[3] I accordingly started on the 18th January with 1 man[4] and arrived on the 27th without much incident. There I remained till the 1st of Feby and started back to this post with an express for below, arriving here on the 9th of that Month, then came the difficulty of having them[5] forwarded from this as no

[3]Iced over river.

[4]Robert Morgan of Dunfermline, Fife, Scotland.

[5]Letters and requisitions.

man could be found here to undertake the journey so Mr. C. had again recourse to me and I agreed. Furthermore I seemed to have greatly got into Mr. Chardons good graces, and he promised that if I would consent to return by the S. Boat[6] in the Summer he would give me command of this post and remunerate me well to which also I agreed on condition that Mr. Laidlaw did not consider me bound to him. I started from this on the 11th and arrived at Fort Pierre on the 24th of February. There I found business had been very good since my leaving and that they were much in want of goods, and that a few could be spared from Fort Union. I again volunteered to return to the latter place and have the goods sent down by boat on the opening of the River[7] and accordingly started on the 7th of March and after a very long and arduous journey arrived at Fort Union on the 6th of April. The River did not break up till the 13th when I left amid the running ice on the 14th and arrived here on the 22nd of [page torn]. On arriving I enquired from the Boat "How is Mr. Chardon and why has he not come down to welcome us" and you can imagine, but not realize my feelings on having this answer bauled back to me. "Mr. Chardon died this morning at 2 Oclock" only 4 hours previous to our arrival.[8] He was in perfect health when I left him on my upward trip on the 27th of March, and his disease was one quite unknown in the country. I think from the description it must have been scurvy.[9] Since my arrival on the 22nd April[10] I have been here in charge of the Fort, and a solitary and lonely life I assure you it is.

Thus you see I have had a good Winters work, having traveled 2700 miles entirely on foot, through deep Snow all the time, and most part of the way with my bedding[,] clothing[,] 10 days meat &c &c on my back, weighing from 25 @ 65lbs. according to the quantity of meat[,] mocassins and other things <u>perishable</u> that I had at the time.

---

[6]Steamboat.

[7]When the ice broke.

[8]Palliser, *Solitary Rambles*, 262–63: "A day or two afterwards poor Mr. Chardon requested me to write his will for him, which I did. He dictated everything correctly and sensibly, and the day after signing it, died surrounded by us all."

[9]Why Dawson believed that Chardon died of scurvy is unclear. Symptoms of scurvy, according to Leach, *The Ship Captain's Medical Guide*, 124–25, include "swollen and spongy gums, dark spots and blue blotches, like bruises, about the legs, and a brawny hardness about the calves of the legs and under-parts of the thighs." Abel, *Chardon's Journal*, 267, says Chardon became "very ill, with a violent attack of rheumatism."

[10]Below this he has written 27th March.

Some hundreds of miles the Snow was an average 2½ feet deep and rendered travelling most fatiguing and in some places where the Snow was 3 and 4 feet deep I would take from 1 to 2 hours to travel a single mile. From the quantity of Snow Game was very scarce so that no dependence could be placed on this source for food, and I had therefore to carry as much as would last me from post to post. One time I fell from the bank of the river where I was walking and hurt my foot so bad as to detain my companion and myself 4 days, and we had to starve 4 days on the rout in consequence. On the 4th day we found a poor frozen Skunk which we roasted whole and it proved to me the sweetest morsel I think I ever eat. At another time, I was seized with Snow blindness but most luckily I managed to get to a trading post on the evening of the same day before I got entirely blind. On coming to the fire you cannot have any idea of the very excruciating agony caused by this attack, and for 5 days I was quite blind from it. At another time my companion gave out (a young Scotchman) and fell behind, and eventually lost himself—I waited the next day to hunt for him but without success, and I assure you my anxiety was very great until on my return I found him at one of the lower posts, he having turned back. After losing him I had to travel 200 miles entirely alone and I assure you that day after day as I plodded on my weary rout, my thoughts were all with you at home, and I derived a sweet pleasure from thinking that perhaps your thoughts might even at that time, be with me. At Sun set I would choose a place to camp (if possible amongst thick brushwood it being warmest there and freest from observation) shovel away the Snow with my feet to make a hole to sleep in, then cook and eat my little meats, consisting of dried Buffo meat generally and then far as I was from human being and surrounded by many dangers, after offering up my sincere and fervent prayers to him who knows the heart, would I lay down and sleep most soundly. My bed when I had to carry it consisted only of a Buffo Robe my Overcoat and some Brushwood, when I had a horse to carry my bedding I added a pair of Blankets. You may wonder how I was able to keep a proper direction in my travels but I very rarely lost sight of the River Missouri and indeed the quantity of Snow on the Prairie compelled me to travel on the Ice a great proportion of the way. Think of such a River as the Missouri, a mile wide in many places, and running on an average 7 miles an hour being entirely frozen over for 1000^s of miles to the thickness of 4 feet and you will be able to form a small idea of the coldness of our climate in winter. Tho traveling on river we had to melt the Snow for water—and frequently suffered greatly from thirst as we could not stop during the day to thaw the Snow and eating it does not much quench the thirst.

The Indians that we trade with at this post, are the Gros Ventres[11] (french for big belly) and Mandans and are allowed to be the best Indians on the river, they decidedly far excel any I have passed through and these are not a few. They are stationary, living in mud lodges within 50 yards of the Fort whereas all the other Indians live in Skin lodges and travel from place to place on the prairie.

The Gros Ventres also raise a great quantity of Corn which none of the other nations on the Mo. River, do with the exception of the Ress[12] a nation 60 miles below this. Corn Buffo Deer is all the food they have to eat, and they thrive well on these. You would pity the poor Squaws having so much to do, but they do not think they work more than their Lords and Masters. What do you think? The former—the Squaws—have to dress all the Robes, attend to all the household and family affairs,[13] carry firewood from a distance of 1 mile at least—hoe all the Corn, Sow & gather it whilst the Latter—the Lords—have to go and kill the meat—their Squaws bring it home—and go to war when they think fit, which is very seldom. All their other time and that is 11/12^{ths} of the year, they play at some of their Games or sit and smoke. A Squaw would rather die from fatigue than suffer the disgrace of seeing her husband carrying anything on his back—all live happily—all have generally plenty to eat and to drink—all are free from care or the anxietys or troubles that possess the whites and on the whole are much more comfortable and happy than the whites, on whom they look as a very inferior race of beings to themselves. I am not yet of course sufficiently acquainted with their language to judge properly of them and mostly all I know of their belief and knowledge is thro the Interpreter.[14] They have some beautiful stories amongst them as to their origin and the romance in

[11] Hidatsa.

[12] Dawson almost certainly meant "Rees."

[13] Dawson may not have realized that the women also owned all of the household goods. They could, and sometimes did, kick out a shiftless husband.

[14] Fort Berthold's primary interpreter was Pierre Garreau.

them is much grander than any story I ever read or heard. Did my space allow I would tell you a beautiful little tale which is at present fresh in my mind, but this I must forgo till I can tell it to you with others in presence. Alas! will this happiness ever be mine? This fort is more beautifully situated than any place on the river. It is on a high Bluff 50 feet perpendicular with a fine level Prairie behind of some miles in extent which terminates in a long ridge of little hills. Do not imagine to yourself however that these hills are part of the Rocky Mountains. I have been about 250 miles further N. W. than this spot yet have I never been within 600 miles of these mountains.

Our Fort commands a beautiful view of the mighty river some 5 miles both ways and I think must be a very healthy spot, at least I have hitherto found it so, but others complain of its being unhealthy. The only thing that can cause this is a custom the Indians have of not burying their dead but errecting them on Scaffolds, the place of which is quite close in the rear of the Fort, and when the wind blows from that quarter the stench is certainly strong.

It has pleased me much to hear of poor Andrew Potts in such high terms.[15] I have met with many that were in the Fort (at the Blackft) when he was killed and one and all of them talk even yet with unfeigned regret of his loss to them and the country. He was an universal favorite. I do not think that his brother Thomas[16] is aware that Andrew was married here, and that he left behind him a fine healthy boy at present about 8 years old.[17] Mr. Culbertson the present manager at the Blackfeet passed here on his way below a few weeks since,[18] and he alluded to me about little Potts, and also regreted much that the poor little fellow is being brought up as he is,[19] I therefore concluded that I would write to you about him, and if you see fit you might inform Thomas of the circumstance, Should he desire his being sent home I shall cheerfully take the management myself

[15]Andrew Petrie Potts, born 20 October 1811, Earlsheugh Farm, Parish of Jedburgh, Roxburghshire, Scotland, the third son of Andrew Potts Sr. (1783–1869) and his wife, Jean Cockburn Potts. He was murdered at Fort McKenzie.

[16]Thomas Potts, 16 Albany Street, Edinburgh, was deputy clerk of the Court of Session, Scotland's supreme civil court.

[17]Jerry Potts.

[18]Alexander Culbertson arrived at Fort Berthold soon after Chardon's death. Dawson packed Chardon's possessions, and Culbertson took the body downriver for burial.

[19]Following his father's murder, Jerry Potts and his mother, Namo-pisi, were taken as the son and wife of Alexander Harvey.

and consider it a means of repaying a small portion of the very great obligation I lie under to Thomas for his kindness to me on my leaving home.[20] It is almost an universal practice with the Clerks and Traders here to marry, and all seem fondly attached to their Wives or Squaws and children. Of course the marriage is not solemnised by a minister or priest, but is according to the only law of the country—and I think it would in all the circumstances be an extra display of bigotry to cavil at the sinfulness of the connection. All who can afford it, send their children below[21] to be educated, and they are recognised in society as much as we are, indeed even more so.[22]

One glorious improvement for this country is the very strict prohibition of all intoxicating liquors, the use of which in former times has caused many deaths, both to the whites and Indians.[23] You will recollect I was a Teetotaler before coming into this country, but now I have released myself from the pledge and gone to the other extreme, that is I have resolved to drink all I can get, which has hitherto been none! so I do not run much risk of hurting myself.

As to my views for the future I have for [hole in letter] none, on the arrival of the Steam Boat if I can make good with the Agent,[24] my agreement with [hole in letter] Chardon, I shall remain another year at least in country, but if I cannot or some equally favorable, I think I may push ahead to California and try what I can do with the small means I have at command.[25] Certainly I shall not return again to civilisation to resume another situation, as I now think it time I were serving myself instead of another, and the sole aim of my life now is to amass something whereso that to return to my dear native land and to my dearer friends.

---

[20]Thomas Potts wrote a letter of introduction for Dawson to Kenneth McKenzie.

[21]To the States.

[22]This may indicate that frontiersmen were regarded as somewhat lowly in the States; however, it is difficult to interpret, since Dawson had not returned to the States since his trip upriver.

[23]The so-called Intercourse Laws forbade importing intoxicating liquors into Indian Country. However, these laws were regularly ignored. Dawson may have arrived when alcohol importation was at an ebb, or he may simply have been trying to convince his mother of this. Later Dawson would be accused of drinking heavily. Dawson is right that liquor caused many deaths for both Indians and traders.

[24]Probably a reference to Alexander Culbertson, who was in charge of the upper Missouri forts.

[25]James Marshall discovered gold at Sutter's Mill on 24 January 1848. San Francisco reported rumors of the discovery the following March. It was first reported in an eastern newspaper in August 1848. Whether word could have already reached Dawson is unclear.

I must here pause a while however to leave a little space till after the S Boat arrives which is now daily expected, Do not think however this is still the 28th of May with me. I have written a little only every day at this, thus dragging out the pleasure of writing it till the 8th June. Fare the well for the present, and I shall now content myself with a contemplation of the good news I hope will be brought me by the Boat.[26] . . .

June 27th

I close this in vastly different spirits from what I commenced it in. The S. Boat[27] arrived on the 24th Inst. and brought me not a word from home. Friends in America have been much kinder. What makes this the more melancholy is that I cannot hear for a long time more. . . . With sincere love to all and praying God to bless one and all I remain

Your very affec Son
Andw Dawson

7

Fort Berthold
10th June 1848.

My Dear Eben

I conceive that none at home so worthily deserve a letter from me than your worthy self, though to be plain this is no very great compliment after all, for some few I could name, deserve it little enough, and mayhaps don't desire it.[1] However have done with such thoughts, it is sufficient that you not only deserve, but, to judge from my own feelings, desire it. . . . Yesterday we, or rather the Indians here, had a visit from a large band of their friends the Crow Indians and after allowing them time to paint and bedeck themselves on the hill about 5 miles distant we (again) sallied out to meet them, myself accompanied by the interpreter and I felt well repaid for my trouble. Such a sight to one inexperienced as I am, is so exciting as you can well conceive, and to add to this, as I was the chief of the whites

[26]Dawson hoped the steamboat would bring letters from home.
[27]The *Martha*, captained by Joseph La Barge.
[1]Dawson frequently imagines that his family and friends in Scotland have forsaken him.

(pro tem:) many honors (savage enough certainly) were paid me. The number of visitors was about 7 or 800 and the visited about 500 all mounted on horseback and besides there were many led horses, and dogs innumerable. The Indians are most part beautifully dressed and all fantastically painted white & black, vermillion & yellow &c &c and as I rode along with their head men, amidst whoopings & howlings I really began to think I might perhaps be dreaming of another world. The Indians themselves get very excited on such occasions. In the evening came the dancing and singing exchanging presents—& which all wound up with their eating themselves to sleep. An Indian can eat seven times as much as any white man, and on the other hand can starve seven times as long, The effects of the visit has been a very busy day today trading. The trade of this country is now chiefly in Robes though we trade still a few smaller skins such as beaver and Woolf. The former however has so fallen of late years in price,[2] as to render it very unprofitable for any one to engage in it and as it was chiefly the white trapper that hunted them,[3] they are now left to themselves to multiply and replenish till a more profitable season.

The trade in Robes this year has been grater than any previous year. All together at the different posts this company will trade over 7000 Packs, or 70,000 Robes, and besides this, there is one other Co. in opposition, who will trade 20,000 Robes.[4] Allow twice this number for the use of the Indians and what is wasted, and we have 270,000 Buffalo destroyed throughout the Season. Certainly a most awful destruction, yet some say that they do not appear to decrease. The Indians themselves do not think they diminish any, and have an idea that others come out of the earth to replace those they kill. As I write this I am surrounded by Indians smokeing &c but they do not trouble me much as they say I am at my medicine,[5]—"ma ma na ky dy"—and should not be spoken to. They are a good humoured set of beings on the whole. I have one to come and give me lessons in their language

---

[2]The previously fashionable beaver top hats had been replaced by silk ones.

[3]Indians resented the presence of white trappers, or "mountain men," who took native pelts. The Blackfeet were especially hostile to independent hunters and trappers. The demise of these trappers was also accelerated by the arrival of fur trading companies, like the AFC, which let the Indians do the hunting and trapping and then traded the pelts to the fur companies, who transported them downriver and sold them at market.

[4]Harvey, Primeau and Company was formed by Alexander Harvey and financially backed by Robert Campbell, after the AFC banished Harvey from Blackfeet country following the Fort McKenzie massacre.

[5]To an Indian, "medicine" meant special powers; in this case, it was Dawson's writing.

every night but my progress is necessarily very slow as it is impossible to let them know what I want a translation of in many cases. I can easily enough acquire the names of nouns but how for instance am I to get him to tell me the Indian for "I am sick" &c &c The Interpreter too is very jealous of anyone attempting to acquire the language, and justly so for it is his only qualification for employment in the country, as he neither can read or write and otherwise is most ignorant, indeed the better the Interpreter is, you will always find the more ignorant he is. It would do you good to see the pantomime between myself and Tutor "Tak a ra" (what is this) I will enquire holding up the article or imitating or describing it as well as I can if absent—then comes the acquiring the pronunciation of the most unpronounceable words you ever heard "Nachotz cola" (no friend) the Indian will say again and again with the most good humoured smile imaginable, and then after many attempts comes the beam of satisfaction for it seems a great satisfaction to him when I can pronounce it well—Suckitz Suckitz he says (good good). The language is exactly what you would conceive a fishing reel made of wood on a large scale would make—abounding in R's—I have another task to overcome and that is to acquire a knowledge of the French but I get fast on with it and already can join in any commonplace conversation. It is the general language of the country amongst the Whites.[6] I have met with one man who can talk fluently in 7 different civilized languages, and no one knows how many Indian languages, yet, can he neither read or write. It is universally the case that the most uneducated man acquires the language the quickest.

The Indians are excellent horsemen, they generally ride without the Saddle and sit so gracefully you would think the horse and rider were but one animal. At full galop they can pick up anything off the ground without dismounting. The most beautiful sight you can well imagine is to see about 500 of them running Buffo on horseback. They find the Bow and arrow much more serviceable to them than the Gun in this kind of hunt & generally use it and in its use are most expert. The Whites on the other hand use the gun alone. A light single barreled smooth bore is the gun most preferred and flint much before percussion. I have met with one man a son of my friend Mr.

---

[6]The traders spoke many languages with pidgin French being common. The universal language, whether among traders, Indians of different tribes, or traders and Indians, was sign language.

Kenneth Mackenzie[7] who can load and fire 13 shots in the time his horse will run a mile at full speed. The manner of loading however is very different from that practised in any other description of hunting. The first charge is done at leisure and in the usual way, but previous to starting on the run, the hunter puts his bullets in his mouth and the powder in his pocket—then down goes a handful at a time and on the top of it the ball without patching or anything. In running Buff° the hunter must gallop up so close to the animal that the powder will sing the hair on discharging—he can take no aim but fire on the instant he points his gun at the Buffo otherwise you will observe the Bullet would run out. A good hunter with a good horse kills from 5 to 15 in a race lasting generally about 15 minutes. I have had only one opportunity of trying my skill but I was badly mounted and could not make up to the Game. After the S. Boat leaving however, should I remain, I shall be more at leisure and I have no doubt in a little time will prove an adept. It is most exciting Sport. The breed of horses in the country is very inferior and there are very few that are called Buff° horses. The Co. bring up some 200 or 300 every year but these are the cheepest they can find below costing about 30$ which they sell for 30, 40 & 50 Robes, the largest number equal to $150 @ $200 a pretty good profit, but you must recollect the expenses are very great. The poor white man suffers very much from the extortion of the Co—every thing he buys cost him about 10,000 P. C.[8] more than it would below. A Clerk however has no need to spend anything but for his clothing as all the luxuries of the country—Sugar Coffee Flour and Tobacco, are furnished him, in moderation for nothing. For a shirt I have to pay $4 and this wont bare a washing. Thanks to the good workmanship of our good Sister however, I have not as yet had to go to this extravagance tho' I am now at "my last shift" and shall have to fork out on the arrival of the Steamer. . . . I made a present the other day to one of our opposition neighbours (a young Scotchman[9] and acquainted with Thomas Potts) of 6 common Clay Tobacco Pipes, which you get in Scotland at 3 for ½d.[10] These six cost me $1.50. Is it not shameful. At this post there is no one I can associate with, as the men's feelings and mine are vastly at variance. I had

---

[7]Owen McKenzie.

[8]10,000 percent.

[9]Perhaps a reference to John McBride. When his service began is unclear. Boller, *Among the Indians*, 46n33.

[10]Half-penny.

a visit however a short time since from a young wealthy Irishman,[11] who has been hunting in the country for his pleasure the past winter and his company was a vast source of comfort. He has left again after Bear but I expect him back tomorrow here to remain till the Steam Boat arrives. He is quite an enthusiast in hunting, and I regret much my duties here did not permit me to accompany him.

Has this letter now got long enough for your head? I will tell you why I ask. I showed it and a much longer one I have written to Mother to my tutor, and he says he knows the one that writes it has a strong head, and so must the one that reads it he thinks, as just by looking at it, it makes his all run round and sick. I have told him it is to his great great father far away and described Scotland as well as I could, & that I have given a good account of him and his friends here, which he says makes his heart glad and he hopes to go and see this white man sometime. To give you some little idea of their ways let me relate—the great chiefs of the village had a medicine making last night—this is now the 15th—and the result is that they say—and all I think most confidently believe, that they know the steam boat wont be here till 10 days yet, it is aground several 100 miles below this,—that there are 2 S Boats[12] and they even go so far as to give the number of men coming up, which as stated by them is a very unusual number. This medicine making I cannot explain to you but it is somewhat after the manner of our conjurers actings at home. They have certainly told many strange things which have turned out true, but you must not think me silly enough to place any faith in their prophecies. Before going to war sometimes, a young man will carefully keep his horse from water, for three days. On the 3rd day he takes him to a sand bar on the river, then has two sticks pushed through his own flesh behind, to which sticks the horse is tied. If he succeed in drawing him from the water without his being able to drink then he is capable of going to war.[13] The band of Crows who paid us a visit had 20 of their numbers killed last winter by the Blackfeet, and they are still morning their loss and shall continue so to do till they kill an equal number of the Blackfeet. Their mourning is shown in many different ways—They will go out a little distance by themselves and

---

[11]John Palliser.

[12]Two steamboats were headed upriver, the *Bertrand* and the *Martha*.

[13]If the warrior can pull the horse from the water before the horse can drink, he is ready to fight.

sit down and cry in a particular manner for days. If they cannot cry well then they take stones and cut and mash themselves fearfully and the blood that flows is not to be washed away till they are revenged & most all of them have their faces or some other part of their body barkened with it.[14] I need not however go on in this strain as I fear it would only lengthen the letter without increasing your interest in it.

Sunday June 18th. I have today been witness to the most horrifying proceedings you could conceive anything having the shape of human beings could be guilty of. About 7 in the morning—we rise very early here breakfasting at 4 O clock—a war party of about 100 Sioux made a rush from the hills on the horses belonging to the Gros Ventres, when the latter were quickly out in pursuit. The result of the whole was the Sioux killed one of the GVs[15] but were unable to carry off any part of his body or scalp, the much prised war trophy, they wounded another, who will recover, and they carried off 22 horses belonging to the Indians & the opposition Co. On the other hand the G.Vs killed one Sioux and secured his body. The poor Sioux was dragged behind a horse for the distance of 3 miles, at full galop, and then delivered over to the Squaws, each of them would cut off a little ps[16] and sticking it on a switch kept dancing and singing before it in a most lamentable manner,—there would at one time be from 200 to 300 Squaws all dancing and singing each with a little ps of the poor Sioux stuck up before them. When they got tired of this kind of revenge they betook themselves to the main part of the body which they cut and disfigured with their Tomahawks firing at it &c &c keeping up a horrible screetching all the time, and finally they burned it up.[17] At this time the news of 1 of the G.Vs being killed was brought, at which they betook themselves to wailing & mourning, but a few Crows still remaining in the village kept up their war dancing and singing before the feet hands & scalp of the Sioux all day. When the body of the Gros Ventres was brought in the squaws collected in a circle all st[letter torn]g with their faces to the east, and commenced such a howling and screeching as to horri[letter torn]. Then came the

[14]Meaning of "barkened" unknown. Perhaps Dawson meant "darkened" or "blackened."

[15]Gros Ventre, also known as the Hidatsa.

[16]An abbreviation for "piece."

[17]Palliser was clearer about the cannibalism. *Solitary Rambles*, 286: "Then commenced a truly disgusting sight; the boys shot arrows into the carcase of their fallen enemy, while their women with knives cut out pieces of the flesh, which they broiled and ate. I turned away chilled with horror."

Widow and another woman and going up to the body called on it in [letter torn] way I could not understand, she then tore her hair and her face till she was bloody all over, the other woman kept cutting her head with a knife. At this time I left. It was truly shocking to me to see human nature in so degraded a form, and it reflects but little credit on the American Government that such is still the case.—I do not think it is so with the Indians under the British Govmt.

It is a long time since you had a letter from me or I from you, and you must have plenty to write me about. If I do not receive a letter from you by the Boat that takes this, do not I beseech you fail to write me immediately on the receipt of this and tell all to write me frequently as I find there are many chances from below of sending Letters. . . . How does Alexander & Abram get along, I do trust well, and that none of them ever think of becoming a wanderer, as their Brother is, at least until I should say so. I do look forward to the time with a certainty, when I may be able to say to one or both come and assist me. . . . Tho I am at present unsettled,[18] I have the utmost cheerfulness as to my future career, and tho it is very far from likely that I shall remain any length of time in this barn[19] country yet it is far from being time lost. I have regained more than my strength which was much weakened in St. Louis, and the energy activity and sprightlyness of my schoolboy days has again returned. Furthermore my income whatever it may prove to be must, considerably exceed my expenditure, which you [obscured by sealing wax] is a very wholesome state of affairs. . . . I fear my letters for home entrusted to the Co. might go astray. . . . This is now the 20th and still no Boat so I begin to fear some accident, but the River has been low for some time past.[20] No further news of the War Party or anything that would prove interesting to you and as my paper is now pretty tolerably well used up I shall bid you good bye for the present. . . .

ever believe me,
your truly affectionate Brother
Andw Dawson

---

[18]New posting orders traditionally arrived with the steamboat. Dawson expected to be transferred since he gained his Fort Berthold position by chance following Chardon's death.

[19]This probably means "barren."

[20]On June 13, the *Martha* was attacked by the Yankton Sioux near Crow Creek. To assuage the bad feelings, the AFC threw several feasts. For more, see Wischmann, *Frontier Diplomats*, 166–69. This predated the Sioux attack near Fort Berthold about which Dawson writes.

8

Fort Berthold
31st December 1848

My Dear Mother

I had intended commencing many long letters for home on the 1st of the year, that is tomorrow, judging I would have plenty time to close them ere the arrival of the express from above, for below. On my return late last night, from the Winter Village of the Gros Ventres,[1] where I had been with a sleigh for a load of Robes, and to see how things were going on with the trader there, I found however that the express had arrived and been waiting here for me for 2 days, being just one month sooner than I was last year and so much sooner than I expected it. I feel much grieved at this as my letters for home must in consequence be fewer than I intended them and much shorter.

I have detained the express 2 days longer, thus I have only today and tomorrow to do all my business of love as well as that of necessity. How exceedingly unkind I was in my last letters home to express even the idea that you all there had neglected me. On the 4th of this month I received all your kind letters of March last, and I assure you it was indeed a feast; I had then been 18 months without a word from home and my anxiety to hear had become almost unsupportable & made me very unhappy. With your letters came a letter of appology from one of the Clerks below for having so long detained them, but if I had had him here at the time I should have made his appologise in another manner. Better late than never however and as I have said they were indeed a treat & one that is not finished yet for I keep reading them daily and every time some passage or other will make me forget the very great distance that separates us, and I feel myself seated as it were amongst you all, and oh! what a pleasure that would be in reallity. On recollecting myself again, then I begin to weep like a little bairn,[2] for I do believe I have become younger in feelings in this country. . . .

This winter has been passed by me so far in a much quieter way than the last tho I cannot say more pleasantly, for I have a pleasure in stirring about, and doing as the Yankee says, something desperate,

---

[1]Hidatsa.

[2]Scottish for child.

I have been almost a prisoner for 2 months past. You must know that our Inds[3] here in winter move either up or down the river to some point of timber where they errect themselves a village for warmth. Returning to their village here again about the end of February. The Village here is situated close by the Fort, and both are on a high bluff—and were it not for the close high pickets arround the Fort, we could never stand the cold in winter. While the Inds are away there is always to be feared the Sioux who keep prowling around all the time in search of horses and <u>scalps</u> and with them a white man's scalp is just as good to dance to as an Inds. This state of things renders us close prisoners, so much so that the temptation of a band of Elk Deer Antelope or Bufo close in sight can scarcely wile the most of the men here from their stronghold, so I get most of the hunting to myself. There was a young Irish gentleman[4] here last winter hunting for his pleasure, and on his return to civilisation I gave him letters to some folks below. . . . he was to ship a few things he had collected here to the care of Aleck in Liverpool, and if he has done so I trust Alexander will attend to all most businesslike.[5] He is a fine fellow and of much influence at home and is moreover very wealthy.[6]—he has sent me a very valuable horse by a Mr. Murray,[7] who visited St. Louis this year, and who you will recollect came to this country with Andrew Potts. Poor Murray however is taken dangerously sick about 1000 miles below this, so I have not as yet received my horse. I have no news of Murray later than the 18th Sept but our next express will bring some account of him and perhaps he may be the bearer of it himself if he has recovered.[8] He is a native of Peebleshire and well known to Thomas Potts.[9] I shall write you in my next if anything has happened to [obscured by sealing wax] as he is one of ourselves. The Irishman (Mr. Palliser) I expect will visit this country again next Summer. . . .

---

[3]Indians.

[4]John Palliser (1817–87), born in Dublin, spent eleven months hunting on the upper Missouri. See *Solitary Rambles*.

[5]Dawson's younger brother Alexander received Palliser's hunting trophies and Indian artifacts, which arrived in Liverpool aboard the *Abbellino,* and then shipped them to Palliser in Dublin.

[6]John Palliser inherited his father's fortune in 1862. In 1859, he received the Royal Geographical Society's gold medal.

[7]James Murray came from Tweed Valley, Peeblesshire, Scotland, where his family lived near the Laidlaws. Murray traded with the Crow at Fort Alexander on the Yellowstone.

[8]Murray died of this illness, and Dawson never got the horse.

[9]Thomas Potts, Andrew Potts's brother.

I shall endeavour to send my letters always thro some friend in the states, as the C°. receives so many by the express that they might omit to prepay mine and in consequence they would not reach you. You will always write to me through the C°. however "P. Choteau Jr. & C° S^t^. Louis" as I think this is the surest way of my getting them. You <u>all</u> must always write to me in <u>March</u> <u>July</u> and <u>November</u> early in each month and do send me a newspaper or two, as they would be a great treat here and come next to a letter. One or two Scotchmen and one or two Lpool Mercurys[10] would do.[11] My friends in the States sent me a lot of Newspapers but I received their letters only, it may fare otherwise with your papers however, at all events give them a trial. My chief amusement this Winter has been trapping Woolves and I have already killed 65, for the skins the Coy allows me .25 .50 & $1 according to their size and this is always a little item in ones income, we must take pay in goods however, and when you know that a small Tin Cup of sugar costs a $1, ½ lb Soap the same &c &c our hunting cannot make us very wealthy, but I take a pleasure in it and would do it independent of the pay. This morning a Woolf has run off with one of my traps, and as I cannot go to hunt it I fear I shall have to pay $10 in consequence, the price of the trap. I have got one of the men to go out after it after promising him $5, if he is successful, so you see not only is the pay poor but the risk pretty heavy. So it is with all things connected with this Company. They are a grassping close niggardly set. Our winter yet has not been so very cold as last but I expect it is to come. As I write it is snowing and blowing like all fury and is such a day as you at home could not show your noses in, yet we do not feel it much. Since the 9th of November the river has been frozen over and the Ice is now about 3 feet thick. Plenty chance for curling here.[12]

I have only one opportunity in the year to arrange money matters below, that is in June or July by the Steam Boat and this time I intend sending a little home to you,—it will be a very little, and perhaps none at all,—there is no saying. This is the third time I have

---

[10]The *Scotsman* and *Liverpool Mercury* were newspapers in Edinburgh and Liverpool.

[11]Traders were anxious to receive newspapers, and those that made it upriver were passed from trader to trader until they wore out.

[12]In curling, contestants slide a stone across a sheet of ice toward a target area. Dawson's brother Ebenezer was first secretary of the Dalkeith Curling Club in 1839. Dawson Family Papers.

intended doing so and possibly will be the third time I may be prevented. Murder will out,—could you believe me so silly as to have lent an "American" on his bond $750! I only mention this now that I am getting over it, and now that I am able to laugh at the matter myself. A young Doctor in St. Louis conceived that by setting up a Drug Store he could get immensely rich in short time, but he had not the wherewithal to do it would I lend him a little money,—a very little money, say $750[13] and he would give me a bond over the whole <u>moveables</u> in the Store and pay me 10 pr cent Interest until he could fork up. Well as I was very soft,—very very soft—and very intimate with him, so intimate that I was engaged to be married to his Sister—another secret you never heard of—I lent him the money and to enable me to do so had to borrow a little of it on 6 pr cent Interest. Well the moveables proved to be too moveable and I never got a cent of the interest or the principal and never got married to the repudiators Sister—so there is an end of the story—"say no more about it." . . . 100s of little Merchants flo in some with a little but most with no capital or principal, who get their goods from N York from other speculators of little principle on a credit of 12 months sell them out to Tom, Dick and Harry in order to do a big business as they say, and at the end of the 12 months find themselves without a cent to pay their debts. Never mind go ahead is the order of the day and they go to N York again without a cent and by dint of cunning & impudence again return with a "large & well assorted equipment of Dry Goods"—Any one can get goods on a credit in America. . . .

I must now wind up My dear Mother to give me time for other letters. . . . if there is any opportunity in the interim I shall write a few lines and take the risk of its reaching.—the only chance I can have is by deserters from the Opposition Coy[14] going down Stream. To you I will always write by the ½ yearly opportunities. . . .

And now my dear Parent faretheewell once again. May God Almighty watch over and guard you, and that he may please to restore us once again to each other is the earnest prayer of your most loving Son.

Andw Dawson

---

[13]Approximately three years' salary for Dawson and the equivalent of $17,200 today.

[14]Harvey, Primeau and Company. It is interesting that Dawson ascribes all possible desertions to the opposition company and none to the AFC.

9

Fort Berthold U.Mo.R.
31st Dec. 1848

My Dear Abram[1]

I have never once written to you since I left home, a very long time since indeed, and you certainly are deserving of a long letter this time but for the reasons I have stated in my letter to Mother I cannot serve you as you deserve, but better small fish than none you know. I feel assured you will not be offended however, and keep writing on and writing on to me long and numerous letters just as if you received the same quantity in return. One and all of you express a desire that I should keep a Journal and send you long and numerous extracts from it.

I do keep a Journal, write in it daily indeed am compelled to do so otherwise I would forget the days, not only of the year and month but of the week, but I judge you would not feel much interest in reading it from beginning to end. But come I will try you with it and so here goes for the first day I put my thumb on "ahem—Wednesday 8th Nov. 1848: Frost continues and prospects of the River being frozen over by tomorrow. Discovered a Bull on the Prairie, back of the point above and the writer with the Interpreter went and killed it. It proved a very old tough sinner but some of the meat is preferable to our present fare so brot home a lot." And now how do you like all that? It proves to be a day having more interest in it than frequently occurs here. As regards the Bull, it was the first Bufo we had seen from the Fort for 4 months, and we had been living on dried Bufo meat for months previously—poor poor fare indeed tho' Bull meat is very little preferable. Of all the meat I ever eat however recommend me to that of a fine fat Bufo Cow. In the Summer Buffo are generally poor, and it is very rarely we see any here, as they keep far out in the Prairie, and frequently we have to send so far as 60 miles to get a Cow. In Winter however, things are altered. The Cows are all fat and come into the timber for warmth, and the timber in this country consists only of a norrow stripe along the bed of the Mo. As I write there are thousands within 3 miles of the Fort and many within 300 yards, so that we can just kill what we want. Our winter is not like yours at home. when it once commences it lasts without

[1]Dawson's younger brother.

thaw for 4 or 5 months, and we thus can freeze our meat and have it fresh all winter. In Summer we preserve it for sometime in the Ice house, but more commonly we have none to preserve, and have to live on what I have mentioned before, dried Bufo meat. This is the Bufo cut up into long large thin slices and dried by the Ind[s] in the Sun or in winter over their fires. One gets very tired of it. Our other fare is Deer Elk Antelope Geese and Ducks in Summer &c &c and just now I can just shoot a cartload of Prairie Hens if I wish. They are much like the Groose[2] at home, but it would sicken you to see how they are cooked here. I often cook one myself as near after the old fashion as possible, but they laugh at me for my pains.[3] You can have no idea what a quantity of meat is wasted.—To supply this Fort I require a Cow a day and we all men women and children, number only 25 sometimes more sometimes less. Think of that—Could you find any family of 25 at home to eat one Cow—and our Bufo are very little less than your Cattle. I mention in my letter to Mother the sickness of a M[r]. Murray[4] a young Scotchman in the country. Had it not been for this circumstance I would have been superseeded in my charge of this post by this time,—but the man who was coming to take charge—(a real bona fide Major with awful beard)[5] got his orders to press on to the Crow post[6] and take charge there in room of[7] Mr. Murray. He informs me that this is the post designed for him and that he shall return on the opening of the River to take charge,[8] unless otherwise instructed by the Supreme powers here—a pack of fools and knaves between you and me, with as much brains amongst them all as you might find in daft Tam's sckull.[9] But this is no business of mine, so that they pay me for my services that is all that is wanted by me, and wait a wee[10]—perhaps,—but we wont say what. Where I may be located next year is in the present state of things uncertain, perhaps should Murray not recover, I may be sent to the

---

[2]Probably grouse.

[3]The Indians covered a bird in clay and cooked it whole. The traditional method for cooking a grouse entailed plucking, removing the innards, and then roasting or boiling.

[4]Letter 8, nn. 7–8.

[5]Charles Larpenteur. Why Dawson called him a "bona fide Major" is unknown, since this title was merely honorific.

[6]Fort Alexander.

[7]Scottish "in place of."

[8]Larpenteur wanted his own post but did not want to serve at Fort Alexander; he hoped to command Fort Berthold.

[9]Reference to Robert Burns's 1790 poem, *Tam o' Shanter.*

[10]Scottish for "a little while."

Crows,[11] but more likely I think if I do not remain here, I shall be sent to the Rees[12] as the party in charge there[13] intends going below in Summer and I begin to talk pretty good Ree. That post[14] is about 65 miles below this by the River and 35 miles across by the Prarie. Never mind, rest assured I will be comfortable where ever I am. This is a land of independence and I am perfectly able to take care of myself, and in case of sickness I have [obscured by sealing wax] good friends in this country that would take care of me and I of them in a like emergency. I said a land of independence and certainly it is. Think of me driving a cart or a sleigh and immediately after having a prince of the royal blood as my guest.[15] You cannot think how very strong and healthy I have become here and in speed can nearly compete with the horse, particularly when I receive such a budget[16] of letters from my good friends as I did on the 4th of this Month, the sight of them was enough at first, and I just gave such a leap when I observed from appearances that all were well at home, as would have endangered the sealing of any common dwellinghouse but here we have no sealing. I took one days pleasure out in looking at them, then I treated myself next day to reading one, and so on and so on till all were read when I began to read all over again and I think I shall not stop so doing till another budget comes to take their place. I feel sorry that the wrathful Ralph[17] should so conduct himself in his humour, but it is well as it is.—none of you I feel assured could ever again feel pleasure in his society, and it is well as it is. You can all live happily without him and therefore leave him to himself or perhaps he will bite you like "Quilp."[18] For my own part I am glad he has

---

[11]Fort Alexander.

[12]Arikara.

[13]Joseph Desautel, James Kipp's nephew.

[14]Fort Clark.

[15]It is not clear whether Dawson is speaking of an actual guest or simply painting a plausible picture of his lifestyle. There are no records of royalty visiting Fort Berthold in 1848. However, many accounts of Dawson mention him hosting "Count Koskiosko" (probably Kosciusko) of Poland, "the grandson of Count Kossuth." According to these accounts, Dawson wryly dubbed him "Count Cask of Whiskey." Most accounts suggest this visit occurred at Fort Benton. The authors have found no records of this. See James Dawson, "Major Andrew Dawson, 1817–1871," 65.

[16]Bundle of letters.

[17]Ralph Erskine Scott, Dawson's uncle with whom he studied accounting.

[18]Charles Dickens, *The Old Curiosity Shop*, 34: Daniel Quilp crossed the London Thames on a wherry boat and on reaching the Surrey side he spotted a boy standing on his head right next to Quilp's little wooden counting house in a dilapidated rat-infested ship-breakers yard called "Quilp's Wharf." "You Dog," snarled Quilp, "I'll beat you with an iron rod, I'll scratch you with a rusty nail, I'll pinch your eyes, if you talk to me. I will!"

wrapped himself up in his dignaty and retired from vulgar gaze. Dignaty forsooth in a room corner. Ralph the wrathful was never suited for centres. Let us draw a picture of him. He has been busy for a long time over a single sheet of paper and this paper he carries with a subdued smirk on his face to his better whole. Wifey dear wify come see what I have been doing he says. This sheet of paper shows exactly what we are worth interest and all included up to exact 12 O'clock this evening. Just see he says what we can leave to our sweet beloved babes, the prattling Ralph the cherubimic Jane the &c &c (for I suppose their name is now legion) just see what would be left them did it please the Almighty to take us both to his bosom this night at exact 12. £13,000:10:11 11/12ths!!![19]—what do you say responds his better whole £13000.10.11 11/12ths—just that! Ralph can you be pleased with that, why I had thought and it must be 10 times more, and so to begin you shall only have ½ a square inch of pudding in future on Sundays instead of a square inch and the servants must have only 1 potatoe instead of 1½ p. diem. The wrathful Ralph, now become the meek Ralph shirks back to his desk—and like King George 3rd when he heard of the Rebellion in America, as I read the other day in old book—he casts his eyes of fire on the floor and twirls his terrible thumbs—resolving that it will be as his dear wifey says and so on. But what is to become of all this hoard? If you live to the allotted age you will see—certainly not much happiness will ever spring from it. But let him sleep now. Christian[20] writes me he calls me a spy and I cannot know how in his estimation I deserve this appelation, but he best knows perhaps I shall be getting a fee some of these days from the ex King of France or from Victoria herself for services rendered. I do confess to having sometimes spied his "wify" dolling out the above mentioned allowance of Potatoes to her Servants, but I can at present think of nothing else nor do I care to remember.[21]

I am delighted to hear of your change of occupation and now you must stick to it.[22] Be sober Abram steady and slow to take offence, above all diligent and anxious to please and with economy you will

[19]13,000 pounds, 10 shillings, and 11 11/12th pence.

[20]Dawson's sister.

[21]This paragraph makes clear how deep Dawson's wounds remained from the falling out. That his uncle called him a "spy" is probably the only clue we will ever have about the cause of their feud.

[22]Abram was constantly in search of his calling in life. He worked in Glasgow, Liverpool, the United States, and Australia before ultimately becoming destitute. Dawson Family Papers.

yet be a great man[23]—a great big man some of these days like what I am going to be, for I feel perfectly assured if I live I shall yet be something. It has done me much good coming to this country, renewed my energy and now I just feel competent to undertake anything. . . .

And now I must also close with you my dear Brother for the present. Do not fail to remember the times of writing to me which I mention in my letter to Mother and do not fail to write me every time. It is only 3 times a year and this is not much for one that loves you so very dearly. Let me mention by the bye—there is a Carpenter in the Country from Perthshire[24] and who I had here in the Summer working for me. He will return to Scotland next Summer and will likely call on Mother to say he has seen me. Be of course very kind to all such visitors they wont be many, but I shall endeavour to make them as many as I can, for I think you all will like to hear of if not from me.

With love to one and all and every wish for your prosperity and happiness. I remain,

My Dear Abram
Your foolishly fond Brother
And[w] Dawson

10

Fort Berthold U. Mo. R.
1st May 1849

My Dear Mother

You see I take time by the forelock[1] this time, not choosing to be cheated out of my half yearly chat with you as I was in January last. In future also you may calculate upon me sitting down to write you every 1st of May and 1st of December with just as much certainty as you used to do of my writing you every Thursday night when first I went to Warrington.[2] How goes the first of this merry month with you all at home? Here it has been blowing & snowing most tremendously all day, and is much liker the 1st of January at home than the

[23]This sentence echoes Ebenezer's lecture to Dawson before he left Scotland. See chapter 2.
[24]Robert Morgan.
[1]To seize an opportunity, to act quickly and decisively.
[2]Dawson worked in Warrington, England, from 1842 until 1844.

1st of May. Such is the weather here however, the prairie shows no signs of vegetation, and the trees are, and will be for a month to come just as naked as in December. Notwithstanding the weather however, I have just returned from Duck hunting, having killed 11, a dish that would delight you all I know, but which are presently being spoild boiling in the kettle. So much for this country's cookery.—I have just finished eating 4 of the above much disparaged Ducks and I think like the little boy I might eat some more if I stood up but I feel sleepy, and inclined to lay down, so my dear Mother good night for the present.—

If the supper above mentioned should astonish you, it would never do for me to speak of some of my other doings it might too greatly shock your nerves, so I will let this subject drop for the present,—note this however, that since 14th January, I have had nothing else to eat save Bufo meat, and for the last 3 weeks only dried meat, and this as I before wrote you is poor poor living to one accustomed to it, worse I think by far than the sailors salt junk.[3] Since January also I have had nothing to drink save water,—out of Sugar out of Tea & Coffee in short out of every thing but dry meat, or as we term it, parchment, & water, and most anxiously longing for the Steam Boat[4] to bring us a little variety.—

Since I last wrote you (31st December '48) at which time I wrote also to Abram, I have received no letters from home, in short all the letters I have received from home, whilst in this Country is your budget of March 1848 and which came to hand last December. In a little while I am in hopes things will be a little more regular, only pay particular attention to writing me at the times specified in my last letter, viz. early in March, July & November. The March letters I will receive p[5] S. Boat in June, the July letters p whites who may have gone below p S. Boat, and who return here about October or later, and the November letters I shall receive p our Winter express which arrives here, in February March or April. This year we have had no express from below Fort Pierre. In November last, my friend Mr Laidlaw left Ft. Pierre for the settlements[6] to bring up a band of horses, and the express, but they write me from Ft. Pierre in March

---

[3]Salted beef.

[4]*Amelia*, captained by D. Finch.

[5]Per.

[6]The States.

last, that he had not then returned and that they were at a loss to account for his delay. I trust all is right with the good old man—and that long before I close this I will hear of his being up, and also receive another big budget from home. M^r^. Culbertson, the Agent for the Company, passed here 24th ult^o^ on his way from the Blk F^t^[7] to meet the Boat, and he promised to send someone up here with some horses from F^t^. Pierre, immediately on his getting there, and if he does I shall receive them about the 24th Inst. The only news therefore that I have from below F^t^. Pierre is through the opposition Co.[8] and from them I learn that my friend Murray, of whom I wrote you in my last, is alas no more. He died 1st November last poor fellow, and his loss will be much felt, he was getting along very well. Had saved a good deal of money, and had the prospect of early having a share in the Company.[9] Thus are Andrew Potts and his friend, both dead and both like myself doubtless, lived fondly in the expectation of once again revisiting their dear native land, but this now can never be with them, and so also may it be the case with me, but may the Almighty in his goodness ordain it otherwise, for I do most ardently long once again to embrace you all. When I last wrote you, I was busy Woolf trapping, and you will recollect had lost a trap that very morning. Well after the express left and I had a little time to myself, I went out day after day after this said trap, and traveled after it I think one way with another, over 300 miles, but no trap is yet found.—This is the more singular as besides the trap the woolf dragged along with it the log to which the trap was attached. Many of the mens traps were lost through out the season, by the breaking of the chain & but all have been recovered either by the men or the Indians, some at the distance of 50 miles from where they were lost, but what can have become of mine no one knows or can imagine.

I did not trap any more, as being short of men, I had to do most of the business between this and the Winter camp[10] myself, and short time after the express left there came another from above, "in great haste" the 2 men that brought it having taken 24 days to travel what

[7]Fort Lewis, aka Benton.

[8]Harvey, Primeau and Company.

[9]James Murray of Scotland. See letter 4, n. 7. Hodges, *Missouri Miscellany*, 12:15: "James Murray, decd. Admr., Moore K. Lurty. Sec. Geo. E. Claybrook and William Laidlaw. 25 Dec. 1848. Page 43." John James Audubon and his family stayed with the Murrays in the Scottish Border Highlands during their 1838 trip. Hart-Davis, *Audubon's Elephant*, 254–55.

[10]The Indians often moved to more secluded locations during the winter. Traders frequently established temporary quarters near "winter camp" to trade.

I accomplished [obscured by sealing wax] last winter one time, in 7.[11] and that is not all, on getting here, they declared themselves worn out and sick and would not budge a foot further. The only other resource left me was to take it[12] myself as far as the Rees,[13] so away I trudged accompanied by my dog [illegible] time, (it is such a dog!)[14] to carry my blanket, mocassins and meat for one day. On reaching friend Desautels (one of the 3 that wrote Thomas Potts of the death of Andrew) I found him even worse of than myself for men, and to make matters as easy as possible I offered my services to take the express through the Sioux country to F^t^. Pierre. This he would not hear of as I was required at my post and so "me and the dog" started back again, having been absent 5 days. Six weeks after, Mr. Desautels wrote me that he had forwarded the express by one of his men, that according to instructions the man had delivered it to the first trading house he came to and started back on his return but had not since been heard of and the express from F^t^. Pierre informs us of his having been killed by the Sioux.[15] Such might have been my fate, and such are the dangers we are all exposed too in this country, but do not let this at all alarm you for my safety, as I do not think I shall ever be required to go expressing again.

I have been here living in the impression that my Indians[16]—the Gros Ventres[17]—would not harm the whites, but I now find I have been mistaken, they are like all other tribes, will take advantage when they can, being like all others most ignorant and superstitious. It does reflect very much against the American Government and people to find such a state of things existing in their own home and that no effort has ever been made either publickly or privately to bring about a better state of things with the many savage tribes on this great river.[18] The Company in which I am, has for its sole object the amassing of as much wealth as possibly it can, and the more ignorance the

[11]Dawson remained enormously impressed by his own running of the express that first winter.

[12]The express.

[13]Fort Clark, about 50 miles downriver. Unfortunately, Dawson gives no clue as to whom he left in charge at Fort Berthold.

[14]Indian dogs routinely carried heavy bundles and pulled travois before the Indians acquired horses.

[15]Such incidents were so unremarkable that no record of this incident could be found.

[16]The traders commonly thought of the tribes they served as "their" Indians.

[17]Hidatsa.

[18]Of course, that far up the river was no longer the United States. Further down, many efforts to Christianize and "civilize" various tribes had been made, but as Dawson himself notes in other letters, the Indians considered their culture vastly superior to that of the whites.

Indians are kept in, the more profitable is the trade, so nothing is done by this Company towards their inlightenment, but the reverse.

This Spring, a good many war parties started from this against the Sioux below—but by that time all the Sioux had started back in the prairie, so they found none but a few white traders, guarding the Robes they had traded throughout the Winter, until an opportunity offered to have them conveyed to the Fort. To these traders, the Indians caused much trouble robbing most all of them, and trying to kill some but did not accomplish it. On the other hand, one of the traders killed one of the Gros Ventres, and on their return here we were all put to much trouble in consequence, and had for some time to keep the Gates of the Fort closed. I presume you know the custom with the Indians, that should one of them get killed they must to appease the "Great Spirit" kill some one in return, whether the murderer or an inocent party it does not matter. So was it our case, one must be killed before they would make peace, but after restricting them the privilege of the Fort, for some days—(they do dearly like to come here and gaze about)—they wanted to smoke, that is make peace, and after making them a few trifling presents, they did smoke, and so far all is right again.

May 18. Today we have had one of the severe thunder storms I think any one ever experienced. I have often read of hail stones as big as a pigeons egg, but never believed it, now however let me hear of them being a ton weight, it will go down quite slick. Well then let me tell you, they were each fully a ton weight, <u>or a little less</u> and in less than no time the ground was covered to the depth of a foot. Every window in the fort was smashed like pipe stems, and the yard became in a little time so flooded that there was no going out. It would have amused you to see the turn out of the poor women from the village each with her kettle or wooden dish, to gather the hail stones before they would melt. The Mo water[19] is you know very muddy and as the Ind^s. have few or no utensils wherein to let it settle they prefer ice or snow when they can get it. All the water they drink in winter is carried from the River in large cakes of Ice.

May 22—You see I get on very slow with my letter, but I have plenty time before the boat arrives, and here again I must make another long pause & <u>ponder</u>—Ponder over what you will say, and what it is I am

[19]Water from the river.

almost too proud to tell you at present,—why my dear worthy Grand Mama, there now lays on my desk a feast for a King, and can I not be allowed a few minutes to "peel & eat." In other words, I have this morning received Christians letter of 30th July and Ebens of 7th Augt. but of course I cannot read them yet for a little while, this would be wasting a good treat too soon. . . .

June 22nd. I have indeed made a very long pause with you. . . . you cannot imagine what a patient fellow I have become.—if things go wrong my consolation is in righting them or in awaiting until they will amend themselves—for instance I expected the Steam Boat by about the 10th on account of its being a new Boat, and the river very high, but it has not come yet.—No impatience however "perhaps it will come tomorrow" is my comfort. . . . when I write one at home I know you consider the letter as for you all and it goes the rounds, and when each have read the three long ones I have written by this opportunity, you must acknowledge you have been bountifully served, otherwise you are more greedy mortals than I took you for.[20] Do not again imagine I shall ever omitt to write you by every opportunity, I could not live out the next six months were I to do so, so if at anytime you do not receive letters from me when they are expected, you must lay it down entirely to the failure of the mail or the expresses in this country and from the many hands my letters have to go through I think it not at all unlikely that some may go missing some time, you will recollect that one of Andrew Potts budgets[21] was lost. Should I be rendered, by any cause whatever, unable to write home, some one would write home for me and at the sametime you expected my letters you would receive theirs explaining why I did not write. I am the more particular in stating this as it will keep you from all anxiety on my account should any of my letters not come to hand. In my last letter I promised to send you a little money by this opportunity, and I have set aside a little for this purpose, but I must await the arrival of the Steam Boat ere I can say I shall send it or not, so until it does arrive I shall say nothing further on this subject.

I know it will give you satisfaction to know that I feel in this country as happy as I could feel anywhere away from home, and that I have every prospect of getting along very well.—It is probable therefore I

[20] Dawson teases quite a lot in this letter.

[21] Bundle of letters.

shall remain in the country for some years, and then should I think I might manage better elsewhere I shall of course make the change. This remains to be found out however, but there is one thing certain, this country is becoming poorer and poorer yearly, the only trade in it now of any importance being the Buf^o Robes. We are curtailed of many comforts too, but we will just enjoy those we have left the more when again we return to them, and the pursuits and occupations of all of us added to our most temperate way of living are such as certainly will secure to us many more years of life. An Indian has just returned with a little meat, and says it was a bull he killed in the near neighbourhood having 4 enemys arrows in him, and other came with his budget of news also, and says he heard the report of 3 canon in the neighbourhood of the Rees,[22] and that it must be the Steam Boat. To add to the excitement of the day we have seen either smoke or a cloud very like smoke,—not at all like a whale—in the direction in which the S Boat will come.—No boat yet however, and it is late, perhaps she may turn up in the morning but whether or not it does arrive I shall not resume this letter to you again until after its arrival as I want a little space to write to you, as with the others, after its arrival.

I close all my letters in much haste. The Steam Boat[23] arrived 19th July since which time I have been busy winding up the last years business and putting the present one on its hinges, and tomorrow I start with a band of horses to Fort Clark which will be my residence for the next year at least. I send you no money at this time as not only is the boat too hurried to transact anything but necessary business but the little I have to send would not help very much and again I may require all can muster up sooner than I expected as a new hope is once more sprung up here that I shall not be so long away from you all as a few days since I was thinking. . . . God bless one and all of you and still preserve and watch over you my own dear Mother, and I now trust the time is not far distant when I shall be reunited to you all.

Ever fondly and affec: Your Son
And^w Dawson
24th July '49

---

[22] Arikara.

[23] *Amelia.*

11

Fort Berthold, U. Mo. R.
28th May 1849.

My Dear Christian

On the first instant, I commenced writing a long letter to our dear Mother, which as usual, was to serve for you also. On the 22nd Inst. however, I received your letter of the 30th July and Ebens of 7th August, which have entirely and most agreeably changed all my plans.[1] . . . I feel in duty bound to write you in place of Eben, at which change I know the latter will take no offence, but quietly await his turn next half year. Half a year! what a long time this is and how many changes it does bring about with you all, but here it finds me almost the same, only I think as time advances, I get younger and stronger, perhaps happier too. . . .

Along with yours and Eben's letters, I received one from my good old friend Mr. Laidlaw, and a letter indeed it is, so full of friendship, and expressing so much interest in my welfare. You can little know what it is to stand alone in this wide world as I do, and to receive a letter from home or from a friend, to read them, I have always to hide myself and then—but I would be too childish were I to relate what does happen. You ask which of all your letters I opened first, alluding to "Mail Bag No. 1" of March 1848,—why tit[2] you should know this without asking, you recollect the copy lines used to instruct us to respect "grey hairs"—so I arranged them in this order, commencing with old "Grandmama's"[3] first, yours next, and so on,[4] . . . and each and all of them had their separate "days of reading." I assure you it was indeed a treat to me that same Mail Bag and how much I felt annoyed at myself giving expression in my letters of last June to the idea of your having neglected me at home; but pardon this, I know you all will have done so long ago, when you fully considered the awful disappointment it was to me receiving no letters from home by the Steam Boat, after so long being without news from you all, and so very very ardently longing for such. I felt like a being entirely [obscured by wax seal]

---

[1]These letters informed Dawson that Christian was to be married.

[2]Nickname for Christian.

[3]"Grandmama" appears to be an affectionate name for his mother adopted after Ebenezer's wife had children. Ebenezer may have referred to her this way.

[4]In other words, Dawson read his letters according to the age of the writer.

alone in the wide world, without one kindred tie and oh what feelings this is to one who had, and now finds he has so many kind friends, as I have. You express a desire to hear of my being permanently situated some where or other in this country, but this cannot be probably for some years, the distance is so great from post to post and the means of communication so very few, that it takes some time before a new hand finds his proper position,—rest perfectly satisfied however, (for I feel confident) that every change I may make will be to the better. On the arrival of the Steam Boat, I believe I shall have to trot either up or down Stream,[5] to make room for this terrible Major.[6]—I alluded to him in my letters of December last, but where, or whether I shall even have to move at all is to me a matter entirely in the dark. M[r]. Laidlaw has been using his interest on my behalf and writes me, my services will be required at Fort Pierre next year, but if I can get out of this without offending the old man, I shall be glad, for I do not at all like that post, and tho the remuneration may be what I cannot get, elsewhere, yet I look to being happy and comfortable before I look to riches, but bide a wee[7] perhaps the wealth may come too. I felt at one time dissatisfied with M[r]. Laidlaw and inclined to doubt the motives of his having brought me in the country, but I find I was very wrong to entertain such ideas of the good old man, and now am confident he will do all he can for my advancement.

When we came up, he had the idea of retiring from the Company, as many things were not conducted quite according to "H & Co."[8] in his opinion, and now that I know them, in mine too. A new coppartnership however was entered into in June last, for 4 years and with it many changes and improvements have taken place and are still taking place. Had M[r]. L retired it was his intention to have started an opposition Comp[y] and in it I would have held a prominent place. Things are better as they are however, for you know that sudden leaps are apt to be dangerous. One grand thing for a man in this country is to gain a familiar knowledge of the Indians, their ideas, different dispositions and tastes, and above all their language.

---

[5]Transfer to another post.

[6]Charles Larpenteur.

[7]Scottish for "wait a little while."

[8]This appears to be "H & Co." but the authors are not totally confident of the transcription. Nor are we able to explain what Dawson meant except that obviously Laidlaw, Dawson, and other traders had concerns about how the AFC handled its finances.

With one language I have already made considerable advancement, can understand anything they will tell me in round about words and can also explain myself "indifferently well" but to hear them talking amongst themselves and understand is more than any white man has ever yet been able to do. I allude to the Rees,[9] those Ind^s^ at Fort Clark some 35 miles below this by land. You may wonder at my striving after this language before that of the Gros Ventres[10] with whom I am at present, and the reason I have is only this, of the 2 the Ree is much the easiest to gain a smattering of, thus I have the Rees often about me, and my interpreter[11] is a Ree half-bred—they are moreover much more numerous than the Gros Ventres and there language is similar to the Pawnees, so the one may be of much more service to me than the other. When we meet I think I will be able to make you laugh by speaking in the most uncouth tongue, it was ever the lot of mortal to listen to, and tell you such stories too, as will make you confess all other fiction you ever read or heard of to be nothing but a trifle to it. Such stories here however are no fiction, but are most firmly believed in by all. On the other hand let me relate to the Indians some of our most common place facts, and they will not believe them—they say "our white brother lies." There are some few of the Sioux who have been taken below at different times by the Steam Boat, and brought up again the following year. These are invariably great men—"the biggest chiefs"—but on their return, on relating the, to him, many great wonders he may have witnessed, he is not believed the whites, say they, have turned his head, let us have another chief in his room, and he is from henceforth a mere nonentity in the nation. There have as yet been no Gros Ventres below, but this morning the "Four Bears"[12] the greatest amongst them, brought me 50 Robes, and said it was as a present to his White friends and that he desired to be taken below by the Steam Boat. He has paid so well, that possibly it may please the avaricious Lords of said Boat, to take him below, and whether or not he on his return, I shall if alive know what may be his treatment, and whether or not he sinks into oblivion. I have written to mother of several war parties having

[9]Arikara.

[10]Hidatsa.

[11]Pierre Garreau.

[12]Four Bears was the war chief Noc-pitt-see-top-pish. Born an Assiniboine, he was captured by the Hidatsa and became one of their greatest leaders.

started below and of the consequences, but it seems tho we have succeeded in making peace with them here it does not include all our white kindred, and three other parties have since started, with the express object of killing a white man,—what may be the result of all it is hard to tell, but I apprehend much trouble again. Certainly they will not rest until they have killed one white man at least. It is their religion and they think it appeases the wrath of the "great spirit" for the death of their brother by an enemy.

31st May.

This awful "Major" to whom I have frequently alluded arrived today with 2 Boats containing his returns from the Crow Post, and tho a right good hearted fellow, he is presently in an awful fume. I have told you in previous letters, that he was to have superseded me in charge of this post, but as I anticipated, since the death of our countryman "Murray,"[13] he has received orders to remain where he was. Of the two posts, this is in his opinion the most comfortable, and he is away below, to endeavour to have things amended, but I think will be unsuccessful. What may become of me I cannot conjecture, but the arrival of the Steam Boat will clear all up. In the meantime I have applied to have the situation of Bookkeeper at the Yellowstone, (Fort Union)—and tho not so prominent a one as my present, it is much more comfortable, and yields more emmolument. It is not vacant at present, but the one who fills the post, has been taken in as partner and as he has professed himself to be very much my friend, I have hinted that it would be very agreeable to me to take the weight of the Books away from his great shoulders.[14]

And what is our dear Mother to do Tit, in this change of yours? Now I suppose she will shut up house, and just toddle about from house to house, and like all good Grandmamas, pay a monthly visit at each, oh that I could only have the pleasure of such a visit, and what bright and new ideas would spring from out my carroty noddle,[15] at the refreshment of such a watering. Here I am too much alone, not a being arround or near me can read or write even his own name and what a pleasure it is to me to have a little conversation with the few

[13]James Murray.

[14]Edwin Thompson Denig (1812–58).

[15]His red hair.

comparitive strangers who pass here at long intervals to their post above, or going below. How infinitly greater however, would be the pleasure of a short visit from a relative, and above all my Mother,—but there is no use dwelling on such a theme, for tho often and often I talk and think with myself of such a pleasure, it can never happen. . . . And now good bye for the present tit, I must reserve the filling up the corners of this last page till the arrival of the Steam Boat, at which time I am kept so busy that I can only spare a few minutes to close my letter for home, and write a few short ones to friends in the States.

24th July 1849.

I close all my letters this evening my dear Tit very hurriedly as I am on the eve of starting to new quarters Fort Clark the Ree Post where I shall be for another year at least, on an increased Salary and I believe far more comfortably as I shall have for a companion a young man[16] my own age and a finer fellow never walked. I have received your and Mr Drummonds[17] joint letter of March last but I cannot read it yet a while. I see however you blame me for not having written home but never do this again Tit as you cannot know how it pains me to think how you again entertain such an idea of me. I write by every opportunity in the year and these are only two—December and May and my December letters to Mother and Abram you could not have received when you wrote as they would then be only about St. Louis and would reach you some time in April. The Winter letters are conveyed by parties on foot, and you should know that our winter is very severe, so that it travels at anything but Railway speed & indeed will generally arrive short time before our Summer express, only this Season our S Boat has been unusually long. One Boat was Sunk, and a second one was burned[18] in St. Louis so that our present one[19] is the third Boat the Company has freighted this year. . . . with many a prayer for your increased happiness ever believe me

your most attached brother
Andw Dawson
24th July 1849

---

[16]Joseph Desautel.

[17]Christian's fiancé.

[18]The St. Louis waterfront suffered a massive fire in 1849 that destroyed the steamboat *Martha*.

[19]The *Amelia*.

12

Fort Berthold, U.Mo.R.
6th June 1849.

My Dear Alexander

Through yourself into the most comfortable of the many easy chairs arround you, rest your feet gracefully, according to the latest touch of your fashions, on the chimney piece, stroke your beardless chin (I know it still is so) and after putting on your specktacles—if you need them as much as I do—prepare for a long chat from your absent brother. All these preparations will make some little amends for the terrible discomfort he is in at present. You know the pleasures of washing day of old, but in place of a washing of clothes, I am presently having the whole of this nice little Fort whitewashed with clay, and, as it rains "just like anything," I am forced to remain indoors, and have myself whitewashed too. On the 22nd ulto I received Ebens letter of the 7th August 48, and in it he mentions just having received from you my letter of June 1848,[1] enclosed in a blank cover.—Just as much as if you had said, "see the ingratitude of this world! For the long and kind letter I wrote Andrew in March last this is all I get for it oh woe! oh woe! oh woe!! I shall never certainly write him again." But hold on, you will write him again and often too, I know, for let me tell you it is a most safe investment much more so than speculating in Railway shares, and will amply repay both principle and interest.

The fact is Aleck, I did feel terribly mortified at the non receipt of letters from home p[er] the Steam Boat last year. Ere its arrival I had written my letters for home, only briefly closing them after its arrival, and it was only on Mr Pallisers behalf, I wrote you at all by that opportunity, and in writing I could not help letting a little of my disappointment "stick out a feet." You will have long since pardoned this however for I know your forgiving disposition and that by this time many a long letter is on the way from you. All I have received from you in this country is, that above alluded to of 24th March 1848, and a very acceptable letter it was as were all the rest that accompanied it. I received them all 4th Dec. 1848.

The poscript to yours amused me much "send me a Newspaper." Why Alec, I have not seen a Newspaper in the country with the

[1]These dates are correctly transcribed but cannot have been accurate.

exception of 4 American ones M[r] Laidlaw sent me by the last express, and these are much too precious documents to send back again,—I have taken pity on my fellow sufferers above, and sent them there. Christian writes me you frequently send me Newspapers but I have never received any. Do not let this dishearten you however in your good work, but keep sending repeatedly for should even one reach me, the pleasure it will afford, should amply repay you for the trouble you may be put to in dispatching 100. They are probably too bulky to send by the express, and possibly I may receive a lot by the Steam Boat.

It does not matter to me how old the date may be, 9/10ths of the writting will be news to me. I am too scantily supplied with reading matter here, all I have being my Bible my Shakespeare a "tea paper copy" of Burns,[2] and a very few others I have picked up in the country. . . . Your remarks about Memphis are very true as to business at present[3] but it once was a good field, and in a year or two will be so again, such are the changes in all Western America. Much better have no capital than a small one in such places. In S[t]. Louis without any capital at all, I had the offer 50 times of being established in business, but as I justly conceived myself a little too green for young Uncle Sam I declined them, but any American, would have accepted of any one of these offers and possibly enough "gone ahead." but what if he did not it matters not a button to him in short he could not live I [obscured by sealing wax] were he to be always successful, or without going through [obscured by sealing wax] 20 Bankruptcies. They are a right stirring bustling hard working people however, happy withal, and blessed with (with, a most inordinate share of self conceit, but I never yet met with one man having a proper knowledge of business amongst them. My late worthy employers Tevis Scott & Tevis used to boast of their Bookkeeper, your humble servant, as being the first in America! And gave me a present of $100. once for making out one [a]/c[4] which required only a little time to do it, for I am sure the ability displayed therein would scarce have drawn 1[ct5] in Liverpool. What would gruff grisly grabbing Garven[6] say to this compliment.

---

[2]Robert Burns. A "tea paper copy" refers to a paper of printing quality 20" × 16" of 10–12 pound per ream. Formerly used by grocers.

[3]Alexander had complained that a business venture with his uncle in Memphis apparently had not paid off.

[4]Account.

[5]One cent.

[6]Garven was Dawson's employer in Warrington.

What a contemptable man this was, for I presume he is long talked of amongst those that were,—the only ability he ever showed was in keeping himself from oblivion long ago, and this was done only by knavery. Aleck when I was in Warrington[7] I was indeed very much to blame in one respect, and in one only but I not only heard, but read on black and white, accusations against me of the grossest nature, but tho they were asserted with the strongest possible faith in the truth thereof they were nearly all lies. These lies had their source from Garven, and George Combe,[8] the former lied because he could not help it, and the other had his own object to serve, and tho I know nothing at all of his career since I saw him, yet I would hazzard the proof of this assertion on what it may have been if known to you. All is past however, and by one and all I feel assured all is forgiven, bye it I have become "a wanderer in a foreign land" and this is indeed a punishment, but I now feel satisfied that my worldly prospects have not suffered much by the circumstance. . . . A long wide space separates me from my Father land, too wide perhaps for me ever to revisit it, tho I live strongly in the faith that I shall do so sometime or other, but if I should come, who of you all Aleck may I find alive to welcome me? It is this idea that makes me so desire to live in peace and love with you all—I may never see one or other of you again. As for the "indignant and wrathful Ralph"[9] his case is a hopeless one, so we will lay him on the shelf. He has long since been dead to me.

I do indeed envy you the many happy trips you make to Dalkeith and your fishing exploits to old Gala.[10] Here I go most every night to the Mo. to fish but it is a poor job. I take my seat upon a stone and trash[11] away for an hour or so, and for all this wonderful display of patience I am rewarded with about one Cat fish about a lb. weight p week! There are plenty fish however in the River, if we could only get ahold of them. I have contrived a wooden net which I think will be a little more successful than the rod and line, and I only want to know whether I shall be removed from this post or not, ere I try its effect. A good dish of fish would be a most acceptable variety to our present fare. But if my fishing be very poor and unprofitable sport,

---

[7]He worked in Warrington from August 1842 through March 1844.

[8]George Combe, Dawson's cousin, recommended him for the job with Garven.

[9]Ralph Erskine Scott, Edinburgh, taught Dawson bookkeeping.

[10]Gala Water in Galashiels on the Scottish Borders. Dawson's father used to take his sons fishing there.

[11]Probably meant "thrash."

don't you envy me my hunting Aleck. I assure you it is a little more exciting than shooting sea Gulls on Ailsa[12] or Rabbits on the Links.[13]

Indeed there can hardly be anything more exciting than running the Bufo and as you are green in the affair let me describe the whole of it from beginning to end, the more so as I do not think I have before done so to anyone. Let it be Summer, for in Winter I assure you it is very far from pleasant, it being then quite cold enough for anyone, Ther:[14] generally 20 @ 30 degrees below zero. Well then we have to be up bright and early Buf° being then 10 or 20 miles distant in the Prairie, and away we set each as he may get ready, riding each his Pack Horse and leading his Runner, and sometimes 1 or 2 more Pack Horses. When the one in advance comes in sight of the Buf° he dismounts and gets ready his long Pipe, preparatory to all smokeing as they may come up. In this same smokeing there is a great deal of humbug gone through, so much must be blown to the Sun, so much to the earth, so much to the Buf° &c &c otherwise they would not in their belief be able to kill many, or perhaps might meet with some accident, When all have assembled and all have smoked, we remount our pack horses and in close single file ride on towards the Buf° taking care to have the wind blowing to us from them. Buf° will smell horses or men 3 miles off but with the slightest precaution they are easily approached on the open Prairie to within 500 yards. On we ride in this order till the Buf° begin to display symptoms of having discovered us, which is easily observed by their rising up some ceasing to eat and others moving of[f] at a slow walk, we again dismount and now all is hurry. Our Pack Horses that may be known to stray, we hobble and the others we cast loose, each having a long cord tied to their neck, then tighten the girths of our runner, mount him and set off. Now the run has commenced.—On we move all pretty closely together, at a slow galop, and tho the Buf° have increased their walk to a galop also, we very soon get to about 30 yards of them, and then is the time to show your horsemanship and the powers of your horse. To be first in the band is a great boast for both the Man and horse, and he has the better chance of a fat Cow, but at this near distance the Buf° can run faster for a while than many of the horses in the field, but a good rider and good horse is soon up with them. Then like the

---

[12]Ailsa Craig is twelve miles offshore in Girvan, Ayrshire.

[13]Coastal golf links in Midlothian and East Lothian.

[14]Thermometer.

man in Islington "he casts his eyes about"[15] for a fat one, drives her all the time at a galop out of the band, and when he gets side by side with her, and so near that he can spit on her, he shoots for the heart,—If the shot be good, she immediately throws up blood and slackens her pace but if not so it is necessary to repeat the dose, and in loading your gun the 2nd time you have only to poor down the powder, then the ball and you are again ready. All this you must do at a galop, as it would be too much for the horse to get behind and then have to make up to the band again. If you want more than 1 Cow, away you dive into the band again, and go through the same opperation. Some whites are so expert, that they will kill 10 @ 15 Cows on one run of about 10 minutes. The Whites invariably use the Gun but the Ind^{s} still adhere to the Bow and Arrow in this kind of hunting, and I think the latter is the more preferable to one accustomed to it. Then commences the butchering, but it would take too long space for me to describe this. The Robe is only valuable in Winter, so that in summer the skin is seldom brought home, and when it is, the Ind^{s} dress it only for clothing. At another time I will give you or some other an account of the way we butcher how the Skin is made a Robe &c &c

Besides the Buf^{o} we have plenty other hunting but of the whole I much prefer that of the Deer. It is much like our good old pastime,—fishing—and requires the same patience and perseverance, as foll . . . [obscured by sealing wax] by the whites in the country. We go into the point of timber alone, and proceed slowly and cautiously with the wind always in our face. Great care must be taken to make as little noise as possible, the breaking of even a small twig will alarm the Deer at 50 yards from you, at which distance there is little chance of your even getting a glimpse of his tail, the brush is so very thick, Walk as if you expected to see a deer at every step you take tho sometimes you may walk a whole day without seeing any at all. When you discover him he is generally from 20 to 25 yards off, but you must calm your great excitement and make believe you have not seen him at all, otherwise he is off in an instant into the thickest brush and tho of course you shoot you seldom kill him. Proceed a few steps as cooly as before making a few unseen preparations then

[15]Here he is alluding to Dickens, *Dombey and Son*, 140: "At the mention of his name, Mr. Carker the manager [from Islington, London] was, or affected to be, touched to the quick with shame and humiliation. He cast his eyes full on Mr. Dombey with an altered and apologetic look, abased them on the ground, and remained for a moment without speaking."

up and bang at him on the instant. With my good "Joe" for which I would not take $1,000 in the country I seldom fail to kill,—The Ind[s] pursue a very different way in this hunting,—They ramble along at a half trot till they have discovered the game, then they "let out" both in lungs and legs, shouting and running like the very devil. Some are very successful in their way of hunting but in killing one deer they commonly shoot about 20 times. . . .

I will now pause till the arrival of the S. Boat before I fill up the short remaining spaces of this epistle.

See all other letters for items. You know not my own dear dear brother, how I have felt since reading your letter.[16] You ask me to come home, and oh how fervently, very very fervently do I wish & long to be there, Had I had this request from you all before I might have been with you all at this moment but until I could return perfectly independantly, or at the unbiassed request of one and all of you I never could turn my thoughts to this step. I feel quite confident that by a long residence in this country I could amass much wealth. but how much happier would poverty with contentment be to me amongst you all than the greatest wealth the world can afford away from you all. Let one and all of you write in this strain and I shall not be very many years of being again with you all, and tho not wealthy, not too proud to work at any thing & without much vanity I do think I can work a little. Ever since I commenced business the only idleness I have had was the few short weeks in Dalkeith last [obscured by sealing wax] bless you [obscured by sealing wax] dear boy. I shall when time and space affords again write on this subject.

Eternally your fond brother
And[w] Dawson

13

F[t]. Berthold U. Mo. R.
28th June 1849

My Dear Eben

I did not think to have the pleasure of writing you this half year, but so it is. My Interpreter, a Ree half-bred,[1] left this on the 11th

[16]Presumably written after the steamboat arrived bearing a letter from Alexander.

[1]Pierre Garreau.

instant for the Ree,[2] for the purpose of Interpreting on arrival of Steam Boat, but yesterday he returned, and with him a man from Fort Pierre who brings the rumour that this Companys and the oppositions Steam Boats[3] are both tied up somewhere on the boarders of the settlements and that all hands on board are dying of Cholera.[4] This is sad news indeed, and altho we have no direct account, I am inclined to fear that it will prove too true,—Something must be detaining the Boat for certain, as from the high stage of water it should have been here by 15th at latest, & to add to my fears, a few American Newspapers I received by last express alluded to there having been several cases suspected to be Cholera in New Orleans. It would be a melancholy thing were the Steam Boats to bring this dreadful plague into the country. From the filthy way in which the Indians live, and indeed many of the whites too, I do believe it would sweep near every inhabitant out of the country, yet such is the greedy desire of the Americans after a few dollars, that I very much fear they will overlook the danger they put the Indians in, and that the boats will yet come,—You will recollect the dreadful effects the Smallpox had amongst the Indians, and this disease was brought in the country by the Boats. It swept away 9/10ths of the Rees Mandans and Gros Ventres, and 9/10ths of the remainder, bear to this day the disfiguring marks of this awful malady.[5] It was along after the disease had passed away ere the Rees in particular forgave it, and many whites were killed by them in token of revenge. The Rees are of all the tribes on the Mo the most troublesome[6] and what might be the result if another malady was brought on them by the whites would be hard to tell if indeed any remained after it had passed, for they with the 2 above mentioned tribes are now very few in numbers, but gradually increasing. In the meantime we have taken the precaution to keep this rumour from the Indians, and in case of the Steam Boat coming up with the disease on board, a fleet messenger will be sent us in

---

[2]The Arikara at Fort Clark.

[3]The *Amelia*, bought to replace the *Martha*, which burned in the St. Louis waterfront fire that spring, and the opposition steamer, the *Tamerlane*.

[4]Nine died on *Amelia* and one on *Tamerlane*. Sunder, *Fur Trade*, 120.

[5]The 1837 smallpox epidemic wiped out nearly 50 percent of the upper Missouri tribes and came very close to eradicating the Mandan. The disease came upriver aboard the steamboat *St. Peters*.

[6]It is doubtful that this would have been the universal opinion. Most traders would have applied this designation to either the Blackfeet or Sioux.

advance, when we will endeavour what we can to have the Indians go back in the Prairie for sometime at least.

You cannot know how anxious I am to have news from home and to know how things go with you there. Whether or not this disease has visited my own dear native land, and if so, what has been its effect, but patience is my only resource. . . .

I have not a very great deal of labour to perform in my present position, either mental or manual, but I can scarce ever call a moment my own, having all the time to be on the watch someway or other, and having continually a large crowd about me from the first dawn of morn till long after sunset when I drive the Indians out of the Fort and close the gates.

For sometime past I have been more crowded and busied than usual, however, so much so in fact that to find a sitting place, I have to pile my chairs (4 in number) on the top of each other, put them thus in my bed, and sit on the top one!! This unusual crowd arises from a visit we have had from the Crow Indians who are not away yet, and tho I have kept writing to you every moment I could find "elbow room" you see how far I have got on, and it is now the 12th of July—the anniversary I think of our Bass Rock excursion. How altered to me alas is the day, but things will mend Eben. No Steam Boat yet, but we have news by our opposition man,[7] that it is not the sickness but the unusual high water, that detains them, and that probably they will be here in about 6 days from now.

Last year I wrote to you of a fight the Gros Ventres[8] had with the Sioux, and this year I have again the same subject to write about, but a much more serious affair, both to whites and Gros Ventres, and one in which I took, was compelled to take, an active part in. It was my first battle with powder and ball,—dont talk about fist fighting if you please—and I trust will be the last. On the 10th Inst. then, over 700 Sioux made a rush from the hills here,—on an alarm of this kind our first thing to do is to run and try to secure the horses. On this occasion ours were not far distant and were soon all secured and in the Fort; and, as I thought that then our part of the danger was over, I went out in the prairie about a mile to witness the fight,—The Sioux came rushing on however, nearer and nearer, but in such a scattered

---

[7]Employee of Harvey, Primeau and Company.

[8]Hidatsa.

manner, that I could not tell Gros Ventres from Sioux, and it was not until the fireing commenced, that I discovered I was right between the 2 enemys, and indeed that I was the principal object aimed at by the Sioux. I saw the Gros Ventres were retreating fast, so I fired off my good old friend "Joe" wheeled and retreated also at no slow pace I assure you. For a half a mile or so I think I can compete with any Indian in speed, but then an Indian can run 24 hours without stopping,—most of them were mounted on this occasion too whilst I was only on foot, but I got into the Fort without hurt, but I must confess a good deal out of breath,—The yard and houses I found crowded with all the women children and cowards of the village and lot others crying for ammunition,—This I told them was not the time to ask for ammunition, they had been daily expecting the Sioux for a month back and ought to have long since been in readiness but it is ever thus with most of the Indian tribes, they never once cast a thought towards the morrow. To gain a little peace I was compelled to give them a barrel of Powder and some balls, and then on running to the bastion I found the Sioux so near as 150 yards from the Fort, and fireing on us as well as the Indian village. They have a most singular way of attack leaping and dancing about like fiends and throwing themselves flat on their belly at the report of every gun. They were all silent unless when one got wounded, when the savage yell, I suppose well known to you, was given and those near rushed to his rescue. To be wounded or killed is an honor. but to allow the scalp to be taken is a great disgrace. I found it quite time enough for me to be active too, so I got the little Canon we have, out of the Fort to an embankment close by and gave them some 15 shots from it, but unskilled as I am in gunnery and having no one to assist me save my old negro cook,[9] all the others refusing to go out of the Fort, I cannot say what execution was done, but the noise alone served a good end as it terrified the most away from my neighbourhood. The Gros Ventres say I did them a great service—and I do believe myself had it not been for the whites and this Fort all the village would have been swept away. The Sioux displayed much courage and a good deal of skill in their attack, but the Gros Ventres being so very few in proportion had recourse to that better part of valour called discretion, and the result shows they were not wrong in doing so.

[9]Perhaps this was Black Hawk, Chardon's slave, who was manumitted in his will.

The fight continued until about 3 o'clock when the Sioux gradually retired followed for about 2 miles by the Gros Ventres who then returned, and then commenced their relating their deeds of glory done. Though the fight lasted so long, the quantity of powder spent, and the very close proximity of the 2 foes, you will be astonished at the small number killed: The Gros Ventres had only 1 little boy killed—poor fellow he was the ugliest object I ever looked upon, having his nose crushed into his skull, and I believe I was the only one who used to pity his case, and occasionally feed him. He had gone to the woods in the morning to gather berries and was there surprised and killed by the Sioux. They rendered him even more ugly cutting off his hands and feet and taking the scalp. Other 5 of the Gros Ventres were wounded very slightly and 27 of their horses stolen 1 killed and 3 wounded, also 33 dogs killed, and what is very vexatious—most all their corn and pumpkins is destroyed.

I think you must have read in some of your fine novels of the respect one savage tribe has for the dead of another tribe,—I have read this somewhere, but none was shown on this occasion at least. I have before alluded to the practice these Gros Ventres have of putting up their dead to rot on scaffolds and these were all torn down old and recent, and cut to pieces with the tomahawk. I do not feel very sorry at this as it may be the occasion of the dead being interred in future,—the present practice being not only unhealthy but at times most unsavory. The pickets and houses of the Fort are quite full of balls. On the other hand the Sioux, so far as known to us had 3 men and 5 horses killed, and a great many men and horses woonded, and one horse stolen. They babbled out to us that they would be in the neighbourhood all summer and would pay us many a visit, and that we should have no Buf° meat to eat, but we have seen nothing of the Gentlemen since, and a fine band of Buf° was discovered on other side this morning, out of which we all got a good supply of fresh meat.

It gives me much pleasure to find Eben that tho you do not advance rapidly to wealth you at least are not going down the hill and are contented. This is right, for let me assure you in my opinion, and I have seen a little more of mankind than you, that you are more comfortable by far and have more reason for happiness, than 9/10^{ths} of the world. For myself, riches do not at all concern me, and it would not matter to me a fig were I to know for certain that I should live on and die just as poor as I am at present, which is not much above par, were it not to come in the way of my again revisiting you all. My intention is to remain in this country some years longer until I have scraped up a few dollars, which I think I can do, and should I then think it best for me to make a change, I shall do so and return to the States to commence business there in some way or other, or to proceed to California for I know a very small capital in a new place is considered a very large one. It is therefore some time yet before I shall probably make a change if ever, so in the meantime it is not worth while me alluding to this subject. I mentioned to Mother a very unprofitable speculation I entered into in S^t^. Louis,[10] which took away then more than I could call my own—$750—but I have got over it, and can now actually whistle, nay could jingle my pockets too if the paper were only converted into the metal. We have no coin here you know. I intend out of this little to send our good old Mother the half, but tho little it is the first, and you know the old saying, small beginnings have big ends and I trust I will be able to carry out the truth of the saying in this instance.

I have given Aleck a short account of a Buffalo "surround" as it is termed, and I promised an account of the way we butcher, but I find this is more than I am able to give, and I do not think would be at all interesting,—The meat is cut out from the bones in stripes, and pieces each p^s[11] having a name, and so expert are the Indians that they will cut up a Cow and in a very few places will you see where the knife has been used at all, they sever the muscels.—These pieces are cut so as easily to be packed on the horse, and when the Buf^o^ is at a distance none of the bones are brought home, being too heavy and unprofitable to carry far, but when near, or even at a good distance when Buf^o^ is scarce every thing is brought home to the very horns, and they find a use for every thing. The Sinews they make use of for sewing purposes, are not taken as I used to think, and I suppose you also, from the legs, but from the back between the "deeprise" and the "filet" as we term the pieces and in every sirloin you eat you have a p^s^ of the sinew. It is quite flat, about 2 to 3 inches broad and when dried is easily torn into threads and is well adapted for sewing skin or any strong stuff. An Indian puts a whole Cow on one horse, gets on the top of the load himself and jogs on homeward rejoicing. for an Indian

[10]See letter 8.

[11]Piece.

always sings when he has the prospects of a good belly full, and he can eat a few I assure you,—I never once saw an Indian refuse to eat when meat is offered to him and I have known him to go to 10 feasts within 2 hours,—he invariably cleans the dish too, but then poor devil he can do for 10 days without eating at all or complaining very much. The bones are pounded fine something like, your manure at home and then boiled in water.—A rich grease rises on the surface, and this is carefully collected and put in bladders. It is much prized here, and is superior to our home butter. The Skin is only valuable for Robe making in Winter, say from the end of September to the 15th of March. When the Cow is full grown the skin is cut up the back as well as the belly and thus raised in 2 ps, not only that it may be the more easily packed on the horse, but it is very inconvenient and takes a much longer time to dress it when whole. The first step in dressing is to stretch it tight on a frame, then the flesh is taken off very clean with a tool commonly made out of an old Gun barrel and resembles a gouge groved. The skin is then allowed to dry on the frame, when it is taken off and scraped to the proper thickness with an instrument resembling the first, but smooth in the edge. It is then softened with a mixture of the brains, a little of the above mentioned grease, and some water, and it lays this way for a day and night. Then when quite soft, it is rubbed between the hands and "see sawed" on a rough cord made of sinew, and occasionally stretch[ed] on the frame and scraped with a ps of tin, and these processes are continued till it becomes quite dry and soft, when you have the Robe completed all but the sewing up the back. Some of the Robes are very prettily garnished with Beads and Porcupine Quill others painted but these are chiefly for the Indians own use and so highly prized by them that they are seldom traded until a good deal worn. It—the Robe—makes a most comfortable and warm hap,[12] and I only wish I could send you one to use in your Journeying North South East and West, and I may be able to do this sometime or other. Should Mr Palliser again come in the country or anyone so circumstanced, you will have the best Robe the country affords should it even cost me my horse, and I have known as much as 2 horses given for a Robe. There are a few a very very few White Bufo in the country and for their Robes you can almost get any price from the Indians as it goes down with them

[12] A comforter or quilt.

as great "Medicine" and keeps off the devil most wonderfully. One about a century old was sent me from above this spring to trade, it was torn and all rotten and full of holes, but for it I got 15 prime new Buf° Robes.[13]

"Further News from the Field"
—July 18th 1849!

A messenger arrived Yesterday from the Rees, with the glorious news that the opposition Boat had arrived there and that ours might be expected daily that there was sickness on board—but that the half of St. Louis as well as the half of the Steam Boats had been burned,[14] which was the only cause of the S. Boats being so long. In the evening the opposition Boat arrived here. From these messengers we learn that the Sioux had 5 men killed and 25 wounded, most of them dangerously and that they blame the Canon for all this.[15] They have resolved to [obscured by sealing wax] up the Fort as well as the Village, and for this purpose are mustering 2000 strong and will be here again in a few days. They have long since determined and try to do both these things long since, but have been unable and will remain unable I think unless we are taken by surprise throughout the night, but to prevent this I have mounted a night guard in both Bastions.[16] Just think of it, Eben,—We muster only 8 whites, 1 old Negro, and 1 Half=Breed, in all 10, and of this number I have to confess most are cowards, yet do some of the right ones, feel perfectly sure of being able to maintain the Fort against 2000 Indians! Yet do the Indians call the Whites, Women, Fish everything but brave.

. . . I feel too excited however with the news of the near approach of the Steam Boat to write any more at present, till it arrives, and unless I remain here another year or go below I shall have no time to write [Abram] I fear after its arrival, but he must not feel hurt at that. In the event of my not writing him this time he will be the first

[13]Catlin, *Letters and Notes*, 1:133–34, mentions the Mandan buying a white buffalo robe from the Blackfeet. It is possible this was the robe Dawson received.

[14]The St. Louis waterfront went up in flames on 17 May 1849 when the steamboat *Highlander* caught fire, which quickly spread to other nearby boats. Twenty-three steamboats were destroyed along with adjacent warehouses and some fifteen blocks of the downtown business district. The losses totalled some $6 million.

[15]"From the Yellowstone River," *St. Louis New Era*, 9 August 1849, carried similar numbers.

[16]Fort Berthold, like most AFC posts, had two opposing bastions.

served after Mother the next time. Adieu then for the present Eben. As with the other letters I shall reserve the remaining space of this one to be filled up after arrival of the Steam Boat.

24th July 1849.

Steam Boat arrived 19th Inst. and I am too hurried with one thing and another to do more than close this. . . . referring you to the tails of the other letters and particularly to Alecks[17] for further items ever believe me, your most fond brother.

Andw Dawson

14

Fort Clark U. Mo. R.
14th June 1850

My Dear Mother

The Steam Boat[1] arrived here the 12th Inst. bringing me the following letters being all I have received from home or indeed anywhere else since those pr[2] S Boat in July 1849 which I have already answered. . . .

I like to hear of the receipt of my own letters and I am therefore particular in acknowledging those of others, and I do so in this letter to you, as I am not sure who else I shall be able to write to as I am exceedingly pressed for time.

From your letters I have been relieved from a load of anxiety which has much oppressed me during my lonely winter. . . . My dear Mother, when I received Alexanders Letter last Summer urgently calling on me to return home to you all once again I readily grasped at the thought of it being possible that such a happiness might be nearer in store for me than I had been calculating on. The Boat had only left however when my eyes were opened to the dream.

No, no, this can not be for yet a little while, but wait only a little longer say for 3 years and I promise to pay you a 6 months visit at all

[17]Letter 12.

[1]The *El Paso* captained by John Durack. Cholera claimed six lives on the upriver voyage. Sunder, *Fur Trade*, 125.

[2]Per.

events. Were I to return to home again at present it would be necessary for me to accept of some subordinate situation or other and there dwindle out the balance of my days in a second oblivion, and after the first excitement of my return home was over, there would be nothing but regrets on all sides. Here I feel happy and as independent as the 4 winds of heaven, and tho I have not yet become the Ir. Co.[3] like my good little brother—God bless him—yet I think I can decern about half, at least, of a bright twinkling little star on the horizon of my future. You seem to think me the most flighty and unsettled being possible—sometimes I am digging Gold in California[4] at another meeting with Aleck in New York[5] &c &c and here I have been in reality for the last 2 years within 60 miles of where I am writing to you from, and likely to remain as much longer, or if I should move you will be duly apprised of it, as to effect any change at all I would have to return to the settlement.[6]

You seem also to want to know "my circumstances"[7]—now these are pretty good, and beyond all other such recent beginners in the country. My salary, which has increased yearly, and will continue to do so, I think, is this year equivalent to a little over £200[8] and I have nothing to pay for living. Clothing and other articles of comfort are however very expensive, and as I look to the comfort of the present as well as that of the future I cannot spend less than half of this sum—so it stands thus:

For the present Mr. Carroty Ead[9]	£100: 0: 0
For the future Mr. Old-un[10]	100: 0: 0
	£200: 0: 0

and as affairs will improve the longer I remain I trust you will be relieved from all anxiety as regards "my circumstances" and our good little "Ir. Co." must I think acknowledge he was in error when he said

[3]Senior manager. His brother Aleck was senior manager for a British company and apparently had expressed doubts about his older brother's prospects.

[4]In letters 6 and 13, Dawson mentioned possibly going to California.

[5]Alexander Dawson was living in New York.

[6]This was only true if he left the AFC. The AFC could and would move Dawson at will to another post.

[7]This and the previous paragraph suggest that Dawson's mother continued to express doubts about his ability to get his life on track, doubts that would have stung him.

[8]Equal to about $24,300 today.

[9]Teasing himself a bit.

[10]For retirement.

it was improbable that I could "get along" where I am,—Now the fact is I have long since seen the folly of my ever thinking of returning permanently to you all, unless I can do so and be independent. Now nothing I long for so much as to return and be at rest with you all, as I have resolved to become independant , and if God grant me life and health, I shall be so,—I assure you my own dear Mother, there is little of the boy left in your Son now, things appear now in there true light, I think, he is in a right way, and never was he possed[11] of better health or more energy. But I tire even you my fond Mother with all this egotism which I only have indulged in in the hopes of relieving you from all anxiety on my account. M[r]. Desautels the party in charge of this Fort leaves for the first time for 15 years on a visit to his [obscured by wax seal] and during his absence I remain in charge. But I shall anxiously look for his return in October next as he is the most agreeable companion, and the best friend I have on this side of the Atlantic. During the past Winter I was resident in the Winter Village about 10 miles from the Fort trading with the Ind[s][12] and I there wrote some few letters for home, but the express passed down earlier than usual and did not call at my post so that I burned the letters.[13] This then is the only letter you will have received from me since that of July 1849—and I am sorry it should be so short.[14] But instead of commencing on the 1st of May as I did last year I put it of[f] till I should receive your letters. . . . Write to me on receipt and I may receive your letter p[r]. Mr. Desautels in October.[15] In December I shall write you as usual, and expect a much longer letter—and now my dear Mother good bye God bless you and that God may still reunite us on earth is the sincerest prayer of your fondest Son

And[w] Dawson

(I have reopened this Letter to ask you if you could not manage to send me, your portrait in Daguerreotype? Now that Aleck is in N.Y. probably,—I think you might arrange it, and it would be a great prize to me. I have asked Aleck for his.)

---

[11]Probably "possessed."

[12]Arikara.

[13]Dawson later shared observations of the Arikara with Edwin Denig, who was preparing culture studies that eventually were published as *Five Indian Tribes*.

[14]This letter marks an interesting shift in Dawson's letters. Having assumed a more responsible position, his letters became shorter. Also, apparently with more access to paper, he abandons the cross-hatched, space-saving style of earlier letters.

[15]Dawson assumed Desautel would stop at AFC headquarters in St. Louis on his return.

15

Fort Clark U. Mo. R.
15th June 1850.

My Dear Abram

Last Summer if I remember right you were the only one of "the circle" I did not write to and this Summer, the other day you are the only one I received 2 letters from. This certainly is reaping where I had not sown, and were I not to write you at this time I would indeed be unhappy for 6 months to come, the next period of my writing home. Your long gossip about family matters my dear fellow will afford me enjoyment for 6 months to come and as all seems well and happy and just as my most sanguine wishes would have them it has made me infinitely happy too. . . . I have been happier and more contented this year than any previous one since my boyhood,—and the one I have just entered on,—we date our years here not from 1st January, but from arrival of Steam Boat,[1] promises to be even happier and more contented,—one grand thing at least to start with is an increase in my Salary—were I to tell you how I stand in the opinion of those who know me in the country it would be savouring a little too much of egotism you would think but let this little hint suffice you, that I think I shall yet shine a little in the world, and that my lustre is to be gathered from this barren soil. Now that I have become accustomed to the ways of the Country I prefer the life here to that of the settlements, but I would be far from advising any one to do as I have done—you know my tastes have ever been for adventure and daring and here I have them fully gratified, but I know that 9 in 10, would not get along here as I have done and feel confident of doing, but on the other hand the same individuals might far surpass me in another field.

Whilst on this subject my dear Chap let me advise you however not to think of ever leaving your native land.

Work hard there and be economical and you have a far better chance of attaining to affluence than by imigrating, I declare Abram I do think if I had remained at home, and worked ½ so hard as I have done since leaving it,[2] I would have been rolling about in my carriage by this time,[3] but then work, work, is my element, and I feel as

[1]The steamboats usually reached the upriver posts around mid-June.

[2]This is Dawson's first admission that his own failings may have caused his previous employment troubles.

[3]A symbol of wealth.

active and as full of energy as a little cricket. By remaining at home too, you are saved the almost unsupportable sacrifice of feelings on being sundered from all those friends you love so dearly, this state of feelings I am only just now getting relieved a little from tho it is now 6 long years since I left you all—still yet many is the solitary communings I have with you all.

I am unable to write you a very long letter at this time but take the will for the deed. In the winter budget I shall give you a much longer screed, and a little more of this countrys incidents. . . .

And now Abram I bid you farewell. God bless you my good fellow and rest ever assured of the love and affection of your sincerely attached brother.

And^{w} Dawson

16

Fort Clark U. M. R.
8th January 1852.

My Dear Mother,

I have first and foremost to give you and not only you, but one and all at home a good scold and then for the news of myself. How very very unkind it is for you to neglect me so very much.

On the 28th May 1851 I received Ebens letter of 2nd March 1851 and Alexanders of the 6th of same month and these 2 letters are the only ones I have received from home in a period of <u>two years</u>. Now is this kind I ask you? I do begin to think the old saying "out of sight &c" holds good with you also but oh how untrue it is with myself for not a day I may not say not an hour, but I am thinking of some of you at home still very dear, oh! how dear to me at least. Did you only know how very desolate I do feel when an express arrives,—we have but three in the year—and find no letters for me from home. I am sure you would think more of me and show it by writing oftner. Do again let me entreat you to write me if not all at once at least one at a time say in the Months of March July & November and these letters would reach me at different intervals throughout the year. This would be very little trouble for you, say one letter from each of you in two years for I still reckon on many friends at home, and this if regularly fulfilled would amply compensate me for the 10 or 12 Letters

I annually write home.[1] I have but two opportunities in the year of writing home, in Summer by the Steam Boat, and in Winter by an express which is annually sent below with our requisition for goods for the ensuing year and I never omit writing some 4 5 or 6 letters home by these opportunities. So far our express has not yet arrived from above but I write this in anticipation of its not being long.

What a dreadful life of anxiety and trouble I have spent since I last wrote you[2] July 1851![3]—arrising from the Cholera having at length visited these poor ignorant dogs. This disease broke out about 25th August and as the S. Boat[4] left for below 18th July I cannot think we[5] are the cause of bringing this scourge in the Country, yet the Indians blame us for it and seem thoroughly convinced it was our desire to kill them. Not one of the whites either having died, although we all had the disease seems to strengthen them in their opinion, and the result of all has been inumerable attempts to kill any one of us, but in particular myself. Now for myself I had never any fear, for with due caution, or to use a Yankeeism having your eye skined,[6] no 10 Indians will attack a white man, but on the other hand 1 Indian will kill 10 men if he can manage it without danger to himself. The result of all our troubles so far has been only one man shot in 2 places and 2 horses shot, all of which however have recovered, and now they seem inclined to let us alone so far as killing is concerned but our difficulties in trade will yet be immense. You are aware there is one other Company opposed to ours in the Country, and would you suppose that through them my troubles have been multiplied 10 fold.[7]

Thinking to escape trouble themselves and also to turn the trade on their side, they told the Indians they were well aware it was me that had killed them and that I would kill many more of them unless they killed me before next Spring, but still I am alive nor need you entertain any fear of these Indians ever being the cause of my death. Still such conduct is most cowardly and mean on the part of an opposition and by this express I shall report all to the authorities below, so that another year I think I shall be deprived of the pleasure of such

[1]Dawson must be alluding to letters written to friends as well as family.
[2]The stress of the previous six months may have contributed to this harsh beginning.
[3]None of Dawson's 1851 letters have survived. For more on this cholera outbreak, see chapter 6. Also see Sunder, *Fur Trade*, 135–36.
[4]The *St. Ange*.
[5]The American Fur Company.
[6]To be careful, to remain vigilant.
[7]Harvey, Primeau and Company.

an opposition. Were it an [obscured by sealing wax] Government we were under I would feel certain such would be the result, but this America!—pooh—

My former letters, those of July 1851 apprised you of how well I was getting along and since then there has been no change in my affairs, and my life since then with the exception of this sickness has been entirely with out incident. In fact this life of an Indian trader is a most monotinous one, still to me at least it has its pleasures and I feel contented and happy in all things excepting in regard to my long separation from you, but the time I have set aside to visit you all is fast running away. Recollect in my last letters I said in 5 years now it is only 4½ years, and at the end of that time tho' I cannot promise to come home to you all for good, I can at least promise to come home for a good long time say a 10 months visit and in that time what with Indian dances, War Songs &c &c I have no doubt you will feel perfectly agreeable to your Indian son making his retreat once more to his far off wilds. . . . About the Scotts[8] write me too for, tho' I cannot esteem any one of them yet I like to know how they are doing. They are a poor proud pack like many more in Scotland, hearts they have but as callous as a piece of baked clay—a brick—and their life entirely taken up in making appearances—had I always been amongst them of course I would have been a victim, but I have travelled and my eyes are opened.

But now adieu—I write you a very short letter but then I write to all the others. God bless you—

Your truly affectionate Son
Andw Dawson

17

Fort Clark
22nd January 1852.

My Dear Aleck

A few days since I wrote to our good old worthy Mother, and now for yourself, not that you are next on my list, for others I should write to before you, but as I shall now and henceforth, until you further instruct me, send all my letters for home to you through your house

[8]Dawson's maternal relatives.

in New York,[1] it is necessary for me as a matter of course to prepare an envelope for the "Budget"[2] and I do not approve of sending blank paper such a distance. . . .

For myself, my housebuilding and my other projects have been all knocked on the head since I wrote you, my Indians having been visited by the Cholera and at least a fourth of them carried off, but my letter to Mother will inform you of all this and of my troubles arrising therefrom. Now I think these Indians will move somewhere else in Summer and as I shall have to move with them my genius for housebuilding must be exercised in another field. I wish you were with me to revise my plan of a Fort,[3] as it is, should it be carried out I think I must send the plan home,—it may interest you, not only as being the production of your absent brother, but as being his residence in exile.

In the morning I commenced this, and see it is now evening and I have got only thus far, with my letter, and you may ask what have I been about since? As it may interest you to know, and give you some little knowledge of our life here I shall tell you. Having come to a fine pause as I thought at the word exile, (read again and judge)—I filled my pipe, lighted it and took a strole out at the Gate to cogitate upon other matter where with to bespatter this "envelope"—when what do I behold!—a fine band of Cows[4] on the other side of the river, distant only about 2 miles. Now at such an occurrence as this every thing else, with me at least is overlooked. I ran in and seizing my good old faithful friend "Joe" who I keep at all times ready for me, away I went it on foot, leaving it to the Clerk and a man to saddle up and bring the horses. The ground was very favorable for me "approaching," and by the time the horses arrived I had killed two fine fat Cows and an Antelope, the meat and skins of all of which are now snuggly stowed away in my meat house, excepting a goodly portion of the "tit bits"[5] the hunters reward, and which are already consumed, if not by the hunter alone, he at least does not complain. And now I feel tired sleepy and comfortable and inclined to take it easy—so good night for the present.

And now I have rested I must tell you of my New Years excursion,

[1]His office.

[2]Bundle of letters.

[3]Hewitt, *Journal of Rudolph Friederich Kurz*, 104: "Dorson [Dawson], the bourgeois at Fort Clarke, is trying to get together here [Fort Berthold] the necessary tools for some building he wishes to do."

[4]Buffalo.

[5]Liver, kidneys, and tongue.

it may serve as a little contrast to the account you give me of that little fellow the "I^r. C^o."[6] travelling about in first class Coaches and dine-ing at first rate Hotels. I cannot forget that little p^s[7] egotism Aleck. Well on the 29th ult^o. long before day light, having bedecked my good "American"[8] with all the finery of the Country away I went it at a good pace I assure you,—tho not quite at first class carriage rate, but then the horse was my own and so might I say was the road my man following mounted on a mule, at quite a respectful distance, not out of respect however, we have not much of that with us here, and feel its want very little—but for convenience as I only knew the way, and the Snow being deep I broke the way for him. It was cold cold however, you cannot know how very cold we have it sometimes in this country, so we had to dismount and take the rest of the journey on foot, and the Snow being nearly 20 Inches deep it was long after Sun down when we got to "Governor"[9] Kipps tho the distance is only about 35 miles. Arrived there Aleck, we soaked our wearied day in a Cup of Strong Coffee. Coffee is an expensive luxury in this Country more so than Champagne is to you, yet nowhere do I think is it ever drunk as strong. It & Tobacco however are our only luxuries, and you will therefore excuse us the extravagance. Our New Years fare was such as none of your grand Hotels can boast of and I question much if that all dreaded personage the Duke of Humbugs would not have envied us our feastings, but we had one great want—Potatoes—I have not tasted a Potatoe Aleck for these four years and you cannot know how I do long now and then for them, M^r. Kipp has 1 Bshl stowed away and I bothered him much to tap his "Cash"[10] but he was firm—they are for seed, and he said wisely "perhaps next New Years day we may eat a few if the crop does not fail." Our return home was similar to our going only this time we had to walk all the way our horse and mule being heavily laden with fine fat Pork a present for me from the "Governor."

How is it Aleck I got no News Papers from you by the Steam Boat last year. I think I wrote you your Papers never came to hand but I believe all you have ever sent I have received, tho they are generally delayed a good deal by the Clerks below. They are a great treat, not

---

[6]Senior manager, Aleck Dawson's position.

[7]Piece.

[8]A horse brought up from the States as opposed to an "Indian" horse native to the country.

[9]James Kipp. "Governor" is purely an honorific.

[10]Cache.

only to me, but all so do not forget a big budget this time. That box also you sent me I have never heard anything of. Has it really been sent. And here Aleck the Envelope is full enough and I must now think of writing some thing to put inside so God bless you my good little fellow and ever believe me to be your most affec: Brother.

And^w Dawson

February 12th

A day or two after writing this letter I was visited by two large bands of Sioux Indians who have engaged all my attention every since till yesterday when much to my relief the last of them got off and left me wearied indeed.

Today our express has arrived from above. . . . My whole time tonight and tomorrow will be taken up with Company business. Let this and Mothers letters however go the rounds and let each think they are addressed to them, for one and all of you are to me equally dear. By the express I receive a letter from a fellow Scotchman[11] from above who says he will pass here in Spring on his way to visit old Scotland. By him I shall write again and shall send some little thing as a remembrance.

Adieu once more
fondly yours
And^w

18

F^t. Clark U. M. R.
26th April 1852.

My Dear Aleck

I wrote you by the winter "Express" that I expected a friend would be here about this time from F^t. Union, on his way to Scotland and that by him I would send you a few little things from this Country as a remembrance of your exiled brother.[1]

Well today he has arrived and today left taking a little bundle for you but he has no letter, not even a line and I had only time to scratch down your address in Liverpool. I hope you will receive the bundle

[11] Robert Morgan, stationed at Fort Union.
[1] Letter 17.

and more than all, that you will see the bearer thereof Robert Morgan as he is to return here again, possibly in fall, and it will be such a pleasure to me to have a talk with one who has so recently been with you all. Of Morgan I do not know anything further than that he came in this country along with Mr. Laidlaw and myself,[2] and he it was that got lost and almost died of starvation and cold when with me in my first years journeyings.[3] Since then I have never met with him till today, but I understand he has been stationed all the time at Fort Union having charge of the men, and thus altho he has not so far got on quite so well as your humble servant he may be the more worthy of the two. We have occasionally corresponded since being in the Country, and I pray show him every attention.

The reason of my being unprepared with a letter for him, is that nearly since I wrote you last, I have had my woman of all works hard at work making a fine Coat for you, but she has been sadly interrupted and in the intervals, has made 37 other kinds of Coats[4] for the trade and had only yesterday finished garnishing the pieces for your Coat when an opposition man arrived with the news that our Mr. Culbertson and party would be here in two days, much too short a time to finish the Coat, so I gave that up as a hopeless job and this morning bundled up the few other things I had in readiness for you intending to write as I now do tonight when in stepped Mr. C. before his time and found me busy marking your bundle and you will see I had not even time to finish that, having only made the A.M. The party's[5] stay was not over 10 minutes the day being very calm and favorable for water travelling and their desire being to beat the opposition man who arrived late last night and started early this morning. I now write these particulars then, in the hopes of by sending this by the Mackinaws[6] it may reach you before my letters by the Steam Boat, and whilst Morgan is still on the other side of the Atlantic. I shall enclose it to your house in New York[7] and at the same time take the opportunity of apologising to them for the trouble I now, have formerly and may still continue to give them in this respect.[8]

---

[2]See Letters 3, 4, and 5.

[3]See Letter 6.

[4]Buffalo robes.

[5]Culbertson, Cadotte, Dolores, Kurz, and Morgan.

[6]Flat-bottomed wooden boats named by Canadian fur traders after Mackinac Island.

[7]Aleck's New York employer.

[8]By sending letters through them to his family.

Should you not have seen Morgan nor have received the things I send before this, you must write to him at his mothers—"M^{rs}. Morgan, High Street Dunfermline Fife Shire, and should you see him after receiving this tell him he will find a letter from me for him lying in the Office in S^{t}. Louis.

The bundle I send you contains:

1 Fine painted Robe.
1 Indian Stone Pipe & Stem & Primer
1 " Tobacco Pouch full of Ind.: weed mixt
1 " Knife Scabberd
2 P^{r}. " Mocassins
6 Dried Salted Buf^{o}. Tongues.

The Robe is the Skin of a Buf^{o} killed in winter by myself and is intended for Mother, she will find it a warm hap for winter though a somewhat singular one. The other things do as you think best with them but let all have a taste of the Tongues. Boil well and cut cold, and you will declare them the sweetest morsel you ever eat. They never reach England, in fact are all bought up in S^{t}. Louis at $6 p doz.[9] Possibly they may be the Tog^{s}. of Buf^{o}. killed by myself but I cannot swear to this, they are all however salted under my inspection.

The Pipe I send is one recently used by the Gros Ventres on their making peace for the thousandth time with the false Sioux. Morgan will instruct you how to smoke &c—The weed that I send is what the Ind^{s}. smoke, a mixture of the inner bark of the Red Wilow and Tobacco and I think you will rather like it. The painting on the Robe will be Greek to you but every line has its meaning to an Ind: and is as plain perhaps more so to him than this Letter to you, but I cannot go into any particulars about it in a letter and when we meet I shall read it to you in part, some I do not know myself. And now my dear little laddie any say is said for the present. Kindest love to Mother and all others. God bless and prosper you dear Aleck.

Your very fond brother
And^{w} Dawson

At another time I will send your Coat whether it ever reach or not.

[9]Thousands of salted buffalo tongues were shipped annually to St. Louis.

19

Fort Clark
6th July 1852.

My Dear Mother

Our Steam Boat[1] arrived here on the 2nd Inst. bringing me Ebens Alecks and your Letters of March last, and these are all I have received from home since May 1851. I have just finished reading them all for the third time and just finished drying my eyes and acting the big baby for the same number of times and sit down to reply to them all and first and foremost to your own worthy self. How thankful do I feel to Providence that my own most immediate relations are all still to the fore, are all still improving in worldly wealth and that the prospect is thus still held out to me that we may all meet once again. In fact my own dear Parent I only live for this, were such a prospect taken from me then would I not only be glad to die but would seek death. When I wrote you in Summer last[2] I hinted that it was most likely I should soon alter my way of life and was thinking of taking unto myself a wife, and I only waited to hear what you would all say before I wrote you more on the subject. Now I thank God your opinions coincide with my own on the subject and that without a priest marriage in my own circumstances can be as sacredly and as honorably performed as amongst you all in Gods most holy Sanctuary. You will now know then that I am married! and feel happy indeed, but much happier in being able to write to you about it, for it is a long time since it took place, in the end of July 1851 shortly after the Steam Boat[3] left. My wife is the boast of all the Country, not for good looks but for worth and I assure you though an Indian is well worthy of a place by your fireside, where she may be sometime or other, the only thing awkward would be her backwardness in speaking our language for though she is nearly perfectly conversant with it she will talk to no one but myself and this only when alone.

In winter I gave her many lessons in reading and have now received a supply of rudimental Books and shall I hope make some further progress in the ensuing winter, but it is a hard job, and often do I

[1]The *Banner State*.

[2]The 1851 letters are missing.

[3]The *St. Ange*.

wish I had brother in law Ralph with me to lend a help.[4] She is widow to my much lamented friend Joseph Desautels[5] who preceeded me in the charge of this Fort, and by him had two little daughters only one of whom is now living. She[6] is only 19—don't feel shocked—her Mother a half breed and much like yourself in age and appearance lives with us. And now Mother what do you think of me. Don't feel offended at my not mentioning this to you by our winters express.

When I first came in the Country I wrote you about a little boy Son of Andrew Potts being here but you never further attended to the subject and I concluded it was offensive and that it might also be so in my own case, and had I not found out differently I should never again have alluded to the matter.[7] I had said to myself should their views of the subject be different from mine this will not satisfy me I have done wrong, tho as I seek their happiness I shall conceal it even at the risk of my own and wifes happiness, but now all is said. I have no family so far but there is every prospect I shall have about August. Mr. Desautels Mother resident in Montreal regularly correspond and she seems anxious for me to send, her little grand-child to her. She has already a child of Mr. Desautels with her by a former wife deceased,—It is probable however on account of the Mother[8] that I shall not send the child so far away, but attend to its education myself, as Mr. Desautels left me money for this purpose.[9]

About myself I get on better far than even I anticipated. When I succeeded to the management of this place I thought I should remain at a stand still, till becoming a partner in the Company say in some 10 or 15 years hence if ever. But it seems not so. This year the partners without a hint to me of it increased my salary $200—and gave me a present worth $100 more in the Country. Now I feel almost ashamed of this because this year I have only made half the profit I did last, but they are aware of the reason being with the Indians and not myself.[10]

We had indeed trying times of it last year with the sickness, but

---

[4]Ralph Drummond, headmaster at Kirkcudbright Grammar School, married Dawson's sister, Christian.

[5]Abel, *Chardon's Journal*, 248–49, nn. 195, 201, and 203, mentions Desautel, who was the Fort McKenzie clerk at the time of the massacre. He died on 15 November 1850 while returning from visiting his family in Montreal.

[6]Dawson's new wife.

[7]Jerry Potts now lived with Dawson at Fort Clark.

[8]Dawson's wife.

[9]What ultimately happened to this daughter is not known.

[10]The outbreak of cholera and the subsequent hostilities engendered dampened returns.

not quite so bad as you may have seen stated in the papers. I understand they had it reported that I and all the men were killed and the Fort and goods destroyed, but I feel no fear of its ever coming to this pass.[11] Even were I entirely alone in the Fort. I have an ugly looking Canon and it only requires me to show his nose out of a port hole to scare away 10000 such cowardly devils.[12] I will conclude—as I shall write to Eben & Aleck also at this time—both of whose letters you will also of course peruse—Abram did not write me at this time and consequently I pass him over and Christian also, but if they will take up the pen immediately on this coming to hand so that I receive their letters in fall, they shall receive my winter budget. God bless you my dear Mother and continue to always think of your absent and oh how very very affectionate Son

And[w] Dawson

20

Fort Clark U.M.R.
6th July 1852.

My Dear Eben

God bless you my dear brother. Say anything to me and it would not give offence for well do I know the intention is otherwise, and how therefore could I become offended when you talk so much in accordance with my own desire. That I have sent nothing[1] to our worthy Mother since I left is the only thing which troubles me in my daily thinking of you, but it is not from want of desire or ability. (I have God be praised now plenty and to spare) but from dread it is that I have never sent. I live with a curious people and hear this—I left my Gun case to be sent up in this Country after me, but it never came or is it now to be heard of. A friend[2] sent me a fine horse from

[11]An extended search of St. Louis papers failed to turn up such an article.

[12]Hewitt, *Journal of Rudolph Friederich Kurz*, 167: "October 8 (1851): An Assiniboin to-day brought the first news I have received from Fort Berthold since I left. Arikara [at Fort Clark] are still dying, he says, like flies under frost. The survivors are in a fury; have razed the block houses of the opposition [Fort Primeau] and stolen their goods; Dorson [Dawson] found it necessary to bring into action his great guns in order to protect himself from the same fate. If this be true, Dorson has no further prospect of trading with the Arikara. Nothing is left for him to do but ship his goods to Fort Pierre."

[1]He is referring to not sending money to repay his debts.

[2]John Palliser.

St. Louis through the Company and I have witnesses to say the Company received it but yet they deny all knowledge of it. I sent a dft.[3] for $20 to St. Louis to a friend[4] to purchase me an American Rifle, and my friend says he never got the dft, but I am charged with it. My trunk clothing books & I left behind me to be sent by S. Boat but to this day I have nor can hear anything of it.[5] My very dear friend Jos. Desautels of whose decease I apprised you[6] had some $1000 property with him for his family. I have been able to recover only about $70 of this. He willed to me $1000 for the benefit of his family. I have so far not fingered a Cent of it &c &c &c and add to all this the very heavy loss I met with through a swindler in St. Louis[7] and I am sure my dear Eben you will not blame me for this dread.

I have often desired to visit St. Louis for this very purpose, and so many things begin to accumulate on my hands and my own individual affairs begin to be of such importance trifling yet however that I shall soon have to visit the settlements, probably next year, but I am very desirous of paying Scotland a visit at the same time.

Bear with me yet a while Eben, I know all about it and could almost be sure that the money is not all I desired but it is the effect it would have upon some scabby loafing scoundrels whose name will be nameless.[8] Should I send too late then indeed I should ever blame myself but God forbid this should prove the case. I am as in youth careless of money too much so, but I have said enough of this.

All the money I have lays in the hands of the Company in St. Louis at interest 5 p C^{t}.[9] and I think it right for you to know this, my yearly savings also shall continue to remain with the Company and these vary from $500 @ $800 as the case may be. This year I shall save $700. Should I apply my money which is not likely in the meantime I shall inform you of it and this much I think to trouble you with in the meantime.

In case of my death my papers would show to a fraction how I stand but these papers might probably be destroyed. You will see from my Letter to Aleck[10] that I have sent one fine Robe and a number of

---

[3]Draft.

[4]John Tevis, Dawson's former employer.

[5]Dawson left some possessions in St. Louis and at Laidlaw's home in Liberty, Missouri.

[6]This letter is missing.

[7]His fiancée and her brother swindled Dawson. See Letter 8.

[8]Most likely a reference to his creditors in Scotland.

[9]Percent.

[10]Letter 18.

other things home this Spring by a Mr. Morgan who is to visit you all and if these should ever reach you let me know what duty you pay for them &c I never thought to try to send you anything without such a chance as this but next year whether I visit St. Louis or not I shall send you two or three Robes and some other things through the House in St. Louis and should I be able to open up a channel this way it will be fine fun,—why I shall be asking Mother to knit me a ½ dozen pairs of Socks. I never got the likenesses[11] Aleck promised me and latterly he has said nothing about them?

You will notice all about my marriage in my Letter to Mother. . . . It was the request of my deceased friend Desautels that I should marry his widow and it was also the request of the whole of the partners in the Company that I should marry someone,[12] and latterly it was my own desire. I find it helps me well along with the business and gives me much more influence with the Indians. I have given up all idea of building here for at least another year as the Indians are still unsettled and talk of finally removing from this in fall, when as a matter of course I shall have to follow them.[13]

You talk of Gala[14] and I can now sing a little about Missouri. Fishing has again become pretty much of an amusement with me for tho at first I detested the idea of sitting down on a Stone and going about it like a Cockney[15] but I find it not only a little amuseing but it affords a most acceptable variety to the table. Commonly then you will see me right in front of the Fort every evening with the most unmanageable looking pole stuck before me and I most intently watching the float. By my side sits Kate—(her name is Kuta meaning "yellow" which was changed by my deceased friend into the above)—and her little girl[16] who either sit sowing or singing as she feels inclined, and a little distance off so as not to frighten the fish are dabbling away our two wild Geese, quite tame however and thus do I spend some one or two hours. Quite a family group you will say,—The best night I have made yet was four fish weighing together 37 Pounds and

[11]Daguerreotypes.

[12]Dawson had gone much longer than most traders before taking an Indian wife.

[13]Fort Clark was becoming more and more rundown. Dawson had hoped to construct new buildings, but the Arikara were dissatisfied with the location and planning to move north to be closer to the tribes around Fort Berthold.

[14]Gala Water, twenty-eight miles south of Dalkeith.

[15]Likely a reference to impoverished Cockneys who used sticks found on the shoreline as fishing poles. They would sit on rocks to avoid sinking into the mud of the Thames.

[16]Kuta's daughter by Joseph Desautel.

commonly I catch 5 or 6 but not quite so large say 2 @ 5 lbs the average. Sometimes however I get none at all. They are Cat fish (do you want to make a pun here) and are excellent eating. But I must knock off so as to leave a little in my noddle[17] for Aleck. . . . believe me your most truly attached brother

And^{w} Dawson

21

Fort Clark U.M.R.
6th July 1852.

My Dear Aleck

Read my Letter to Mother and then pause in your lecture on morality. Why one would think we in this "far west" were indeed heathens and devoid of all sense of shame entirely now this is just where you go wrong, for we are indeed so very far west as to have got past a good deal of the imorality and ludeness of the world and become in at least a small measure purified. Now this is a fact. We have so much leisure here for reflection so much time for self accusation that one and all of us seem to ponder on our every action and to choose that path which apparently leads to our own happiness and comfort, and with reflection and prudence this path must invariably be that of honor and rectitude. For example I am married but without the marriage ceremony having been performed, still nevertheless am I married and what is more I am happy.

Happy only that I am so far away from you all. . . . In the evening of the 26th of April I wrote you a letter of explanation but this Letter I had no opportunity of sending but by the Mackinaw Boats which passed here on the 13th June so that, that Letter and this will probably reach you both about the same time if indeed the former ever reaches at all. Do not omit then to write to M^{r}. Morgan immediately on receipt of this, if you have heard nothing from him. He is to be found at his Mothers "M^{rs}. Morgan High Street Dunfermline Fife Shire" but as he intends returning here again in fall his stay in Scotland will not be long, probably he may have left when this reaches you. The Bundle I sent contains a fine Robe killed by myself and

[17]Head.

dressed and painted by my old Mother in Law. An Indian Pipe & Tobacco Pouch full of the weed as smoked by the Indians, two p^r^. Mocassins and some other Garnished work by my wife and Six Salted Buf^o^ Tongues. Next year it is very probable I shall visit S^t^. Louis, but whether or not, I shall run the risk of sending through the House in St. Louis[1] and yours in New York,[2] two more Robes and your Coat &c and even if they do get lost, why, it will not ruin us. This year I have 5 fine Robes but these I promised to parties on board the Boat before I opened your letters, and so very suspicious have I become of the men I am dealing with that until I opened your letters the thought never entered my head of sending anything through them, and when I do send I shall look upon the chance as very small of their ever reaching. Should you see Morgan after you receive this tell him he will find a letter from me for him in the office in S^t^. Louis.

And so you are going to mount a Gig[3] are you? . . . I wish I could send you a pony I have to put in the Gig. it is let me tell you the best little animal in all the Country and so well is it acquainted with the Buf^o^. that I expect you could kill on it yourself your first trial. It was a marriage present from one of my B. in Laws, and can you think Aleck, the poor fellow cried when he gave it to me, oh my comrade says he you will learn to know how I love this horse you will ride it in the big summers and you and my sister will eat the fattest Cow the Antelope also if you desire it is yours &c &c

Now all he said was pretty true and pretty cunning, for the fellow now laughs and boasts how he fooled his comrade the "Big Knife"[4] (your humble servant) out of his fine American Horse.

Still I am contented. The horse I gave was much more valuable in the eyes of an Indian whilst the horse I received is the most valuable in the eyes of the whites and so suits me that I shall never part with it unless indeed you were to pay me a visit. You ask me to keep a Journal and send it to Mother, now keep quiet. This is just exactly what I have done every day since coming in the Country and it has now become so bulky as to be far beyond Mail size. Yet perhaps I will send it to you sometime or other, or perhaps bring it myself. . . . When I have $5000 which is a big capital in Western America, and which I

---

[1]Pierre Chouteau, Jr., & Company.

[2]Aleck's New York employer.

[3]A two-wheeled carriage drawn by one horse.

[4]The Indians called Dawson "Big Knife" because of his sword.

will have perhaps before you think of it. I shall either be a partner in the Company or I shall return to civiliz life for good and there make a spoon or spoil a horn.[5] But until I have $5000 I shall stick to the Buf^{o}. though I may pay you all a visit. Remember me to all who care about me. . . . God bless you.

Your (obscured by wax seal) fond Br.
And^{w} Dawson

22

Fort Clark
12th January 1853

My Dear Abram

Morgan arrived here fresh from the land of Cakes[1] on the 22nd ultimo but brought me no letter, no token that he had seen any of my friends there which made me very unhappy, and I had determined giving you all a fine blowing up. I have just done reading however my last letters from home received in July last from Mother Eben & Aleck and in consequence just done having a fine <u>blubber</u> to myself & feel my mind much altered. I have only to say then if you always write me such feeling and such good letters as these are, I have no reason to complain of a little irregularity now and then, tho I cannot describe to you how sometimes I am disappointed for I have so repeatedly told you all the proper months for writing me. Morgan had determined to see my Mother but thought all the time she was at Dalkeith[2] and he was equally unfortunate in finding Eben but let this all pass as it now cannot be helped, and I am coming myself sometime soon to see you all face to face. Think of it! M^{r}. Culbertson the Agent & principal partner of this Company and myself have engaged to pay a visit to Scotland England Ireland and France in the Summer of <u>1855</u> should we be all spared and so look out. His arrangements will not admit of his going sooner and I have agreed to wait that time. He talks of taking his family—Carriages &c &c along, but as I am waxing old and consequently careful—I have good reason to be

[5]A phrase meaning to either succeed in an enterprise or fail miserably.
[1]Colloquial for Scotland.
[2]Dawson's mother split her time between her children's homes.

so—I shall be careful he bears his own expenses and me mine. At the sametime as Morgan arrived I received a letter from a Mr. Richardson of Phila. stating he had received a parcel from a passenger pr. S. B. Manchester for me, and asking what he shall do with it. I presume this is something you had intended to send by Morgan, but it appears singular Morgan should have arrived by the same Steam Boat and know nothing about it. He tells me Aleck took out his berth for him and pointed it out, but on his coming to take possession he found it occupied and on applying to the Steward was shown the same No. in the fore cabin Aleck having paid £15:15—whereas the berth pointed out by him was only £13:13—this may account for his not bringing the parcel. As it is I doubt now if I shall ever see it, as long before Mr. Richardson can hear from me he may have sold it as the saying is "to pay expenses." but I shall try what I can to recover it. . . . I cannot imagine to myself what kind of a looking fellow you now are grone. I had calculated you were at least 6 ft 5 by this at the rate you were going ahead when I left but this is not the case. Morgan tells me I am the giant still.[3] As for Aleck I cannot form any conjecture of his appearance at all—of nights I frequently paint you all severally to myself but then comes that belly and I am done. My same informant states it to be a respectable belly a gentlemanly belly, but then "bellies" are of such varieties that they must be seen to be realised. It is only in its infancy also and what varieties of shapes it is yet to assume before reaching the "Falstaff"[4] climax is to me most interesting matter for study.[5] To wind up the group with him that is far awa' I have no belly, Abram and for a true picture I refer you to Aleck who drew me to the life in his last letter only he used the Artist's privilege a little too much viz flattery.[6] This is no country for bellies I assure you, though our food is all that I can desire yet the exercise required to procure it is a sure preventative against rotundation. Querry? How fast or how far could a Falstaff travel through a 5 ft Snow. Of all the animal food ever masticated give me

[3]Dawson was well over six feet, taller than his brothers.

[4]Sir John Falstaff appears in three Shakespeare plays. Primarily a comic character, he is quite fat.

[5]Dawson's younger brothers, Abram and Aleck, apparently both had considerable bellies.

[6]Alexander Dawson visited his brother on the upper Missouri and then returned with James to the UK, where the boy attended school. Exactly when is unclear, but this may help fix the date.

the Buf°—nothing in my opinion approaches it, and as for Venison out upon it,—Had his right royal highness the Duke of Humbug eat half as much of it as I have he would quit his praise of it and adopt the more homelier "Mutton." How I sometimes long to taste again one of Mothers giggots[7] notwithstanding the Buf°. This year our life here so far has been without incident. The American government begin now to pay a little attention to this portion of their vast territory and have adopted measures to endeavour to civilise these Indians in some little measure. Amongst other things they have agreed to pay my Indians here in goods $1500—annually so long as they keep peace towards us poor traders and do not molest us in our pursuits—and this fall I paid them their first present.[8] This step of itself will have most beneficial effects as regards the whites here but I much fear that sometime Uncle Sam will fail to fulfil his part of the contract and then will things be worse than ever.[9] Individually in one respect I have been unfortunate in having lost my own horses and those of my Indian connections[10] from sickness 5 in all and I as their chief will have to replace these horses, and this costs money—but then they will give me in return the most of their next years hunt. On the other hand "Kuta" my wife presented me with a fine little Andrew[11] on the 6th of September who is strong and hearty as the daddie would desire and strange to say he has got a black head, with only the slightest possible tinge of the "gamboge"[12] in it. He will make a roarer if he goes on as he does and at present he is a great source of happiness to his delighted papa. . . . The express I expect from above sometime during this Month and am busy getting my papers, business as well as private in order for it. May God Almighty bless and prosper you my dear boy and continue to lend his helping hand as most manifestly he has done to one and all of us and believe me to remain

My Dear Abram
Your fond and affectionate brother
And^w Dawson

---

[7]Boiled leg of mutton.

[8]These conditions resulted from the 1851 Fort Laramie (Horse Creek) Treaty.

[9]Even that year, agreed upon annuities failed to reach some upper Missouri tribes.

[10]Best guess. This word is written over and hard to decipher.

[11]The child's name was James. Whether they changed it later or Dawson was referring to a little version of himself is unclear. It is also possible this was a major slip. Recently, Dawson had fathered a son by a Sioux woman, whom he named Andrew.

[12]Yellow tinge; pigment from a gum resin.

23

Fort Clark
15th January 1853.

My Dear Christian

You will scarcely believe me when I write that to find out whereabouts in all this wide world Kirkcudbright lies I had to refer to Bradshaws Railway Map[1] (the only one I have of the sweet old Isle) for my recollection of places &c even near at home are saddly faded. . . . The Indians have their own notions and ideas about things present past and future, and one is that in whatsoever direction they point the skulls of the Bulls they kill, in that direction they will surely sometime follow,—Now were such a custom to prevail amongst the whites, the Bulls Skull of the Dawsons family would certainly be pointed Southwards. . . .

I would regret much however, had we no tie to the good old place[2] and I do trust Eben will prove a fixture there. . . .[3]

And not only has this change in your locality estranged us a little from each other my dear Tit.—Since your marriage you have become an exceedingly bad correspondent and though it is true my letters to you individually have been very few, yet I regularly write home to some one or other, and a letter to one I consider as a letter to all,—moreover you did not use to be so nice of old for, for one letter I would write you I used to receive some 10. Stir yourself up then, and try and manage to save a little time from family affairs at least once a year to write him who is ever thinking of you. You I think requested I would keep a Journal of incidents occurring &c and promised Mr. Drummond[4] would put it in shape for publication, but you must wait for such a thing till I come home. I have a journal here about big enough for a Cart load but whether or not there is a gleaning of matter in it to interest a public reader will remain for after consideration.

It is to be supposed however that I could communicate to a public much more correct information about the Prairie life manners &c

[1]George Bradshaw published the world's first railway timetables in 1839 in Manchester, England.

[2]Dalkeith.

[3]The first Dawson to live in Dalkeith was James Dawson (c.1749–1815), and the last was Ebenezer Erskine Dawson (1887–1949), the grandson of Dawson's brother, Eben.

[4]Christian's husband's family had an interest in publications.

than some that have attempted it. Just think of it—Dickens visited what we call the Lookingglass prairie—a dry lake near St. Louis 9 miles long, and from that presumes to discourse as from personal observation of the boundless Prairies of North America.[5] I have often laughed at the incident of his visiting that Prarie. A party at his own request was made up to take him there and away they started in "buggies." These are vehicles on 4 wheels and covered but can only accommodate 2 persons, but at every half mile or so the party would stop and the person riding with Dickens descend and another take his place, so that all would have the honor of saying they had ridden in the same buggy with the imortal Boz[6] and much honor they got by it when he came to write about them.

Cap[n]. Maryatt[7] also states that the Indians are all "straight toed" owing to the long grass of the Prairies it being a hard matter to walk through it with the foot at an angle. Now the grass of the prairies in general is not over 4 inches long is very thin and is no impediment at all to walking or running and the reason of the Indians being straight or intoed[8] is their manner of sitting from infancy on the ground. Thus the women sit differently and have their toes crooked differently from the men and of the two the women walk the most through the prairie. Cap[n]. Maryatt must have visited the "bottoms" near Council Bluffs where the grass is over your head when on horseback.[9]

My Letters will have long since informed you how comfortable I am now situated in the Country and of my having taken unto myself a wife. Indeed Christian I am very happy. My Salary is more than I ever expected it to be and more than double my expenditure so that I am now able to lay past something against the winter of life, and to enable me, which is now my only desire to spend it with you all and like Goldsmiths hare to "die at home at last."[10] None but those who

---

[5]Charles Dickens, *American Notes*, 140: "a day was fixed, before my departure, for an expedition to the Looking-Glass Prairie, which is within thirty miles of the town [St. Louis]." Today, near Alhambra, Illinois.

[6]Charles Dickens (1812–70) became a household name after publishing *Sketches by "Boz"* in the 1830s.

[7]Captain Frederick Marryat, R.N., a friend of Dickens, wrote *Diary in America, with Remarks on Its Institutions* (1839).

[8]Pigeon-toed or knock-kneed.

[9]See Letter 4.

[10]Oliver Goldsmith, *The Deserted Village* (1770):

"And, as a hare, whom hounds and horns pursue,
Pants to the place from whence at first she flew,
I still had hopes, my long vexations passed,
Here to return—and die at home at last."

have really experienced it can understand the sacrifice it is to have such dear friends as I have, and to live at such a distance from them. I have stated I am very happy but still I have my sad moments and then "Kuta" cannot get a word out of me either English, French or Indian "ah" she will say "you are again thinking of your Mother &c" and she is right. Kuta presented me on the 6th of September last with a fine little boy, and you cannot think how spoiled the little fellow will be if things go on as they do. It is the first Grand-Son the old woman[11] has ever had and has rendered her perfectly crazey. I have been fortunate in my choice at least all the Country says so and that I have the best family in it,—and to be candid I think they talk right. . . . God bless one and all of you and believe me ever to be your most fond Br.

Andw Dawson

24

Fort Clark U.M.R.
18th January 1853.

My Dear Mother

Now that I have leisurely perused for I daresay the hundredth time your last letter to me what a fund do I find it to contain for serious reflection how thankful should we all be for the Almightys goodness manifestly displayed towards you and your family. Some who I left surrounded by all the comforts this passing world affords, I find pennyless and worse, whereas we that were pennyless have become though not affluent at least comfortable and that is better than great riches. . . .

This is a most remarkable healthy country to live in and it is very rarely one of us have a complaint, Still we have our deaths also and these are generally most melancholy. A Mr Bruguiere[1] paid his relations in Montreal a visit this Summer for the first time in 17 years and on his return to the country, died in the Prairie with only Morgan[2] and another man with him. How was he interred? The only impliments the party had were their hunting knives and the ground was frozen to the depth of 4 feet, so they wrapt the body in a lodge skin

---

[11] Kuta's mother.

[1] Jacques Bruguière.

[2] Robert Morgan.

and put it on a tree to preserve it from the wolves,[3] and there he sleeps on his great sleep doubtless as quietly as in a marble sepulchure but still there is something distressing in such a funeral particularly to the feelings of the relatives. This is the third death, under similar circumstances since I have been in the Country. My good old friend Mr Laidlaw is now also no more. He died at his home of Cholera in the fall of 1851 and it is strange I heard nothing of it until last August. I wrote the good old man by the Steam Boat[4] last year, long after his death. Although very wealthy at one time he died "without effects" and has left a large family very destitute.[5] I wrote you some time or other that my trunk was in his house and tho it contained clothing &c of some considerable value that portion of my property had long since ceased to be a matter of any interest to me as I am aware the Moths must have long since appropriated it to themselves but my writing desk,—you will know it was my fathers—is also there, and I am a good deal anxious about it. I shall pay someone by the Steam Boat to go and try and secure it, for me, and to place in the Companys hands in St. Louis. It was intention to have visited St. Louis myself this ensuing Summer but my plans have been altered. . . . And I am again coming home to see you all? "heigh ho"! What a feeling this love of home is, to those in exile. Even at so short a distance as Edinburgh is how I used to long for my Saturdays walk,[6] my dinner ready waiting for me as I would most punctually step in at 3 Oclock, is still fresh before me & a thousand other things. Then in Warrington a short time after my unfortunate visit to that place I threw a woman a half crown, who was grinding away at "Sweet Home" on a barrel organ before my window. I had often a visit from the same personage but she did not know the "open system"—she would try to open my heart with all kinds of funny tunes, but she got badly remunerated as she never again tried me on "Sweet home." In St. Louis also I had my adventure. A poor widow Scotchwoman was referred to me for assistance as being a Countryman but she did not know my name. Where are you from was my first question? From Dalkeith Sir. Here I had slight palpitation but suspected imposture so continued my questioning. Was

[3]Mimicking Indian tree burials.

[4]*St. Ange.*

[5]William Laidlaw, age fifty-five, died bankrupt on 10 October 1851. His farm was sold in 1850 and his effects in 1851 to pay creditors. Laidlaw's Will and Testament, Clay County Archives and Historical Library, Liberty, Missouri.

[6]Dawson walked seven miles to Dalkeith every weekend while living in Edinburgh.

your husband from there also—"yes and we were married there" did he learn any trade? "Yes he served an apprenticeship in Dalkeith." Here considerable interest—With whom? "with Mr Dawson." Here palpitations distinctly audible and I could scarcely ask what as? "A Brushmaker" was her prompt answer.[7] Palpitations not very distinct. Did you know any other Dawsons there? "I know widow Dawson Sir." Here I could question no further, the poor woman had said enough for me and I dismissed her with $5.

And in this Country I could strip my Coat to help a countryman, and if from Dalkeith the Pants and Shirt might follow the Coat and me stand alone a beautiful (?)[8] representation of our forefather in the garden.[9] Quite an interesting spectacle I hear you say but doubtless not very comfortable in winter.

"Kuta"—I have abolished the name of Kate, for tho it is pretty enough yet there is something snappish wiry, frosty, truly disagreeable to my feelings associated with it that I never wish to hear it mentioned,—has been working hard in her own way all winter at a Coat for Aleck and will have it finished in time for me to send off as I promised by the Steam Boat,—I also intend to send home two Robes which may surpass the last one. Should these reach you we will then have a little road opened between us, and I look forward with delight to receiving innumerable little boxes from home filled with all manner of little things which a mother only knows the use of and how to pack away. But seriously it would please me and Kuta also I know were you to send her some little thing. I had a Coat already made for Aleck, but parted with it to a Gentleman on board the Steam Boat.

Last year I had a very uneasy time of it here and I now must confess a very dangerous one on account of the sickness, but the Indians have now got somewhat tranquil and attend better to their business—Robe making—though at best they are lazy dogs. Last year I had to give away many things for nothing to keep them anyways within bounds, and then they made but very few Robes, the result of all which was a very poor trade on my part, and the profit a most inadequate one, but happily the Company appreciated all the circumstances, and instead of blame as I fully expected, I was highly

---

[7] *Old Dalkeith Industries* mentions a brush-making factory, James Dawson & Co., founded in 1779. These Dawsons were not related.

[8] Question mark in original.

[9] Apparently referring to Adam in the Garden of Eden.

commended. This year however things go on smoothly and well and I anticipate a big trade and a most profitable one. Buf^o^ are in Millions close in the neighbourhood of their two Camps, and though the Indians do not go after them so often as I would like it yet they are making a few Robes, and I shall get at least 9/10ths of them.

You are aware that since I have been in the Country there has been an opposition Company trading all the time, but this has become such a poor affair as scarce to deserve the name of opposition. Last Summer they were unable to bring up any Steam Boat, and have now consequently no goods or at least no desirable ones.[10] In winter these Indians separate into two Camps and station themselves in some of the points of the Missouri where it is warmer—wood plenty and near—and where they expect most Buf^o^. In each of these Camps I have a trader whose principal business is to trade Tongues and Meat and say some 10 packs of Robes each,[11]—but the chief business is made here in March April and May when the Indians return and drop their Robes in the Summer Village. All the other nations except the "Gros Ventres"—by the way I do not know how they can have got this name[12] for you will see from my Letter to Abram it is only you people at home that have bellies—dress their Robes as they get them, and the reason is plain,—they have no settled place of residence like the Rees and Gros Ventres, who both raise Corn—but are continually wandering about in search of Buf^o^ and to carry their Robes about with them would require many more horses than they have. We number only 4 Scotchmen in the Country and with the exception of Morgan are all in charge of posts or Forts being the only 3 Clerks in the country so honored.[13] The other Forts being in charge of partners.

---

[10]Harvey, Primeau and Company's 1851 returns were mediocre. By January 1852, the company was rumored to be out of trade goods and heavily in debt. Within a few weeks, they had suspended payments, and the AFC believed they might be on their last legs. In late June, Joseph Sire informed Pierre Chouteau that the opposition still had made no preparations to outfit their upriver posts. Finally, in late July, Harvey renewed their trading license and headed upriver with fewer supplies and fewer employees. Sunder, *Fur Trade*, 144–45.

[11]One hundred robes.

[12]Early French explorers saw the Hidatsa rubbing their bellies to indicate hunger and misinterpreted that as big bellies.

[13]Despite extensive research, the authors cannot positively identify the other two Scottish clerks to whom Dawson refers. Dawson's inclusion of "posts" raises the possibility that he was including temporary establishments from which there are no surviving records. We could find no other reference to an August 1852 gathering at Fort Berthold. Our best guess is that he might have been referring to Charles Morgan, mentioned by Kurz and about whom little was found, and the opposition trader mentioned in Letter 7, since his reference is not limited to AFC employees.

Last August we contrived all 3 to assemble at Fort Berthold. Morgan you know was absent—and as one of the party had returned from the settlements by the Steam Boat, and had secured a proper quantity of grog—a very rare thing in this country we had 3 days and 3 nights of most blissful riot but you must not think the worse of us for this, we were totally reasonable notwithstanding, and the health of one and all at home were twenty times drunk,[14] and every time I will vouch with much more sincerity than is to be found round your Mahogany boards.[15] Note—none of us fell under the table as we took the precaution of spreading our Cloth upon the floor! So much for Scotia[16] and her Sons. This winter I have been so situated as to be unable to leave the Fort for any length of time and until yesterday have killed no Buf° though they have for a long time past been in sight of the Fort at a little distance. Yesterday however—this is now the 22nd—two lost Cows tempted me too much, so out I went after them and killed the fattest, but as I was on foot I gave the Skin and Carcus to a couple of Indians taking only the Tongue for my share. You would be surprised to see what a load an Indian can carry on foot. I have seen many a one on their way to Camp still 4 miles off with the meat of a whole Cow—half he will sew up in the skin which in these times of plenty Snow is easily dragged behind him, and the other half he packs about his person, and with this load will travel 3 miles an hour. But of all the shameful sights, though I am now a little accustomed to it—the way the women are worked is the worst, yet to them it is an amusement, and sooner than see her husband pack wood or hay or anything of that sort she would I think break her back—it is a great disgrace to the women to see their husbands working though hunting and packing the meat &c is considered the husbands duty but frequently the women have to assist in packing the meat also.

This Winter, the Snow has been much greater than any year since I have been in the Country and it is almost impossible to use horses.[17] Their hunts therefore are for the most part on foot and they are very expert at this. The most of Indians will out run a horse in two days, and the most of horses can out run the Buf°—then in the Snow the

---

[14]They drank twenty times to their loved ones' health.

[15]Dining tables.

[16]Scotland.

[17]Arriving in St. Louis in May, Alexander Culbertson reported a brutal winter with mules freezing to death and trading posts isolated by mountainous snowdrifts. Sunder, *Fur Trade*, 150.

Buf° make but poor way whereas at present the crust on the snow is sufficient in most places to bear a man and this gives him a giant advantage. Two or three times the Indians this year have succeeded in driving the Buf°. into a ravine where the Snow is 20 or 30 feet deep and there slaughtered the whole band all in a heap. My other letters will inform you that I have now procured you a little grandson[18] in this far of[f] wild land a very fine little healthy fellow he is, but I have said too much about this stranger already in my other letters, were I to say more you would think me crazey. But I must stop here now my dear Mother, Kuta is getting decidedly too impatient and wants to know what all this singular writing she calls it is about and to interpret it is a three days work for me at least. Our express has not yet arrived from above, but when it does I will add you a short postscript at least with latest date. God ever bless you my dear Mother is the sincerest prayer of your most loving Son

And[w] Dawson

1st February

Our express arrived late last night and will start for below tomorrow—All well God again bless and preserve you. AD

25

Fort Clark
3rd July 1853.

My Dear Mother

Our Steam Boat arrived here the 29th ult°. and by it I experienced the unspeakable pleasure of receiving at long last "letters from home." yours and Alecks of March last. When you wrote these my winter letters to you all do not seem to have arrived but doubtless by this time they have turned up, but whether or not, they contained nothing but good news. In fact I never have anything else to report to you, and always the longer the better. . . .

I have this year made an engagement with the Company for two years and though I have done so on an increased Salary of $100 annually I begin to wish I had not done so though I cannot tell why I

[18]James Scott Dawson.

should fear. Two years however at my time of life is a long interval to remain in status quo. Formerly my engagements with the Company were for only one year and every new one was more advantageous than its forerunner. I am aware however that I have reached the very utmost climax of Clerkship in this country the ne plus ultra,[1] and a step further would see me Mr. Co.[2] but I have no reason to anticipate this step will soon be taken if indeed ever. Did I remain long enough in the Country I presume this would be the result—but the question is, is this worth waiting so long for. My resolution has ever been to leave the Country when I seriously think I can employ myself and capital to more advantage elsewhere.

Thus far I have never thought I could, indeed much beyond anticipation has my success in the country been, and I now find all other Clerks be they grey headed or otherwise under me.[3] I am thus plain with you my much loved Mother not from any desire to boast but from the sincere desire of lending one little drop of comfort to your old age and I know such a statement is well calculated to do so. Know me then for the next two years as the same old musty fusty dusty Clerk as ever at the end of which time Mr. Culbertson has just been reminding me of what I hourly think of, that he and I are to visit you all.—This year I am to have a young Scotchman of the name of Constable as my Clerk.[4] He is a native of Edr.[5] and some relation of the Publishers[6] I believe but I have got to find all this out yet on his return by the Boat. What a talk we will have the instant the Boat is off, particularly if he is recently from the Land of Cakes. My old friend John Tevis of St. Louis has also paid me a visit this time and will pass the winter in the Country, hunting deer buffalo & health.

This is getting to be a little more bustling place than hitherto and I trust will continue increasing in this respect. This year a troop of Soldiers has gone above by land and are to proceed over the Mountains to the Pacific. There is a talk that another troop will visit us next year and build a Fort about the YellowStone where they will remain, and at present a Government Agent with some 10 men is exploring

---

[1]The highest point.

[2]Head of the Upper Missouri Outfit.

[3]Dawson was the highest earning AFC clerk.

[4]David Archibald Constable, born 29 January 1829, in Belgium. His family lived in Edinburgh.

[5]Edinburgh.

[6]Constable's grandfather, Archibald Constable (1774–1827), was an Edinburgh publisher who started *Farmer's Magazine*, *Scots Magazine*, and *Edinburgh Review*. He bought *Encyclopædia Britannica* in 1812.

the Prairie and will reach me in about 25 days.[7] I only wish he would discover some Gold mine to complete things. We in the Country would have the first chance at it.

I only write to you at this time as I am much pressed being all alone for the present. I sat down to write several times before the arrival of the Boat, but I had so many letters at home and on the way unanswered that I was at a loss what to say. In winter however I shall write to one and all of you commencing with your own worthy self. . . . Tell Aleck that I have now got the Coat[8] and the two Robes I have previously written about but one and all advise me not to run the risk of sending them at present as they would most certainly never reach and I am somewhat of that opinion. They are prime and valuable. M^r^. Culbertson has at this time offered me an American Horse value $150 for the Coat alone, but I consider it Alecks property and were I to part with it I do not know if I could soon replace it. It was a winters work for poor Kuta. When Mr. Tevis goes below I think I shall entrust them to him to have forwarded to Alecks house[9] in New York. . . .

. . . Here we are all well. My little boy just begins to stand up and is daily of greater interest to me. I have called him James.

He is not quite the "finest child that ever was" but I assure you he is "some" and much surpassing in good looks any of the family I have yet seen.

. . . Remember me to one and all. . . . God bless and protect you.

Believe me ever My Dear Mother
Your truly affec Son
And^w^ Dawson

26

Fort Clark
3rd January 1854.

My Dear Christian

. . . Your worthy husband came into and alas has departed from the family circle without my acquaintance yet I morn his loss equally

---

[7] Exactly how Dawson is using "government agent" is unclear, but he almost certainly does not mean Indian agent. Most likely he is referring to scientific expeditions, led by Dr. John Evans, Fielding Bradford Meek, and Ferdinand Vandeveer Hayden, who were then exploring the Badlands.

[8] See Letter 18, n. 4.

[9] Aleck's New York employer.

with you all, and not the less so from the very desolate situation you must be placed in.[1] But be of good cheer my worthy sister, think of the trials of our worthy good old Mother and how these trials are now being rewarded, by an "age of ease"[2] and by the well doing of all her children. You have many bulwarks to look to and none of these I feel assured will fail you, as has been the case with Mother. Ten years since I was an outcast from home without a comforting voice from friend or foe except yours and Mothers, and I then dared to tell this mighty man Garven[3] that a germ of honest pride was still left to me. "Honest pride"![4] was echoed back to me in a voice I have since heard slightly immitated by the Bears of the far west, and then came the cry of the curs in pursuit, ask John Scott.[5] "honest pride," "honest pride" till I had almost thought myself it could not be so,—Now however let me cry back to them in Brain's own voice[6] "yes honest pride"—and nothing my dear tit[7] will be more gratifying to it than in helping to shield you from the chill of this cold world. One and all of you have been helping our dear Mother and each other I feel assured all this time and my hand has not been with you. but see my position comparest with yours. All alone in a far off country,[8] I have had my trials and I may add my fears for the future, but I now am comfortable, happy, I may almost say independent for which much standing wealth is not required in this country. My former letters will have apprised you that I am coming home in 1845[9] to be again introduced to you all, for I do not expect to know any of you, and then you will also know me better.

On the 13th ult°. Kuta presented me with another little pledge, this time a girl[10] right fat and healthy as should be. My little boy who I call James,—not Andrew as I think I told you before,[11]—is beginning to speak a very little and moves about in the position of man. He is

---

[1] Ralph Drummond died in Kirkcudbright on 27 May 1852, leaving behind six children, including a newborn. ScotlandsPeople; Dalkeith Census 1851.

[2] Oliver Goldsmith, *The Deserted Village*: "A youth of labour with an age of ease."

[3] Dawson's Warrington employer.

[4] Robert Burns, *The Cotter's Saturday Night:* "With honest pride, I scorn each selfish end."

[5] A Liverpool relative.

[6] One's own voice.

[7] Christian's nickname.

[8] Christian lived in Liverpool, away from her family.

[9] Dawson meant 1855.

[10] The daughter was named Grace, although she apparently went by Maggie. See epilogue.

[11] Letter 22, n. 11.

a fine little boy, and relieves daddy a good deal from the eating pain of home sickness.

I fondly hope I will be able to return to you all permanently and bring my family with me, there to spend "green old age" and "die at home at last." This is my day dream, and the only source of all my little unhappyness. Were I able to shake off the remembrance of bonnie Scotland and to cease to think of it as home I would feel as happy as it is permitted us poor mortals to be. but no I am talking nonsense, were it not for the thoughts of home I would be the most miserable mortal on earth. This is strange contradiction, but it is the fact. The same thoughts cause me both pleasure and pain something in the same way as Professor Wilson talks of the joy of grief.[12] This winter for the first time since I have been in the country we have had quite a scarcity of Buf^{o}. and at present one and all of us Whites and Indians are starving, our chief support being Prairie Hens. Of these this year we have an immense abundance and every [page torn] morning we slaughter from 15 to 20 Brace.[13] It [page torn] a bird exactly similar in every respect to your grouse and in a stew is tolerable enough eating yet with this as our only food we find it very hard times, and the above though it will appear to you an ample supply is to us scanty enough. I have often written to you about the immense quantity of Meat we consume in this Country and you cannot wonder at it as it is nearly all we have. Take your soups your vegetables your desserts &c &c from the dinner board and set some 50 ^{lbs} fine B.[14] Steaks and these only to some 10 young men hale strong and hearty as we in this country all are and I question if you will find much left. The scarcity of Buf^{o}. arises from the exceeding mild winter we have had and also from the Prairie on both sides of the River being burned up far and near. Notwithstanding this latter cause had we plenty Snow and very cold say our usual weather Buf^{o}. would make for the river for protection. Thus far however I have experienced about as cold a winter in Scotland and the ground is still black.[15] I fear much the partners in this Company will find no dividend to their credit next year, but we

---

[12]Wilson, *Works of Professor Wilson*, 3:297: "*North*. The joy of grief! That is a joy known but to the happy, James. The soul that can dream of past sorrows till they touch it with a pensive delight can be suffering under no severe trouble."

[13]A pair.

[14]Buffalo.

[15]No snow.

have no accounts yet from the Upper Country, though I anticipate they will turn out far from flattering. And now my dear tit let me say adieu nor complain of the shortness of my letter. I shall write to one and all of you and put these together and you will have a longer letter than I have ever received from home at any one time. God bless you

Your fond brother
And^{w} Dawson

27

Fort Clark
5th January 1854

My Dear Eben

It at present blows and snows,—and oh! how cold it is—as to preclude all kinds of outdoor business, and so here I sit me down to knock you off a screed,[1] not that you deserve it, for you are much my debtor in the correspondence account, but because in my summer letters I promised to write one and all of you by this winters express.

Just think of it, and take shame. Each and all of you will have at this time whole 5 letters from him who I know pretty well is now nearly out of mind at home, and this too when you are daily cheered and comforted with almost hourly intercourse with each other, whilst he poor hapless devil, scarce able to sleep at nights from thinking of home and those there, will be rewarded at the end of say some six months, with <u>one</u> letter from some one or other of you. However as I have said some 150 times before I must not complain, for fear I should be deprived of even this one letter also.

I have little news or none to communicate, and to fill these five letters requires some little ingenuity as I know all will be read by each of you, and the same song sung five times does sound rather tiresome even should the party be <u>foo</u>.[2] My life here is so void of variety however that a journal for one year would with a few interlineations[3] do for nearly all the others.

Amongst these interlineations since I last wrote home I have to

[1] A hurried letter.
[2] A drunken celebration.
[3] To insert between lines.

place the birth of a fine sonsie[4] lassie just as like her dad as Queen Victoria but his notwithstanding,[5] and promises to make a fine looking lady. Wee Jamie also is thriving finaly and with all his prattle and romping causes me anything but trouble. . . . This winter has been the mildest I have passed in the Country and the consequence is we have hitherto had no Buf° and as it is our staple support we at this time look a lean rawboned society I assure you. The weather we have had for a few days past however is just what is wanted, in it nothing can live in the "large"[6] but travel to the Missouri for shelter from the timber and broken ground. Indeed the Indians already report to me that they have discovered Buf° in abundance close to their village and when the weather moderates a little we may expect to get where withal to fatten up again. It would do your heart good to see the vast bands of Buf° we sometimes have all around us, and it would do me also some good to see you well mounted and chasing them. Your luck would not be much for the first few attempts, it is generally the "lean kine"[7] that falls to begginners, and these are only eat in times such as the present, a very few surrounds however would soon enable you to tell fat from lean. By the S Boat[8] the Agent[9] left me as Clerk here a David Constable a fine straight forward "up and down" Scotcham. He is a grandson of the Publishers[10] and Nephew of M^rs^. or Miss Skipton a wealthy lady who resides at Lasswade. Should she be of your acquaintance you can mention this to her, and you can add I think a good deal of him. He left Scotland in a pit[11] and has come here like some others to fight his own battles where there are no John Scotts.[12] Many a talk we have of the Land of Cakes. He is at present with four others in winter quarters trading. This year my business here is considerably increased, the Sioux having moved so close on account of Buf° and I have now a large Camp with 400 lodges and three traders to attend to. Should Buf° come in large numbers it is

[4]Having a pleasant body.
[5]Grace apparently looked nothing like Dawson.
[6]In the open prairie.
[7]Thinnest and slowest moving buffaloes.
[8]*Robert Campbell.*
[9]Alexander Culbertson.
[10]Archibald Constable and Company, Edinburgh.
[11]This probably refers to the tradition of putting two fighters in a pit to wage battle.
[12]A relative on his mother's side whom Dawson believed betrayed him during his Warrington employment.

not too late even yet for me to make the biggest business ever has been made at this Fort.

. . . And now adieu—kiss all your little ones for me and the wife should she be in good humour, why you can give her a smack too, if not why whip her till she is so—"were such the wife had fallen to"[13] &c &c &c but my dear Eben I do love thee [obscured by sealing wax]

Your most affec brother
And[w] Dawson

28

Fort Clark
10th Jany 1854.

My Dear Abram

This fall I received the small parcel sent by you & Aleck in 52 containing your two likenesses and six Calico Shirts. Some of Alecks letters makes mention I think of a Coat or something else being in the parcel, but the above is all I received, and it would have been amply welcome even had the shirts gone the way of the Coat. Your likenesses are a great treasure to me, and you cannot know how I behave with them,—every night at least I have a peep before going to bed and then a song for auld lang sine. This love for home makes me at times very childish and somehow I dont feel ashamed at it. America is a thousand times better place for a young man "going ahead" than the old country yet my advice to all possessed of such feelings as ours is to stay at home. Though you are poor still if you have a livelihood I say again stay at home. Mechanics and others who have no tie there would do well all to come to America. In S[t]. Louis they rank with and live like gentlemen no matter what their trade, at home you know their position—£3."." p week[1] is an average wage for tradesmen and then provisions are very cheap compared with the old country prices.—Your parcel came to hand very much damaged and all wet, yet I feel that the likenesses are uninjured. In yours I can trace a very faint resemblance of the boy I left, yet though I

---

[13]Robert Burns, *The Henpecked Husband*: "Were such the wife had fallen to my part, I'd break her spirit or I'd break her heart."

[1]The equivalent of $780 per annum.

might have recognised you "in the old house at home" I would certainly have passed you in the Street. Aleck again is another person altogether and he might have "wintered with me" without my having the slightest suspicion that he was my own dearly loved brother. You are two fine looking fellows and only want me in the middle to set you off![2] Eben too how does the world bear with him worthy fellow and why was his phiz[3] not in the group? Above all however I would have prized a likeness of Mother, but I suppose I shall have to wait for these until I come to visit you in 1855. Just think of it! it begins to sound quite close already, only next year.

This Country begins to be opened up and I think that in 5 or 10 years it will be no place for a large Company such as this I am engaged in. Government is to bring a Steam Boat of its own next Summer,[4] and hear there is some rumours of a company of Soldiers to be stationed somewhere near the YellowStone.[5] If so there will follow a considerable influx of Steam Boats and with them petty traders.[6] In which case you will most assuredly have to count me in the number. Could I have found a safe and certain conveyance for goods here and also for my returns from this I would have been on my own hook for some years, and a right profitable business I could make of it, but in the present state of affairs the risks the trouble, and the expenses are too great for this. I have as the Yankees say however. My eyes skinned.[7] The whole country has been surveyed the last Sum^{r}. and fall with the view of ascertaining the best rout for a "Pacific Railway" and though I have no expectation of the rout being chosen anywhere in this neighbourhood,[8]—on account of the Climate. yet it must pass through some portion of the Indian Country and some of its effects found here. Turn up what may however, I feel waxing old, but as healthy and as nimble as a Cat, and feel the necessity of some strenuous exertions [page torn] a comfortable build for the winter

[2]Dawson was taller than his brothers.

[3]Physiognomy, i.e., why wasn't his daguerreotype included?

[4]Isaac Ingalls Stevens, head of the Northern Pacific Railroad Survey Party, had proposed that the government purchase their own steamboat to save money in transporting annuities. The government declined his advice.

[5]Soldiers did come into the area following the Grattan massacre, but this was eight months away. The 1851 Horse Creek Treaty allowed troops to be stationed in Indian country.

[6]Independent traders.

[7]Paying close attention.

[8]The northern route was not chosen.

of life. I [page torn] on [word illegible] and confidently however of attaining this end if God continues me in my present strength.

At present I am comfortable and have all my wants supplied with a third of my income, yet this income is dependant on the will of others, at least at the expiration of two years.[9] . . . I have heard so much of the disappointments caused by the California excitement.[10] And thus as I have said before stick at home. A "Lampie" gasses are sustenance from the Rock.[11] Do let me entreat you to write me a long letter on receipt of this and make it just as much about yourself as you feel inclined, the more the better, and this is always an easy subject for any one to write upon. I wrote Eben and Christian some 5 or 6 days since in very starving times, but now ours is the land of plenty overflowing with fat. such are the changes we experience in this Country. The very cold weather still continues and Buf^o^ I understand are on the move this way in immense crowds, though I have not yet seen them nor have I indeed seen a Buf^o^ for the last six months, yet the news must be true, as the Inds. have brought me plenty meat. Adieu—

Ever your [obscured by sealing wax] brother
And^w^ Dawson

29

Fort Clark
17th January 1854

My Dear Mother

I have written to one and all at home and had reserved what I thought ample leisure time to have a long talk with you, filling and refilling such a sheet as this in the chat, but to my disappointment! half an hour since in popped our "Express" from above and tomorrow morning must start for below along with a good deal of work from me still unexecuted. My information was that this express would leave the Blackfeet[1] 1st of January where as it left Fort Union

---

[9]The length of his contract.

[10]Only a few of those who followed the gold rush came out ahead.

[11]Probably refers to a miner's lamp, but the reference is unclear. The word transcribed as "gasses" could be "gains" or "games."

[1]Fort Lewis, aka Benton.

that date. Never mind however you must take the first reading of the enclosures for yourself out of which you will pick all the news I have to give which you will find is not much, although I feel assured that to you it is sufficient to know that he who loves you so much is well, I should say very well, comfortable, and happy as it is possible for him to be so away from you. As you will find from some one of these enclosures "Kuta" on the 13th ulto presented me with another little pledge this time a girl and people say a real beauty but now that I have them of my own I feel no ways altered in the opinion I held of old that children are like Eggs all alike only some larger than others and it requires a few moons for me to be able to distinguish any beauty or ugliness they may possess. Little James is the size for me and he begins to be not a little amusing with his prattle and antics. In Summer by our Steam Boat[2] I shall make ample amends for this short epistle even at the sacrifice of some of the others. In the meantime with love to one and all and sincere prayers for a long and happy life for you my beloved Mother believe me to remain with fond affection

Your Most dutiful Son
Andw Dawson

30

On Board S.B. Sonora
Mth White River U M R
29th June 1854.

My Dear Mother

Three days since I received at my old place at Fort Clark by this Steam Boat your and Christians satisfactory letters of March last, and am highly delighted with all or rather the general part of the news therein contained.

. . . The day previous to the arrival of Steam Boat, an express arrived by land at Fort Clark bringing me orders from our Agent[1] to prepare myself to start for the Blackft. country to winter there and I am now in a dream as it were on my way there, for so much had I become a fixture at old Fort Clark, the idea of my moving to any

[2]*Sonora* captained by Joseph La Barge.

[1]Alexander Culbertson.

other place never entered into my head. This to me my dear Mother is an important crisis in my career in the country and I may say in life, the result of any next years trading for the Company will be either my making or marring. and as I know that all relating to your far distant son is much more important to you than any other news I could give you I here insert an extract from our Agents letter to me to show you the nature of my present change.

"Fully satisfied of the judicious and careful management of Fort Clark since it has been under your charge, we find your service will be now more necessary and beneficial to the Outfit by giving you a larger field to work upon. It has consequently been agreed upon by the gentlemen of the house as well as myself to place Mr. Galpin[2] in charge of Fort Clark and you to accompany me to the Blackfeet preparatory to taking the permanent charge of Fort Benton."[3]

Fort Benton does four fifths of all our trade and this confidence in me in thus placing me as it were at the head of the business over many my seniors[4] is very complimentary and to you I have no doubt will be very pleasing. The Agent and one or two other interested parties on board furthermore have at this time verbally stated to me, that next year a new contract of copartnery will be entered into when a share in the Company will be placed at my command. What only grieves me midst all these glad news is that now I am uncertain whether I shall be able to fulfil my intention of visiting you next year or not. Should I not visit you however depend upon hearing from me much more substantially than you ever have hitherto, and in another year I shall probably be able to visit you with much more comfort and satisfaction than I could do as a Clerk. Kuta and little James with wee Gracie are all on board accompanying me to my new abode. I had almost said home but no no I have but one home and that is in your house.

. . . In Spring I shall return with my Returns to meet the Steam Boat by Mackinaw Boat and shall write you a journal from the day I

[2]McDonnell, "Fort Benton Journal," 305n282. Charles E. Galpin came upriver in 1839.

[3]Culbertson was scaling back his Company involvement, spending winters at his new home in Peoria, Illinois.

[4]In particular, Dawson was promoted over Malcolm Clarke, who came upriver in 1839 as Culbertson's protégé. For years, he had overseen Fort Benton in Culbertson's absence. Exactly why Culbertson chose Dawson over Clarke is unclear. Perhaps Culbertson, knowing he would often return to Fort Benton, preferred to have someone in charge who would show him continued deference. Dawson better fit that bill. Clarke was so angered by Dawson's promotion that he soon quit the AFC.

leave Fort Benton until I meet the Boat and you will also hear from me from Fort Benton by winter Express as usual. My old friend Tevis from S[t]. Louis is again on board and will winter with me to endeavour to recruit his health.[5] Excuse me writing any more at present as my head is just as much in a whirl as Alecks can be at present.[6] Recollect I have not travelled on a Steam Boat for the last 8 years and my life has been such a quiet and sedate one all that time that the present noise and racket is driving me stupid. God bless one and all of you my dear mother and fondest love to Christian and my new sister-in-law.

Most sincerely your attached Son
And[w] Dawson

31

F[r]. Benton
26th Feb[y]. 1855.

My Dear Mother

Since I wrote you from on Board our Steam Boat last June this is the first opportunity I have had of again writing. We arrived at Fort Union on the 3rd July and the day following started with two Mackinaw Boats each containing some 27 Tons Frt[1] for this place where we arrived after a most tedious trip on account of low water, on the 19th September following making in all 78 days. The distance is estimated at 750 miles though it is scarce half of this by land and had you been with me to see the rapids[2] we have to get over, the shoals we have to work through the loading and unloading and the portages &c &c we have to make you would indeed say it was something of an undertaking. This is the poorest spot I should imagine on the face of creation, and the "furthest from nowhere" in the known Globe. The Fort itself however is by far the best, & the most commodious on the river but it is miserably situated in what you can conceive to be an immense Basin the diameter of which is about 2 miles, so that in no direction

---

[5]Tevis, age thirty-four, had recently retired. Whether ill health contributed to this is unknown, but the open prairies were widely believed to provide a health-restoring climate. He died in 1890. *Necrology Scrapbook*, 1:22.

[6]Aleck had recently married.

[1]Freight.

[2]The rapids were Birds, Lone Pine, Dauphin's, Pablo's, Kettle, Dead Man's, and Kipp's. McDonnell, "Fort Benton Journal," 298n264.

does our view from the Fort, extend over 1 mile, on the edge of this Basin however we have a fine view of the Rocky Mountains towering over all arround, but near as this prospect is, so occupied have I been that I have only been there once. We are only 20 Miles below the Great Falls of the Missouri which I hope I will be able to visit before I leave for good. Shortly after I wrote you last I was given to understand that it is requisite for the partners in this Company to make arrange one year in advance,[3] in consequence of the goods having mostly to be purchased in England. Arrangements were therefore entered into at Fort Union, for the next year, that is to commence after the returns of this current year are made, which at this Fort will be in May next. By these arrangements I was included as a partner in the Company and though my interest is not the greatest thing in the world still it is a step to advancement and I have the pleasure to state that my prospects are very flattering. My interest in the Company is 1/24th and independent of it I get a Salary of $500, my goods at Cost and Charges and am exempted from all risk of loss. You are aware that in 1853 I engaged as Clerk for 2 years on a considerable Salary and never dreamt of any change being made till the expiry but not so. Mr Culbertson cancelled it, and drew out another, adding $200 to my previous salary and allowing me any goods at Cost and charges.

All these things I mention to you my dear Mother not in a boasting light but in the belief that if all others have forgot me, you at least yet retain some interest in the welfare of your now long absent son. Aleck has I presume been married, nay is perhaps a father by this time, and Tom Dick and Harry have had honorable intimation of the important circumstance, but not a word of it all does he think to send to his Brother. My old S^{t}. Louis master and friend John Tevis accompanied me by the Boats for the benefit of his health and passes the winter with me. Mr Culbertson also arrived on the 28th of September and introduced me to these Red Skins and opened the trade with them, but they both left together by land on 26th December and remain at Fort Union awaiting my present express which Mr Culbertson proceeds on with to S^{t}. Louis. I am thus all alone in the management here but I can get along nicely. So far I have not picked up a dozen words of the Blackfoot language yet I can manage to talk pretty fluently to them on my hands. I presume I have informed you some

[3]Dawson was not a partner when he first planned his visit home.

time that all the Indians on the Missouri have signs in common and one nation can converse fluently with another by these signs although their language is very different.

I write you my dear mother at this time under very great anguish. Kuta my good loving obedient wife and companion lays by me on her death bed. She has not enjoyed one days health since she left home and now her disease has assumed such forms as makes it impossible for me longer to deceive myself. She is in the last stage of a consumption[4] and the dropsey[5] has in the few last days laid its fingers on her. On the opening of our River next Month, it is my intention to send her below in a skiff with three men, if she then is able to bear the fatigue which I much fear. The trip may do her some good and prolong life a little and furthermore she is desirous of seeing her Mother. Her symptoms are too well known to me however for me to entertain any hope. If you could but only know her goodness my dear mother, how you would morn with me. My two little children are in excellent health, but at present are sadly neglected.

Contrary to my expectations I will have to remain here this Summer, having been ordered to receive Govr. I I Stevens of Washington Territory who is to arrive here from the Pacific in June next, to hold some treaty with the Indians. In 1856 however I shall go below but probably not farther down than Fort Pierre, unless I am ordered to S^t^. Louis, and in 1857 if I am spared, nothing will prevent me visiting the Land of Cakes. My visit to Scotland therefore is delayed for two years, it is very seriously for my interest to do so, but as I have said I shall not be longer disappointed, indeed I am getting too anxious to live quietly without such a trip, and then my children will be requiring some arrangements for their education.[6]

By the Boats in May I shall again write you and for the first time since I left, shall then send you a little money. God grant it will not be the last. I would do so at present but it would be irregular at this time.—Present my love to one and all and believe me ever to remain

My Dear Parent
Your Most Affec Son
And^w^ Dawson

---

[4]Tuberculosis.
[5]An excessive accumulation of serous fluids in tissue spaces.
[6]Most traders sent their children downriver to be educated.

32

Judith River 90 Miles below Fr. Benton
11th October 1855.

My Dear Mother—

My last letter to you was dated I think 2nd March[1] wherein I alluded to the dangerous sickness of my beloved Kuta.—She died 9 days afterwards that is on the 11th of March 1855.[2] She was a faithful, loving, obedient and most affectionate Wife as ever breathed the breath of life,—and she is dead. The same letter informed you that I had orders to remain at Fort Benton over the Summer, but this event so unnerved me and unfitted me for any manner of business that I left with my two little children, for my old quarters at the Rees[3] on the 3rd of May and reached that place on the 2nd of June where I remained till the arrival of our Steam Boat 5th July.[4] My children "James" and "Grace" I have left for the present in the care of their Grandmother at the Rees, and as I have many warm and true friends[5] there, they will be comfortable enough for a little time, and in a year or two at the most, should we be all spared I shall take them with me to the settlements. Since 5th July or at least since the return of the Steam Boat from Fort Union, I have been wending my way at a Snales pace up Stream to Fort Benton and have got thus far. The United States Government this year hold a treaty with the Blackfeet and other Indian tribes in this neighbourhood, and our Coy. has secured the contract for the transportation of the goods required and they make an immense pile[6] I assure you requiring four large Keel Boats, the largest that ever entered on these waters, and to add to our difficulties the water as a matter of course is lower "than it was ever known to be." My labors anxieties and troubles are at long last however at an end. The Council is to be held here and I now only wait the arrival of the Commissioners[7] to get their

---

[1]Letter 31.

[2]McDonnell, "Fort Benton Journal," 25: "Sun. 11 March 1855: Mr. Dawsons Wife died and was interred back of the Fort."

[3]Fort Clark.

[4]*St. Mary*.

[5]Charles Galpin, David Constable, and Kuta's family.

[6]Ewers, *Blackfeet*, 221: council gifts included "blankets, cotton prints, sugar, coffee, rice, flour, and tobacco."

[7]Isaac Ingalls Stevens, governor of Washington Territory, and Alfred Cumming, superintendent of Indian affairs. The treaty conference was originally planned for Fort Benton, but when the goods were delayed, the council was moved to the mouth of the Judith River.

receipts for the goods, when I shall start to Fort Benton by land to relieve Mr Culbertson and who will probably attend the treaty.[8] This contract, now successfully implemented will nett our Company a little over $35000. a pretty little business of itself, but add to this one of our Forts—"Pierre"—which we used to Inventory at $5000. has been sold to Govn^{t}. for $45000.[9] and you will agree that I have been lucky for my first year as the Ir. Co.[10] It is true that our business as Indian traders will be considerably injured by this war with the Sioux Indians[11] and other Govn^{t}. movements, but this year we can afford it, and perhaps another year something else will cast up. In my last letter I stated my determination to visit home in 1857 and already I begin to count the time when I shall start. Confidently expect me, as nothing but Gods direct decree will prevent me and oh how fervently I do pray that God to preserve you all till that moment at least, in the same healthy and prosperous condition I believe you all to be in at present. My best friend, M^{r}. Culbertson, a great friend too of poor Andrew Potts[12] will probably accompany me. The Shells Aleck sent me, met with the same fate as those I sent him, still I secured enough to discover they were not what I wanted, being porcelain and not shell.[13] This matter will do to lie over however till I visit you as my interest in the matter is very different now as a partner from what it was then as a Clerk.[14]

. . . I promised to send you a little present this Summer, but this

---

[8]Culbertson's exasperation with the quarrelling commissioners led him to consider not attending the council, which he had been working to arrange for almost four years.

[9]The Army arrived on the upper Missouri following the 1854 Grattan massacre. Needing to house the troops, the government bought Fort Pierre. Charles Galpin handled the sale for the AFC. The property had long been neglected, and the AFC vastly overcharged the government. This so infuriated General William Harney that he refused to help Culbertson and Cumming when, on their downriver journey, the Sioux stole their mules. When they asked Harney for help, he replied: "All summer I and my men have suffered and boiled to chastise these wretches while you have been patching up another of your sham treaties." Bradley, "Affairs at Fort Benton," 275–76.

[10]Company manager.

[11]That spring, a band of Yankton had detained Culbertson's party for two days, threatening to kill all white men. Alfred Vaughan to Alfred Cumming, 19 May 1855, NAM, M234/885.

[12]The two served together at Fort McKenzie.

[13]"A shell, called by the traders Ioquois, is sought after by them more eagerly than anything else of the kind. They are procured on the coast of the Pacific and find their way to our tribes across the mountains through the different nations by traffic with each other. . . . These shells are about 2 inches long, pure white, about the size of a raven's feather at the larger end, curved, tapering, and hollow, so as to admit of being strung or worn." Denig and Hewitt, *Assiniboine*, 196.

[14]Dawson apparently had hoped his brother could secure Ioquois and that, as a clerk, he could sell them for his own profit. As a partner, this was no longer possible.

Summer I did nothing and I know you will forgive me. . . . I have frequently stated that when I write to one I do so to all, and as I have tried the other plan of writing to all and find it no more profitable I mean at this time at least to try the first plan as I have little time at my command having the wants of some 170 men to attend to. So pass this the rounds. Remember me however more particularly to Christian whose position I have a particular simpathy with.[15] Think of me often my Dear Mother. I almost believe I can tell when you are thinking of me and at these moments, old and grey headed as I am I can do nothing but weep and one of these moments is the present.

Your Most Affec Son
And[w] Dawson

33

Fort Benton
4th Jany 1856.

My Dear Mother

I have been delaying starting the Express for S[t]. Louis for sometime in the hopes that six Wagons I started for Fort Union on the 17th Nov[1] would arrive when I might also reply to any letters I might receive by them. A recent very heavy fall of Snow however convinces me that it would not be prudent to wait any longer, for the probability is that these Wag[ns] must now be delayed for some weeks to come, and in a moment I have determined on starting off said Express tomorrow[2] thus leaving me little enough time to write letters, yet time sufficient to say all that is necessary which is that here I still am in good health having experienced no change except of position since I wrote you in October from the Council Grounds at Judith River. In good health but alas how lonely. This fall I was induced to take a trip to the Missouri Falls[3] along with Major Hatch[4] the now Indian Agent and who

---

[15]Both had lost their spouses.

[1]McDonnell, "Fort Benton Journal," 52–53: "November 1855. Fri. 16: Had Wagns. Harness etc. all arranged for men to make an early start for Ft. Union to fetch up Corn of which we are much in want."

[2]Ibid., 58: "January 1856. Sat. 5: Started Mr. Wray and one man with Express for St. Louis to be delivered at Ft. Union."

[3]Great Falls of the Missouri.

[4]McDonnell, "Fort Journals," 270n76: Major Edwin A. C. Hatch (1825–82) was born in New York and lived in St. Paul, Minnesota, before being appointed agent for the Blackfeet in 1855.

resides with me. and well did I consider myself repaid for the trouble. The sight is very grand not I suppose to be compared to Niagara, but in America most every one has seen those latter falls but how very few have seen the former. Our trip lasted 5 days though the distance is only 25 miles yet we set out not to hurry but to enjoy ourselves. Let my Brothers read this. On a small Creek we call the "high wood" we camped at noon and whilst lunch was being prepared Hatch told me to come along and he would teach me a Yankee trick. Having hooks with him he took one and gave me another having each about 2 f^{t}. whip cord attached to it. we then went to one of the deepest pools about, all of which were covered with Ice some 9 In. thick in which we each cut a hole about one foot square. Having baited our hooks with a little p^{s}. fresh venison and without rods having hold of our short lines with our hands in we bobbed to the hole but scarce were the hooks in when out came from each hole a real Scotch trout[5] at least a pound weight, then in again and out in and out, the same bait doing all the time until we had 7 doz of the finest trout you ever saw the very least weighing 14 Oz and all caught in less than 30 minutes—what fun and how I thought of you all and of the days gone by, but now since my beloved wifes death when is home ever absent from my thoughts? Another incident occurred to us on the trip which is allied to the miraculous and which I shall also relate. I need not tell you I am an excellent shot, though I am far better than I used to be Major Hatch is about as good,—you know I could not say <u>as good</u>. Well about dusk and after supper when enjoying ourselves around the Camp fire close under one of the falls—there are 10 in all[6]—one of the men came running to say there were Geese close on the bank about 50 yards from us. I immediately seized my gun as did also Hatch and on advancing some 10 steps we immediately discovered what we thought were the Geese. when Hatch fired, the object only moved a very little, whereon I also fired, when on the instant up started one of my men being the object we were fireing at, god what excitement I did experience for the next few moments. a thousand times I could shoot the same shot without missing but God be praised this time I had missed, the Major had missed and the man was unscratched.

I anticipate making the biggest and most profitable trade that ever

[5]Loch Leven Trout or Salmo Levensis.

[6]Most count five falls (Great, Crooked, Rainbow, Colter, and Black Eagle), not ten. Cutright, *Lewis and Clark*, 156.

has been made in this country this year. Plenty money plenty Robes plenty everything, but still I am unhappy. Next year I am coming to see you all as I have promised, when this may again change me for the better. I shall go below with my returns so far as my little family[7] and on meeting the S Boat, though there is still an uncertainty if a Boat will be up for this year,[8] shall make arrangements for my intended visit, and will then be able to write you definitely when to expect me,—My intention is to try and arrange to start from here in a skiff so early as the river opens and proceed straight on to Scotland, but I shall be better able to state my plans in Summer—coming I am however rest assured of that if God spares me.

God bless you one and all Ever believe me

Your truly affec Son
And^w Dawson

34

Fort Benton
4th January 1859.

My Dear Mother

Exactly 4 months today I was with you[1] and now where am I and where are you?[2] what a world of water and of land separates us and yet how closely in feeling am I with you.

I arrived here on the 16 ult^o. after walking nearly the whole distance from F^t Union through snow. I had one horse stolen by the Assinniboines and one other I had to leave on the way done out. The other trojans[3] hardly reached here, another day would have brought all to hault but now they are having good times in a better climate

[7]He was headed for Fort Clark, where his children lived with Kuta's mother.

[8]There was much unrest on the upper river in 1855, apparently leading Dawson to question whether a steamboat would appear. However, in April, the *Clara* left St. Louis carrying government supplies, AFC freight, military troops, and a "jolly" party of French noblemen and their wives on a "pleasure trip." On June 7, the *St. Mary* headed upriver with Charles Chouteau, Alexander Culbertson, Alfred Vaughan, Lieutenant Gouverneur K. Warren, and Elkanah and Sarah Mackey on board. Both journeys were relatively uneventful. Sunder, *Fur Trade*, 175–76, 179.

[1]Dawson sailed from New York to Liverpool in August 1858 to visit family in England, Scotland, and Ireland.

[2]Dawson's mother died at age sixty-five, on 20 January 1859, before this letter arrived.

[3]Strong horses.

and doing nothing. I froze my nose cheeks and ears pretty badly, but these are incidents so common to the "Voyageur"[4] as scarcely to call forth a remark. Otherwise throughout my entire trip was just as I would have wished. Whilst the excitement of it lasted my spirits kept good but now I feel lonely very very lonely. but let us cheer up and hope again soon to be reunited.

I had hoped at this time to have been able to write you with some comfort and at much length, but my red friends will not have it so. The news of my return has already spread throughout the land and one and all are crowding in to welcome me back as they say, but actually to pick up from me what they can. which is a good deal, for as they all bring me some little present my heart is in their language made soft.

At present I am in a crowd—it is midnight and I start my "Express" tomorrow, and as I have still much business to do I must again neglect all others at home with the exception of this to you which will also do for them. In a short note I wrote you by Mr. Culbertson from Fort Union[5] I quite omitted to mention having spent two days with my children and the old lady. All were well and it pleased the grand-mama very much to hear you had sent her the present of a dress. The dress is still in St. Louis but will be up with my trunk on the Steam Boat. I have made all arrangements to have my children taken to St. Louis in Summer and have found them a home for the present with a Captn La Barge[6] with whom I have been long well acquainted and who I feel assured will show them every attention and kindness.

Our trade last year proved very much of a failure in the result and there was very little money for anyone. This year however I am delighted to state—for every dollar brings me so much nearer home—that there is every prospect at present of our making very handsome returns, and as my interest is just double what it was previously[7] I hope to make a long stride towards you all in money matters this year, and I fondly hope that my expectations will not be frustrated in being home with you all in three years. Misrule and extravagance has had its sway here in my absence, but still when Robes are plenty our profits are such that we can overlook a little extravagance. I may perhaps not be able this year to pick you up a set of Sables or

[4]The low-level company employee who transported goods between outposts.
[5]This letter did not survive.
[6]Both Joseph and John La Barge, brothers and steamboat captains, were Dawson's friends.
[7]Dawson's partnership share had apparently increased.

some such furs as I came late and these are only to be had from other side the mountains but you will get them sometime. Perhaps I may procure them in time in Spring.

If you have an opportunity I wish you to tell Thomas Potts that in my absence "Jerry" has been enticed away to Red River[8] but I fully expect to see him back here again. In the meantime I hold the Pistol that was sent for him and which I will give a good account of. I will write to Tom at a more leisure moment.

How I do wish I had a scrap from [word obscured by tear] of you at home, it would relieve a little of my lonely feeling, or had I even your likenesses that I brought to S[t]. Louis they would make me feel amongst you all again. I shall start from here with my returns in May for F[t] Union, from whence I shall proceed on by Skiff to meet the S Boat[9] and may probably get as far down as Fort Pierre. Next year I shall again visit S[t]. Louis.

My warmest love to one and all and with every prayer for your comfort and happiness I am

My Dear Mother
Your Most devoted Son
And[w] Dawson

35

Saint Louis, Mo.
24th April 1861.

My Dear Brother Eben

I arrived here yesterday from Fort Benton. . . . What changes have occurred in our family circle since I was with you—when will death stay its hand with us.[1] May time my brother again restore you to peace and happiness for well I know that nothing else can.

---

[8]The Red River Settlements, also known as Selkirk's Settlement, in Manitoba, North Dakota, and Minnesota. A colonization project established by Thomas Douglas, the 5th Earl of Selkirk, in 1811 on a land grant from the Hudson's Bay Company. Many dispossessed and impoverished Scots originally settled here until the agricultural experiment failed and the HBC ended its subsidies. After that, the métis dominated the region. In 1869–70, the Red River Rebellion, led by Louis Riel, began here. The Red River Settlements were also home to Dawson's Sioux son, Andrew, who was raised there by Robert Morgan. See epilogue.

[9]*Spread Eagle.*

[1]Many significant events occurred in the two years between letters 34 and 35: his mother's death, his own crippling accident, his marriage to Pipe Woman, the birth of his fourth child, Thomas, and the death of Eben's wife.

You are very urgent in your request for my return home[2] and you cannot know how very ardently I do long to be able to do so. By night and day it is my sole consuming thought, but still it cannot be for yet a little while longer, perhaps never. When at Home with you in '58 all seemed bright and prosperous with me and I then hoped to be able to return in five years at the very furthest but the Commercial panic which then occurred[3] and which I never expected would affect our Robe trade, has indeed been more severe with us than perhaps with any other branch of business and in place of the large fat dividends which I had handled in anticipation I have had nothing from the business but my paltry salary of $1000. pr an[n4] ever since—and which is scarce more than I require for family expenses. This year past however we have had no opposition in our trade[5] and our returns are much increased which coupled with a large and most profitable business done by me with the Soldiers last year[6] will certainly make us a handsome dividend and I am further in hopes that we will now get along with our trade without opposition in which event a few years more I am in hopes would make me rich enough to return spend the balance of my days with you and like Goldsmiths hare "die at home at last."[7] Let us hope on my dear brother and pray God most fervently again to reunite us.

We have the most exciting bombastic furious times here that any Country ever experienced what with these safron visaged lank southerners and those gaunt boney tobacco chewing Yankees of the North. I do not anticipate that much blood will be shed in all their squabling and when all the funds are expended and every one has

---

[2]Ebenezer was concerned about Dawson's health. Perhaps because of his accident, Dawson's handwriting appears shakier than normal in this letter.

[3]A declining international economy coupled with overexpansion of the domestic economy led to the Panic of 1857. As businesses collapsed, thousands lost their jobs. The downturn was especially severe in the West as commercial credit dried up, emigration fell off, and land values declined. Also causing uncertainty was the Supreme Court's *Dred Scott* decision, signaling the end of the Missouri Compromise and likely a war to end slavery.

[4]Per annum.

[5]Alexander Harvey died 20 July 1854. Harvey, Primeau and Company survived for a few years, but without Harvey's driving force, they finally disbanded.

[6]Sunder, *Fur Trade*, 216: "By late September [1860], [Dawson] had forwarded forty thousand pounds of military supplies, under government contract, across the Rockies to support the soldiers who were marching west from Fort Benton over the Mullan Road to Walla Walla . . . and had continued to sell thousands of dollars' worth of supplies, including food, small tools, and whiskey, to Mullan's surveying parties."

[7]Letter 23, n. 10.

become bankrupt they will again come together and again together spout of the glories of this great growing and inseparable Union. In the meantime however business is a dead letter.

My trip down from Fort Benton this year was even quicker than that of last year but having been more prudent than is my wont I feel now that it is over just in as good health and as strong as ever I was in my life. There has been a strong effort made by some parties to obtain my position in the Country but it would require just twenty such to be successful without my willingness. I intend to make capital out of their failure and am in hopes of having my Salary increased two fold.

. . . I leave for F^t Benton again on the 1st prox.[8] and will write to Aleck from on board the S. Boat where I shall have more leisure than it is to be expected I can have here. Write me often on the 28th of January I received at Fort Benton yours of last August, and you cannot know how gratifying it is for me in my solitude to hear from any of you at home. Again this Winter I expect there will be opportunities of sending letters to me though I do not think it probable that I shall be sending my Winter Express here. I did not do so last year for now that we have no opposition I do not consider the advantage of sending one will compensate for the risk and expense attending it.

. . . With love to one and all I remain

My Dear Eben
Your Most affect Bro.
And^w Dawson

36

S.B. Spread Eagle Near Sioux City
May 15th 1861.

My Dear Aleck

On arrival in S^t. Louis on the 23rd ult^o. I received your very much prized letter of the 12th Dec. last having enclosed Discharge to our dear Mothers Trustees for me to execute. . . . It is truly wonderful and much credit does it reflect to the memory of the lamented deceased

---

[8]Dawson delayed his return to attend Kenneth McKenzie's funeral. McKenzie died 27 April 1861.

that notwithstanding all her trials, the immense expense of educating and keeping in control us her unruly Sons that her estate should show such a result, but Aleck we had a Mother such as no other man had. Let us in accordance with her last desire continue in love one with the other and in welldoing and to cherish her memory. . . . I have seen a few of the Ioquois[1] you sent out to Constable[2] and have the whole lot on board boxed up for the Upper Country they are not quite the thing, are a good deal under 1½ inch, on the average and are apparently somewhat different in shape from our Ioquois,—still I feel certain they will go well and yield you at least a very handsome profit, but I regret you have sent no invoice of them. In the circumstances therefore I left the matter to Constable to settle. Make to yourself a reasonably profitable demand on him in settlement of these, and he has my instructions to remit to you. In the meantime I would not advise the purchase of any more until I can report the result of the speculation now on hand. As to the Gold Watches and Pistols I can do nothing for you in that matter but this I do know that if Constable had 1000 of the latter in these present times of excitement he might realize a handsome fortune to both of you, and I have advised him most strongly to make a demand on you for a large consignment. In St. Louis there was not a pistol to be had for love or money. Nothing is talked of but soldiering and even here on the S Boat the passengers have formed themselves into a Company and go through daily drill.[3] I fear much that utter bankruptcy will be the result to one and all. You and Eben both press me hard to return to you all and live the balance of my days at home, and what I said and had almost hoped to realise when I was with you would certainly have induced one to think that I would be ready to do so about this time but it is not so my expectations have been sadly disappointed and now even at this length of time my whole wealth is summed up in these little figures $10,000[4]—this invested at 10 p[r] C[t5] would give me an income of £200. certainly not enough for an old foggie like myself with two

[1]Letter 32, n. 13.

[2]David Constable had retired and was living in St. Joseph.

[3]Dawson's friend, John Mason Brown, organized the drills. A graduate of Yale and a lawyer, Brown visited Fort Benton in 1861 and 1862 before becoming a colonel, commanding the Second Brigade of the Fifth Federal Division.

[4]Roughly the 2010 equivalent of $236,000.

[5]Per cent.

incumbrances to retire on,[6]—but wait still a wee—we have again this year the Country entirely to ourselves and a continuance of this luck for a two or three years more will certainly swell my little pile out sufficiently to take me home. By the return of this Boat I send little Jimmy below and have arranged with a family in St. Joseph to provide for him. Constable will also kindly look to his comfort. The little fellow now talks English pretty well and writes and reads a little. I have always omitted to write you that on my return from my visit to you all I put up a box of different things with the intention of sending home—Beaver Skins . . . Bear Skins . . . Robes . . . a fine Robe and fine Indian Suit for Thomas Potts &c &c and a few things for her that has left us for ever, and on account of her loss[7] it was that they were never sent. On examining the Box this year in St. Louis I find everything motheaten rotten and ruined. I may perhaps get up another box for some of those friends left still left us but as the great incentive is now at an end this is very doubtful.

In your letter you come down very hard on me on the bender question[8] and perhaps with some justice for it is to be supposed that one leading my life must indulge some little on reaching the land of gaiety and profusion. The truth is however that from whatsoever cause occurring I was indeed very sick last year when in St. Louis. I wrote you and others however several times from the Boat not one of which letters are acknowledged.[9]

I shall not probably be sending any Express from Benton this winter and will not have an opportunity of sending my usual winter letter. I think however that I shall find a chance to write home by way of the Pacific[10] and I shall not omit to write to Christian on the return of this Boat. . . . with much love to you my dear brother and to all

I remain
Your truly affec Brother
Andw Dawson

---

[6]Probably a reference to his failing legs. Could also refer to his two sons, James and Thomas, who were with him in Scotland after his retirement.

[7]His mother's death.

[8]Dawson's brothers expressed concern that he drank heavily.

[9]These letters have not survived. This seems to be an attempt by Dawson to change the subject.

[10]The post went via Salt Lake to San Francisco and then by sea to New York.

37

Fort Union
31st July 1861.

My Dear Christian

My last letter home was to Aleck from our Steam Boat written when she was about Sioux City and in which I promised to write to you from Ft. Benton by the return of the Boat. It is ever so however, Man proposes and God disposes.[1] On the 22nd of June our Boat the Chippewa was totally consumed by fire, not a wreck saved, Cargo private baggage and Boat all gone. One minute perhaps after the fire originated—how no one knows—it was discovered when Mr. Chouteau[2] and myself were instantly at the hatches. The Hold we found in one blaze from stern to stern so quickly does fire spread on a boat and with 200 kegs Powder[3] on board there was no time to loose. The word was quickly passed for one and all to save themselves and the Boat was immediately put in to shore—all got safely landed & without even taking time to tie the Boat rushed from it as far as they considered prudent—she then rounded off from shore and floated down stream one entire sheet of flame—in ten minutes after the ignition she blew up and all was over. The report was very great but thank god though no property was saved no lives were lost. One man alone was badly burned who however has recovered. Had the Boat been tied up or not drifted into the Stream curiosity or a desire to save something would have induced many to approach her nearer, who would most certainly have been killed. We had quite a number of passengers on board[4] an Englishman of the name of Scholfield from Shefield and his Wife also a young lady companion from N York and the next business was to get all safely to this place. Most fortunately I had a 70 foot boat some 20 miles above where the accident occurred which I sent off for in the night and by noon the next day we were all crowded on board floating down stream, and notwithstanding all our losses, the party was far from being sad—where all were lossesers[5]

---

[1]Thomas à Kempis, *The Imitation of Christ*, book 1, chapter 19: "For man proposes, but God disposes; neither is the way of man in his own hands."

[2]Charles Chouteau.

[3]Each keg contained ten pounds of gunpowder.

[4]One of the passengers was William de la Montagne Cary (1840–1922). The *Chippewa* explosion cost Cary eighty sketches and drawings.

[5]Losers.

none seemed to feel it. Arrived here more comfortable arrangements were made for the ladies and others and the day following M^r^. Chouteau started with all for below since which time I have heard nothing of the party. Immediately on getting rid of them I started to F^t^. Benton for my Wagons and returned here a few days since with twenty two all of which I have good loading for and shall start back for the old place as soon as my animals are a little rested.[6] The entire loss to the Company M^r^. Choteau estimates @ $67000[7]—on which there is no Insurance, but my arrangements with the Company free me from any loss they may annually make and payment in any case of a Salary of $1000. so that that sum is all I expect to work for for the next 12 months—still the inconvenience to one and all Indian's and Whites is very great. My private loss was considerable trunk clothing private stores &c &c and what perhaps I regret the most my old Joe Manton Gun is gone.[8] My private letters, pocket book Mem^o^ Book Journals[9] &c &c are also all gone but what I deem very fortunate I had left all your likenesses the razors I got of you[10] and some few other things at Benton—which are of course saved to me. So much for this disaster. This is going to be a sad year of trouble and anxiety to me I know. Since I wrote the above I have had a mutiny amongst my men which has resulted in the discharge of four of them. The present opportunity of writing you occurs from there still being some 4000 Robes in the Country belonging to last years business[11] and which I was anxious to send below—I had a boat all arranged Crew appointed and all ready for an early start tomorrow when at the eleventh hour the men refused to go.[12] I am short of men and I fear to appoint another crew as the result might prove the same—their refusal to go and in consequence their discharge for I allow no man to dictate what they will or will not do. I will now therefore retain those Robes for another year and attempt to forward my letters by land.[13]

---

[6]Most of the Fort Benton supplies were lost with the *Chippewa*, so Dawson gathered what he could from the existing Fort Union stock.

[7]The equivalent of slightly more than $1.58 million in 2010 dollars.

[8]Letter 5, n. 5.

[9]These were the journals Dawson promised to keep and which his family had expressed interest in seeing published. See Letters 21 and 23.

[10]Apparently Christian had given him some razors.

[11]The Sioux attacked Fort Union in late August 1860, which may explain why the robes remained. Sunder, *Fur Trade*, 215.

[12]Most likely, the men feared the Sioux, who were causing disruptions up and down the river.

[13]This letter may have gone overland to San Francisco and then by boat around Cape Horn to New York. The envelope has not survived.

By our Steam Boat the "Spread Eagle" I sent little Jimmy to the States, having whilst there myself arranged a home for him at S[t]. Joseph under the care of my friend Constable.

Doubtless he is now making great progress at School and I feel every confidence in the family he is with making him very comfortable and happy,[14] but he was poor fellow very sorry to learn I shall be down again next Spring when I shall see that all is right with him. I do wish to god my dear Sister that I too was in a position to leave this miserable country. I am getting most heartily tired of it but there is now no recourse. I must keep in it for a yet a year or two more—nay perhaps what I often fear I may die in it. My little girl Grace is still in the Country. I would that she were out of it, but the Grandmother is very much averse to part with her. . . . I should like to write at this time to your little family[15] but it would feel a task. Kiss them all for me and tell Andrew his Spotted Horse is still alive and is now very fat. James has also a Spotted Poney on the same pasturage. God Bless you my dear Sister. I will be in S[t]. Louis by 1st May 1862. Write—

Most truly your affec brother
And[w] Dawson

---

[14]It is not clear with whom James Dawson was living. Letter 36 makes clear he did not live with the Constables.

[15]Christian had four children at home.

PART III
Lodge Talks

Introduction to Lodge Talks

THE PRECISE ORIGINS OF THESE "LODGE TALKS," FOUND IN the Dawson Small Collection at the Montana Historical Society Archives, are unknown. Dated December 1858, the handwriting confirms that Andrew Dawson wrote them.

A note appended to "Lodge Talk, N°. 2" suggests their genesis: "We were snugly domiciled in the comfortable & commodious Agricultural Fort which Col. Vaughan, the efficient Agent for the Blackfeet Indians, had lately erected in the valley of Sun River; and there were gathered round the burning logs in the hospitable drawing room Col. A. J. Vaughan, a host, & the host, in himself, Major Owens, the enterprizing Agent for the Flathead Indians in Washington Ter., Mr. MacDonald, the quiet, intelligent & courteous Agent of the Hudson's Bay Co's Fort at Colville in Oregon Ter. And several spirited & lively young men, companions of the latter gentlemen." This Lodge Talk relates a storytelling session at a Christmas gathering of trappers. It is not unreasonable, then, to suspect that Dawson and his companions had also gathered to celebrate Christmas and that they, too, entertained themselves with the time-honored tradition of storytelling.

But assuming all that is correct, questions still remain. Why did Dawson reduce these stories to writing? These are not random notes to keep a narrator on track. Quite the contrary. These were carefully crafted, diligently recorded, meticulously edited, and dated. Moreover, Dawson must have preserved them long after that gathering and then taken them to Scotland when he retired. They apparently were brought back to the States, along with a bundle of letters written to Dawson in the 1860s, by Thomas Dawson, who returned to the States following his father's death. Ultimately Thomas donated them to the Montana Historical Society.

This is quite an effort for writings that appear to have originated as simple stories to share around the campfire, all of which suggests a more interesting possibility. Dawson's sister, Christian, had urged her brother to keep a journal, suggesting that her husband might be able to arrange for its publication.[1] Dawson had also noticed that one of his clerks, David Constable, came from a family of influential publishers.[2] But those early publication opportunities faltered when Dawson's brother-in-law died and then Dawson's journals sank with the *Chippewa*. Nonetheless, it seems quite possible that Dawson took such care with these stories because he hoped to see them published someday. If that is true, their inclusion in this volume is even more special. As with Dawson's letters, "Lodge Talks" have been transcribed to be as faithful as possible to Dawson's original writings. The authors originally hoped to present these as Dawson left them, complete with his numerous edits. Space limitations made that impossible. Instead, our transcription represents our best interpretation of his final draft. We encourage those interested in Dawson's variations to consult the originals at the Montana Historical Society.

If, indeed, these stories were presented orally, Dawson's use of a heavy dialect in "Lodge Talk N° 2" is fascinating. One can only smile imagining the recitation by Dawson, whose Scottish brogue remained so heavy that, seven years earlier, Rudolph Kurz had mistaken his name for "Dorson."[3]

"Lodge Talk N° 2" is also interesting for its discussion of sharing hoarded whiskey, which suggests that, even in 1858, the illicit liquid may have been more precious, at least among trappers, than is often assumed. "Lodge Talk, N° 1," while slightly more prosaic, is revealing for its suggestion that tribes continued to take women of their enemies captive well into the 1850s, long after government-negotiated treaties might have been expected to end such practices. In addition, the woman's experience with the wolf illustrates well the Indian belief in an animal's anthropomorphic qualities.

Regardless of how these stories were created or what the intention was behind their transcription, they remain entertaining more than 150 years later.

---

[1]Letter 23.

[2]Letters 25 and 27.

[3]See Kurz journal entries from August and October 1851.

Lodge Talk 1

Dec. 19th 1858 ~

With the indispensible & ever agreeable after supper pipe in my hand, I slipped quietly away from the enjoiments of civilized life & intelligent companions, & entered a lodge which was pitched near by, intent upon a quiet smoke & social chat, while resting upon the luxurious couch of robes which surrounded the cheerful fire in its center. The evening was cold enough to render a seat by the fire a place of comfort, though it was early in November & the days warm & pleasant as Indian summer days usually are; owing to the close proximity of snow clad peaks & the prevalence of icy winds.

Having but recently journeyed some days with the inmates of the lodge & more than once rested beneath its friendly shelter, I confidently lifted the raw skin flap which served for a door & entering without ceremony seated myself as usual on the nearest vacant robe. I found the space around the fire at present occupied by Mr. Tallman & Mr. La Fontaine, & the wife of each; The former clever, sociable mountain men, & the latter strong, hearty & good-looking half-breed women, the best of companions for the hardy & rugged Trapper. After the usual summary of local talk, Mr. Tallman at my request related the story of his wife's recent capture by the Crows & her escape from captivity & death & miraculous return to her people, the whole forming a history of truthful events to myself of far more thrilling interest & novelty than the most exagerated tissues of fiction. Strange & in some respects incredible as it is, I have every assurance of its truth & give it as a simple narration of facts.

On the fifth day of June last [1858] a small party of Trappers &

Hunters crossed the dividing ridge between the Gallatin fork of the Missouri & the head waters of the Yellowstone river & pitched their lodges on an island in a tributary of the latter. The party consisted of some four or five white men from the Bitter root valley in Washington Territory, among whom was Mr. Tallman, with their halfbreed wives and one or two Flathead Indians. Knowing that they were in a dangerous locality & liable to be visited by war parties of the Crows, who were continually hovering around the main Flathead camp which was only [illegible] miles distant to steal horses or "count a coup"[1] by some other feat of successful daring, the camping ground was selected with unusual care & a due regard for concealment & security. The pointed chosen was admirably suited for this purpose, being a small island formed by a bend of the main stream on one side, & a narrow slough or cut-off on the other, the shore & in fact the whole island, save a small circular space in its center, a level grassy spot, being covered with Cottonwood timber & thickets of willow & other undergrowth. The bluff on the opposite side of the main channel was high & almost perpendicular, such as is usually called a "cut bank," while that on the opposite side of the slough was equally as high, though of easy ascent, the slope being very gentle/gradual. The lodges were pitched upon the small grass plat near the center of the island & were completely concealed from view by the tall cottonwoods & thick willows, which so closely surrounded them that their location could be revealed to the wandering warrior only by the thin blue smoke that ascended from the little fire necessary to cook a slice of venison. Satisfied with the quiet security of their retreat the whole party rested lightly & slept soundly that night, & were up with the dawn, busily intent upon fixing and arranging their traps, preparatory to setting them.

As the day advanced the party separated each intent upon the accomplishment of some particular object, & among others two of the women, Mrs Tallman & Mrs Silverthorn[2] mounted their horses & started to haul roots. They had proceeded but a little way from the camp when they were startled by the dreaded cry of the Crow warrior, & dreading the result of turned immediately to regain the

[1]To "count a coup" meant to touch an enemy.

[2]Probably Mrs. John Silverthorne. Silverthorne is believed to have been the first person to bring gold to trade in Fort Benton. See chapter 9.

camp. Her companion succeded in reaching the lodges, but Mrs T. was intercepted & taken prisoner by the Crows. The victory was an easy one, as the attacking party numbered near fifty strong, athletic warriors, & the result was one Flathead Ind. Killed & thirty or forty horses stolen. The victors in turn becoming cautious lest their new gained booty should be wrested from them by a stronger party from the neighboring camp, & feeling satisfied with the result of the expedition, hastily gathered the band of horses before them & rode off, taking their prisoner with them. Determined to risk no chance of pursuit they pushed along at a headlong speed, fairly flying over the rolling prairie, for hours & hours at atime urging theirs horses to a full run. Thus they continued in the saddle, forcing their animals on, throughout the day & throughout the long, dreary night that followed, nor stopped to rest or eat, or even pulled a rein till near sun set the following day. With a firmness of purposes that knew no compromise, & a rigidity of muscle that Knew no tire, they recognized no demands of hunger, & no necessity for rest, but snatching a few drops of water from the little stream as they crossed it, & conveying it to the mouths in the bent up palm they alleviated for the moment the fever of impatience & passed quickly on.

Thus they traveled on & on without ceasing till many a weary mile was between them & the scene of their late foray, & they had reached the bank of the Yellow stone, but a little distance above the main Crow camp which was at the mouth of A-thousand-yards river.[3] Here owing to the proximity of their own people feeling perfectly secure in the possession of their prisoner & their booty, they halted for the first time in near 36 hours & setting free their weary & jaded animals rested themselves. Their rest & quiet however was of short duration, for but a little time after Sunset they were joined by a war party of 18 Crows who were just returned from a successful foray into the Snake country. These latter brought with them 3 Snake children prisoners, & several scalps, & with the enthusiasm & glee peculiar to the savage warrior alone, both parties prepared to celebrate their success by joining in the wild & exciting scalp dance.

Having built a large fire, which was kept in a continual blaze by additional wood thrown upon it from time to time, by the squaws

---

[3]Unable to further identify. The Crow lived in the Yellowstone River valley of what is now southern Montana.

attendant upon the parties the warriors took their places in a circle round it. They were stripped to the breech cloth & their long & sinewy limbs & passion lighted countenances shown with a fearful distinctness as they gathered round the blazing pile. At a given signal, the dance began, & as if by magic, so sudden & complete was the transition, the whole band seemed instantly transformed into a legion of dusky devils. Starting from their quiet attitudes, they danced & rushed around the fire, twisting & turning their agile frames & facile limbs into every possible grotesque shape, and convulsing their apathetic features by the most furious contortions of countenance, every throat yelling & screaming forth the savage & discordant scalp song & war hoop, forming a fearful accompaniment to a fiend-like dance. Wild & exciting as the commencement was, goblin like they seemed only maddened more & more as their infernal orgies progressed, till in the wild frenzy of their glee they brandished the bloody tomahawk & naked scalping Knife towards the captive woman, hissing forth from their frothy lips a song of death or uttering with hideous delight their shrill & piercing cries of triumph. At a little distance from the infuriated dancers, & securely bound with a cord, the prisoner woman sat, a mute though deeply interested spectator of the savage ceremony. Still with the native courage of the Indian she did not despair & while her enraged captors were menacing her with a death of torment, she was keenly alive to even the smallest chance of escape. Thus when wearied with watching this maddened throng circling round the blazing fagots she cast her eyes upon ground about her & spied a small piece of tin, part of an old wristlet, glistening in the glow of fire light. Watching an opportunity when the attention of the idlers around was absorbed by some more startling scene in the dance, she yielded to impulse & hastily snatching up the little bit of shining metal, immediately secreted it in her bosom. When the watchers turned again to observe her, her countenance gave no token of a change in her forlorn situation, though inwardly she congratulated herself on the possession of a something that might aid in her escape, & exultingly awaited the termination of revel that a change of position might bring a new clew to freedom. Patiently & long she waited, for the charms of the scalp dance held the dusky warriors enthralled in its uncouth mazes till near day-light. At length however the over-strained muscles became wearied, & the most exciting themes of song were exhausted, & the jaded & worn revellers bethought themselves of rest. With undiminished vigilance for the security of their prisoner, they stripped her of all clothing save her shirt, & binding her arms with a raw skin cord which passed completely round her body, they laid her in a lodge on a bed directly opposite the door, & placed beside her on either side a squaw, who laid on the extended ends of the cord, in such a manner that any movement of the captive would surely waken them. Then having securely fastened the door by lacing a strong cord many times across it, they gave themselves up to sleep without a care, satisfied that the escape of the woman was impossible.

Soon the long & severely overtaxed senses & limbs of the warriors yielded to the sweet relaxation of quiet slumber, & all save one throughout the whole camp were sleeping profoundly. In proportion to the long endurance & restless activity of the attack, the hasty retreat & subsequent dance, was the complete & death-like inertness of the oblivious war-party when thus buried in sleep, & therefore no sense was wakeful enough to note the quiet movement of the hand, or the low grating of the rough edged bit of tin as the captive took it from her bosom & commenced sawing & scraping her rawhide bonds. From time to time carefully observing if her operation on the cord produced any change in the stupor of her enemies, Mrs T. assiduously continued her efforts & gradually weakened her bonds till at length the sharp metal cut completely through them & left her arms at liberty. Resting quietly for a moment, lest too much haste might mar her success, she again assayed to free her body from the cord, & having succeded in this quietly crawled to the door. Here she was intercepted by the laced cord which she knew it would be impossible for her to loosen without being detected. Her only chance was, to pass under the lacing, and with the same quiet & continuous determination that she exhibited in using her implement of tin, she unhesitatingly thrust her head beneath it & slowly dragging herself out of the logy stood up once more in the open air unbound & free. Calmly Casting her eye about her she beheld by the dim starlight the shadowy forms of the wearied Crows reclining around her in the listless attitude of deep sleep, while not a sound or movement of the body gave evidence of a single observer of her freedom. Quietly threading her way through the unconscious sleepers her first care was to secure an animal which might carry her beyond the reach of pursuit, for she Knew her absence would soon be noted, & she so hotly pursued that escape on foot was impossible. Approaching the band of animals which were picqueted around the camp, she first caught a mule, which she endeavored to lead off. The mule however showed no disposition to go, but jumped & snorted, till the woman was forced to let him loose. She next caught a large, strong looking horse, which she mounted using the cord with which he had been tied for a bridle, & started off up the bank of the Yellowstone. She had proceeded but a little way when she discovered to her sorrow the horse was much too slow & lazy for a speedy flight & her chances of escape on him a very slim one. She thought her safety now unbound & free though she was, must depend entirely upon the speed & willingness of her horse & she must be well mounted indeed to out fly her pursuers when once they undertook the chase. Therefore with a mind strongly resolved to risk everything to secure a steed which would prove equal to the task circumstances might assign him, she turned back & cautiously entered the Crow camp again. Taking the cord from his mouth she turned the lazy horse loose & stood for an instant observing the animals near her resolving in her mind which one seemed best suited for her purpose. However delay was quite as dangerous as a slow horse & she therefore quickly selected a fine looking gray mare, which she mounted & again started up the river bank, leaving the camp of her enemies at the dawn of the day, still wrapped in quiet slumber. This time she discovered to her great joy that her horse was both quick & free, & urging him to full speed she bounded over the ground with a brave heart & exulting hope of home. Though alone, utterly destitute of provision & clothing, with near 300 miles of wild & rugged mountain land between herself & home, & seated upon the horse's bare back, with no bridle, save short rawhide cord, she did not despair, but felt proudly glad that she was free & homeward bound. But her enthusiastic dream of home & friends was suddenly chilled as the shrill & piercing cry of rage yelled forth by the disappointed Crows when they discovered her escape, came distinctly to her ear, borne on the still air of morning, & she felt again that home & friends alas, were yet far away.

However, Nerving herself to meet the exigencies of the chase, she shook the cord impatiently over the horses neck & urged him on at his utmost speed, resolved if possible to out ride her enemies. & With a readiness which seemed to indicate an instinctive Knowledge of her intentions the noble animal responded to her lightest touch & leaped over the ground with an ease & quickness that well might challenge pursuit. Thus on she sped, with every sense on the alert to detect the various chances of the race in time to avail herself of stratagems[4] if open flight should prove too dangerous, when by the dreadful distinctiveness of the savage outcry behind her she became conscious of the too near approach of the leaders in pursuit. Feeling that swift as was rate at which she passed over the way her enimies were following yet more rapidly & would undoubtedly overtake her, she determined to conceal herself while yet they were out of sight. To hide herself & horse was a matter of no small difficulty, yet with the intuitive perception of the Indian, she Knew the only hope of concealment from the lynx eyed Crows was on the river side; and suddenly wheeling her hose she rode straight to the water's edge. Although the stream was high & swollen by the melting snows in the mountains, & the water cold as ice, still without hesitation she rode into the rushing torrent, selecting her path toward a dense thicket of willow bushes which extended out into the swollen river as far as the edge of low-water. Winding about through the willows & studiously avoiding the possibility of a trace of her course being left to betray her whereabouts, she at length halted her horse in the thickest of the bushes where the water was nearly up to his back & dismounting stood beside him, about submerged in the muddy current, to await the result of her stratagem. Meantime like an avalanche of demons the pursuing hord of Crows rushed past along the neighboring bank, howling like wild beasts suddenly robbed of their prey. On they went, each in turn, according to the speed of his horse, till full fifty hurried by eagerly intent upon the recapture or death of their prisoner. Little dreaming that she they sought was shivering in the cold stream beside them & but a few paces distant, they strained their eager eyes far in advance, expecting every instant to detect her fleeting form appear in the distance ahead. Thus they passed on, & the heart of the concealed woman throbbed with joy once more as the hooping of the Crows became indistinct, & finally inaudible. Still she dare not leave her hiding place disagreeable as it was, for well she knew her enemies

[4]This word is obscured by a tear in the paper but appears to be "stratagems."

would be scattered far & near in search of her, nor give up the hunt till every visible place of concealment was thoroughly searched. Thus she stood nearly up to the throat in icy water for several hours when by the tramp of horses & the voices of their riders on the shore she became aware of the return of her pursuers & hoped that the chase was abandoned. A little while after they had repassed she thought she could hear the hum & bustle of raising camp, which in time grew more & more indistinct, till it ceased entirely. Conjecturing that the war parties had given her up at least for the time & were on their way down the river to the main camp, she mounted her horse & rode out of the water on to the dry bank. Taking a hasty survey of the country to assure herself that no straggling Crow was near to detect her resumed her former rapid flight up the bank of the yellowstone. Thus she continued without interruption till Gradually becoming more confident that pursuit was given over & all the Crows had returned to the camp, she slackened the pace of her horse & allowed him to assume a more moderate gait, which he could maintain for a longer time. During the remainder of the day & the following night she continued her way up the river bank, journeying along without accident. The next morning however she left the valley of the river & struck off in a N.westerly direction for the Rocky Mountains, then only a few miles distant, deeming herself safer from wandering war parties, in their dense forests & deep canons, than in the open prairie or near the timbered streams, & preferring to encounter the fierce wild beast lurking in the one to the relentless enemy roaming about the other.

As the day wore on & noon approached, her unprotected limbs & body began to suffer severely from the burning heat of the meridian sun & soon were swollen & puffed up in large blisters beneath his scorching rays[.] If the cold waters of the yellowstone were freezing to her the day before, she felt that the intense heat of the Sun was no less disagreeable to day; but as a hardy frame & stern resolution had enabled her safely to encounter the one, she hoped the same hardihood & a like determination would successfully endure the other. Therefore she jogged along seemingly more mindful of the appearance & approach of an enemy than of the pain occasioned by her blistered limbs. Thus on she went, pursuing a way through the rough & rugged Spurs of the mountains, sometimes along the steep & stoney mountain side & sometimes in the deep defile at its base, through dense forests of tall & stately pines, & over bald & barren spots, unmindful of sleep or hunger, throughout the second day & second night of her journey home.

On the third day when leaving some timber through which she had followed a small trail, she was discovered by 5 large Grizzly bears, which immediately rushed toward her. Fortunately there was a clear & open space for a considerable distance before her, & she whipped her horse into a full gallop, thinking easily to leave her ugly pursuers far behind. But in this she was mistaken, for her horse was much worn & jaded by incessant traveling over a rough road, & responded very reluctantly to every endeavor to urge him on, while the fierce monsters in pursuit were spurred on by Keen hunger & the sight of that which might satiate their appetites & followed her with an alarming rapidity. Turn which way she would, over hills, across gullies & on the level ground the 5 rapacious bears followed with ravenous pertinacity, the distance between herself & them apparently growing no greater. The chase was maintained thus for 3 or 4 miles, when the hunted woman becoming somewhat alarmed, lashed her unwilling steed into his fastest run, & gradually left the unwelcome visitors farther & farther behind, till they stopped & gave up the pursuit. Discovering that she was no longer followed she allowed her horse to resume his pace, wishing to favor him as much as possible.

As the night approached she felt very weary & drowsy, having slept none since her capture, but an undefined fear awakened in her bosom by the late narrow escape from the jaws of the ferocious bears made her loath to stop, & she continued traveling slowly on throughout the entire night. By degrees however this new feeling of terror passed away & she became so much reassured that in the morning of the 4th day she yielded to an increasing inclination to sleep, & tying one end of the cord which served as a bridle securely round her wrist laid down on the grass in a small open space in the timber. She was soon asleep, but slept neither soundly nor long, for her mind so long disquieted & tortured by the anxieties of her situation continued conning over the perils of the way, though the body was listless & inert. Thus she dreamed that something told her to get up immediately & leave that spot, as it was dangerous for her to remain there longer, & awaking suddenly she beheld a large wolf sitting near where she lay. As she started up the wolf howled, & mounting her horse she left the little prairie as soon as possible. While still thinking of the strange & vivid dream & the howling of the wolf, she came to a dense thicket of pines on the summit of a small mountain & wishing to avoid passing through them she wound around the edge of the timber on the hill side. While passing along the mountain side with every sense on the alert to detect the expected danger, she saw a party of Indians some distance below her wending their way as nearly as could judge directly toward the small prairie in which she had stopped a short time before. The appearance of this party & the direction they were going immediately suggested a satisfactory solution of her dream & the howling of the wolf, & she firmly believes now that the Indians were Crows & that the wolf warned her of their coming & told her to get up & travel on. Whether this simple solution of the incidents be true or false, her belief in the miraculous whispering of the medicine wolf is certainly very beautiful and very natural. During the remainder of that day & on the day following she saw several parties of Indians on the prairie beneath her & their being in the neighborhood completely forbade any rest or sleep for her & therefore she moved slowly along without halting till on the 6th day she reached the valley of the Vermillion, a stream emptying into the Mo. river. Stopping here for a short time she made search for something to eat, as her hunger had become almost insupportable. She found 8 roots of the carrot species, each about twice as large as her thumb, which she ate & continued her journey toward to Mo.[5] On the following day she arrived at the bank of the river & found the water high & swollen from the melting snow in the mountains. Still it must be crossed, & without hesitation she whipped her weary & jaded horse into the rapid stream & swimming by his side guided him safely to the opposite shore. Drenched & chilled by the icy waves she mounted her horse & started again along the base of the mountains, feeling well satisfied to have the watery barrier behind her. Thinking herself comparatively safe from wandering Crows, she assayed a more rapid gait & open road; but alas, her good & faithful horse was no longer able to maintain even the slow, jogging pace at which she had come, & was so completely exhausted & worn out that he could move at all with the greatest difficulty. The loss of her horse would be indeed like parting with the only hope of life, as she had yet many miles of mountain road before her & well Knew her own limbs, engulfed by hunger & exhausted by want of rest would not endure the rugged journey on foot. Stop she could not, for starvation stared her

[5]Missouri.

in the face & every moments delay was fraught with a double danger. Therefore she plied the whip continually, determined to ride on till the poor horse could no longer stand. as every step he would bear her now was a step the less between herself & home. Toiling along thus over the uneven ground, sad & dispirited by the sluggish weakness of her only friend, she was suddenly started by a loud neigh, & looking up beheld a beautiful spotted horse with head erect & prancing step trotting cautiously toward her. As She looked upon his fat & vigorous form, & sleek & glossy skin, a sudden hope thrilled & animated her sinking heart, but it was fleeting as it was sudden, for the beautiful animal had been free so long he had doubtless become wild & would not be caught. Her own poor brute stood perfectly still & answered the salutation of the prancing animal with a faint & supplicating response, as if beseeching friendly relief from him. Circling round two or three times the wild horse gradually came nearer & nearer, till at length by a sudden movement she cast one end of her bridle cord over his neck, when as if still accustomed to the useages of a master, he very unexpectedly remained quiet while she fixed it in his mouth. Scarcely thinking an adieu to the meagre remnant of her former gallant friend, she quickly mounted her new steed & with a beating heart set off in a gallop. She found her newly acquired horse to be as gentle & tractable as he was beautiful, & as free & willing as he was swift & strong; & becoming impatient & eager to end her perilous journey & satisfy her gnawing appetites, she urged him on at a rapid pace. Early on the following morning she came to a newly made Flathead trail, & longed to follow it to the camp of her nation, but she dare not do so as she Knew the Crows were continually hanging about the trail of her friends & would possibly intercept her. Preferring to risk even starvation rather than a meeting with her savage captors, she reluctantly crossed the broad path & continued along the base of the mountains.*

On the eighth morning she crossed the high summit of the mountains & about noon came to the valley of a small stream called Little Blackfoot on their western slope. Here she was once more in her own country on the home side of the Rocky mountains, in a locality familiar to her, & felt now perfectly safe from pursuit. As the dread of danger gradually melted away before the friendly look of objects

*During the day she was twice detected & pursued by huge & ferocious bears, at one time by 3 & again by one, but her good steed was fresh & nimble, & soon left the grizzly monsters far behind.

around her, & a feeling of glad security soothed her sorely taxed & anxious mind, weary nature asserted more pointedly her demand for sleep & rest. Therefore tying the bridle end securely round her wrist as she did before, she laid herself down on the luxuriant grass to take her second nap. This time no feeling of insecurity & danger kept her excited mind busy to disturb her by rude visions of approaching enemies, but soothed & relaxed by sweet thoughts of safety, home & friends, every sense & every nerve yielded to seductive sleep & both mind & body were steeped in death like oblivion. For ten days she had slept none, save the few moments of disordered rest she had enjoyed when so suddenly roused by her wondrous vision & her poor & emaciated form had scarcely rested for a moment during her long & perilous flight, her mind nervously tortured by ever changing fears & hopes, every sense continually racked to detect a danger, & her unsatisfied appetite feeding upon her vitals & adding to the pain & fever of her burned & blistered person. And now that she was in a safe & secure retreat, the very Keenness & intensity of her former suffering seemed to act as an opiate & lull her to a deeper slumber, for & she lay asleep all the afternoon & all the following night & did not awake or move till the warm sun was shining in her face the next morning. She found her good horse had improved the time as well as he was able, for not a sprig of grass or sign of vegetation was left within the limits of his cord, every thing nipped to the bare ground by his busy teeth. Resuming her journey with a glad heart, she followed down the Little Blackfoot for a few miles, when she came to a broad & well beaten trail. Turning into this to her well known path, she rode along at a brisk pace, & late in the afternoon reached a camp of her friends at Camache prairie,[6] the Flathead root ground, that being the eleventh day since her capture by the Crows. As she approached the lodges her people could scarcely recognize her, her thin & emaciated body, & her almost fleshless limbs, blistered & scorched by the sun, & torn & lacerated by the thorny bushes, seeming so little like her former self, but when known she was gladly welcomed home, & every comfort & attention the camp could afford was lavishly bestowed on the poor & exhausted wanderer.

Thus were her trials & tribulations at an end & death perfected

[6]This site is also mentioned by Garrett B. Hunt in *Indian Wars of the Inland Empire*, but its exact location is not known.

her escape from captivity her fearful & remarkable journey miraculously accomplished, & the brave woman once more happy & contented enjoying the kind & soothing joys of home & friends.

Original Notes for Story

5th June 1858

5th June 1858 crossed divide between Gallatin Fork Mo. & Yellowstone, & camped on Tributary of Yellowstone.

June 6th morning—2 Squaws caught horses to get roots. T. gone to traps. Camp attacked by 40 or 50 Crows. 1 Squaw cut off from Camp & captured. 1 Flathd Killed & 30 or 40 horses stolen. Crows travelled without stopping till Sunset 7th & Came to main Crow Camp at mouth 1000 Yr river—were joined by war party 18 from Snake Country, with scalps & 3 Children prisoner. Both parties stopped in sight Camp & danced scalp dance till near day light. T's Squaw was bound with raw skin & placed at back of lodge an old squaw on each end of cord. lodge door was laced across with raw hide cords. When all was quiet sawed cord loose with piece tin, old rist band, picked up while Cs dance war dance. Crawled out under door, caught a mule—went stiff legged, jumped & snorted—let him go; caught a horse—tryed & found him too slow & lazy—Went back & took gray mare—Started up river—Soon Missed & pursued—rode into river & hid among willows, horse standing in water nearly up to his back—Crows Hunted every where & gave up—raised camp & went into main camp. She started up river into Mountains. 4th day laid down to sleep—waken by a dream telling her to move (indecipherable) found large wolf sitting near—howled. mounted horse & rode on—Saw a party Cs going to spot she had left—Chased by grizzly bears 3 times—Once by 5, by 3 & by 1—One chase 3 or 4 miles. Came to vermillion—found 8 roots, of carrot species, big as 2 thumbs—found Mo. high—Swam it—horse broke down—saw a spotted wild horse came up to her voluntarily—bridled it & started on. Saw Flthd trail but did not follow it. afraid C's would be watching—Saw several [indecipherable] at different times—Crossed mountains—reached Little Blackfoot—about noon laid down to sleep & did not wake till next morning. Next day reached Flthd Camp at Camache prairie root grounds—out eleven days from Crows—only 8 roots to eat.

Lodge Talk 2

Dec. 26–29th 58

Christmas with its holidays & its merrymaking, its happy scenes & jolly times is welcomed & enjoyed once a year by civilized man through out the world. And though a thousand miles or more without the pale of civilization far remote from its customs & its usages, & perfectly destitute of its conveniences & comforts, we long for its coming & welcome its presence in the lodge with as much true hearted gladness as greeted its arrival at the old homestead. To us it is still a day of festivity & feasting, & if it brings not the time honored reunion board,[1] loaded with its wealth of good cheer, its roast beef & fattened turkey, soups & seasonings & all the tempting et ceteras of a family feast, round which the present & past generations were wont to gather in the years gone by, it still affords the humbly spread saddle cloth with its kettles of boiled meats & strong coffee, with its well roasted rib & panful of slap-jacks.

The Christmas of 18—[2] found me in one of a goodly party assembled round the high blazing fire in a lodge that was pitched by the side of a clear rapid stream in the mountains. The day was cold & freezing & the chill & icy wind that followed the deep gorge was whistling & sighing mournfully through the tall pines around & about us, & circled round the lodge in eddying gusts, seeking in vain to fan the warm fire within. It was indeed one of those occasional & supremely bitter days that occur in this latitude & locality, preceded & followed generally by unusually pleasant weather, & yet being themselves the

[1]Dining table.

[2]Why this date is not completed is a mystery. The authors believe this occurred in 1858, since that date appears at the top.

severest of the season & possessing the keenness & rigor of the whole winter. In a word it was what old Mott styled "cold as sin & smelt like fire." The party consisted chiefly of old mountain men, trappers & hunters, the chief of whom was a tall, muscular old man, whose whitened & grey beard locks seemed strangely at variance with the strong & sinewy limbs & robust frame, known as old Mott, & in whose lodge we now were. Besides these who were perfectly at home were one or two temporary sojourners in the land, myself among the number. The last rays of the setting sun were lingering on the mountain tops, having long since left the deep valley, & the night was fast blending with the winter twilight, when everything having been made ready & the party complete by the return of one or two who had been absent during the day, we were notified to draw our butcher knives & make ready for a feast. The humble kettle with its wholesome & abundant food was placed in our midst & each attacking its smoking contents in turn again & again, we used our knives & teeth with a will till our hearty appetites were perfectly satisfied. Then falling back listlessly on the soft robes & thick bear skins that were spread around the fire for the double purpose of a bed & a seat, each one almost simultaneously drew out a pipe & tobacco sack intent on the customary smoke.

"A dram of old sperits wouldn't go bad a bit now, to warm a feller's blood & sorter help his belly smash up all that are supper. But cuss the luck, 'taint in the country." The melancholy reflections which the speaker conjured up by his remarks, & particularly the closing sentence, seemed to operate strongly on the whole party, & we laid back in solemn silence & puffed forth yet stronger volumes of smoke. The silence & puffing continued without interruption for some minutes, when the host having exhausted his first pipe, took from under his pillow a skin bag, which contained his meagre wardrobe. Rummaging in this for a moment he slowly drew forth a small iron hooped keg, capable of holding a little more than one gallon, which he placed gently in his lap, & returned the sack to his pillow. This suspicious looking keg was eyed with considerable interest & excited some curiosity. "I tell yer what it is, boys, I've got a gallon of sperrits here, & if yer a mind to jine me, we'll drain it till its gone." "To be sure we'll jine yer & sartin.[3] But where in the name of ingin sinse did yer fetch that feller from? I'd a sworn there was nit a drop in the country."

[3]Certain.

"Why yer sees, I was allers used to drinkin' a dram Christmas & now I've done it so long & so reglar I'm feelin' sort a religion like on the subject & cannot git over the time at all without licker. So, soon as one Christmas' gone I begins to watch for licker to drink the next; and I never lets a chance pass of gittin some, though it ain't more'n a swallow at once, without tryin' it, & I allers puts what I gits in this little feller & hides him till Chrismas comes agin." Said old Mott, patting the keg affectionately. "Now, yer sees I was down to the Fort last summer & I thought I'd jist smell around abit & see if I couldn't scare up a drop or so of licker for my little chrismas feller here. Well, while I was think' t myself who I'd ax to tell me where to git it, sure enough up comes a new feller as had jist come from the states & begins a talkin' to me. His face looks purty red & thinks I old feller I'll jist take a sniff at your breath on a ventur,—a kind a speriment like yer know & if I likes the smell o' the wichd[4] yer blows, why may be I'll jist come right out & ax yer 'bout the critter. Well, he talks & talks, & I keeps a answerin' of him, & all the time sorter edgin up to 'im, till I gits my nose purty tolable close to hisn. Then I watches when he blows out & I sniffs up sorter stiff like, detarmined to make the pint sartin. Blow me if he didn't smell like a reglar tavern, & I know'd then I was on a purty fresh trail, so I thought I'd sorter feel round him a bit & keep tryin' him till I found out all about it. Well, I didn't say nothin' for more'n a minit & then I says to the feller, 'Stranger, can't yer sell me some licker, for yer've got a manifactry some where down there 'mongst yer innards.' The way he took the hint is wonders, & so he sorter laughed & to me says "my friend, I've got a little licker left, but I've promised it all & I don't see as I can spare any," and then he laughed agin. Bit I was detarmined to have some, so we stuck to each other till he 'greed to give me 4 bottles as a sorter favor like & I 'greed to pay him for them. So, I got my gallon licker & he got one purty good horse & the vally[5] of a better one. Any how here's the licker & its been paid for—so lets dram away at it while we've got it." A most thorough & minute search brought to light the equivalent of 4 cups of different sizes, shapes & material. When the stopper was drawn from the bung of the keg & while pouring out the precious fluid careful not to spill a drop, Mott suddenly said, "Now

[4]Unsure of transcription.
[5]Perhaps meaning "value."

boys, every drop of this licker's to be drunk to Little Ben & no body else. I allers drinks my Chrismas drams to him, 'cause I allers thinks o' him more'n more when Chrismas comes." All willingly assented to this, though some of us had yet to learn who Little Ben was & what was the ty that bound the speaker so firmly to him.

When all had taken a pretty stiff dram & the alchol began to warm them up a little one of the party said to old Mott "your notion's a good un, old man, 'bout drinkin' this licker to Little Ben. And so I popose that you tell us a story 'bout him & then when yer done, we'll git Bob over there to sing up the song that little Ben writ about the mountains. What do yer say, wont that be purty good." "Well, I dont care to tell yer somethin' bout him, if its 'greeable to the party. And then as yer say, when I'm done, Bob'll sing us Little Ben's song, & we'll swaller the ballance o' the licker & go to bed." Of course it was perfectly agreeable to the whole party & therefore the programme of the evening's festivity was fixed without more ado. "Let's all take another drink, afore I begin, to sorter bring back old times, & then you fellers keep now & then punchin' up the fire to make it kinder comfortable like & I'll tell yer some of what I knows 'bout Little Ben." The alacrity with which the company sat upright, plainly showed a willingness to do anything to get old Mott started with his story, even to taking a drink with him before he commenced, & I had no doubt that if the old man by chance should become exhausted at any time during his narration & should again suggest a dram to revive & refresh himself, that the whole party would promptly join him & drink him to life again. In due time each had taken his dram, & settled himself comfortably on the robes, & the fire made to burn brightly & cheerfully by additional fuel, when with the keg still resting safely & snugly in his lap, the old trapper began his story of Little Ben.

"I've been sorter turnin' the thing over in my mind, 'bout what I'd better tell about, and I've concluded to tell yer what an infernal scrape Ben got into when he went huntin' the Wild Widder"—"Then it's a woman story you're goin' to tell us" interrupted a young hunter. "Woman git out. I tell ye it's the wild widder, Ben's hoss & no woman." "What a singular name for a horse. Do you know why he named it so—" "Yes I knows that too. He called his chestnut mare the Wild Widder because she was a purty beast, & that was the name of his wife too. But that's 'ntirely 'nother story, which maybe I'll tell yer all 'bout 'nother time. But I cant now, for its no use mixin' up differ'nt tales why yer popose to tell only one"—I could resist the inclination to clinch the old man's promise to tell the other story too at another time, & therefore told him I considered him pledged to relate it the convenient opportunity & begged him not to forget it. "Now don't yer go to feelin a bit uneasy & git resty-like, fearin' I'll ever forgit that story. I cant do it no how, for I tell yer its all writ down on paper as purty as print—& as plain too to them as can read it. Little Ben was reglar colicy bred feller, I guess, (it is presumed Mr. Mott meant college bred) for he used to be most allers a readin' or a writin' somethin'. He writ that story down & if you want to hear it you can read it yerself any time yer please & welcome. so now I'll jist go on agin with my story 'bout the fix Ben got into once.

Long time ago, afore the blasted red devils was sorter civilized & friendly, when a man's hair was considered purty vallyble by the ingin in these parts & a body was killed & skinned reglar like a beaver for his fur, Ben 'n me was once trappin down on the Missouri. We was right at the mouth of a little river that come into the-big un from a way up north somewhere, & was purty well fixed for the trappin's bisness, so we was haulin in lots o beaver & cache'er them all time so's we'd have 'em safe in case we was discovered by the injuns & 'ould have to run fer it. Well, we didn't see nor hear of any body's bein round our camp for a long time, but we kept watchin & careful jist the same as if we expected 'em all the time; for we knowed them red fellers was not likely to makin' much fuss when they was prowlin' 'bout after scalps. Early one night we was a layin' snug in our blanket, think o' things in genral, when I seed a Crow flyin' over us, & jist when he was right over our heads he gives one squawk, as if kinder skeered like. Now I knowed that Crow wasn't flyin' 'bout that time a night for nothin' & so I jist pulled Little Ben & wispered to him. I was sartin injins was 'bout. Well up we gits without making no noise & he crawls one way while I slips off 'nother, goin to see if we'd hear anything of the varmints. We was out lookin' round more'n an hour, & as we didn't find any sign of injins we slipped back to camp. Ben he'd been to see the hosses & found them all right & feedin' quiet, the widder & all. So we jist laid down agin & was most asleep when the 'nfernal Crow flew back agin & squawked jist once as did afore when he went over. Now I thinks it's all right, if we was to be fooled once, we wasn't goin' to be fooled twice by a black Crow—& so I says nothing to Ben but turns over to go to sleep. I tried & kep tryin' to sleep, but some how or 'nother I was resty & oneasy, & I'd a good notion once or twice to wake Ben up, but then I thought he'd only laugh at me, & so I'd let him sleep on, thinkin' I wouldn't disturb him unless I hurd somethin'—Mornin' come at last & I gits up & starts a little fire to cook our meat while Ben goes out first thing to see the horses. I cooked the meat & sat down to wait for him & waited till I got tired, & then eat a bite & thought I'd go & raise the traps, wonderin' all the time what was keepin' Ben. I was gone I reckin more'n hour & when I come back I knowed he hadn't come yet for the meat was there jist as I left it. Directly in he comes a lookin' might queer & sober like & I knowed then somethin' happened, so I jist axed him what was the matter. "Injins about" says he. "The 'nfernal scoundrels stole my widder last night. But I'll follow 'em to the devil afore I'll let 'em keep the beauty." Now the Wild Widder was a sure enough beauty purty as a posey, & jist like an arrow when she was a runnin, she'd git over the ground so fast. There wasn't no hoss ever I seed eatin grass as could near come up to her, & them Atelopes I've seed her ketch in two mile, though they allers had considerable start. I tell yer she was a reglar wind-streaker & Little Ben loved her jist the same as if she was his gal. "Did yer see any injin signs" I axed him. "I seed this" says he as he throwed the end of a cabris[6] over to me, "No wolf gnawin' bout that." I looked at it & it was cut as clean as a razor, showin that the thief had a purty sharp knife. "How many hosses did the devils take" says I. "Only my Widder—the rest o the band is all right." When he got done eatin his breakfas he begin to fix his rifle & fixins without saying a word. I looked at him wonderin what he was goin to do but never said nothing as I sposed he'd tell me when he got ready. So he takes some dry meat & 1 or 2 pair shoes & tyins it up in his blanket with a cabris, so's he could sling it on his back, he sits down & says to me "Mott, I'm agoin to bring my hoss back or else I'll give the cussed injins my hair 'long with the beast. I don't want no scalp as long as an injin got the widder; & if he keeps one he must git the other too. So you jist wait here for me & take care o' the tricks till I come back; & if I shouldn't come purty soon, afore yer go jist leave word here for me how long you staid & where yer goin to, & if I live I'll foller yer

[6]Probably a corruption of the word "cabestro," meaning a hair rope, lariat, or cinch.

as soon as I kin. I don't think there's more'n one been here yet, for if there'd been more of 'em I'm a thinkin' they'd have took all the hosses & tried git our hair too & besides yer know that Crow squawked jist only oncet. But that feller as did come's a blasted good judge of hoss flesh, to pick the widder out in the dark, & if he's as smart 'bout other things may be he'll jist bring a dozen injins back with im. So I'd advise yer not to stay here more'n 2 or 3 days afore yer move, unless yer want them devils to find yer. And now I'll jist shake yer hand good bye, for a day or two, & go and git my hoss." I knowed 'twant no use my sayin anythin' agin his doin as he pleased, for it'd only vex 'im without doin' a bit of good, so I jist said good bye & sorter squeezed his hand, and he shouldered his rifle & blanket fixins & started off on foot injin fashion goin to steal his own hoss. When he was gone I begin to feel queer & lonesome like, & got to thinkin' bout the injins comin' back. So I jist waited there 4 days, & then dug a little hole in the ground right where we had our fire & put in it some little sticks with notches on 'em that'd tell him all 'bout it, & covered it up putin' the ashes over it & the chunks round nat'ral like, & took all our tricks & moved down the river to the Fort. Little Ben he hunted round up long the big river first & didn't see no tracks nor no fresh sign of injins, so he crosses over the prairie & comes back to the little un agin, away up above where we camped & went pokin' about 'long up the bank watchin like a hawk for ingin sign. He hunted 'bout mighty close at first I tell yer, for he wanted to see which way the feller went in the start, as he knowed the trail wouldn't be fresh long, cause he was afoot & the rascal'd gain on him all the time.

A little afore sundown he sees some crows a eatin something out in the prairie bottom & he walks up to see what it was. He finds them pickin some deer bones & when he sees them he thinks they both might fresh & so he looks round till he finds where the animal was killed. Here the sign was so fresh that this could be no mistake & he says to 'imself "that varmint's been killed today & I'll jist try to find out what killed it." So he begins gatherin up all the bones & puttin 'em together sorter like an animal's bones is fixed natrally, (for he knowed every bone in a thing's body jist as if he'd made it) & when he got 'em all in a pile he missed 3 of the critters ribs. "That's purty good" says he "here's 3 ribs gone, jist enough for one injin to eat for supper, after eatin the liver raw. I'll take the 3 that's left like them that's gone & foller up the timber for a day or two & see if I don't find out where them ribs was cooked & eat." So he picks out 3 of the bones & follers up the timber on the little river till it gits dark, & then he lays down in his blanket & goes to sleep, for he didn't want to pass any new sign in the dark. When day was breakin the next morning he was a settin on his blanket all tied up proper for carryin, eatin his allowance of dry meat, & when it was fairly light he was up & gone agin. Findin' them ribs missin' the day afore made him sorter confident & as he knowed the feller that took 'em would most like eat 'em the first time he stopped he felt sure he'd find where he made his fire to cook 'em. So he follered on, & the timber begin to get more 'n more scattered, till there want more on the river 'cept little bunches like in the bends. When he'd come to places where there want no timber he'd push ahead like smoke & then in the timber he'd go slow & careful. But he didn't find nothing new that day & he went to bed at night without him a bit wiser than he was afore. Next mornin he starts agin afore sun up & goes ahead jist the same as if he had a fresh trail to foller & about noon he comes to a purty tolable big bunch of timber right where a creek come into the river. He goes into the timber mighty quick & jist right at the mouth of the little creek he sees where there'd been a little fire & lookin round he found a burnt stick that was used to cook meat with. Pickin this up he scraped the bark off the end that had been stuck in the ground & it was so green yet that it was sappy jist as if he'd a cut it off a bush. He knowed then somebody'd been about there not many hours afore, & thinking about the ribs he commenced huntin round the fire to see if he could find any. Well he hunted & hunted till he was purty near sartin there wasn't no bones there, when he sees somethin like a bone jist peekin up 'bove the water bout 10 ft out in the river. The more he looked at the thing the more he thought it was a bone & to make sartin he laid down his rifle, pulled off his shoes & waded right after it. The mud was purty deep but the water wasn't a foot, & when he pulled the thing up he found it was a deer's rib sure enough & stickin right straight up in the mud & meat stickin all over it yet, which was fresh like & didn't smell a bit. When Ben gits on shore agin he takes one of the ribs he fetched 'long with im & lays it 'long side of the tother one he got in the river & if it hadn't been for the skin hangin on one he couldn't tell em apart they was so exactly alike. But he wasn't satisfied with 'pearances only, so he comes a reglar anatomy trick & measures 'em both with a string, first the length, then round here & then round there, till he was scientific sartin that they was as near the same size as two balls run in my bullet moulds. "I thought I'd find yer somewhere on this river, & now that I've seed yer once yer may go back where the red devil flung yer to keep yer from tellin tales I reckin, & I'll jist look round & find out how yer come here as quick for I haint seed no hoss tracks yet, & I know no two feet ever brought yer way up here" & with that he flung all the bones into the water & went up long the creek bank 'bout 50 yards when he seed fresh hoss tracks where he'd been down to water; so he followed the back track a little furder & came right slap on to the stake where the hoss had been tied, & when he looked at the big ring round the stake where the grass was eat off, he laughed right out he was so glad. "If my widder wa'n't tied to that stake & didn't eat that grass off, then Ben's a fool that's all & haint got no sense, for no ingin nor nobody else never tied a hoss with a cabris that long & there never was no such cabris no how 'cept mine that's on the old gal. But yer never come here up the bottom, so I'll take yer back track a little & see how yer did come—maybe it'll larn me how yer goin to travel." Talkin' this way to 'imself he follered the back track till he seed it goin straight out to the hills, when he turned back agin. "Bout what I'd expect of an ingin who's cunnin enough to throw the bones inter the river where he's eat the meat. That feller jist travels on the high prairie, cause he can see furder when he's on top of the hills & like to look if any body's follerin 'im. But I'll foller 'im if he flys, now that I'm started right." When little Ben was a sayin this I aint doubtin' he meant what he said, & so, boys, spose we kinder licker all round agin, that is them that's not asleep, wishin' im a purty pair o' wings in case it comes to fly in sure enough. The way talkin' makes a feller dry's awful, 'specially me that's not used to it—

Mott's supposition was acted upon instantly & no body was asleep just at that particular moment, so each one took a pull at the whiskey & filled his pipe for another smoke, when the old man said to the one nearest the pile of wood: "Now Phil, don't yer go to settin there & gapin at me so while I'm talking, & let the fire go most out agin as yer did afore, but jist look sharp a bit & keep the chunks a blazin, for I tell yer its winter in these hills now. If it want for the drams we've took we'd be a most froze by this time for all the fire you've kep." Phil took the hint & piled the wood on till the fire burned bright & high promising not to forget it again, when the old man continued. "Now since you've got a fire that's calcilated to keep a feller warm, Little Ben jist took the widder's track where it crossed the little creek & followed it on up the bottom for a good ways, when it struck right off agin to the hills. "Yer[7] longin' to take a look agin, are yer, & a goin to git on the hills. Well yer may go, & I'll jist sleep in that little timber up ther afore I foller yer, for its 'bout my last chance on this river I reckin.'" It wasn't dark yet by a good deal, but he didn't see no timber 'bove that little bunch as far's he could see, & so he went to it just as he said he would, intendin' to sleep there. It was a purty little piece of timber 'bout as big as a tater patch in the states & had may be a dozen big trees in it, as Ben sits down in the shade to rest 'imself, waitin till the night come to go to sleep. While he was settin there wide awake, he sees about 20 ingins hikin[8] over the hill & comin straight for the same timber. Then he knowed he was in a fix, for if he left the woods the red fellers'd see him & soon ketch him with their hosses, & if he staid in them they'd be mighty apt to find 'im as there wasn't no place to hide, no big logs nor nothing o' that sort. But he must git out o' that purty quick or they'd scalp him right where he was a sittin, & so he begins a lookin for a hole to hide in on the ground & when he didn't find none there, he jist begin lookin up in the trees. Well the first thing he seed was an old scaffold made of poles & bark & sich like, stickin way up in one of the big trees, what has a dead injin on it all fixed off & buried proper. "I never hurd tell of a feller's buryin' 'imself jist like a deadman to save his life afore, but I reckin' its 'bout the only chance I've got, so I'll jist climb up there & lay myself out till them fellers is gone" and with that he clim right up takin his rifle & blanket with 'im, & movin' the ingin bones off to one side he jist laid himself down on the scaffold & pulled the bark coverin' over im natral & proper's if he was buried sure enough. Well the ingins come right to the timber & turnin' thar hosses loose camped almost under the tree where he was dead. He knowed it was a war party for they hadn't no lodges nor children with 'em & only jist a few squaws to cook & mend shoes & so on. So he thought he'd lay quiet that night & they'd most likely leave there in the mornin', when

[7] Inconsistent quotations in original.

[8] Unsure about transcription.

he could go on agin after the widder. But when the mornin' come the rascals jist drive[9] their hosses down to drink & then turned 'em all out on the prairie agin & never let on a bit like they was agoin. They laid around eatin & sleepin all day & there wasn't no chance for Ben to move, so he jist laid still & watched em. Some of 'em were peekin & peerin' round all the time, the same's if they 'spected to see somethin' interesting & two of 'em come right under the tree & looked up at the scaffold for a long time talkin' to one 'nother, bout the feller as was burried up there I reckin. I mean the dead 'un, not Ben. Howsomever ingins never disturb a dead man & go poking' mong his bones for nottin, its clean agin their medicine, & as they didn't see anything wrong 'bout the fixins up in the tree they went off when they got tired lookin at it. When night comes agin, Ben begin's to feel purty tired of layin stretched without movin', & gits mighty anxious to be goin after his hoss, but he thinks the ingins is rested now & if he sticks it out till mornin' they're sartin to go then, & climbin' down that tree in the dark'd be a risky bisness as he couldn't help makin some fuss, so he stays there 'nother night. Purty soon in the mornin' the ingins are a bringin the hosses in & he 'spects to see 'em mount & go, but they jist lets 'em drink & drives 'em back again the same as afore, 'cept 3 or 4 what some fellers rode off, a scoutin round, I 'spose. Things was gittin to be purty tolable serous with Ben, I tell yer, when he seed 'em layin round jist as easy & comfortable like as if they was at home & was goin to stay there, for he knowed he'd feel most oncommon hungry & thirsty afore he could come to life agin, but he couldn't help imself poor fellow & he was bound to lay still another day whether he liked it or not. But he vowed come what would he git down the next night if it killed him, for he'd better be killed & scalped by an ingin than to lay up there & die by inches. He was a sufferin' a heap from bein so long stretched out in the same way a most without movin' at all, & was gittin' purty tolable dry for water to'ards sun down, when he seed an ingin comin' over the prairie like a streak o' lightnin', he almost flew his hoss was gittin over the ground so fast. I tell yer Ben didn't think no more o drink then, fer he knowed that was his hoss & he determined to lay there a week but what he'd git her. Sure enough up comes an ingin settin' on the wild widder as proud & big as life. Ridin' into camp he got down & showed his hoss

[9] Unsure about transcription.

to the other fellers, mighty proud like of the purty beast & they all crowds round, lookin at her & talking away's as if they was might well pleased with her too. Ben watched when he took the widder down to drink & throwed water on her to cool her off & seed him tie her to a stake right near where the ingins slept, takin particular of how she was tied & all 'bout it. When it got dark the cussed ingins kep walkin round & talkin' & smokin, jist's if they didn't want any more sleep after sleepin' all day, & Ben was gittin mity oneasy fearin they want keep awake all night. And they did come purty near it for after they was abed they went on talkin till purty near day light. So whenever he'd think they was asleep & begin to think 'bout movin all at once he'd hear some o'em talking away as usual. Things went on so a long time, when he seed the mornin star gittin up over the hills & he knowed daylight was mighty close. So he jist determined to make an attempt & if he could git once on his hoss' back he wouldn't ax 'em no odds; if he couldn't, why he'd jist blow that scoundrel's brains out as stole the critter & then die a fitin. He moves off the bark kiverin[10] mighty quiet & careful & set up a bit & took a good look at the sleepin' varmints; then he cuts the cabris in two what he had round his blanket, & with one piece he slings his rifle fast round his shoulder, & ties the other piece round one of the big limbs the scaffold was sittin on. "As I aint exactly sartin as I'll ever need yer agin, I wont run the risk of takin' yer 'long, for yer'd only bother me whether I'm fitin or movin. So you may jist lay there & I'll slip down this rope, for I think I kin git down it quicker and quieter than I kin climb down the tree." and so he left his blanket & dry meat on the scaffold & swung 'imself on to the cord, slippin' down to the ground as quiet & easy as you please. Day was jist breakin', but the widder wasn't far off, so he thought he crawl up to her & if the ingins waked up he run to jump on her any how if he could. He gits down on his belly & crawls like snake through the grass, goin' mighty slow & careful to'ard the hoss, & purty soon gits a hold of the cabris she's tied with without disturbin' any body. Takin' out his knife he cuts it in two leavin' part tied to the stake & then feelin happy & tolable safe when he'd got a hold on the widder's bridle agin, he jist stands up straight & walks up to her the same' if there wasn't no ingins bout. As you may spose them fellers wasn't deaf & the first step he took waked one of 'em up & his yellin' waked 'em all afore he could take the 2^{d} but as good luck would

[10]Covering.

have it a long jump set him all right on his hoss without any more steppin about it, & so he was up as soon as they was. In a minit he was a flyin over the ground goin' might near as fast as the arrys[11] they was a shootin' at him, & next minit 7 ingins was a howlin after him. Well he lets the widder go long easy like & turns round to see how many's follerin im. He sees there's only 7 of 'em, & the first one is the same ugly feller as stole the hoss. "I'll jist stop yer thieving, yer red devil yer" & he slips his rifle round all right for shootin quick, & then stops his hoss stock still.

The ingins thought they had him sure & set up a yellin like mad. When they'd got near enough Ben's rifle jist burnt her powder & the foremost feller give up the chase, fallin down like he was shot.

Away went the widder agin & on come the ingins, as he loaded up agin ready for shootin. "I don't want to kill yer, but if yer determined to die, I guess I'll have to 'commodate yer if I can." So here goes at the head devil agin"[12] & with that he stopped & his rifle told the head feller he'd follered long enough & he jist fell down like he was shot too. The ingins wouldn't stop no how but kep comin' on so Ben says agin, "This is might purty ground for runnin & I'm thinking its 'bout as good & Christian like fer shootin ingins as 'tis runnin' buffalo & so if yer a mind to keep a follerin I'll jist see if the purty gal here & me don't git yer all"—So when the time come he laid another feller out ready fer buryin, when the 4 that was left begin to think they couldn't ketch that hoss no how & stopped on the spot. When he saw they had stopped he stopped too & he says "So yer goin to quit & spoil my fun are yer, jist when I'd begun to like it too. But I'll be blamed if yer shall, for as yer'er follered me without leave I'll foller yer a little & see if the widder's as good behind yer as before." and he jist wheeled right round & rode straight at 'em. They knowed that was no place for them, & they tried to run back a little faster than they come, but they wasn't fast enough neither way, & purty soon Ben was a shootin at 'em agin from behind & when the noise of his gun reached 'em there was only 3 left settin up who could hear it distinctly. The three that was left each struck off in a different direction from tother, hopin' I reckin that he'd foller on the others. When Ben seed them separate he stopped & looked at 'em a good bit, every feller of 'em a whippin' his hoss like fire & tryin the best he knowed

[11] Arrows.

[12] Inconsistent quotations in original.

how to git somewhere else immediately. "Now I reckin I kin ride 'long home quiet & respectable like. So I'll jist go down & jine old Mott agin." He came to the old camp & dug up the sticks I left for 'im & then followed me to the Fort, all safe & sound, where I was mighty glad to see 'im wearin fer all right & natral I tell yer. Now my story's told & I'm done talking, so yer may jist wake up boys & jine me in 'nother drink & we'll have the song Ben used to sing.

The whole party joined the old man in another bumper & resumed their places again, when he held the keg to his ear & shook it saying as he did so, "There's jist about one big dram all round, & when Bob gits done singin we'll swaller it & go to bed considerin that Chrismas' quit when the licker gives out."

Without any hesitation Bob sung the following song to the mountains, with a clear manly voice & in good style, apparently to the entire satisfaction of the company.

A toast to the mountains—to the cloud piercing peaks
With a base upon earth upreaching to heaven,
When first the faint gilding of the rosy morn breaks,
Where linger the latest the soft hues of even.
"Tis the land of the skies, where the bold & the free
Wish to live while they live & to die when they die.—
"Tis a dear mountain land for the Trapper to be,
And a fairy like place for the Hunter to lie.
Then fill to the mountains, & fill full to the brim,
For be it a bumper to the land of the skies,
And breathe each a heartwish in his goblet to swim
That their peaks round his home may eternally rise.

A cup to the mountains—where the Wolf & the Bear
Each a king of his kind, ever fearlessly roam—
Where each cavernous rock is to one a safe lair,
And each forest of pine to the other a home.
But we care not for them, though they lurk near the path
We so buoyantly tread every day of our life—
Let them jump if they dare—what to us is their wrath
While our gun throws a ball & our belt bears a knife
Then fill to the mountains & fill full to the brim &c

A drink to the mountains, where the sure footed Goat
And the snowy fleec'd Sheep feed on the steep cliff side,
And each gouge out a path with its own tiny foot
Where naught save an Eagle with its young dare abide.

They're food for the Hunter & their warm snowy fleece
  Is a soft downy coat impervious to cold—
And what more do we want till our merry times cease,
  Or for what need we care till our life-story's told.
    Then fill to the mountains & fill full to the brim &c

Again to the mountains—where alone the proud bird
  Of heaven daring wing & of sun piercing eye,
From the morn to the night forever is heard
  To sing to its banner where it floats in the sky.
America's Eagle, the fierce bird of the free,
  Is hovering round us, ever watchful & near,—
Then who'll leave the mountains while an eagle they see,
  And who'll not be merry when his screaming they hear.
    Then fill to the mountains & fill full to the brim &c

And off to the mountain—to the forests of pine
  Which so stately & tall like a fringe deck their brow,
Where the bright tinted moss & the green branches twine
  Till the shade of a bird never reaches below
'Neath the evergreen arch, by the swift morning brook
  Where no summer sun's heat nor the wintry winds come
May there ever be pitched & in each cozy nook,
  The lodge of the Trapper & the Hunter's lov'd home.
    Then fill to the mountains & fill full to the brim
      For be it a bumper to the land of the skins,
    And breathe each a heartwish in his goblet to swim
      That their peaks round his home may eternally rise.

[This separate note, on another sheet, apparently explains these "Lodge Talks."]

I say civilized life & intelligent companions, for though in the rough bosom of the far off Rocky Mountains, we were snugly domiciled in the comfortable & commodious Agricultural Fort which Col. Vaughan, the efficient Agent for the Blackfeet Indians, had lately erected in the valley of Sun River; and there were gathered round the burning logs in the hospitable drawing room Col. A. J. Vaughan, a host, & the host, in himself, Major Owens, the enterprizing Agent for the Flathead Indians in Washington Ter., Mr. MacDonald, the quiet, intelligent & courteous Agent of the Hudson's Bay Co's Fort at Colville in Oregon Ter. And several spirited & lively young men, companions of the latter gentlemen.

Bibliography

Archival Collections

Missouri Historical Society, St. Louis (MOHS)

Collections here include a wealth of information about the Chouteau family, the American Fur Company, and all of their employees. The vertical file is an especially handy resource, providing quick and easy citations to documents referencing persons of note. The Chouteau Collection—which has now been merged to include many related collections—contains much original correspondence as well as a lot of miscellany. The Collection of Fur Trade Ledgers, old St. Louis newspapers, and letters received by the Office of Indian Affairs, all on microfilm, were of great assistance. The Jo Leonard file on William Laidlaw was also helpful.

Montana Historical Society, Helena (MTHS)

The collections here includes a great deal of information pertaining to the fur trade era and Pierre Chouteau, Jr. & Co. as well as the town of Fort Benton and Montana's gold rush and territorial period. They also have a wonderful vertical file with clippings on a wide variety of subjects that patrons are free to browse. Small Collection 294 includes much valuable information on the Dawson family. We also utilized Small Collection 1430, Carolyn Abbott Tyler Reminiscences, 1862–85 and Edith Toomer's "Biography—Major Alexander Culbertson," microfilm 250, reel 16. Electronic copies of Andrew Dawson's complete letters will also be deposited here.

Research Library, Fort Union Trading Post National Historic Site, Williston, North Dakota

Collection includes a variety of materials pertaining to the upper Missouri fur trade and the American Fur Company. This includes the microfilmed papers of Pierre Chouteau, Jr. & Co. as well as some of the National Archives microfilms dealing with this period. Author Wischmann's research papers from the writing of *Frontier Diplomats: Alexander Culbertson and*

Natoyist-siksina' among the Blackfeet are housed here. In addition, the fort's extensive library holdings are a handy repository for anyone interested in the fur trade era. Electronic copies of Andrew Dawson's complete letters will also be deposited here.

Joel F. Overholser Historical Research Center,
Schwinden Library and Archives,
Fort Benton River and Plains Society, Fort Benton, Montana

This wonderful resource must not be overlooked by anyone researching any topic affecting this area. In addition to a noteworthy collection of books covering the fur trade, Fort Benton, and territorial Montana, this facility houses the papers of the late Joel F. Overholser. Overholser was a recognized authority on the history of Fort Benton and the surrounding region. Through more than fifty years of research, he amassed extensive files on a wide range of topics. Moreover, nearly everyone who was ever interested in a Fort Benton–related topic got referred to Overholser, and Overholser kept all that correspondence. Thus his papers provide insights into topics that Overholser himself may not have seriously pursued. Electronic copies of Andrew Dawson's complete letters will also be deposited here.

Government Documents

Letter from the Secretary of the Interior, House MiscDoc 59, 33rd Congress, 1st sess., 741 (1854).

Letter from the Secretary of War, Military Road from Fort Benton to Fort Walla Walla, House ExDoc 44, 36th Cong., 2nd sess. (1861).

Report of the Commissioner of Indian Affairs, Senate ExDoc 1, 33rd Cong., 2nd sess., 746 (1855).

Report of the Commissioner of Indian Affairs, Senate ExDoc 1, 36th Cong., 2nd sess., 235 (1860).

Report of the Commissioner of Indian Affairs, House ExDoc 1, 38th Cong., 1st sess., 129 (1863).

Report of the Construction of a Military Road from Fort Walla Walla to Fort Benton, 1863, House ExDoc 43, 37th Cong., 3rd sess. (1864).

Report of the Secretary of the Interior, Senate ExDoc 2, 34th Cong., 3rd sess., 875 (1856).

Report of the Secretary of the Interior, House ExDoc 1, 35th Cong., 1st sess., 942 (1857).

Report of the Secretary of the Interior, House ExDoc 1, 35th Cong., 2nd sess., 997 (1857).

M234/30: Letters Received by the Office of Indian Affairs, Blackfeet Agency, 1855–69.

M234/754: St. Louis Superintendency, Letters Received by the Office of Indian Affairs, 1846–47.

M234/884: Letters Received by the Office of Indian Affairs, Upper Missouri Agency, 1836–51.

M234/885: Letters Received by the Office of Indian Affairs, Upper Missouri Agency, 1852–64.

Books

Abel, Anne Heloise, ed. *Chardon's Journal at Fort Clark, 1834–1839.* Pierre: Department of History, State of South Dakota, 1932; reprint, Lincoln: University of Nebraska Press, Bison Books, 1997.

Audubon, John James. *Audubon's Birds of North America: The Complete 500 Paintings.* Introduction by Sheila Buff. Secaucus, NJ: Wellfleet Press, 1990.

———. *Audubon's Mammals: The Quadrupeds of North America.* Foreword by William Kammer. Edison, NJ: Wellfleet Press, 2005.

Audubon, Maria R., and Elliott Coues. *Audubon and His Journals.* 2 vols. New York: Charles Scribner's Sons, 1897.

Barbour, Barton H. *Fort Union and the Upper Missouri River Fur Trade.* Norman: University of Oklahoma Press, 2001.

Berry, James Jesse. *Arikara Middlemen: The Effects of Trade on an Upper Missouri Society.* Ann Arbor: UMI Dissertation Service, 1978. UMI number: 7821722.

Boller, Henry A. *Among the Indians: Eight Years in the Far West, 1858–1866.* Chicago: R. R. Donnelly & Sons, 1959.

Bowers, Alfred W. *Hidatsa Social and Ceremonial Organization.* Bureau of American Ethnology, Bulletin 194. Washington, DC: Government Printing Office, 1965.

———. *Mandan Social and Ceremonial Organization.* Chicago: University of Chicago Press, 1950.

Burns, Robert. "Tam o' Shanter." In *The Complete Works of Robert Burns,* 2:313–23. Ed. William Scott Douglas. Edinburgh: William Paterson, 1883.

Calloway, Colin S. *White People, Indians, and Highlanders: Tribal Peoples and Colonial Encounters in Scotland and America.* Oxford: Oxford University Press, 2008.

Catlin, George. *Letters and Notes on the Manners, Customs, and Conditions of North American Indians.* 2 vols. New York: Dover, 1973.

Chalmers, John. *Audubon in Edinburgh and His Scottish Associates.* Edinburgh: NMS Publishing with the assistance of the Royal College of Surgeons, 2003.

Chittenden, Hiram Martin. *The American Fur Trade of the Far West.* 2 vols. New York: Francis P. Harper, 1901.

———. *The History of Early Steamboat Navigation on the Missouri River.* New York: Francis P. Harper, 1903.

Chittenden, Hiram Martin, and Alfred Talbot Richardson. *Life, Letters & Travels of Father Pierre-Jean de Smet, S.J., 1801–1873.* 4 vols. New York: Francis P. Harper, 1905.

Coues, Elliott. *The History of the Lewis and Clark Expedition.* 3 vols. New York: Dover, 1964.

Crighton, Andrew. *Memoirs of Rev. John Blackader: Compiled chiefly from unpublished manuscripts and memoirs of his life and ministry written by himself while prisoner on the Bass; and containing illustrations of the Episcopal persecution from the Restoration to the death of Charles II.* Edinburgh: Archibald Constable, 1823.

Cruise, David, and Alison Griffiths. *The Great Adventure: How the Mounties Conquered the West.* Toronto: Penguin, 1997.

Cutright, Paul Russell. *Lewis and Clark: Pioneering Naturalists.* Lincoln: University of Nebraska Press, 1989.

Denig, Edwin Thompson. *Five Indian Tribes of the Upper Missouri: Sioux, Arickara, Assiniboines, Crees, Crows.* Norman: University of Oklahoma Press, 1961.

Denig, Edwin Thompson, and John Napoleon Brinton Hewitt. *The Assiniboine.* Norman: University of Oklahoma Press, 2000.

Dickens, Charles. *American Notes, Pictures from Italy, and A Child's History of England.* London: Chapman and Hall, 1891.

———. *Dealings with the Firm of Dombey and Son, Wholesale, Retail and for Exportation.* London: Chapman and Hall, 1890.

———. *The Old Curiosity Shop.* London: Chapman and Hall, Limited, 1890.

———. *Sketches by "Boz."* London: J. Macrone, 1836.

Douglas, William Scott. *The Complete Works of Robert Burns.* 6 vols. Edinburgh: William Paterson, 1883.

Erskine, Ebenezer, and James Fisher et al. *The* REPRESENTATIONS *to the Commission of the late General Assembly.* Edinburgh: Thomas Lumisden and John Robertson, Fish-market, 1733.

Ewers, John C. *The Blackfeet: Raiders on the Northwestern Plains.* Norman: University of Oklahoma Press, 1958.

Fardy, B. D. *Jerry Potts: Paladin of the Plains.* Langley, BC: Mr. Paperback, 1984.

Forster, John. *The Life of Charles Dickens.* 3 vols. London: Chapman and Hall, 1874.

Fraser, The Rev. Dr. Donald. *The Life and Diary of the Reverend Ebenezer Erskine, A.M., to Which Is Prefixed a Memoir to His Father, the Rev. Henry Erskine, A.M.* Edinburgh: William Oliphant & Son, 1831.

———. *The Life and Diary of the Reverend Ralph Erskine, A.M., of Dunfermline, One of the Founders of the Secession Church.* Edinburgh: William Oliphant & Son, 1834.

Green, James. *Green's St. Louis Directory.* St. Louis: James Green, 1844.

Hafen, LeRoy R. *The Mountain Men and the Fur Trade of the Far West.* Glendale, CA: Arthur H. Clark, 1966.

Hamilton, James McClellan. *From Wilderness to Statehood: A History of Montana, 1805–1900.* Portland: Binfords & Mort, 1957.

Harrod, Howard L. *Mission among the Blackfeet.* Norman: University of Oklahoma Press, 1971.

Hart-Davis, Duff. *Audubon's Elephant: The Story of John James Audubon's Epic Struggle to Publish "The Birds of America."* London: Weidenfeld & Nicolson, 2003.

Herman, Arthur. *How the Scots Invented the Modern World: The True Story of How Western Europe's Poorest Nation Created Our World and Everything in It.* New York: Three Rivers Press, 2001.

Heusser, Albert H. *George Washington's Map Maker: A Biography of Robert Erskine.* New Brunswick: Rutgers University Press, 1966.

Hewitt, J. N. B., ed., and Myrtis Jarrell, trans. *Journal of Rudolph Friederich Kurz: An Account of His Experiences among Fur Traders and American Indians on the Mississippi and the Upper Missouri Rivers during the Years 1846 to 1852.* Lincoln: University of Nebraska Press, 1970.

Hodges, Nadine. *Missouri Miscellany.* Vol. 12. *Abstracts of Wills and Administrations of Clay County, Missouri.* Signal Mountain, TN: Mountain Press, 2003.

Holterman, Jack. *King of the High Missouri: The Saga of the Culbertsons.* Helena: Falcon Press, 1987.

Hunt, Garrett B. *Indian Wars of the Inland Empire.* Charleston, SC: Nabu Press, 2010.

Kane, Paul. *Wanderings of an Artist among the Indians of North America.* Toronto: Radisson Society of Canada, 1925.

Kappler, Charles J., ed. *Indian Affairs: Laws and Treaties.* 2nd ed. Vol. 2. Washington, D.C.: Government Printing Office, 1904.

Killoren, John J., S. J. *"Come Blackrobe": DeSmet and the Indian Tragedy.* Norman: University of Oklahoma Press, 1994.

Ladner, Mildred D. *William de la Montagne Cary: Artist on the Missouri River.* Norman: University of Oklahoma Press and Tulsa: Thomas Gilcrease Institute of American History and Art, 1984.

Lambert, Kirby, Patricia Burnham, and Susan R. Near. *Montana's State Capitol: The People's House.* Helena: Montana Historical Society, 2002.

Larpenteur, Charles. *Forty Years a Fur Trader on the Upper Missouri: The Personal Narrative of Charles Larpenteur, 1833–1872.* Lincoln: University of Nebraska Press, 1989.

Lass, William E. *A History of Steamboating on the Upper Missouri River.* Lincoln: University of Nebraska Press, 1962.

Laveille, E., S. J. *The Life of Father de Smet, S. J. (1801–1873).* New York: P. J. Kennedy & Sons, 1915.

Leach, Harry. *The Ship Captain's Medical Guide.* 14th ed. London: Simpkin, Marshall, Hamilton, Kent, 1906.

Lepley, John G. *Blackfoot Fur Trade on the Upper Missouri.* Fort Benton: River and Plains Society, 2004.

Luttig, John C. *Journal of a Fur-Trading Expedition on the Upper Missouri, 1812–1813.* Edited by Stella M. Drumm. St. Louis: Missouri Historical Society, 1920.

Maclean, Fitzroy. *Scotland: A Concise History.* London: Thames & Hudson, 2000.

Macleod, The Rev. Norman. *Parish of Dalkeith: Presbytery of Dalkeith, Synod of Lothian and Tweeddale, written jointly with Peter Steele,* M.A.*, lately Rector of Dalkeith Grammar School, Statistical Account of Edinburghshire, by the Ministers of the Respective Parishes.* Edinburgh: William Blackwood and Sons, 1845.

Malone, Michael P., Richard B. Roeder, and William L. Lang. *Montana: A History of Two Centuries.* Seattle: University of Washington Press, 1976.

McChristian, Douglas C. *Fort Laramie: Military Bastion of the High Plains.* Vol. 26. Norman: University of Oklahoma Press, 2009.

McDermott, John Francis, ed. *The Early Histories of St. Louis.* St. Louis: St. Louis Historical Documents Foundation, 1952.

Meyer, Roy W. *The Village Indians of the Upper Missouri: The Mandans, Hidatsas, and Arikaras.* Lincoln: University of Nebraska Press, 1977.

Milton, John R. *South Dakota: A Bicentennial History.* New York: W. W. Norton, 1989.

Necrologies. Vols. I and IA, 1885–1910. St. Louis: Missouri Historical Society.

Nester, William R. *From Mountain Man to Millionaire: The "Bold and Dashing Life" of Robert Campbell.* Columbia: University of Missouri Press, 1999.

Overholser, Joel. *Fort Benton: World's Innermost Port.* Helena: Falcon Press, 1987.

Packer, Lester, and Jürgen Fuchs, eds. *Vitamin C in Health and Disease.* New York: Marcel Dekker, 1997.

Palliser, John. *Solitary Rambles and Adventures of a Hunter in the Prairies.* London: John Murray, 1853.

Paul, R. Eli. *Blue Water Creek and the First Sioux War, 1854–1856*. Norman: University of Oklahoma Press, 2004.

Primm, James Neal. *Lion of the Valley: St. Louis, Missouri, 1764–1980*. Columbia: University of Missouri Press, 1998.

Ravenswaay, Charles Van. *St. Louis: An Informal History of the City and Its People, 1764–1865*. St. Louis: Missouri Historical Society Press, 1991.

Richards, Kent D. *Isaac I. Stevens: Young Man in a Hurry*. Provo: Brigham Young University Press, 1979.

Robertson, R. G. *Competitive Struggle*. Boise: Tamarack Books, 1999.

Ronda, James P. *Lewis & Clark among the Indians*. Lincoln: University of Nebraska Press, 1984.

Schooling, Sir William. *The Hudson's Bay Company, 1670–1920*. London: Hudson's Bay House, 1920.

Schuler, Harold H. *Fort Pierre Chouteau*. Vermilion: University of South Dakota Press, 1990.

Smellie, Alexander. *Men of the Covenant*. 2 vols. London: Andrew Melrose, 1908.

Sprague, D. N., and R. P. Frye. *The Genealogy of the First Métis Nation*. Winnipeg: Pemmican Publications, 1988.

Stack, David. *Queen Victoria's Skull: George Combe and the Mid-Victorian Mind*. New York: Continuum Books, 2008.

Stuart, Granville. *Forty Years on the Frontier*. Lincoln: Bison Books, 2004.

Sunder, John E. *The Fur Trade on the Upper Missouri, 1840–1865*. Norman: University of Oklahoma Press, 1965.

Swagerty, William R. Introduction to *Chardon's Journal at Fort Clark, 1834–1839*, ed. Anne Heloise Abel. Lincoln: University of Nebraska Press, Bison Books, 1997.

Szasz, Margaret Connell. *Scottish Highlanders and Native Americans: Indigenous Education in the Eighteenth-Century Atlantic World*. Norman: University of Oklahoma Press, 2009.

Terrell, John Upton. *Furs by Astor*. New York: William Morrow, 1963.

Thwaites, Reuben Gold. *Early Western Travels, 1748–1846*. 32 vols. Cleveland: Arthur H. Clark, 1906.

Touchie, Rodger D. *Bear Child: The Life and Times of Jerry Potts*. Victoria: Heritage House, 2005.

Tubbs, Stephenie Ambrose, and Clay Jenkinson. *The Lewis and Clark Companion: An Encyclopedic Guide to the Voyage of Discovery*. New York: Holt Paperbacks, 2003.

Utley, Robert M. *The Lance and the Shield: The Life and Times of Sitting Bull*. New York: Henry Holt, 1993.

Williams, Randy Hugh. *Ethnohistory of a Fur Trade Community: Life at Fort Clark Fur Trade Post, 1830–1860*. Ann Arbor: UMI Dissertation Service, 1998. UMI Number: 9924943.

Wilson, Gilbert Livingstone. *Agriculture of the Hidatsa Indians.* Minneapolis: University of Minnesota Studies in Social Sciences, no. 9, 1917; reprint, New York: American Museum Press, 1979.

Wilson, John. *The Works of Professor Wilson of the University of Edinburgh.* 12 vols. Edinburgh: William Blackwood and Sons, 1866.

Wischmann, Lesley. *Frontier Diplomats: The Life and Times of Alexander Culbertson and Natoyist-siksina'.* Spokane: Arthur H. Clark, 2000.

Wood, W. Raymond. *Reprints in Anthropology, Volume 25: No. 39—An Interpretation of Mandan Cultural History.* Washington, DC: Government Printing Office, 1967.

Articles

"Being First Annual Report of the State Historical Society of North Dakota to the Governor of North Dakota for Year Ending June 30, 1906." *Collections of the State Historical Society of North Dakota*, vol. 1. Bismarck, ND: Tribune, State Printers and Binders, 1906.

Bradley, Lt. James H. "Account of the Building of Mullen's Military Road." *Contributions to the Historical Society of Montana* 8 (1917): 162–69.

———. "Affairs at Fort Benton." *Contributions to the Historical Society of Montana* 3 (1900): 201–87.

———. "The Oregon Trail: Capture of an Emigrant Train by the Piegan Chief, Little Dog." *Contributions to the Historical Society of Montana* 9 (1923): 335–40.

Dawson, James. "Major Andrew Dawson, 1817–1871." *Contributions to the Historical Society of Montana* 7 (1910): 61–72. Also included in SC 294, MTHS.

Dempsey, Hugh A. "Jerry Potts: Plainsman." *Montana: The Magazine of Western History* 17, no. 4 (October 1967): 2–17.

Greenfield, Charles D. "Little Dog, Once-Fierce Piegan Warrior, Was Wise and Just Beyond His Time." *Montana: The Magazine of Western History* 14, no. 2 (1964): 23–33.

McAdow, Perry W. "Perry W. McAdow and Montana in 1861–1862." *Montana Magazine of History* 2, no. 1 (January 1952).

McDonnell, Anne. "The Fort Benton Journal, 1854–1856, and Fort Sarpy Journal, 1855–1856." *Contributions to the Historical Society of Montana* 10 (1940): 1–327.

Schieffelin, Maj. W. H. "Crossing the Rockies in '61." *Recreation* 2 (1895): 15–21.

Seltzer, Olaf C. "Wreck of the Chippewa." *Montana: The Magazine of Western History* 15, no. 3 (1965).

"Trudeau's Journal." *South Dakota Historical Collections* 7 (1914): 403–75.

Index